One-Way Street

WALTER BENJAMIN was born in Berlin in 1892 and died in Spain in 1940. He studied philosophy and literature in Berlin, Freiburg, Munich and Bern. After the First World War he worked as a freelance critic and translator, notably of Baudelaire and Proust. He moved to Paris to escape the Nazi takeover and committed suicide in September 1940 while attempting to escape from occupied France to Spain. During his lifetime he was a friend of figures such as Theodor Adorno (with whom he shared many of the ideas expressed in these texts), Bertolt Brecht, Hannah Arendt and Gershom Scholem.

One-Way Street

and Other Writings

Walter Benjamin

Translated by
Edmund Jephcott
and
Kingsley Shorter

Introduction by
Susan Sontag

VERSO
London • New York

This edition first published by Verso 2021
First published by Verso 1979
Updated edition first published by Verso 1997
© Verso 1979, 1997, 2021
Introduction © Susan Sontag 1979, 1997, 2021
All texts in this volume are included in Walter Benjamin, *Gesammelte Schriften*, Bd I-IV
(Frankfurt: Suhrkamp Verlag, 1974–76), with the exception of *Berliner Chronik*
(Frankfurt: Suhrkamp Verlag, 1970)
© Suhrkamp Verlag

The following texts first appeared in English, wholly or in part, in Walter Benjamin,
Reflections (New York: Harcourt Brace Jovanovich, 1978): 'One-Way Street'
(selections); 'On Language as Such and on the Language of Man'; 'Fate and Character';
'Critique of Violence'; 'Theologico-Political Fragment'; 'The Destructive Character';
'On the Mimetic Faculty'; 'Naples'; 'Moscow'; 'Marseilles'; 'Hashish in Marseilles';
'Surrealism'; 'Karl Kraus'; and 'A Berlin Chronicle'
© Harcourt Brace Jovanovich, 1978

Verso
UK: 6 Meard Street, London W1F 0EG
USA: 20 Jay Street, New York, NY 11201
Verso is the imprint of New Left Books

ISBN-13: 978-1-83976-165-2
ISBN-13: 978-1-83976-166-9 (UK EBK)
ISBN-13: 978-1-83976-167-6 (US EBK)

British Library Cataloguing in Publication Data
A catalogue record for this book is available from the British Library

Library of Congress Cataloging-in-Publication Data

Names: Benjamin, Walter, 1892–1940, author. | Jephcott, E. F. N.,
translator. | Shorter, Kingsley, translator. | Sontag, Susan, 1933-2004,
writer of introduction.
Title: One-way street : and other writings / Walter Benjamin ; translated
by Edmund Jephcott and Kingsley Shorter ; introduction by Susan Sontag.
Description: London ; New York : Verso, 2021. | Includes bibliographical
references and index. | Summary: ' "One-Way Street" is a cornerstone of
the Benjamin legacy, exhibiting the richness and multidimensional nature
of his thought. Included here are his famous essays on the history of
Surrealism and photography; the personal and confessional writing on
cities in "Hashish in Marseille" and "Naples"; and his powerful and
fragmented recollections of fin de siècle Berlin; alongside his
foundational essays on language, violence, psychology, aesthetics, and
politics'— Provided by publisher.
Identifiers: LCCN 2021012987 (print) | LCCN 2021012988 (ebook) | ISBN
9781839761652 (paperback) | ISBN 9781839761676 (ebk)
Subjects: LCSH: Benjamin, Walter, 1892–1940—Translations into English. |
LCGFT: Essays.
Classification: LCC PT2603.E455 O54 2021 (print) | LCC PT2603.E455
(ebook) | DDC 834/.912—dc23
LC record available at https://lccn.loc.gov/2021012987
LC ebook record available at https://lccn.loc.gov/2021012988

Typeset in Fournier by MJ & N Gavan, Truro, Cornwall
Printed and bound by CPI Group (UK) Ltd, Croydon CR0 4YY

Contents

Introduction
Susan Sontag

In most of the portrait photographs he is looking down, his right hand to his face. The earliest one I know shows him in 1927—he is thirty-five—with dark curly hair over a high forehead, moustache above a full lower lip: youthful, almost handsome. With his head lowered, his jacketed shoulders seem to start behind his ears; his thumb leans against his jaw; the rest of the hand, cigarette between bent index and third fingers, covers his chin; the downward look through his glasses—the soft, day-dreamer's gaze of the myopic— seems to float off to the lower left of the photograph.

In a picture from the late 1930s, the curly hair has hardly receded, but there is no trace of youth or handsomeness; the face has widened and the upper torso seems not just high but blocky, huge. The thicker moustache and the pudgy folded hand with thumb tucked under cover his mouth. The look is opaque, or just more inward: he could be thinking—or listening. ('He who listens hard doesn't see,' Benjamin wrote in his essay on Kafka.) There are books behind his head.

In a photograph taken in the summer of 1938, on the last of several visits he made to Brecht in exile in Denmark after

1933, he is standing in front of Brecht's house, an old man at forty-six, in white shirt, tie, trousers with watch chain: a slack, corpulent figure, looking truculently at the camera.

Another picture, from 1937, shows Benjamin in the Bibliothèque Nationale in Paris. Two men, neither of whose faces can be seen, share a table some distance behind him. Benjamin sits in the right foreground, probably taking notes for the book on Baudelaire and nineteenth-century Paris he had been writing for a decade. He is consulting a volume he holds open on the table with his left hand—his eyes can't be seen—looking, as it were, into the lower right edge of the photograph.

His close friend Gershom Scholem has described his first glimpse of Benjamin in Berlin in 1913, at a joint meeting of a Zionist youth group and Jewish members of the Free German Student Association, of which the twenty-one-year-old Benjamin was a leader. He spoke 'extempore without so much as a glance at his audience, staring with a fixed gaze at a remote corner of the ceiling which he harangued with much intensity, in a style incidentally that was, as far as I remember, ready for print'.[1]

He was what the French call *un triste*. In his youth he seemed marked by 'a profound sadness', Scholem wrote. He thought of himself as a melancholic, disdaining modern psychological labels and invoking the traditional astrological one: 'I came into the world under the sign of Saturn—the star of the slowest revolution, the planet of detours and delays.'[2] His major projects, the book published in 1928 on the German baroque drama (the *Trauerspiel*; literally, sorrow-play) and his never completed *Paris, Capital of the*

Nineteenth Century, cannot be fully understood unless one grasps how much they rely on a theory of melancholy.

Benjamin projected himself, his temperament, into all his major subjects, and his temperament determined what he chose to write about. It was what he saw in subjects, such as the seventeenth-century baroque plays (which dramatize different facets of 'Saturnine acedia') and the writers about whose work he wrote most brilliantly—Baudelaire, Proust, Kafka, Karl Kraus. He even found the Saturnine element in Goethe.[3] For, despite the polemic in his great (still untranslated) essay on Goethe's *Elective Affinities* against interpreting a writer's work by his life, he did make selective use of the life in his deepest meditations on texts: information that disclosed the melancholic, the solitary. (Thus, he describes Proust's 'loneliness which pulls the world down into its vortex'; explains how Kafka, like Klee, was 'essentially solitary'; cites Robert Walser's 'horror of success in life'.) One cannot use the life to interpret the work. But one can use the work to interpret the life.

Two short books of reminiscences of his Berlin childhood and student years, written in the early 1930s and unpublished in his lifetime, contain Benjamin's most explicit self-portrait. To the nascent melancholic, in school and on walks with his mother, 'solitude appeared to me as the only fit state of man'. Benjamin does not mean solitude in a room—he was often sick as a child—but solitude in the great metropolis, the busyness of the idle stroller, free to daydream, observe, ponder, cruise. The mind who was to attach much of the nineteenth century's sensibility to the figure of the *flâneur*, personified by that superbly self-aware melancholic Baudelaire, spun much of his own sensibility

out of his phantasmagorical, shrewd, subtle relation to
cities. The street, the passage, the arcade, the labyrinth are
recurrent themes in his literary essays and, notably, in the
projected book on nineteenth-century Paris, as well as in his
travel pieces and reminiscences. (Robert Walser, for whom
walking was the centre of his reclusive life and marvellous
books, is a writer to whom one particularly wishes Benjamin
had devoted a longer essay.)[4] The only book of a discreetly
autobiographical nature published in his lifetime was titled
One-Way Street. Reminiscences of self are reminiscences
of a place, and how he positions himself in it, navigates
around it.

'Not to find one's way about in a city is of little interest,'
begins his still untranslated *A Berlin Childhood Around the
Turn of the Century*. 'But to lose one's way in a city, as one
loses one's way in a forest, requires practice. ... I learned
this art late in life: it fulfilled the dreams whose first traces
were the labyrinths on the blotters of my exercise books.'
This passage also occurs *in A Berlin Chronicle*, after Benjamin suggests how much practice it took to get lost, given an
original sense of 'impotence before the city'. His goal is to
be a competent street-map reader who knows how to stray.
And to locate himself, with imaginary maps. Elsewhere in
Berlin Chronicle Benjamin relates that for years he had played
with the idea of mapping his life. For this map, which he
imagined as grey, he had devised a colourful system of signs
that 'clearly marked in the houses of my friends and girl
friends, the assembly halls of various collectives, from the
"debating chambers" of the Youth Movement to the gathering places of the Communist youth, the hotel and brothel
rooms that I knew for one night, the decisive benches in

the Tiergarten, the ways to different schools and the graves that I saw filled, the sites of prestigious cafés whose long-forgotten names daily crossed our lips'. Once, waiting for someone in the Café des Deux Magots in Paris, he relates, he managed to draw a diagram of his life: it was like a labyrinth, in which each important relationship figures as 'an entrance to the maze'.

The recurrent metaphors of maps and diagrams, memories and dreams, labyrinths and arcades, vistas and panoramas, evoke a certain vision of cities as well as a certain kind of life. Paris, Benjamin writes, 'taught me the art of straying'. The revelation of the city's true nature came not in Berlin but in Paris, where he stayed frequently throughout the Weimar years, and lived as a refugee from 1933 until his suicide while trying to escape from France in 1940—more exactly, the Paris re-imagined in the Surrealist narratives (Breton's *Nadja*, Aragon's *Le Paysan de Paris*). With these metaphors, he is indicating a general problem about orientation, and erecting a standard of difficulty and complexity. (A labyrinth is a place where one gets lost.) He is also suggesting a notion about the forbidden, and how to gain access to it: through an act of the mind that is the same as a physical act. 'Whole networks of streets were opened up under the auspices of prostitution,' he writes in *Berlin Chronicle*, which begins by invoking an Ariadne, the whore who leads this son of rich parents for the first time across 'the threshold of class'. The metaphor of the labyrinth also suggests Benjamin's idea of obstacles thrown up by his own temperament.

The influence of Saturn makes people 'apathetic, indecisive, slow', he writes in *The Origin of German Trauerspiel.*[5]

Slowness is one characteristic of the melancholic temperament. Blundering is another, from noticing too many
possibilities, from not noticing one's lack of practical sense.
And stubbornness, from the longing to be superior—on
one's own terms. Benjamin recalls his stubbornness during
childhood walks with his mother, who would turn insignificant items of conduct into tests of his aptitude for practical
life, thereby reinforcing what was inept ('my inability even
today to make a cup of coffee') and dreamily recalcitrant in
his nature. 'My habit of seeming slower, more maladroit,
more stupid than I am, had its origin in such walks, and
has the great attendant danger of making me think myself
quicker, more dexterous, and shrewder than I am.' And
from this stubbornness comes, 'above all, a gaze that appears
to see not a third of what it takes in'.

One-Way Street distills the experiences of the writer and
lover (it is dedicated to Asja Lacis, who 'cut it through the
author'),[6] experiences that can be guessed at in the opening
words on the writer's situation, which sound the theme of
revolutionary moralism, and the final 'To the Planetarium',
a paean to the technological wooing of nature and to sexual
ecstasy. Benjamin could write about himself more directly
when he started from memories, not contemporary experiences; when he writes about himself as a child. At that
distance, childhood, he can survey his life as a space that can
be mapped. The candour and the surge of painful feelings in
Berlin Childhood and *Berlin Chronicle* become possible precisely because Benjamin has adopted a completely digested,
analytical way of relating the past. It evokes events for the
reactions to the events, places for the emotions one has
deposited in the places, other people for the encounter with

oneself, feelings and behaviour for intimations of future passions and failures contained in them.[7] Fantasies of monsters loose in the large apartment while his parents entertain their friends prefigure his revulsion against his class; the dream of being allowed to sleep as long as he wants, instead of having to get up early to go to school, will be fulfilled when—after his book on the *Trauerspiel* failed to qualify him for a university lectureship—he realizes that 'his hopes of a position and a secure livelihood had always been in vain'; his way of walking with his mother, 'with pedantic care' keeping one step behind her, prefigures his 'sabotage of real social existence'.

Benjamin regards everything he chooses to recall in his past as prophetic of the future, because the work of memory (reading oneself backward, he called it) collapses time. There is no chronological ordering of his reminiscences, for which he disavows the name of autobiography, because time is irrelevant. ('Autobiography has to do with time, with sequence and what makes up the continuous flow of life,' he writes in *Berlin Chronicle*. 'Here, I am talking of a space, of moments and discontinuities.') Benjamin, the translator of Proust, wrote fragments of an opus that could be called *A la recherche des espaces perdues*. Memory, the staging of the past, turns the flow of events into tableaux. Benjamin is not trying to recover his past, but to understand it: to condense it into its spatial forms, its premonitory structures.

For the baroque dramatists, he writes in *The Origin of German Trauerspiel*, 'chronological movement is grasped and analysed in a spatial image'. The book on the *Trauerspiel* is not only Benjamin's first account of what it means to convert time into space; it is where he explains most clearly what feeling underlies this move. Awash in melancholic awareness of 'the disconsolate chronicle of world history', a process of incessant decay, the baroque dramatists seek to escape from history and restore the 'timelessness' of paradise. The seventeenth-century baroque sensibility had a 'panoramic' conception of history: 'history merges into the setting'. In *Berlin Childhood* and *Berlin Chronicle*, Benjamin merges his life into a setting. The successor to the baroque stage set is the Surrealist city: the metaphysical landscape in whose dreamlike spaces people have 'a brief, shadowy existence', like the nineteen-year-old poet whose suicide, the great sorrow of Benjamin's student years, is condensed in the memory of rooms that the dead friend inhabited.

Benjamin's recurrent themes are, characteristically, means of spatializing the world: for example, his notion of ideas and experiences as ruins. To understand something is to understand its topography, to know how to chart it. And to know how to get lost.

For the character born under the sign of Saturn, time is the medium of constraint, inadequacy, repetition, mere fulfilment. In time, one is only what one is: what one has always been. In space, one can be another person. Benjamin's poor sense of direction and inability to read a street map become his love of travel and his mastery of the art of straying. Time does not give one much leeway: it thrusts us forward from behind, blows us through the narrow funnel of the present into the future. But space is broad, teeming with possibilities, positions, intersections, passages, detours, U-turns, dead ends, one-way streets. Too many possibilities, indeed. Since the Saturnine temperament is slow, prone to indecisiveness, sometimes one has to cut one's way through with a knife. Sometimes one ends by turning the knife against oneself.

The mark of the Saturnine temperament is the self-conscious and unforgiving relation to the self, which can never be taken for granted. The self is a text—it has to be deciphered. (Hence, this is an apt temperament for intellectuals.) The self is a project, something to be built. (Hence, this is an apt temperament for artists and martyrs, those who court 'the purity and beauty of a failure', as Benjamin says of Kafka.) And the process of building a self and its works is always too slow. One is always in arrears to oneself.

Things appear at a distance, come forward slowly. In *Berlin Childhood*, he speaks of his 'propensity for seeing everything I care about approach me from far away'—the way, often ill as a child, he imagined the hours approaching his sickbed. 'This is perhaps the origin of what others call patience in me, but which in truth does not resemble any virtue.' (Of course, others did experience it as patience, as a virtue. Scholem has described him as 'the most patient human being I ever came to know'.)[8]

But something like patience is needed for the melancholic's labours of decipherment. Proust, as Benjamin notes, was excited by 'the secret language of the salons'; Benjamin was drawn to more compact codes. He collected emblem books, liked to make up anagrams, played with pseudonyms. His taste for pseudonyms well antedates his need as a German Jewish refugee, who from 1933 to 1936 continued to publish reviews in German magazines under the name of Detlev Holz, the name he used to sign the last book to appear in his lifetime, *Deutsche Menschen*, published in Switzerland in 1936. In the amazing text recently published by Scholem, 'Agesilaus Santander', Benjamin speaks of his fantasy of having a secret name; the name of this text—which turns on the figure in the Klee drawing he owned, *Angelus Novus*—is, as Scholem has pointed out, an anagram of The Angel Satan (*Der Angelus Satanas*). He was an 'uncanny' graphologist, Scholem reports, though 'later on he tended to conceal this gift'. (Benjamin discusses handwriting in 'On the Mimetic Faculty'.)

Dissimulation, secretiveness appear a necessity to the melancholic. He has complex, often veiled relations with others. These feelings of superiority, of inadequacy, of baffled feeling, of not being able to get what one wants, or even name it properly (or consistently) to oneself—these can be, it is felt they ought to be, masked by friendliness, or the most scrupulous manipulation. Using a word that was also applied to Kafka by those who knew him, Scholem speaks of 'the almost Chinese courtesy' that characterized Benjamin's relations with people. But one is not surprised to learn, of the man who could justify Proust's 'invectives against friendship', that Benjamin could also drop friends brutally, as he did his comrades from the Youth Movement, when they no longer interested him.[9] Nor is one surprised to learn that this fastidious, intransigent, fiercely serious man could also flatter people he probably did not think his equals, that he could let himself be 'baited' (his own word) and condescended to by Brecht on his visits to Denmark. This prince of the intellectual life could also be a courtier.

Benjamin analysed both parts in *The Origin of German Trauerspiel* by the theory of melancholy. One characteristic of the Saturnine temperament is slowness: 'The tyrant falls on account of the sluggishness of his emotions.' 'Another trait of the predominance of Saturn', says Benjamin, is 'faithlessness'. This is represented by the character of the courtier in baroque drama, whose mind is 'fluctuation itself'. The manipulativeness of the courtier is partly a 'lack of character'; partly it 'reflects an inconsolable, despondent surrender to an impenetrable conjunction of baleful constellations [that] seem to have taken on a massive, almost thing-like cast'. Only someone identifying with this sense of historical catastrophe, this degree of despondency, would have explained why the courtier is not to be despised. His faithlessness to his fellow men, Benjamin says, corresponds to the 'deeper, more contemplative faith' he keeps with material emblems.

What Benjamin describes could be understood as simple pathology: the tendency of the melancholic temperament to project its inner torpor outward, as the immutability of misfortune, which is experienced as 'massive, almost thing-like'. But his argument is more daring: he perceives that the deep transactions between the melancholic and the world always take place with things (rather than with people); and that these are genuine transactions, which reveal meaning. Precisely because the melancholy character is haunted by death, it is melancholics who best know how to read the world. Or, rather, it is the world which yields itself to the melancholic's scrutiny, as it does to no one else's. The more lifeless things are, the more potent and ingenious can be the mind which contemplates them.

If this melancholy temperament is faithless to people, it has good reason to be faithful to things. Fidelity lies in accumulating things—which appear, mostly, in the form of fragments or ruins. ('It is common practice in baroque literature to pile up fragments incessantly', Benjamin writes.) Both the baroque and Surrealism, sensibilities with which Benjamin profoundly identified, see reality as things. Benjamin describes the baroque as a world of things (emblems, ruins) and spatialized ideas ('allegories are, in the realm of thought, what ruins are in the realm of things'). The genius of Surrealism was to generalize with ebullient candour the baroque cult of ruins; to perceive that the nihilistic energies of the modern era make everything a ruin or fragment—and therefore collectible. A world whose past has become (by definition) obsolete, and whose present churns out instant antiques, invites custodians, decoders, and collectors.

As one kind of collector himself, Benjamin remained faithful to things—as things. According to Scholem, building his library, which included many first editions and rare books, was 'his most enduring personal passion'. Inert in the face of thing-like disaster, the melancholy temperament is galvanized by the passions aroused by privileged objects. Benjamin's books were not only for use, professional tools; they were contemplative objects, stimuli for reverie. His library evokes 'memories of the cities in which I found so many things: Riga, Naples, Munich, Danzig, Moscow, Florence, Basel, Paris … memories of the rooms where these books had been housed. …' Book-hunting, like the sexual hunt, adds to the geography of pleasure—another reason for strolling about in the world. In collecting, Benjamin experienced what in himself was clever, successful, shrewd, unabashedly passionate. 'Collectors are people with a tactical instinct'—like courtiers.

Apart from first editions and baroque emblem books, Benjamin specialized in children's books and books written by the mad. 'The great works which meant so much to him', reports Scholem, 'were placed in bizarre patterns next to the most out-of-the-way writings and oddities.' The odd arrangement of the library is like the strategy of Benjamin's work, in which a Surrealist-inspired eye for the treasures of meaning in the ephemeral, discredited, and neglected worked in tandem with his loyalty to the traditional canon of learned taste.

He liked finding things where nobody was looking. He drew from the obscure, disdained German baroque drama elements of the modern (that is to say, his own) sensibility: the taste for allegory, Surrealist shock effects, discontinuous utterance, the sense of historical catastrophe. 'These stones were the bread of my imagination,' he wrote about Marseilles—the most recalcitrant of cities to that imagination, even when helped by a dose of hashish. Many expected references are absent in Benjamin's work—he didn't like to read what everybody was reading. He preferred the doctrine of the four temperaments as a psychological theory to Freud. He preferred being a communist, or trying to be one, without reading Marx. This man who read virtually everything, and had spent fifteen years sympathizing with revolutionary communism, had barely looked into Marx until the late 1930s. (He was reading *Capital* on his visit to Brecht in Denmark in the summer of 1938.)

His sense of strategy was one of his points of identification with Kafka, a kindred would-be tactician, who 'took precautions against the interpretation of his writing'. The whole point of the Kafka stories, Benjamin argues, is that they have *no* definite, symbolic meaning. And he was fascinated by the very different, un-Jewish sense of ruse practised by Brecht, the anti-Kafka of his imagination. (Predictably, Brecht disliked Benjamin's great essay on Kafka. intensely.) Brecht, with the little wooden donkey near his desk from whose neck hung the sign 'I, too, must understand it', represented for Benjamin, an admirer of esoteric religious texts, the possibly more potent ruse of reducing complexity, of making everything clear. Benjamin's 'masochistic' (the word is Siegfried Kracauer's) relation to Brecht, which most of his friends deplored, shows the extent to which he was fascinated by this possibility.

Benjamin's propensity is to go against the usual interpretation. 'All the decisive blows are struck left-handed', as he says in *One-Way Street*. Precisely because he saw that 'all human knowledge takes the form of interpretation',[10] he understood the importance of being against interpretation wherever it is obvious. His most common strategy is to drain symbolism out of some things, like the Kafka stories or Goethe's *Elective Affinities* (texts where everybody agrees it is there), and pour it into others, where nobody suspects its existence (such as the German baroque plays, which he reads as allegories of historical pessimism). 'Each book is a tactic', he wrote. In a letter to a friend, he claimed for his writings, only partly facetiously, forty-nine levels of meaning. For moderns as much as for cabalists, nothing is straightforward. Everything is—at the least—difficult. 'Ambiguity displaces authenticity in all things', he wrote in *One-Way Street*. What is most foreign to Benjamin is anything like ingenuousness: 'the "unclouded", "innocent" eye has become a lie'.

Much of the originality of Benjamin's arguments owes to his microscopic gaze (*as* his friend and disciple Theodor Adorno called it), combined with his indefatigable command over theoretical perspectives. 'It was the small things that attracted him most', writes Scholem. He loved old toys, postage stamps, picture postcards, and such playful miniaturizations of reality as the winter world inside a glass globe that snows when it is shaken. His own handwriting was almost microscopic, and his never realized ambition, Scholem reports, was to get a hundred lines on a sheet of paper. (The ambition was realized by Robert Walser, who used to transcribe the manuscripts of his stories and novels as micrograms, in a truly microscopic script.) Scholem relates that when he visited Benjamin in Paris in August 1927 (the first time the two friends had seen each other since Scholem emigrated to Palestine in 1923), Benjamin dragged him to an exhibit of Jewish ritual objects at the Musée Cluny to show him 'two grains of wheat on which a kindred soul had inscribed the complete Shema Israel'.[11]

To miniaturize is to make portable—the ideal form of possessing things for a wanderer, or a refugee. Benjamin, of course, was both a wanderer, on the move, and a collector, weighed down by things; that is, passions. To miniaturize is to conceal. Benjamin was drawn to the extremely small as he was to whatever had to be deciphered: emblems, anagrams, handwriting. To miniaturize means to make useless. For what is so grotesquely reduced is, in a sense, liberated from its meaning—its tininess being the outstanding thing about it. It is both a whole (that is, complete) and a fragment (so tiny, the wrong scale). It becomes an object of disinterested contemplation or reverie. Love of the small is a child's emotion, one colonized by Surrealism. The Paris of the Surrealists is 'a little world', Benjamin observes; so is the photograph, which Surrealist taste discovered as an enigmatic, even perverse, rather than a merely intelligible or beautiful, object, and about which Benjamin wrote with such originality. The melancholic always feels threatened by the dominion of the thing-like, but Surrealist taste mocks these terrors. Surrealism's great gift to sensibility was to make melancholy cheerful.

'The only pleasure the melancholic permits himself, and it is a powerful one, is allegory', Benjamin wrote in *The Origin of German Trauerspiel*. Indeed, he asserted, allegory is the way of reading the world typical of melancholies, and cited Baudelaire: 'Everything for me becomes Allegory.' The process which extracts meaning from the petrified and insignificant, allegory, is the characteristic method of the German baroque drama and of Baudelaire, Benjamin's major subjects; and, transmuted into philosophical argument and the micrological analysis of things, the method Benjamin practised himself.

The melancholic sees the world itself become a thing: refuge, solace, enchantment. Shortly before his death, Benjamin was planning an essay about miniaturization as a device of fantasy. It seems to have been a continuation of an old plan to write on Goethe's 'The New Melusina' (in *Wilhelm Meister*),[12] which is about a man who falls in love with a woman who is actually a tiny person, temporarily granted normal size, and unknowingly carries around with him a box containing the miniature kingdom of which she is the princess. In Goethe's tale, the world is reduced to a collectible thing, an object, in the most literal sense.

Like the box in Goethe's tale, a book is not only a fragment of the world but itself a little world. The book is a miniaturization of the world, which the reader inhabits. In *Berlin Chronicle*, Benjamin evokes his childhood rapture: 'You did not read books through; you dwelt, abided between their lines.' To reading, the delirium of the child, was eventually added writing, the obsession of the adult. The most praiseworthy way of acquiring books is by writing them, Benjamin remarks in 'Unpacking My Library'.[13] And the best way to understand them is also to enter their space: one never really understands a book unless one copies it, he says in *One-Way Street*, as one never understands a landscape from an airplane but only by walking through it.

'The amount of meaning is in exact proportion to the presence of death and the power of decay', Benjamin writes in the book on the *Trauerspiel*. This is what makes it possible to find meaning in one's own life, in 'the dead occurrences of the past which are euphemistically known as experience'. Only because the past is dead is one able to read it. Only because history is fetishized in physical objects can one understand it. Only because the book is a world can one enter it. The book for him was another space in which to stroll. For the character born under the sign of Saturn, the true impulse when one is being looked at is to cast down one's eyes, look in a corner. Better, one can lower one's head to one's notebook. Or put one's head behind the wall of a book.

It is characteristic of the Saturnine temperament to blame its undertow of inwardness on the will. Convinced that the will is weak, the melancholic may make extravagant efforts to develop it. If these efforts are successful, the resulting hypertrophy of will usually takes the form of a compulsive devotion to work. Thus Baudelaire, who suffered constantly from 'acedia, the malady of monks', ended many letters and his *Intimate Journals* with the most impassioned pledges to work more, to work uninterruptedly, to do nothing but work. (Despair over 'every defeat of the will' —Baudelaire's phrase again—is a characteristic complaint of modern artists and intellectuals, particularly of those who are both.) One is condemned to work; otherwise one might not do anything at all. Even the dreaminess of the melancholic temperament is harnessed to work, and the melancholic may try to cultivate phantasmagorical states, like dreams, or seek the access to concentrated states of attention offered by drugs. Surrealism simply puts a positive accent on what Baudelaire experienced so negatively: it does not deplore the guttering of volition but raises it to an ideal, proposing that dream states may be relied on to furnish all the material needed for work.

Benjamin, always working, always trying to work more, speculated a good deal on the writer's daily existence. *One-Way Street* has several sections which offer recipes for work: the best conditions, timing, utensils. Part of the impetus for the large correspondence he conducted was to chronicle, report on, confirm the existence of work. His instincts as a collector served him well. Learning was a form of collecting, as in the quotations and excerpts from daily reading which Benjamin accumulated in notebooks that he carried everywhere and from which he would read aloud to friends. Thinking was also a form of collecting, at least in its preliminary stages. He conscientiously logged stray ideas;

developed mini-essays in letters to friends; rewrote plans for future projects; noted his dreams (several are recounted in *One-Way Street*); kept numbered lists of all the books he read. (Scholem recalls seeing, on his second and last visit to Benjamin in Paris, in 1938, a notebook of current reading in which Marx's *Eighteenth Brumaire* is listed as No. 1649.)

How does the melancholic become a hero of will? Through the fact that work can become like a drug, a compulsion. ('Thinking which is an eminent narcotic', he wrote in the essay on Surrealism.) In fact, melancholics make the best addicts, for the true addictive experience is always a solitary one. The hashish sessions of the late 1920s, supervised by a doctor friend, were prudent stunts, not acts of self-surrender; material for the writer, not escape from the exactions of the will. (Benjamin considered the book he wanted to write on hashish one of his most important projects.)

The need to be solitary—along with bitterness over one's loneliness—is characteristic of the melancholic. To get work done, one must be solitary—or, at least, not bound to any permanent relationship. Benjamin's negative feelings about marriage are clear in the essay on Goethe's *Elective Affinities*. His heroes—Kierkegaard, Baudelaire, Proust, Kafka, Kraus—never married; and Scholem reports that Benjamin came to regard his own marriage (he was married in 1917, estranged from his wife after 1921, and divorced in 1930) 'as fatal to himself'. The world of nature, and of natural relationships, is perceived by the melancholic temperament as less than seductive. The self-portrait in *Berlin Childhood* and *Berlin Chronicle* is of a wholly alienated son; as husband and father (he had a son, born in 1918, who emigrated to England with Benjamin's ex-wife in the mid-1930s), he appears to have simply not known what to do with these relationships. For the melancholic, the natural, in the form of family ties, introduces the falsely subjective, the sentimental; it is a drain on the will, on one's independence; on one's freedom to concentrate on work. It also presents a challenge to one's humanity to which the melancholic knows, in advance, he will be inadequate.

The style of work of the melancholic is immersion, total concentration. Either one is immersed, or attention floats away. As a writer, Benjamin was capable of extraordinary concentration. He was able to research and write *The Origin of German Trauerspiel* in two years; some of it, he boasts in *Berlin Chronicle*, was written in long evenings at a café, sitting close to a jazz band. But although Benjamin wrote prolifically—in some periods turning out work every week for the German literary papers and magazines—it proved impossible for him to write a normal-sized book again. In a letter in 1935, Benjamin speaks of 'the Saturnine pace' of writing *Paris, Capital of the Nineteenth Century*, which he had begun in 1927 and thought could be finished in two years.[14] His characteristic form remained the essay. The melancholic's intensity and exhaustiveness of attention set natural limits to the length at which Benjamin could explicate his ideas. His major essays seem to end just in time, before they self-destruct.

His sentences do not seem to be generated in the usual way; they do not entail. Each *sentence* is written as if it were the first, or the last. ('A writer must stop and restart with every new sentence', he says in the Prologue to *The Origin of German Trauerspiel*.) Mental and historical processes are rendered as conceptual tableaux; ideas are transcribed in *extremis* and the intellectual perspectives are vertiginous. His style of thinking and writing, incorrectly called aphoristic, might better be called freeze-frame baroque. This style was torture to execute. It was as if each sentence had to say everything, before the inward gaze of total concentration dissolved the subject before his eyes. Benjamin was probably not exaggerating when he told Adorno that each idea in his book on Baudelaire and nineteenth-century Paris 'had to be wrested away from a realm in which madness lies'.[15]

Something like the dread of being stopped prematurely lies behind these sentences as saturated with ideas as the surface of a baroque painting is jammed with movement. In a letter to Adorno, Benjamin describes his transports when he first read Aragon's *Le Paysan de Paris*, the book that inspired *Paris, Capital of the Nineteenth Century*: 'I would never read more than two or three pages in bed of an evening because the pounding of my heart was so loud that I had to let the book fall from my hands. What a warning!'[16] Cardiac failure is the metaphoric limit of Benjamin's exertions and passions. (He suffered from a heart ailment.) And cardiac sufficiency is a metaphor he offers for the writer's achievement. In the essay in praise of Karl Kraus, Benjamin writes: 'If style is the power to move freely in the length and breadth of linguistic thinking without falling into banality, it is attained chiefly by the cardiac strength of great thoughts, which drives the blood of language through the capillaries of syntax into the remotest limbs.' Thinking, writing are ultimately a question of stamina. The melancholic, who feels he lacks will, may feel that he needs all the destructive energies he can muster.

'Truth resists being projected into the realm of knowledge', Benjamin writes in *The Origin of German Trauerspiel*. His dense prose registers that resistance, and leaves no space for attacking those who distribute lies. Benjamin considered polemic beneath the dignity of a truly philosophical style, and sought instead what he called 'the fullness of concentrated positivity'—the essay on Goethe's *Elective Affinities*, with its devastating refutation of the critic and Goethe biographer Friedrich Gundolf, being the one exception to this rule among his major writings. But his awareness of the ethical utility of polemic made him appreciate that one-man Viennese public institution, Karl Kraus, a writer whose facility, stridency, love of the aphoristic, and indefatigable polemic energies make him so unlike Benjamin.[17]

The essay on Kraus is Benjamin's most passionate and perverse defence of the life of the mind. 'The perfidious reproach of being "too intelligent" haunted him throughout his life', Adorno has written.[18] Benjamin defended himself against this philistine defamation by bravely raising the standard of the 'inhumanity' of the intellect, when it is properly—that is, ethically—employed. 'The life of letters is existence under the aegis of mere mind as prostitution is existence under the aegis of mere sexuality', he wrote. This is to celebrate both prostitution (as Kraus did, because mere sexuality was sexuality in a pure state) and the life of letters, as Benjamin did, using the unlikely figure of Kraus, because of 'the genuine and demonic function of mere mind, to be a disturber of the peace'. The ethical task of the modern writer is to be not a creator but a destroyer—a destroyer of shallow inwardness, the consoling notion of the universally human, dilettantish creativity, and empty phrases.

The writer as scourge and destroyer, portrayed in the figure of Kraus, he sketched with concision and even greater boldness in the allegorical 'The Destructive Character', also written in 1931. The date is suggestive: Scholem has written that the first of several times Benjamin contemplated suicide was in the summer of 1931. (The second time was the following summer, when he wrote 'Agesilaus Santander'.) The Apollonian scourge whom Benjamin calls the destructive character 'is always blithely at work … has few needs … has no interest in being understood … is young and cheerful, … and feels not that life is worth living but that suicide is not worth the trouble'. It is a kind of conjuration, an attempt by Benjamin to draw the destructive elements of his Saturnine character outward—so that they are not self-destructive.

Benjamin is not referring just to his own destructiveness. He thought that there was a peculiarly modern temptation to suicide. In 'The Paris of the Second Empire in Baudelaire', he wrote, 'The resistance which modernity offers to the natural productive élan of a person is out of proportion to his strength. It is understandable if a person grows tired and takes refuge in death. Modernity must be under the sign of suicide, an act which seals a heroic will. … It is *the* achievement of modernity in the realm of passions …'. Suicide is understood as a response of the heroic will to the defeat of the will. The only way to avoid suicide, Benjamin suggests, is to be beyond heroism, beyond efforts of the will. The destructive character cannot feel trapped, because 'he sees ways everywhere'. Cheerfully engaged in reducing what exists to rubble, he 'positions himself at the crossroads'.

Benjamin's portrait of the destructive character would evoke a kind of Siegfried of the mind—a high-spirited, childlike brute under the protection of the gods—had this apocalyptic pessimism not been qualified by the irony always within the range of the Saturnine temperament. Irony is the positive name which the melancholic gives to his solitude, his asocial choices. In *One-Way Street* Benjamin hailed the irony that allows individuals to assert the right to lead lives independent of the community as 'the most European of all accomplishments', and observed that it had completely deserted Germany. Benjamin's taste for the ironic and the self-aware put him off most of recent German culture: he detested Wagner, despised Heidegger, and scorned the frenetic vanguard movements of Weimar Germany such as Expressionism.

Passionately, but also ironically, Benjamin placed himself at the crossroads. It was important for him to keep his many 'positions' open: the theological, the Surrealist/aesthetic, the communist. One position corrects another: he needed them all. Decisions, of course, tended to spoil the balance of these positions, vacillation kept everything in place. The reason he gave for his delay in leaving France, when he last saw Adorno in early 1938, was that 'there are still positions here to defend'.

Benjamin thought the freelance intellectual was a dying species anyway, made no less obsolete by capitalist society than by revolutionary communism; indeed he felt that he was living in a time in which everything valuable was the last of its kind. He thought Surrealism was the last intelligent moment of the European intelligentsia, an appropriately destructive, nihilistic kind of intelligence. In his essay on Kraus, Benjamin asks rhetorically: Does Kraus stand 'at the threshold of a new age? Alas, by no means. He stands at the Last Judgment.' Benjamin is thinking of himself. At the Last Judgment, the Last Intellectual—that Saturnine hero of modern culture, with his ruins, his defiant visions, his reveries, his unquenchable gloom, his downcast eyes—will explain that he took many 'positions' and defended the life of the mind to the end, as righteously and inhumanly as he could.

Susan Sontag 1979

Publisher's Note

The background and organization of the materials included in this volume need a few words of explanation. At its head stands Benjamin's work *One-Way Street* (I), the one other complete book after *The Origin of German Tragic Drama* that he succeeded in publishing in his life-time, and the work that marks the main watershed in his intellectual and political development. There follow five groups of shorter texts corresponding to successive phases in his writing before and after this turning-point. These obey a chronological order, with some minor variations. They start with a selection of Benjamin's metaphysical writings, largely from the early years 1916 to 1921 (II); proceed to a series of townscapes written between 1924 and 1928 (III); present a trio of major aesthetic essays of the later Weimar period, dating from 1929 to 1931 (IV); then move to the autobiographical writing of 1932 that was his closing project before the victory of Nazism (V); and finally conclude with a representative theoretical study from the time of his exile in France, composed in 1937 (VI). Some brief remarks may serve to clarify this sequence.

Benjamin's early philosophical formation was in the neo-Kantian idealism that dominated the German universities in the years before the First World War, although his own admiration for Kant was tempered by his attraction towards the romantic aesthetic theories of Schlegel and Novalis, constructed in part against the legacy of Kant. His deepest convictions at this date, however, seem to have been religious —in theological affinity closest to Jewish mysticism, and in speculative focus trained primarily on language. Politically, he had broken with the elitist and nationalist *Jugendbewegung*, of which he had been an active member as a student, when its leaders rallied to the imperialist war effort in 1914. During the war, the last part of which he spent in neutral Switzerland, he shared the radical anarchist sympathies of his friend Gerhard Scholem. The group of early texts below (II) reflects this youthful outlook. Benjamin was 24 when he wrote the first. Highly gnomic and abstract, they were not as entirely isolated or idiosyncratic as they might appear to a contemporary reader. The great metaphysical interest in language evinced in *On Language as Such and on the Language of Man* and *Fate and Character* had a counterpart in the contemporary work of the young Heidegger, whose quest for origins took by contrast a medieval rather than biblical direction. The messianic conception of social revolution as the descent of an eschatological salvation, marked in *Critique of Violence* and the *Theologico-Political Fragment*, was likewise not confined to Benjamin. His elders Ernst Bloch and Georg Lukács had independently developed a very similar mystico-political radicalism in the years before the First World War. Lukács had been attracted by Christian and Hassidic doctrines of redemption (the latter under the influence of Buber), and even Hindu notions of caste.[1] Bloch's first major work, Der Geist der Utopie, published in 1918, was an exalted call for a new terrestrial order and a new church to link it to the supernatural order above, which saw the Bolshevik Revolution as the work of 'praetorians enthroning Christ as Emperor' in Russia.[2] Benjamin met Bloch during their common refuge in Switzerland, forming a close friendship with him. *Fate and Character* was published in Bloch's expressionist review *Dit Argonauten*, as was Benjamin's first significant literary essay, on Dostoevsky's *The Idiot* (a central book for this generation); the *Theologico-Political Fragment* expressly invokes *Der Geist der Utopie*.

In the post-war epoch, all three men discovered Marxism. Lukács abandoned the universe of religion altogether, becoming a major theorist and militant in the ranks of the Third International. Bloch fused religious and political themes into a single millenarian cosmology. Benjamin's encounter with Marxism occurred later, and its results were more cryptic. His development reveals an unmistakable evolution towards a more coherent materialism. But there was no inward rupture with his earlier mysticism, so that he could write short texts in the 1930s directly continuous in idiom and preoccupation with those of a decade before. *The Destructive Character* and *On the Mimetic Faculty*, included in this collection, are cases in point—pendants respectively to *Fate and Character* and *On Language as Such and on the Language of Man*;[3] while the unpublished *Theologico-Political Fragment* of 1920–21 so clearly adumbrates themes in *Theses on the Philosophy of History* of 1940 that Adorno could long believe it to have been composed as late as 1938.

On the other hand, with very few exceptions—the essay on Karl Kraus and the *Theses*—Benjamin did not attempt any syncretism of the two sources of his beliefs either. His thought retained what Scholem has aptly called a 'two-track' cast.[4] Characteristically, mystical and materialist motifs were distilled into separate writings, whose precise inter-relationship remained enigmatic, often exasperatingly so, to his secular and religious admirers alike. The balance, however, was to shift qualitatively between the two in the trajectory of his work.

After the War, Benjamin's first major publication was a long essay on Goethe's *Elective Affinities*, composed in 1922. Arcane in style and metaphysical in register, it fitted no conventional category of literary criticism, contemporaneous or subsequent. The Austrian poet and playwright Hugo Von Hofmannsthal warmly approved the essay and published it in his recently founded review *Neue Deutsche Beiträge* in 1924–25. Hofmannsthal's cultural authority might have seemed to ensure Benjamin's national debut in German intellectual life; this was, at least, probably Benjamin's own expectation. In fact, however, the *Neue Deutsche Beiträge* proved to be a fiasco as a journal: the mixture of conservative nostalgia and religious restorationism that dominated its pages consigned it to a virtually private backwater in Weimar culture.[5] Its circulation was so small that Benjamin's essay found no resonance in German letters at the time. His first attempt to establish himself as a critic drew, in effect, a blank. His second was more ambitious. From March 1923 to April 1925 he worked on a post-doctoral thesis for the University of Frankfurt on German baroque drama. If accepted, this would afford him a secure academic career. The final work was, however, too complex and esoteric for the professors to whom it was submitted. Forewarned of rejection, Benjamin withdrew the text. Eventually published in 1928 as *The Origin of German Tragic Drama*, its ultimate fame was to be entirely posthumous. At the time of its appearance, it was greeted with silence and incomprehension in Germany. The dual failure of his work on Goethe and the Baroque to win even an initiated public was to be one of the main precipitants of the abrupt change of direction in Benjamin's work after 1925.

There were two others. In the closing stages of his work on the German *Trauerspiel*, Benjamin had stayed for some months in Capri in late 1924, in the company of Bloch. There he met and fell in love with Asja Lacis, 'a Russian revolutionary from Riga, one of the most remarkable women I have ever met'.[6] He now determined to study Lukács's *History and Class Consciousness*, of which Bloch had just written a review, and the political practice of contemporary communism. The beginning of his movement towards Marxism thus coincided with the completion of *The Origin of German Tragic Drama*. In the autumn of 1925, after the failure of his thesis at Frankfurt, he visited Asja Lacis in Riga. He was now, Scholem reports, actively considering whether to join the KPD or not.[7] This sharp political turn, meanwhile, was accompanied—perhaps in part prompted—by a transformation in his economic situation. Benjamin had hitherto been financially supported by his father, a well-off art dealer in Berlin, with attendant tensions between the two. The onset of the great inflation of 1923 struck at his father's fortune, leading him to suggest that Benjamin take up employment in a bank. The project of the *Habilitationsschrift* had thus also been an attempt to escape familial dependence through a university appointment. In the aftermath of its failure, Benjamin had to look for alternative ways of earning his living. The solution he adopted was to be journalism. From 1926 onwards, the character of his output underwent a drastic outward alteration—in a word, from hermeticism to publicism. He became a prolific book-reviewer, travel-reporter and radio-scriptwriter, forsaking his more esoteric diction for an often disconcertingly concrete language, metaphysical for more topical terrains.

One-Way Street, for the most part written between August 1925 and September 1926, represents the staccato announcement of these changes. Its first lines ('Filling Station') proclaim the end of 'the pretentious universal gesture of the book', in favour of forms alternating between action and writing, 'leaflets, brochures, articles and placards'. Elsewhere ('Attested Auditor of Books') it declares: 'Printing, having found in the book a refuge in which to lead an autonomous existence, is pitilessly dragged out onto the street by advertisements and subjected to the brutal heteronomies of economic chaos. This is the hard schooling of its new form.' Composed of a mosaic of aphoristic paragraphs, captioned by placards of urban scenery, *One-Way Street* is deliberately at the antipodes of the treatise form of *The Origin of German Tragic Drama*. Its debts to surrealism (intercalation of dreams) and to photomontage are obvious: pointers to the profound transformation in Benjamin's conception of contemporary art that was eventually to find formulation in the subversive functionalism of his essays of the thirties. Simultaneously, *One-Way Street* set out the programme of what was to be his critical practice in the

Weimar press: 'The critic is the strategist of literary struggle'. The political overtones of the phrase—what Scholem
noted as the 'background thunder of Marxist vocabulary'
in the passages Benjamin read to him before publication[8]—
were not fortuitous. The original kernel of the work was,
in fact, the section subtitled 'A Tour of German Inflation'.
First sketched in 1923, it condensed Benjamin's reactions
to the economic misery of the time, and the degradation
of social and personal experience that accompanied it. The
material crisis of the German intelligentsia evoked here was
to be one of the most constant themes of his journalistic
interventions, recurring again and again in his book reviews
of the later twenties. The political conclusions he drew from
it were now intransigently radical. Where he had written
with contemplative resignation in the early draft of 1923:
'But no-one may ever make peace with poverty when it falls
like a gigantic shadow upon his countrymen and his house.
Then he must be alert to every humiliation done to him and
so discipline himself that his suffering becomes no longer
the downhill road of hate, but the rising path of prayer',[9]
he now reversed the terms of the same passage, to read: 'so
discipline himself that his suffering no longer becomes the
downhill road of grief, but the rising path of revolt'. The
change can stand as the motto of his political radicalization.

The pivotal position of *One-Way Street* within Benjamin's work, however, is not due only to its compact register
of the sudden mutation in his critical, aesthetic and political
options in the mid-twenties. It above all lies in the fact that in
the same swift movement with which Benjamin passed from
the banks of tradition to those of the avant-garde, he also
discovered the heuristic method that was to be peculiarly

his thereafter—'the attempt to establish', as he was later to write, 'the image of history even in its most inconspicuous fixtures of existence, its rejects'.[10] The kaleidoscope of urban objects, warnings, buildings, amusements, signs was designed to throw sudden light on the modern epoch. To Hofmannsthal, he wrote: 'Precisely in its eccentric elements the book is, if not a trophy, a document of an inner struggle whose object can be resumed thus: to grasp the actual as the obverse of the eternal in history and to take an imprint of this hidden side of the medal.'[11] His next words usher in the project that was to preoccupy him for the remainder of his life: 'For the rest the book owes much to Paris, and represents my first attempt at confrontation with it. I continue it in a second work, entitled "Parisian Arcades"'. *One-Way Street*, in other words, directly inaugurates the second great phase of Benjamin's major work—his prolonged study of Baudelaire's Paris. He was lucidly conscious of this turning-point at the time, analysing his development in a letter to Scholem: 'Once I have finished … the work with which I am at present circumspectly, provisionally occupied—the highly remarkable and extremely precarious essay *The Parisian Arcades: a Dialectical Fairyland*—this will close for me a productive cycle—that of *One-Way Street*—rather in the sense that the Tragedy book closed my germanistic cycle. In it the worldly themes of *One-Way Street* will march past in an infernal intensification'.[12] The prediction was to hold good. The microcosmic miscellany of the quotidian would continue to provide the sparks for the larger historical illuminations of Benjamin's work, of which *One-Way Street* ends with one of the most memorable: perhaps the first and certainly the finest—because most temperate and rational—expression of that rejection of the notion of the mastery of nature by technology that was afterwards to become a hallmark of Frankfurt Marxism.

Townscapes were to be a recurring motif in Benjamin's writing henceforward. The group published in this volume (III) starts with a description of Naples written in collaboration with Asja Lacis while the two were on Capri together in late 1924. It was not published until August 1925, when its appearance as his first contribution to the *Frankfurter Zeitung* marked the real inception of his journalistic practice. The essay on Moscow likewise owes its origin to Benjamin's relationship with Lacis, whom he visited in the Soviet capital from December 1926 to February 1927. First excerpted in *L'Humanité*, it is of particular interest as a vivid report of Benjamin's personal reactions to what he saw of the USSR in the final months of Stalin's drive to eliminate the Left Opposition, whose leaders had been deprived of their posts in the party a few weeks before he arrived.[13] (His unpublished diary of this period, soon to appear in the *Gesammelte Schriften*, may throw new light on his precise political attitudes towards the conflicts in the international communist movement of the time. Scholem recounts that it was during this stay in Moscow that Benjamin finally decided against joining the KPD.)[14] The two texts on Marseilles, written in late 1928, are of a very different character, reflecting Benjamin's affinity to Surrealism and experimentation with induced hallucinations.

The aesthetic essays (IV) which follow all date from the final years of the Weimar Republic. By this time Benjamin was an experienced, although never exactly established, contributor to the *Frankfurter Zeitung*, the liberal daily with

the most respected feuilleton section in Germany, and the
Literarische Welt, the cultural weekly created by Rowohlt
Verlag, the house which had published *The Origin of German
Tragic Drama* and *One-Way Street*.[15] His articles in the
latter could be somewhat more candid politically than in
the former, a paper ultimately controlled by heavy industry. As Adorno was to note in his obituary of Benjamin, it
was for his critical articles as a publicist in these two organs,
each of which enjoyed a wide circulation, that Benjamin
was known in Germany during his life-time.[16] The essay on
Surrealism, in its delicate blend of sympathy and severity,
represents Benjamin's major reflection on the relationship
between the aesthetic avant-garde in Western Europe and
revolutionary politics. The text on Photography, whose
innovations had been eagerly seized upon by the Surrealists, was one of the first serious treatments of it as a medium
outside the professional milieu itself. Its concerns look
directly forward to Benjamin's great study of *The Work
of Art in the Age of Mechanical Reproduction* of 1936. The
essay on Kraus is distinct in form and intention from either
of these two. Dedicated to Gustav Glück, the friend who
was the real-life model for *The Destructive Character*, it was
designed to show Kraus as a negative hero of destruction,
'the last bourgeois', through whose tormented figure the
positive forces of history could sweep. Long premeditated
and highly wrought, it is Benjamin's one sustained attempt
to found mystical and materialist themes into a single form.

Challenged by Max Rychner, the editor of the *Neuer
Schweizer Rundschau*, as to where he stood in the irreconcilable conflict between mere materialist 'collectivism' and
the 'primordiality of religion and metaphysics', Benjamin

replied in a long letter of 1931 that, seen in retrospect, *The Origin of German Tragic* Drama, 'although dialectical, was certainly not materialist. But what I did not know at the time I was writing it, soon afterwards became ever clearer to me: that between my very special point of view as a philosopher of language and the outlook of dialectical materialism there exists a mediation, however tense and problematic. With the saturation of bourgeois science, on the other hand, there exists none whatever.'[17] Declaring that he felt more in common with the 'crude and rudimentary analyses of Franz Mehring than with the most profound periphrases from the ambit of the ideas produced by the school of Heidegger today', he described his own position with an unwonted lack of obliquity: 'I have never been able to study or think otherwise than in a way that I would define as theological —that is, in accord with the Talmudic doctrine of the forty-nine levels of meaning in every paragraph of the Torah. Well: experience has taught me that the shallowest of communist platitudes contains more of a hierarchy of meaning than contemporary bourgeois profundity, which is always no more than apologetic ... I can tell you at the same time that you will find a more grounded reply to your question than that which I can give you *expressis verbis*, between the lines of my essay on Karl Kraus which will shortly appear in the *Frankfurter Zeitung*.'[18] Scholem, receiving from Benjamin a copy of this letter, wrote back trenchantly that for all his admiration of the essay on Kraus he felt obliged to say that Benjamin was deceiving himself if he thought that a sympathetic reader 'could find any justification of your sympathies for dialectical materialism "between the lines" of this essay'.[19] Reproaching Benjamin for the 'fantastic discrepancy' between a terminology 'possibly close to communist vocabulary' and metaphysical conclusions 'absolutely independent of any materialist method', he criticized his friend's recent productions for the impression they gave of 'adventurism, ambiguity and acrobatics'. In replying, Benjamin defended his political choice 'to hang the red flag out of my window',[20] but was in effect unable to demonstrate that his essay on Kraus had actually achieved the synthesis he claimed. A literary *tour de force*, its intellectual purpose was lost even on those readers to whom it was most addressed. Kraus himself took characteristic umbrage at it, denouncing it for 'abysmal feuilletonism' and declaring that although 'surely well-intentioned', the 'author seems to know much about me that was hitherto unknown to myself, although I even now do not yet clearly apprehend it and can only express the hope that other readers have understood it better (perhaps it is psychoanalysis).'[21] Benjamin kept a dignified silence at this attack. Three years later, when Kraus rallied to the clerical fascism of Dollfuss, he noted 'the capitulation to Austro-fascism, the embellishment of the white terror against the Viennese workers, the admiration for the rhetoric of Starhemberg' in *Die Fackel*,[22] and asked: 'Is there anyone further who can fall? A bitter consolation—but on this front we can suffer no more losses worth mentioning besides this one. The demon has proved stronger than the man or the monster: he could not be silent and so—betraying himself—has accomplished the ruin of the demon'.[23]

The final years of the Weimar period were ones of acute personal crisis for Benjamin, who was divorced from his wife Dora Pollak in 1930, shortly after Asja Lacis

returned permanently to Russia. In April 1932 he sailed to
Ibiza, where he spent the next three months in isolation.
Approaching the age of 40, he now set down the private
autobiographical memoir (V) that was published long after
his death under the title *Berlin Chronicle*. In July, he moved
to Nice, where he wrote his will and decided to take his life.
This crisis suddenly past, he spent the rest of the summer in
Italy. There he completed a entirely reworked version of his
recollections for publication as a book to be entitled *Berlin
Childhood Around 1900*. The Nazi seizure of power a few
months later gave the quietus to this project. The later text
utilizes only about two-fifths of the materials in the earlier,
and these in radically altered form. The *Berlin Chronicle* is
throughout far more directly personal than the *Berlin Childhood*, where Benjamin's experience is transmuted into a
series of more objective notations of his native city. It is also
much more sharply political, pervaded by Benjamin's socialist convictions. These virtually disappear in the 'milder and
more conciliatory lighting' of the version intended for publication.[24] The *Chronicle* is the most intimate document of
Benjamin's yet to be published.

Exile after 1933 cut short Benjamin's journalism. His
publicistic period was now effectively over. The main outlet
for his writing was henceforward the *Zeitschrift für Sozialforschung*, produced by the Institute for Social Research
directed by Max Horkheimer. After the Nazi victory in
Germany, the Institute had moved, first to Geneva, and
then to New York. Its review was—unlike any to which
Benjamin had hitherto regularly contributed—an academic journal; but at the same time it was also one with a
coherent political complexion—essentially, if informally,

Marxist. The tension between these two dimensions of the *Zeitschrift für Sozialforschung*, rendered more acute by its exposed position in an American environment thoroughly hostile to any form of socialism, was not without its effects on the editorial relationship of the journal to its contributors, among them Benjamin. But there can be no doubt that for the first time in his life, Benjamin found in the later thirties an arena of collegial publication that by and large understood, appreciated and supported his work. The form of his writing consequently changed in these years. His contributions to the *Zeitschrift*, although on occasion muted by the tactical apprehensions of his editors in New York, were far more directly political and more deliberately theoretical than anything he had written in the Weimar period. The long essay on Eduard Fuchs (VI) which concludes this volume was one of the most significant fruits of this intellectual collaboration. Its origin lay in Horkheimer's admiration for the figure of Fuchs, a veteran militant of German Social Democracy who was also a notable art historian, for whom he had testified at one of the numerous trials in which Fuchs had been prosecuted for his studies of erotic art. Some time in 1934, Horkheimer approached Benjamin to commission an essay from him on Fuchs for the *Zeitschrift*. Benjamin, who knew and liked Fuchs, then a fellow-exile in his late sixties in Paris, was reluctant to undertake the work, partly because of the amount of reading it involved, and partly because of his lack of sympathy with the positivist culture of which Fuchs, representative of an older generation of German Marxism, partook. Commitment to the project was followed by postponement and tergiversation. Eventually, he resumed serious study for it in late 1936, and completed the writing of the essay fairly quickly in the first two months of 1937. Despite his complaints in correspondence about the commission, he was unexpectedly satisfied with the final results. Leo Lowenthal, speaking for the editorial board of the *Zeitschrift*, secured the omission of the first paragraph as too pronouncedly political in tone.[25] Horkheimer, for his part, responded enthusiastically to the essay, which was published in the journal in October 1937. *Eduard Fuchs, Collector and Historian* is Benjamin's most considered and important statement on historical materialism—to be read together with the *Theses on the Philosophy of History*, of which it anticipates some of the themes and even passages, but in a more comprehensive and discursive space.

The dates at the end of each text in this volume are those of their composition (sometimes approximate), not publication. Apart from *A Small History of Photography* and *Eduard Fuchs, Collector and Historian*, translated by Kingsley Shorter, the translations included in the volume are by Edmund Jephcott.

NLB

I

One-Way Street

> This street is named Asja Lacis Street after her who as an engineer cut it through the author

Filling Station

The construction of life is at present in the power of facts far more than of convictions, and of such facts as have scarcely ever become the basis of convictions. Under these circumstances true literary activity cannot aspire to take place within a literary framework—this is, rather, the habitual expression of its sterility. Significant literary work can only come into being in a strict alternation between action and writing; it must nurture the inconspicuous forms that better fit its influence in active communities than does the pretentious, universal gesture of the book—in leaflets, brochures, articles, and placards. Only this prompt language shows itself actively equal to the moment. Opinions are to the vast apparatus of social existence what oil is to machines: one does not go up to a turbine and pour machine oil over it;

one applies a little to hidden spindles and joints that one has to know.

Breakfast Room

A popular tradition warns against recounting dreams on an empty stomach. In this state, though awake, one remains under the sway of the dream. For washing brings only the surface of the body and the visible motor functions into the light, while in the deeper strata, even during the morning ablution, the grey penumbra of dream persists and, indeed, in the solitude of the first waking hour, consolidates itself. He who shuns contact with the day, whether for fear of his fellow men or for the sake of inward composure, is unwilling to eat and disdains his breakfast. He thus avoids a rupture between the nocturnal and the daytime worlds—a precaution justified only by the combustion of dream in a concentrated morning's work, if not in prayer, but otherwise a source of confusion between vital rhythms. The narration of dreams brings calamity, because a person still half in league with the dream world betrays it in his words and must incur its revenge. Expressed in more modern terms: he betrays himself. He has outgrown the protection of dreaming naïveté, and in laying clumsy hands on his dream visions he surrenders himself. For only from the far bank, from broad daylight, may dream be recalled with impunity. This further side of dream is only attainable through a cleansing analogous to washing yet totally different. By way of the stomach. The fasting man tells his dream as if he were talking in his sleep.

No. 113

> The hours that hold the figure and the form
> Have run their course within the house of dream.

Cellar.—We have long forgotten the ritual by which the house of our life was erected. But when it is under assault and enemy bombs are already taking their toll, what enervated, perverse antiquities do they not lay bare in the foundations. What things were interred and sacrificed amid magic incantations, what horrible cabinet of curiosities lies there below, where the deepest shafts are reserved for what is most commonplace. In a night of despair I dreamed I was with my first friend from my school days, whom I had not seen for decades and had scarcely ever remembered in that time, tempestuously renewing our friendship and brotherhood. But when I awoke it became clear that what despair had brought to light like a detonation was the corpse of that boy, who had been immured as a warning: that whoever one day lives here may in no respect resemble him.

Vestibule.—A visit to Goethe's house. I cannot recall having seen rooms in the dream. It was a perspective of whitewashed corridors like those in a school. Two elderly English lady visitors and a curator are the dream's extras. The curator requests us to sign the visitors' book lying open on a desk at the farthest end of a passage. On reaching it, I find as I turn the pages my name already entered in big, unruly, childish characters.

Dining Hall.—In a dream I saw myself in Goethe's study. It bore no resemblance to the one in Weimar. Above all, it was very small and had only one window. The side of the writing desk abutted on the wall opposite the window. Sitting and writing at it was the poet, in extreme old age. I was standing to one side when he broke off to give me a small vase, an urn from antiquity, as a present. I turned it between my hands. An immense heat filled the room. Goethe rose to his feet and accompanied me to an adjoining chamber, where a table was set for my relatives. It seemed prepared, however, for many more than their number. Doubtless there were places for my ancestors, too. At the end, on the right, I sat down beside Goethe. When the meal was over, he rose with difficulty, and by gesturing I sought leave to support him. Touching his elbow, I began to weep with emotion.

For Men

To convince is to conquer without conception.

Standard Clock

To great writers, finished works weigh lighter than those fragments on which they work throughout their lives. For only the more feeble and distracted take an inimitable pleasure in conclusions, feeling themselves thereby given back to life. For the genius each caesura, and the heavy blows of fate, fall like gentle sleep itself into his workshop labour. About it he draws a charmed circle of fragments. 'Genius is application.'

Come Back! All is Forgiven!

Like someone performing the giant swing on the horizontal bar, each boy spins for himself the wheel of fortune from which, sooner or later, the momentous lot shall fall. For only that which we knew or practised at fifteen will one day constitute our attraction. And one thing, therefore, can never be made good: having neglected to run away from home. From forty-eight hours' exposure in those years, as in a caustic solution, the crystal of life's happiness forms.

Manorially Furnished Ten-Room Apartment

The furniture style of the second half of the nineteenth century has received its only adequate description, and analysis, in a certain type of detective novel at the dynamic centre of which stands the horror of apartments. The arrangement of the furniture is at the same time the site plan of deadly traps, and the suite of rooms prescribes the fleeing victim's path. That this kind of detective novel begins with Poe—at a time when such accommodations hardly yet existed—is no counter-argument. For without exception the great writers perform their combinations in a world that comes after them, just as the Paris streets of Baudelaire's poems, as well as Dostoevsky's characters, only existed after 1900. The bourgeois interior of the 1860s to the 1890s, with its gigantic sideboards distended with carvings, the sunless corners where palms stand, the balcony embattled behind its balustrade, and the long corridors with their singing gas flames, fittingly houses only the corpse. 'On this sofa the aunt cannot but be murdered.' The soulless luxuriance of the furnishings becomes true comfort only in the presence of a dead body. Far more interesting than the Oriental landscapes in detective novels is that rank Orient inhabiting their interiors: the Persian carpet and the ottoman, the hanging lamp and the genuine Caucasian dagger. Behind the heavy, gathered Khilim tapestries the master of the house has orgies with his share certificates, feels himself the Eastern merchant, the indolent pasha in the caravanserai of otiose enchantment, until that dagger in its silver sling above the divan puts an end, one fine afternoon, to his siesta and himself. This character of the bourgeois apartment, tremulously awaiting the nameless murderer like a lascivious old lady her gallant, has been penetrated by a number of authors who, as writers of 'detective stories'—and perhaps also because in their works part of the bourgeois pandemonium is exhibited—have been denied the reputation they deserve. The quality in question has been captured in isolated writings by Conan Doyle and in a major production by A. K. Green; and with *The Phantom of the Opera*, one of the great novels about the nineteenth century, Gaston Leroux has brought the genre to its apotheosis.

Chinese Curios

These are days when no one should rely unduly on his 'competence'. Strength lies in improvisation. All the decisive blows are struck left-handed.

At the beginning of the long downhill lane that leads to the house of—, whom I visited each evening, is a gate. After she moved, the opening of its archway stood henceforth before me like an ear that has lost the power of hearing.

A child in his nightshirt cannot be prevailed upon to greet an arriving visitor. Those present, invoking a higher moral standpoint, admonish him in vain to overcome his prudery. A few minutes later he reappears, now stark naked, before the visitor. In the meantime he has washed.

The power of a country road is different when one is walking along it from when one is flying over it by airplane. In the same way, the power of a text is different when it is read from when it is copied out. The airplane passenger sees only how the road pushes through the landscape, how it unfolds according to the same laws as the terrain surrounding it. Only he who walks the road on foot learns of the power it commands, and of how, from the very scenery that for the flier is only the unfurled plain, it calls forth distances, belvederes, clearings, prospects at each of its turns like a commander deploying soldiers at a front. Only the copied text thus commands the soul of him who is occupied with it, whereas the mere reader never discovers the new aspects of his inner self that are opened by the text, that road cut through the interior jungle forever closing behind it: because the reader follows the movement of his mind in the free flight of daydreaming, whereas the copier submits it to command. The Chinese practice of copying books was thus an incomparable guarantee of literary culture, and the transcript a key to China's enigmas.

Gloves

In an aversion to animals the predominant feeling is fear of being recognized by them through contact. The horror that stirs deep in man is an obscure awareness that in him something lives so akin to the animal that it might be recognized. All disgust is originally disgust at touching. Even when the feeling is mastered, it is only by a drastic gesture that overleaps its mark: the nauseous is violently engulfed, eaten, while the zone of finest epidermal contact remains taboo. Only in this way is the paradox of the moral demand to be met, exacting simultaneously the overcoming and the subtlest elaboration of man's sense of disgust. He may not deny his bestial relationship with animals, the invocation of which revolts him: he must make himself its master.

Mexican Embassy

Je ne passe jamais devant un fétiche de bois, un Bouddha doré, une idole mexicaine sans me dire: c'est peut-être le vrai dieu. (I never pass by a wooden fetish, a gilded Buddha, a Mexican idol without reflecting: perhaps it is the true God.)

Charles Baudelaire

I dreamed I was a member of an exploring party in Mexico. After crossing a high, primeval jungle, we came upon a system of above-ground caves in the mountains where an order had survived from the time of the first missionaries till now, its monks continuing the work of conversion among the natives. In an immense central grotto with a Gothically pointed roof, Mass was celebrated according to the most ancient rites. We joined the ceremony and witnessed its climax: toward a wooden bust of God the Father fixed high on a wall of the cave, a priest raised a Mexican fetish. At this the divine head turned thrice in denial from right to left.

To The Public: Please Protect and Preserve These New Plantings

What is 'solved'? Do not all the questions of our lives, as we live, remain behind us like foliage obstructing our view? To uproot this foliage, even to thin it out, does not occur to us. We stride on, leave it behind, and from a distance it is indeed open to view, but indistinct, shadowy, and all the more enigmatically entangled.

Commentary and translation stand in the same relation to the text as style and mimesis to nature: the same phenomenon considered from different aspects. On the tree of the sacred text both are only the eternally rustling leaves; on that of the profane, the seasonally falling fruits.

He who loves is attached not only to the 'faults' of the beloved, not only to the whims and weaknesses of a woman. Wrinkles in the face, moles, shabby clothes, and a lopsided walk bind him more lastingly and relentlessly than any beauty. This has long been known. And why? If the theory is correct that feeling is not located in the head, that we sentiently experience a window, a cloud, a tree not in our brains but, rather, in the place where we see it, then we are, in looking at our beloved, too, outside ourselves. But in a torment of tension and ravishment. Our feeling, dazzled, flutters like a flock of birds in the woman's radiance. And as birds seek refuge in the leafy recesses of a tree, feelings escape into the shaded wrinkles, the awkward movements and inconspicuous blemishes of the body we love, where they can lie low in safety. And no passer-by would guess that it is just here, in what is defective and censurable, that the fleeting darts of adoration nestle.

Construction Site

Pedantic brooding over the production of objects—visual aids, toys, or books—that are supposed to be suitable for children is folly. Since the Enlightenment this has been one of the mustiest speculations of the pedagogues. Their infatuation with psychology keeps them from perceiving that the world is full of the most unrivalled objects for childish attention and use. And the most specific. For children are particularly fond of haunting any site where things are being visibly worked upon. They are irresistibly drawn by the detritus generated by building, gardening, housework, tailoring, or carpentry. In waste products they recognize the face that the world of things turns directly and solely to them. In using these things they do not so much imitate the works of adults as bring together, in the artefact produced in play, materials of widely differing kinds in a new, intuitive relationship. Children thus produce their own small world of things within the greater one. The norms of this small world must be kept in mind if one wishes to create things specially for children, rather than let one's adult activity, through its requisites and instruments, find its own way to them.

Ministry of the Interior

The more antagonistic a person is toward the traditional order, the more inexorably he will subject his private life to the norms that he wishes to elevate as legislators of a future society. It is as if these laws, nowhere yet realized, placed him under obligation to enact them in advance at least in the confines of his own existence. The man, on the other hand, who knows himself to be in accord with the most ancient heritage of his class or nation will sometimes bring his private life into ostentatious contrast to the maxims that he unrelentingly asserts in public, secretly approving his own behaviour, without the slightest qualms, as the most conclusive proof of the unshakable authority of the principles he puts on display. Thus are distinguished the types of the anarcho-socialist and the conservative politician.

Flag ...

How much more easily the leave-taker is loved! For the flame burns more purely for those vanishing in the distance, fuelled by the fleeting scrap of material waving from the ship or railway window. Separation penetrates the disappearing person like a pigment and steeps him in gentle radiance.

... at Half-Mast

If a person very close to us is dying, there is something in the months to come that we dimly apprehend—much as we should have liked to share it with him—could only happen through his absence. We greet him at the last in a language that he no longer understands.

Imperial Panorama

A Tour of German Inflation

1. In the stock of phraseology that lays bare the amalgam of stupidity and cowardice constituting the mode of life of

the German bourgeois, the locution referring to impending catastrophe—that 'things can't go on like this'—is particularly noteworthy. The helpless fixation on notions of security and property deriving from past decades keeps the average citizen from perceiving the quite remarkable stabilities of an entirely new kind that underlie the present situation. Because the relative stabilization of the prewar years benefited him, he feels compelled to regard any state that dispossesses him as unstable. But stable conditions need by no means be pleasant conditions, and even before the war there were strata for whom stabilized conditions amounted to stabilized wretchedness. To decline is no less stable, no more surprising, than to rise. Only a view that acknowledges downfall as the sole reason for the present situation can advance beyond enervating amazement at what is daily repeated, and perceive the phenomena of decline as stability itself and rescue alone as extraordinary, verging on the marvellous and incomprehensible. People in the national communities of Central Europe live like the inhabitants of an encircled town whose provisions and gunpowder are running out and for whom deliverance is, by human reasoning, scarcely to be expected—a case in which surrender, perhaps unconditional, should be most seriously considered. But the silent, invisible power that Central Europe feels opposing it does not negotiate. Nothing, therefore, remains but to direct the gaze, in the perpetual expectation of the final onslaught, on nothing except the extraordinary event in which alone salvation now lies. But this necessary state of intense and uncomplaining attention could, because we are in mysterious contact with the powers besieging us, really call forth a miracle. Conversely, the assumption that things cannot go on like this will one day find itself apprised of the fact that for the suffering of individuals as of communities there is only one limit beyond which things cannot go: annihilation.

2. A curious paradox: people have only the narrowest private interest in mind when they act, yet they are at the same time more than ever determined in their behaviour by the instincts of the mass. And more than ever mass instincts have become confused and estranged from life. Whereas the obscure impulse of the animal—as innumerable anecdotes relate—detects, as danger approaches, a way of escape that still seems invisible, this society, each of whose members cares only for his own abject well-being, falls victim, with animal insensibility but without the insensate intuition of animals, as a blind mass, to even the most obvious danger, and the diversity of individual goals is immaterial in face of the identity of the determining forces. Again and again it has been shown that society's attachment to its familiar and long-since-forfeited life is so rigid as to nullify the genuinely human application of intellect, forethought, even in dire peril. So that in this society the picture of imbecility is complete: uncertainty, indeed perversion of vital instincts, and impotence, indeed decay of the intellect. This is the condition of the entire German bourgeoisie.

3. All close relationships are lit up by an almost intolerable, piercing clarity in which they are scarcely able to survive. For on the one hand, money stands ruinously at the centre of every vital interest, but on the other, this is the very barrier before which almost all relationships halt; so, more and more, in the natural as in the moral sphere, unreflecting trust, calm, and health are disappearing.

4. Not without reason is it customary to speak of 'naked' want. What is most damaging in the display of it, a practice started under the dictates of necessity and making visible only a thousandth part of the hidden distress, is not the pity or the equally terrible awareness of his own impunity awakened in the onlooker, but his shame. It is impossible to remain in a large German city, where hunger forces the most wretched to live on the bank notes with which passers-by seek to cover an exposure that wounds them.

5. 'Poverty disgraces no man.' Well and good. But *they* disgrace the poor man. They do it, and then console him with the little adage. It is one of those that may once have held good but have long since degenerated. The case is no different with the brutal, 'If a man does not work, neither shall he eat.' When there was work that fed a man, there was also poverty that did not disgrace him, if it arose from deformity or other misfortune. But this deprivation, into which millions are born and hundreds of thousands are dragged by impoverishment, does indeed disgrace. Filth and misery grow up around them like walls, the work of invisible hands. And just as a man can endure much in isolation, but feels justifiable shame when his wife sees him bear it or suffers it herself, so he may tolerate much as long as he is alone, and everything as long as he conceals it. But no one may ever make peace with poverty when it falls like a gigantic shadow upon his countrymen and his house. Then he must be alert to every humiliation done to him and so discipline himself that his suffering becomes no longer the downhill road of grief, but the rising path of revolt. But of this there is no hope so long as each blackest, most terrible stroke of fate, daily and even hourly discussed by the press,

set forth in all its illusory causes and effects, helps no one uncover the dark powers that hold his life in thrall.

6. To the foreigner cursorily acquainted with the pattern of German life who has even briefly travelled about the country, its inhabitants seem no less bizarre than an exotic race. A witty Frenchman has said: 'A German seldom understands himself. If he has once understood himself, he will not say so. If he says so, he will not make himself understood.' This comfortless distance was increased by the war, but not merely through the real and legendary atrocities that Germans are reported to have committed. Rather, what completes the isolation of Germany in the eyes of other Europeans, what really engenders the attitude that they are dealing with Hottentots in the Germans (as it has been aptly put), is the violence, incomprehensible to outsiders and wholly imperceptible to those imprisoned by it, with which circumstances, squalor, and stupidity here subjugate people entirely to collective forces, as the lives of savages alone are subjected to tribal laws. The most European of all accomplishments, that more or less discernible irony with which the life of the individual asserts the right to run its course independently of the community into which it is cast, has completely deserted the Germans.

7. The freedom of conversation is being lost. If it was earlier a matter of course in conversation to take interest in one's partner, this is now replaced by inquiry into the price of his shoes or his umbrella. Irresistibly intruding on any convivial exchange is the theme of the conditions of life, of money. What this theme involves is not so much the concerns and sorrows of individuals, in which they might be able to help one another, as the overall picture. It is as if

one were trapped in a theatre and had to follow the events on the stage whether one wanted to or not, had to make them again and again, willingly or unwillingly, the subject of one's thought and speech.

8. Anyone who does not simply refuse to perceive decline will hasten to claim a special justification for his own continued presence, his activity and involvement in this chaos. As there are many insights into the general failure, so there are many exceptions for one's own sphere of action, place of residence, and moment of time. A blind determination to save the prestige of personal existence, rather than, through an impartial disdain for its impotence and entanglement, at least to detach it from the background of universal delusion, is triumphing almost everywhere. That is why the air is so thick with life theories and world views, and why in this country they cut so presumptuous a figure, for almost always they finally serve to sanction some wholly trivial private situation. For just the same reason the air is so full of phantoms, mirages of a glorious cultural future breaking upon us overnight in spite of all, for everyone is committed to the optical illusions of his isolated standpoint.

9. The people cooped up in this country no longer discern the contours of human personality. Every free man appears to them as an eccentric. Let us imagine the peaks of the High Alps silhouetted not against the sky but against folds of dark drapery. The mighty forms would show up only dimly. In just this way a heavy curtain shuts off Germany's sky, and we no longer see the profiles of even the greatest men.

10. Warmth is ebbing from things. The objects of daily use gently but insistently repel us. Day by day, in overcoming the sum of secret resistances—not only the overt

ones—that they put in our way, we have an immense labour to perform. We must compensate for their coldness with our warmth if they are not to freeze us to death, and handle their spines with infinite dexterity, if we are not to perish by bleeding. From our fellow men we should expect no succour. Bus conductors, officials, workmen, salesmen—they all feel themselves to be the representatives of a refractory matter whose menace they take pains to demonstrate through their own surliness. And in the degeneration of things, with which, emulating human decay, they punish humanity, the country itself conspires. It gnaws at us like the things, and the German spring that never comes is only one of countless related phenomena of decomposing German nature. Here one lives as if the weight of the column of air supported by everyone had suddenly, against all laws, become in these regions perceptible.

11. Any human movement, whether it springs from an intellectual or even a natural impulse, is impeded in its unfolding by the boundless resistance of the outside world. Shortage of houses and the rising cost of travel are in the process of annihilating the elementary symbol of European freedom, which existed in certain forms even in the Middle Ages: freedom of domicile. And if medieval coercion bound men to natural associations, they are now chained together in unnatural community. Few things will further the ominous spread of the cult of rambling as much as the strangulation of the freedom of residence, and never has freedom of movement stood in greater disproportion to the abundance of means of travel.

12. Just as all things, in a perpetual process of mingling and contamination, are losing their intrinsic character

while ambiguity displaces authenticity, so is the city. Great cities—whose incomparably sustaining and reassuring power encloses those at work within them in the peace of a fortress and lifts from them, with the view of the horizon, awareness of the ever-vigilant elemental forces—are seen to be breached at all points by the invading countryside. Not by the landscape, but by what in untrammelled nature is most bitter: ploughed land, highways, night sky that the veil of vibrant redness no longer conceals. The insecurity of even the busy areas puts the city dweller in the opaque and truly dreadful situation in which he must assimilate, along with isolated monstrosities from the open country, the abortions of urban architectonics.

13. Noble indifference to the spheres of wealth and poverty has quite forsaken manufactured things. Each stamps its owner, leaving him only the choice of appearing a starveling or a racketeer. For while even true luxury can be permeated by intellect and conviviality and so forgotten, the luxury goods swaggering before us now parade such brazen solidity that all the mind's shafts break harmlessly on their surface.

14. The earliest customs of peoples seem to send us a warning that in accepting what we receive so abundantly from nature we should guard against a gesture of avarice. For we are able to make Mother Earth no gift of our own. It is therefore fitting to show respect in taking, by returning a part of all we receive before laying hands on our share. This respect is expressed in the ancient custom of the libation. Indeed, it is perhaps this immemorial practice that has survived, transformed, in the prohibition on gathering forgotten ears of corn or fallen grapes, these reverting to the

soil or to the ancestral dispensers of blessings. An Athenian custom forbade the picking up of crumbs at the table, since they belonged to the heroes. If society has so degenerated through necessity and greed that it can now receive the gifts of nature only rapaciously, that it snatches the fruit unripe from the trees in order to sell it most profitably, and is compelled to empty each dish in its determination to have enough, the earth will be impoverished and the land yield bad harvests.

Underground Works

I saw in a dream barren terrain. It was the market-place at Weimar. Excavations were in progress. I too scraped about in the sand. Then the tip of a church steeple came to light. Delighted, I thought to myself: a Mexican shrine from the time of pre-animism, from the Anaquivitzli. I awoke laughing. (Ana = ἀνά; vi = vie; witz [joke] = Mexican church [!].)

Coiffeur for Fastidious Ladies

Three thousand ladies and gentlemen from the Kurfür-stendamm are to be arrested in their beds one morning without explanation and detained for twenty-four hours. At midnight a questionnaire on the death penalty is distributed to the cells requiring its signatories to indicate which form of execution, should the occasion arise, they would prefer. This document would have to be completed 'to the best of their knowledge' by those who hitherto had merely offered their unsolicited views 'in all conscience'. By first light, that hour held sacred of old but in this country dedicated to the executioner, the question of capital punishment would be resolved.

Caution: Steps

Work on good prose has three steps: a musical stage when it is composed, an architectonic one when it is built, and a textile one when it is woven.

Attested Auditor of Books

Just as this time is the antithesis of the Renaissance in general, it contrasts in particular to the situation in which the art of printing was discovered. For whether by coincidence or not, its appearance in Germany came at a time *when* the book in the most eminent sense of the word, the book of books, had through Luther's translation become the people's property. Now everything indicates that the book in this traditional form is nearing its end. Mallarmé, who in the crystalline structure of his certainly traditionalist writing saw the true image of what was to come, was in the *Coup de dés* the first to incorporate the graphic tensions of the advertisement in the printed page. The typographical experiments later undertaken by the Dadaists stemmed, it is true, not from constructive principles but from the precise nervous reactions of these literati, and were therefore far less enduring than Mallarmé's, which grew out of the inner nature of his style. But they show up for this very reason the topicality of what Mallarmé, monadically, in his hermetic room, had discovered through a pre-established harmony with all the decisive events of our times in economics, technology, and public life. Printing, having found in the book a refuge in which to lead an autonomous existence, is pitilessly dragged out onto the street by advertisements and subjected to the brutal heteronomies of economic chaos. This is the hard schooling of its new form. If centuries ago it began gradually to lie down, passing from the upright inscription to the manuscript resting on sloping desks before finally taking to bed in the printed book, it now begins just as slowly to rise again from the ground. The newspaper is read more in the vertical than in the horizontal plane, while film and advertisement force the printed word entirely into the dictatorial perpendicular. And before a child of our time finds his way clear to opening a book, his eyes have been exposed to such a blizzard of changing, colourful, conflicting letters that the chances of his penetrating the archaic still-ness of the book are slight. Locust swarms of print, which already eclipse the sun of what is taken for intellect for city dwellers, will grow thicker with each succeeding year. Other demands of business life lead further. The card index marks the conquest of three-dimensional writing, and so presents an astonishing counterpoint to the three-dimensionality of script in its original form as rune or knot notation. (And today the book is already, as the present mode of scholarly production demonstrates, an outdated mediation between two different filing systems. For everything that matters is to be found in the card box of the researcher who wrote it, and the scholar studying it assimilates it into his own card index.) But it is quite beyond doubt that the development of writing will not indefinitely be bound by the claims to power of a chaotic academic and commercial activity; rather, quantity is approaching the moment of a qualitative leap when writing, advancing ever more deeply into the graphic regions of its new eccentric figurativeness, will take sudden possession of an adequate factual content. In this picture writing, poets, who will now as in earliest times be first and foremost experts in writing, will be able to participate only by mastering the fields in which (quite unobtrusively) it is being constructed: the statistical and technical diagram. With the foundation of an international moving script they will renew their authority in the life of peoples, and find a role awaiting them in comparison to which all the innovative aspirations of rhetoric will reveal themselves as antiquated daydreams.

Teaching Aid

Principles of the Weighty Tome, or How to Write Fat Books.
I. The whole composition must be permeated with a protracted and wordy exposition of the initial plan.
II. Terms are to be included for conceptions that, except in this definition, appear nowhere in the whole book.
III. Conceptual distinctions laboriously arrived at in the text are to be obliterated again in the relevant notes.
IV. For concepts treated only in their general significance, examples should be given; if, for example, machines are mentioned, all the different kinds of machines should be enumerated.
V. Everything that is known a priori about an object is to be consolidated by an abundance of examples.
VI. Relationships that could be represented graphically must be expounded in words. Instead of being represented in a genealogical tree, for example, all family relationships are to be enumerated and described.

VII. A number of opponents all sharing the same argument should each be refuted individually.

The typical work of modern scholarship is intended to be read like a catalogue. But when shall we actually write books like catalogues? If the deficient content were thus to determine the outward form, an excellent piece of writing would result, in which the value of opinions would be marked without their being thereby put on sale.

The typewriter will alienate the hand of the man of letters from the pen only when the precision of typographic forms has directly entered the conception of his books. One might suppose that new systems with more variable typefaces would then be needed. They will replace the pliancy of the hand with the innervation of commanding fingers.

A period that, constructed metrically, afterward has its rhythm upset at a single point yields the finest prose sentence imaginable. In this way a ray of light falls through a chink in the wall of the alchemist's cell, to light up gleaming crystals, spheres, and triangles.

Germans, Drink German Beer!

The mob, impelled by a frenetic hatred of the life of the mind, has found a sure way to annihilate it in the counting of bodies. Whenever given the slightest opportunity, they form ranks and advance into artillery barrages and price rises in marching order. No one sees further than the back before him, and each is proud to be thus exemplary for the eyes behind. Men have been adept at this for centuries in the field, but the march-past of penury, standing in line, is the invention of women.

Post No Bills

The Writer's Technique in Thirteen Theses.

I. Anyone intending to embark on a major work should be lenient with himself and, having completed a stint, deny himself nothing that will not prejudice the next.

II. Talk about what you have written, by all means, but do not read from it while the work is in progress. Every gratification procured in this way will slacken your tempo. If this regime is followed, the growing desire to communicate will become in the end a motor for completion.

III. In your working conditions avoid everyday mediocrity. Semi-relaxation, to a background of insipid sounds, is degrading. On the other hand, accompaniment by an étude or a cacophony of voices can become as significant for work as the perceptible silence of the night. If the latter sharpens the inner ear, the former acts as touchstone for a diction ample enough to bury even the most wayward sounds.

IV. Avoid haphazard writing materials. A pedantic adherence to certain papers, pens, inks is beneficial. No luxury, but an abundance of these utensils is indispensable.

V. Let no thought pass incognito, and keep your notebook as strictly as the authorities keep their register of aliens.

VI. Keep your pen aloof from inspiration, which it will then attract with magnetic power. The more circumspectly you delay writing down an idea, the more maturely developed it will be on surrendering itself. Speech conquers thought, but writing commands it.

VII. Never stop writing because you have run out of ideas. Literary honour requires that one break off only at an appointed moment (a mealtime, a meeting) or at the end of the work.

VIII. Fill the lacunae of inspiration by tidily copying out what is already written. Intuition will awaken in the process.

IX. *Nulla dies sine linea*—but there may well be weeks.

X. Consider no work perfect over which you have not once sat from evening to broad daylight.

XI. Do not write the conclusion of a work in your familiar study. You would not find the necessary courage there.

XII. Stages of composition: idea—style—writing. The value of the fair copy is that in producing it you confine attention to calligraphy. The idea kills inspiration, style fetters the idea, writing pays off style.

XIII. The work is the death mask of its conception.

Thirteen Theses Against Snobs.

(Snob in the private office of art criticism. On the left, a child's drawing, on the right a fetish. Snob: 'Doesn't this make Picasso seem such a waste of time?')

I. The artist makes a work.	The primitive expresses himself in documents.
II. The art-work is only incidentally a document.	No document is as such a work of art.
III. The art-work is a masterpiece.	The document serves to instruct.
IV. On art-works, artists learn their craft.	Before documents, a public is educated.
V. Art-works are remote from each other in their perfection.	All documents communicate through their subject-matter.
VI. In the art-work content and form are one: meaning.	In documents the subject matter is wholly dominant.
VII. Meaning is the outcome of experience.	Subject-matter is the outcome of dreams.

VIII. In the art-work subject matter is a ballast jettisoned during contemplation.	The more one loses oneself in a document, the denser the subject matter grows.
IX. In the art-work the formal law is central.	Forms are merely dispersed in documents.
X. The art-work is synthetic: an energy-centre.	The fertility of the document demands: analysis.
XI. The impact of an artwork increases with repeated viewing.	A document overpowers only through surprise.
XII. The virility of works lies in assault.	The document's innocence gives it cover.
XIII. The artist sets out to conquer meanings.	The primitive man barricades himself behind subject-matter.

The Critic's Technique in Thirteen Theses.

I. The critic is the strategist in the literary battle.

II. He who cannot take sides should keep silent.

III. The critic has nothing in common with the interpreter of past cultural epochs.

IV. Criticism must talk the language of artists. For the terms of the *cénacle* are slogans. And only in slogans is the battle-cry heard.

V. 'Objectivity' must always be sacrificed to partisanship, if the cause fought for merits this.

VI. Criticism is a moral question. If Goethe misjudged Hölderlin and Kleist, Beethoven and Jean Paul, his morality and not his artistic discernment was at fault.

VII. For the critic his colleagues are the higher authority. Not the public. Still less posterity.

VIII. Posterity forgets or acclaims. Only the critic judges in face of the author.

IX. Polemics mean to destroy a book in a few of its sentences. The less it has been studied the better. Only he who can destroy can criticize.

X. Genuine polemics approach a book as lovingly as a cannibal spices a baby.

XI. Artistic enthusiasm is alien to the critic. In his hand the art-work is the shining sword in the battle of minds.

XII. The art of the critic in a nutshell: to coin slogans without betraying ideas. The slogans of an inadequate criticism peddle ideas to fashion.

XIII. The public must always be proved wrong, yet always feel represented by the critic.

No. 13

Treize—j'eus un plaisir cruel de m'arrêter sur ce nombre. [Thirteen— stopping at this number, I felt a cruel pleasure]

Marcel Proust

Le reploiement vierge du livre, encore, prête a un sacrifice dont saigna la tranche rouge des anciens tomes; l'introduction d'une arme, ou coupe-papier, pour établir la prise de possession. [The tight-folded book, virginal still, awaiting the sacrifice that blooded the red edges of earlier tomes; the insertion of a weapon, or paper-knife, to effect the taking of possession.]

Mallarmé

I. Books and harlots can be taken to bed.

II. Books and harlots interweave time. They command night as day, and day as night.

III. Neither books nor harlots show that minutes are precious to them. But closer acquaintance shows what a hurry they are in. As our interest becomes absorbed, they too are counting.

IV. Books and harlots have ever been unhappily in love with each other.

V. Books and harlots—both have their type of man, who both lives off and harasses them. In the case of books, critics.

VI. Books and harlots are public establishments—for students.

VII. Books and harlots—seldom does one who has possessed them witness their end. They are apt to vanish before they expire.

VIII. Books and harlots are fond of recounting, mendaciously, how they became what they are. In reality they did not often notice it themselves. For years one follows 'the heart' wherever it leads, and one day a corpulent body stands soliciting on the spot where one had lingered merely to 'study life'.

IX. Books and harlots love to turn their backs when putting themselves on show.

X. Books and harlots have a large progeny.

XI. Books and harlots—'Old bigots—young whores'. How many books were once notorious that now serve as instruction for youth.

XII. Books and harlots have their quarrels in public.

XIII. Books and harlots—footnotes in one are as banknotes in the stockings of the other.

Ordnance

I had arrived in Riga to visit a woman friend. Her house, the town, the language were unfamiliar to me. Nobody was expecting me, no one knew me. For two hours I walked the streets in solitude. Never again have I seen them so. From every gate a flame darted, each cornerstone sprayed sparks, and every streetcar came toward me like a fire engine. For she might have stepped out of the gateway, around the corner, been sitting in the streetcar. But of the two of us I had to be, at any price, the first to see the other. For had she touched me with the match of her eyes, I should have gone up like a magazine.

First Aid

A highly embroiled quarter, a network of streets that I had avoided for years, was disentangled at a single stroke when one day a person dear to me moved there. It was as if a searchlight set up at this person's window dissected the area with pencils of light.

Interior Decoration

The tract is an Arabic form. Its exterior is undifferentiated and unobtrusive, like the façades of Arabian buildings, the articulation of which begins only in the courtyard. So, too, the articulated structure of the tract is invisible from outside, revealing itself only from within. If it is formed by chapters, they have not verbal headings but numbers. The surface of its deliberations is not pictorially enlivened, but covered with unbroken, proliferating arabesques. In the ornamental density of this presentation the distinction between thematic and excursive expositions is abolished.

Stationers

Street-plan.—I know one who is absent-minded. Whereas the names of my suppliers, the location of my documents, the addresses of my friends and acquaintances, the hour of a rendezvous are at my finger-tips, in her political concepts, party slogans, declarations and commands are firmly lodged. She lives in a city of watchwords and inhabits a quarter of conspiratorial and fraternal terms, where every alleyway shows its colour and every word has a password for its echo.

List of wishes.—'Does not the reed the world—With sweetness fill—May no less gracious word—Flow from my quill!' This follows 'Blessed Yearning' like a pearl that has rolled from a freshly opened oyster-shell.

Pocket diary.—Few things are more characteristic of the Nordic man than that, when in love, he must above all and at all costs be alone with himself, must first contemplate, enjoy his feeling in solitude, before going to the woman to declare it.

Paperweight.—Place de la Concorde: the Obelisk. What was carved in it four thousand years ago today stands at the centre in the greatest of city squares. Had that been foretold to him—what a triumph for the Pharaoh! The foremost Western cultural empire will one day bear at its centre the memorial of his rule. How does this apotheosis appear in reality? Not one among the tens of thousands who pass by pauses; not one among the tens of thousands who pause can read the inscription. In such manner does all fame redeem its pledges, and no oracle can match its guile. For the immortal stands like this obelisk: regulating the spiritual traffic that surges thunderously about him, and the inscription he bears helps no one.

Fancy Goods

The incomparable language of the death's head: total expressionlessness—the black of the eye-sockets—coupled to the most unbridled expression—the grinning rows of teeth.

Someone who, feeling himself abandoned, takes up a book, finds with a pang that the page he is about to turn is already cut, and that even here he is not needed.

Gifts must affect the receiver to the point of shock.

When a valued, cultured and elegant friend sent me his new book and I was about to open it, I caught myself in the act of straightening my tie.

He who observes etiquette but objects to lying is like someone who dresses fashionably but wears no vest.

If the smoke from the tip of my cigarette and the ink from the nib of my pen flowed with equal ease, I should be in the Arcadia of my writing.

To be happy is to be able to become aware of oneself without fright.

Enlargements

Child reading.—You are given a book from the school library. In the lower classes they are simply handed out. Only now and again do you dare to express a wish. Often, in envy, you see coveted books pass into other hands. At last desire was granted. For a week you were wholly given up to the soft drift of the text, that surrounded you as secretly, densely and unceasingly as snowflakes. You entered it with limitless trust. The peacefulness of the book that enticed you further and further! Its contents did not much matter. For you were reading at the time when you still made up stories in bed. The child seeks his way along the half-hidden paths. Reading, he covers his ears; the book is on a table that is far too high, and one hand is always on the page. To him the hero's adventures can still be read in the swirling letters like figures and messages in drifting snowflakes. His breath is part of the air of the events narrated, and all the participants breathe with his life. He mingles with the characters far more closely than grown-ups do. He is unspeakably touched by the deeds, the words that are exchanged, and, when he gets up, is blanched over and over by the snow of his reading.

Belated child.—The clock over the school playground seems as if damaged on his account. The hands stand at: 'Late'. And in the corridor, from classroom doors as he passes, come murmurs of conspiracy. The teachers and pupils behind them are friends. Or all is silent, as if they were waiting. Inaudibly he puts his hand to the doorhandle. The spot where he stands is steeped in sunlight. Violating the peaceful hour he opens the door. The teacher's voice clatters like a mill-wheel; he stands before the grinding stones. The voice clatters on without a break, but the mill-hands now shake off their load to the newcomer; ten, twenty heavy sacks fly towards him, that he must carry to the bench. Each thread of his jacket is flour-white. Like those of a wretched soul at midnight, his every step makes uproar, and no one sees. Once arrived at his seat, he works quietly with the rest until the bell sounds. But it avails him nothing.

Pilfering child.——Through the chink of the scarcely open larder door his hand advances like a lover through the night. Once at home in the darkness, it gropes towards sugar or almonds, sultanas or preserves. And as the lover, before kissing her, embraces his girl, his hand enjoys a tactile tryst with the comestibles before his mouth savours their sweetness. How invitingly honey, heaps of currants, even rice yield to his hand. How passionate this meeting of two who have at last escaped the spoon. Grateful and tempestuous as one who has been abducted from the parental home, strawberry jam, unencumbered by bread rolls, abandons itself to his delectation as under the open sky, and even the butter responds tenderly to the boldness of this wooer who has penetrated her boudoir. His hand, the juvenile Don Juan, has soon invaded all the cells and spaces, leaving behind it running layers and streaming plenty: maidenliness renewing itself without complaint.

Child on the roundabout.——The board carrying the docile animals moves close to the ground. It is at the height which, in dreams, is best for flying. Music starts and the child moves with a jerk away from his mother. First he is afraid at leaving her. But then he notices how doughty he himself is. He is ensconced as the just ruler over a world that belongs to him. Tangential trees and natives line his way. Then, in an Orient, his mother re-appears. Next, emerging from the jungle, comes a treetop, exactly as the child saw it thousands of years ago—just now on the roundabout. His beast is devoted: like a mute Arion he rides his silent fish, or a wooden Zeus-bull carries him off as an immaculate Europa. The eternal recurrence of all things has long become child's wisdom to him, and life a primeval frenzy of domination, with the booming orchestrion as the crown jewels at the centre. As the music slows, space begins to stammer and the trees to rub their brows. The roundabout becomes uncertain ground. And his mother appears, the much-rammed stake about which the landing child winds the rope of his gaze.

Untidy child.—Each stone he finds, each flower picked and each butterfly caught is already the start of a collection, and every single thing he owns makes up one great collection. In him this passion shows its true face, the stem Indian expression which lingers on, but with a dimmed and manic glow, in antiquarians, researchers, bibliomaniacs. Scarcely has he entered life than he is a hunter. He hunts the spirits whose trace he scents in things; between spirits and things years are passed in which his field of vision remains free of people. His life is like a dream: he knows nothing lasting; everything seemingly happens to him by chance. His nomad-years are hours in the forest of dream. To it he drags home his booty, to purify it, secure it, cast out its spell. His drawers must become arsenal and zoo, crime museum and crypt. 'To tidy up' would be to demolish an edifice full of prickly chestnuts that are spiky clubs, tinfoil that is hoarded silver, bricks that are coffins, cacti that are totem-poles and copper pennies that are shields. The child has long since helped at his mother's linen-cupboard, his father's bookshelves, while in his own domain he is still a sporadic, warlike visitor.

Child hiding.——He already knows all the hiding places in the apartment and returns to them as to a house where everything is sure to be just as it was. His heart pounds, he holds his breath. Here he is enclosed in the world of matter. It becomes immensely distinct, speechlessly obtrusive. In such manner does a man who is being hanged become aware of the reality of rope and wood. Standing behind the doorway curtain, the child becomes himself something floating and white, a ghost. The dining table under which he is crouching turns him into the wooden idol in a temple whose four pillars are the carved legs. And behind a door he is himself door, wears it as his heavy mask and as a shaman will bewitch all those who unsuspectingly enter. At no cost must he be found. When he pulls faces, he is told, the clock need only strike and he will remain so. The element of truth in this he finds out in his hiding place. Anyone who discovers him can petrify him as an idol under the table, weave him forever as a ghost into the curtain, banish him for life into the heavy door. And so, at the seeker's touch he drives out with a loud cry the demon who has so transformed him— indeed, without waiting for the moment of discovery, he grabs the hunter with a shout of self-deliverance. That is why he does not tire of the struggle with the demon. In this struggle the apartment is the arsenal of his masks. Yet once each year, in mysterious places, in their empty eye-sockets, their fixed mouths, presents lie. Magic discovery becomes science. As its engineer the child disenchants the gloomy parental apartment and looks for Easter eggs.

Antiques

Medallion.—In everything that is with reason called beautiful, appearance has a paradoxical effect.

Prayer-wheel.—Only images in the mind vitalize the will. The mere word, by contrast, at most inflames it, to leave it smouldering, blasted. There is no intact will without exact pictorial imagination. No imagination without innervation. Now breathing is the latter's most delicate regulator. The sound of formulae is a canon of such breathing. Hence the practice of meditating Yoga, which breathes in accord with the holy syllables. Hence its omnipotence.

Antique spoon.—One thing is reserved to the greatest epic writers: the capacity to feed their heroes.

Old map.—In a love affair most seek an eternal homeland. Others, but very few, eternal voyaging. These latter are melancholics, for whom contact with mother earth is to be shunned. They seek the person who will keep far from them the homeland's sadness. To that person they remain faithful. The medieval complexion-books understood the yearning of this human type for long journeys.

Fan.—The following experience will be familiar: if one is in love, or just intensely preoccupied with another, his portrait will appear in almost every book. Moreover, he appears as both protagonist and antagonist. In stories, novels, and novellas he is encountered in endless metamorphoses. And from this it follows that the faculty of imagination is the gift of interpolating into the infinitely small, of inventing, for every intensity, an extensiveness to contain its new, compressed fullness, in short, of receiving each image as if it were that of the folded fan, which only in spreading draws breath and flourishes, in its new expanse, the beloved features within it.

Relief.—One is with the woman one loves, speaks with her. Then, weeks or months later, separated from her, one thinks again of what was talked of then. And now the motif seems banal, tawdry, shallow, and one realizes that it was she alone, bending low over it with love, who shaded and sheltered it before us, so that the thought was alive in all its folds and crevices like a relief. Alone, as now, we see it lie flat, bereft of comfort and shadow, in the light of our knowledge.

Torso.—Only he who can view his own past as an abortion sprung from compulsion and need can use it to full advantage in the present. For what one has lived is at best comparable to a beautiful statue which has had all its limbs knocked off in transit, and now yields nothing but the precious block out of which the image of one's future must be hewn.

Watchmaker and Jeweller

He who, awake and dressed, perhaps while hiking, witnesses the sunrise, preserves all day before others the serenity of one invisibly crowned, and he who sees daybreak while working feels at midday as if he has himself placed this crown upon his head.

Like a clock of life on which the seconds race, the page-number hangs over the characters in a novel. Which reader has not once lifted to it a fleeting, fearful glance?

I dreamt that I was walking—a newly-hatched private tutor—conversing collegially with Roethe, through the spacious rooms of a museum whose curator he was. While he talks in an adjoining room with an employee, I go up to a glass showcase. In it, besides other lesser objects, stands a metallic or enamelled, dully shining, almost life-size bust of a woman, not dissimilar to Leonardo's Flora in the Berlin Museum. The mouth of this golden head is open, and over the lower teeth jewellery, partly hanging from the mouth, is spread at measured intervals. I was in no doubt that this was a clock.— (Dream-motifs: blushing [Scham-Roethe]; *Morgenstunde hat Gold im Munde* [German saying: the morning hour has gold in its mouth, i.e. 'the early bird catches the worm'—tr.]; '*La tête, avec l'amas de sa crinière sombre/Et de ses bijoux précieux,/ Sur la table de nuit, comme une renoncule,/Repose*'. [The head, heaped with its dark mane and precious jewels, rests on the night-table like a ranunculus.] Baudelaire.)

Arc Lamp

The only way of knowing a person is to love them without hope.

Loggia

Geranium.—Two people who are in love are attached above all else to their names.

Carthusian pink.—To the lover the loved one appears always as solitary.

Asphodel.—Behind someone who is loved, the abyss of sexuality closes like that of the family.

Cactus bloom.—The truly loving person delights in finding the beloved, arguing, in the wrong.

Forget-me-not.—Memory always sees the loved one smaller.

Foliage plant.—Should an obstacle prevent union, at once the fantasy of a contented, shared old age is at hand.

Lost-Property Office

Articles lost.—What makes the very first glimpse of a village, a town, in the landscape so incomparable and irretrievable is the rigorous connection between foreground and distance. Habit has not yet done its work. As soon as we begin to find our bearings, the landscape vanishes at a stroke like the facade of a house as we enter it. It has not yet gained preponderance through a constant exploration that has become habit. Once we begin to find our way about, that earliest picture can never be restored.

Articles found.—The blue distance that never gives way to foreground or dissolves at our approach, which is not revealed spread-eagle and long-winded when reached but only looms more compact and threatening, is the painted distance of a backdrop. It is what gives stage sets their incomparable atmosphere.

Halt for Not More than Three Cabs

I stood for ten minutes waiting for an omnibus. 'L'Intran… Paris-Soir … La Liberté', a newspaper vendor called incessantly in an unvarying tone behind me. 'L'Intran … Paris-Soir … La Liberté'—a three-cornered cell in a hard-labour prison. I saw before me how bleak the corners were.

I saw in a dream 'a house of ill repute'. 'A hotel in which an animal is spoiled. Practically everyone drinks only spoiled animal-water.' I dreamt in these words and at once woke with a start. Through excessive fatigue I had thrown myself on my bed in my clothes in the brightly-lit room, and had at once, for a few seconds, fallen asleep.

There is in tenement blocks a music of such deathly-sad wantonness that one cannot believe it to be for the player: it is music for the furnished rooms where on Sundays someone sits in thoughts that are soon garnished with these notes like a bowl of over-ripe fruit with withered leaves.

Monument to a Warrior

Karl Kraus.—Nothing more desolating than his acolytes, nothing more god-forsaken than his adversaries. No name that would be more fittingly honoured by silence. In ancient armour, wrathfully grinning, a Chinese idol, brandishing drawn swords in each hand, he dances a war-dance before the burial vault of the German language. He, 'merely one of the epigones that live in the old house of language', has become the sealer of its tomb. In day and night watches he endures. No post was ever more loyally held, and none ever was more hopelessly lost. Here stands one who fetches water from the tear-seas of his contemporaries like a Danaide, and from whose hands the rock which is to bury his enemies rolls like that of Sisyphus. What more helpless than his conversion? What more powerless than his humanity? What more hopeless than his battle with the press? What does he know of the powers that are his true allies? But what vision of the new seers bears comparison with the listening of this shaman, whose utterances even a defunct language inspires? Who ever conjured up a spirit as Kraus did in the 'Forsaken', as if 'Blessed Yearning' had never been composed? Helpless as only spirits' voices are when summoned up, a murmur from the chthonic depths of language is the source of his soothsaying. Every sound is incomparably genuine, but they all leave us bewildered like messages from the beyond. Blind like the manes language calls him to vengeance, as narrow-minded as spirits that know only the voice of the blood, who care not what havoc they wreak in the realm of the living. But he cannot err. Their commands are infallible. Whoever tries his arm with him is condemned already: in this mouth the adversary's name itself becomes a judgment. When his lips part, the colourless flame of wit darts forth. And none who walks the paths of life would come upon him. On an archaic field of honour, a gigantic battleground of bloody labour, he rages before a deserted sepulchre. The honours at his death will be immeasurable, and the last that are bestowed.

Fire Alarm

The notion of the class war can be misleading. It does not refer to a trial of strength to decide the question 'Who shall win, who be defeated?', or to a struggle the outcome of which is good for the victor and bad for the vanquished. To think in this way is to romanticize and obscure the facts. For whether the bourgeoisie wins or loses the fight, it remains doomed by the inner contradictions that in the course of development will become deadly. The only question is whether its downfall will come through itself or through the proletariat. The continuance or the end of three thousand years of cultural development will be decided by the answer. History knows nothing of the evil infinity contained in the image of the two wrestlers locked in eternal combat. The true politician reckons only in dates. And if the abolition of the bourgeoisie is not completed by an almost calculable moment in economic and technical development (a moment signalled by inflation and poison-gas warfare), all is lost. Before the spark reaches the dynamite, the lighted fuse must be cut. The interventions, dangers, and tempi of politicians are technical—not chivalrous.

Travel Souvenirs

Atrani.—The gently rising, curved baroque staircase leading to the church. The railing behind the church. The litanies of the old women at the 'Ave Maria': preparing to die first-class. If you turn around, the church verges like God Himself on the sea. Each morning the Christian Era crumbles the rock, but between the walls below, the night falls always into the four old Roman quarters. Alleyways like air shafts. A well in the market-place. In the late afternoon women about it. Then, in solitude: archaic plashing.

Navy.——The beauty of the tall sailing ships is unique. Not only has their outline remained unchanged for centuries, but also they appear in the most immutable landscape: at sea, silhouetted against the horizon.

Versailles Façade.——It is as if this *château* had been forgotten where hundreds of years ago it was placed *Par Ordre the Roi* for only two hours as the movable scenery for *a féerie*. Of its splendour it keeps none for itself, giving it undivided to that royal condition which it concludes. Before this backdrop it becomes a stage on which the tragedy of absolute monarchy was performed as an allegorical ballet. Yet today it is only the wall in the shade of which one seeks to enjoy the prospect into blue distance created by Le Nôtre.

Heidelberg Castle.——Ruins jutting into the sky can appear doubly beautiful on clear days when, in their windows or above their contours, the gaze meets passing clouds. Through the transient spectacle it opens in the sky, destruction reaffirms the eternity of these fallen stones.

Seville, Alcaȝar.——An architecture that follows fantasy's first impulse. It is undeflected by practical considerations. These rooms provide only for dreams and festivities, their consummation. Here dance and silence become the *leitmotifs*, since all human movement is absorbed by the soundless tumult of the ornament.

Marseilles, Cathedral.——On the least frequented, sunniest square stands the cathedral. This place is deserted, despite the proximity at its feet of La Joliette, the harbour, to the south, and a proletarian district to the north. As a reloading point for intangible, unfathomable goods, the bleak building stands between quay and warehouse. Nearly forty years were spent on it. But when all was complete, in 1893, place and time had conspired victoriously in this monument against its architects and sponsors, and the wealth of the clergy had given rise to a gigantic railway station that could never be opened to traffic. The façade gives an indication of the waiting rooms within, where passengers of the first to fourth classes (though before God they are all equal), wedged among their spiritual possessions as between cases, sit reading hymnbooks that, with their concordances and cross references, look very much like international timetables. Extracts from the railway traffic regulations in the form of pastoral letters hang on the walls, tariffs for the discount on special trips in Satan's luxury train are consulted, and cabinets where the long-distance traveller can discreetly wash are kept in readiness as confessionals. This is the Marseilles religion station. Sleeping cars to eternity depart from here at Mass times.

Freiburg Minster.——The special sense of a town is formed in part for its inhabitants——and perhaps even in the memory of the traveller who has stayed there——by the timbre and intervals with which its tower-clocks begin to chime.

Moscow, St Basil's.—What the Byzantine madonna carries on her arm is only a life-size wooden doll. Her expression of pain before a Christ whose childhood remains only suggested, represented, is more intense than any she could display with a realistic image of a boy.

Boscotrecase.—The distinction of the stone-pine forest: its roof is formed without interlacements.

Naples, Museo Nazionale.—Archaic statues offer in their smiles the consciousness of their bodies to the onlooker, as a child holds out to us freshly picked flowers untied and unarranged; later art laces its expressions more tightly, like the adult who binds the lasting bouquet with cutting grasses.

Florence, Baptistry.—On the portal the 'Spes' by Andrea de Pisano. Sitting, she helplessly stretches her arms for a fruit that remains beyond her reach. And yet she is winged. Nothing is more true.

Sky.—As I stepped from a house in a dream the night sky met my eyes. It shed intense radiance. For in this plenitude of stars the images of the constellations stood sensuously present. A Lion, a Maiden, a Scale and many others shone lividly down, dense clusters of stars, upon the earth. No moon was to be seen.

Optician

In summer fat people are conspicuous, in winter thin.

In spring attention is caught, in bright sunshine, by the young foliage, in cold rain by the still leafless branches.

How a convivial evening has passed can be seen by someone remaining behind from the disposition of plates and cups, glasses and food, at a glance.

First principle of wooing: to make oneself sevenfold; to place oneself sevenfold about the woman who is desired.

In the eyes we see people to the lees.

Toys

Cut-out models.—Booths have put in like rocking craft to both sides of the stone jetty on which the people jostle. There are sailing vessels with high masts from which hang pennants, steamers with smoke rising from their funnels, barges that keep their cargoes long stowed. Among them are ships into which one vanishes; only men are admitted, but through hatchways you can see women's arms, veils, peacock-feathers. Elsewhere exotic people stand on the deck apparently trying to frighten the public away with eccentric music. But with what indifference is it not received. You climb up hesitantly, with a broad rolling gait as on ships' stairways, and as long as you are aloft you realize that the whole is cut off from the shore. Those who re-emerge from below, taciturn and benumbed, have seen, on red scales where dyed alcohol rises and falls, their own marriage come into being and cease to be; the yellow man who began wooing at the foot of this scale, at the top of it deserted his blue wife. In mirrors they have seen the floor melt away beneath their feet like water, and stumbled into the open on rolling stairways. Into the quarter the fleet has brought unrest: the women and girls on board have brazen airs, and everything edible has been taken aboard in the land of idle luxury. One is so totally cut off by the ocean that everything is encountered here as if at once for the first and the last time. Sea-lions, dwarfs and dogs are preserved as in an ark. Even the railway has been brought in once and for all, and circulates endlessly through a tunnel. For a few days the quarter has become the port of a south-sea island, its inhabitants savages swooning in covetous wonderment before the things that Europe tosses at their feet.

Targets.—The landscapes of shooting-ranges in fairground booths ought to be described collectively as a corpus. There is, for example, a polar waste against which are set bundles of white clay-pipes, the targets, radiating like spokes. Behind this, and before an unarticulated strip of woodland, two for- esters are painted, while right at the front, in the manner of movable scenery, are two sirens with provocative breasts in oil colours. Elsewhere pipes bristle from the hair of women who are seldom painted with skirts, usually in tights. Or they protrude from a fan they spread in their hands. Moving pipes revolve slowly in the further regions of the clay-pigeon booths. Other stands present theatricals directed by the spec- tator with his rifle. If he hits the bull's-eye the performance starts. On one occasion there were thirty-six such boxes and above the stage of each was written what they held in store: '*Jeanne d'Arc en prison*', '*L'hospitalité*', '*Les rues de Paris*'. On another booth: '*Exécution capitale*'. In front of the closed gate a guillotine, a judge in a black robe and a priest holding a crucifix. If the shot hits the mark the gate opens and a board is extended on which the miscreant stands between two police- men. He places his neck automatically under the blade and is decapitated. In the same way: '*Les délices du mariage*'. A penurious interior opens. The father is seen in the middle of the room holding a child on his knee and with his free hand rocking a cradle containing another. '*L'Enfer*'—when its gates part a devil is seen tormenting a wretched soul. Next to him another is dragging a priest towards a cauldron in which the damned must stew. '*Le bagne*' ['clink']—a door with a gaoler in front of it. When the target is hit he pulls a bell-cord. The bell rings, the door opens. Two convicts are seen manhandling a big wheel. They seem to have to turn it. Yet another constellation: a fiddler with his dancing bear. When you shoot successfully the bow moves. The bear beats a drum with his paw and lifts one leg. One thinks of the fairy-tale of the brave little tailor, and could also imagine Sleeping Beauty awakened with a shot, Snow White freed of the apple by a shot or Little Red Riding-Hood released by a shot. The shot breaks in magically upon the existences of the puppets with that curative power that hews the heads from monsters and reveals them to be princesses. As is the case with the great door without an inscription: if you have hit the mark it opens and before red plush curtains stands a Moor who seems to bow slightly. He holds in front of him a golden bowl. On it lie three fruit. The first opens and a tiny person stands inside it and bows. In the second two equally diminutive puppets revolve in a dance. (The third did not open.) Below, in front of the table on which the remaining scenery stands, a small horseman with the inscription: '*Route minée*'. If you hit the bull's-eye there is a bang and the rider somersaults with his horse, but stays—needless to say—in the saddle.

Stereoscope.—Riga. The daily market, a huddling city of low wooden booths, stretches along the jetty, a broad, dirty stone embankment without warehouse buildings, by the waters of the Dvina. Small steamers, often showing no more than their funnels above the quay wall, have put in at the blackish dwarf-town. (The larger ships are moored downstream.) Grimy boards are the clay-grey foundation on which, glowing in the cold air, sparse colours melt. At some corners there stand all the year round, alongside huts for fish, meat, boots and clothes, petty-bourgeois women with the coloured paper rods that penetrate as far as the West only at Christmas-time. Like being scolded by the most-loved voice—such are these rods. For a few coppers multi-coloured chastising switches. At the end of the jetty, fenced off and only thirty paces from the water, are the red-and-white mounds of the apple-market. The apples on sale are packed in straw, those sold lie without straw in the housewives' baskets. A dark-red church rises beyond, outshone in the fresh November air by the cheeks of the apples.—Several shops for boating-tackle in small houses near the jetty. Ropes are painted on them. Everywhere you see wares depicted on signboards or on house-walls. One shop in the town has cases and belts larger than life on its bare brick walls. A low corner-house with a shop for corsets and millinery is decorated with ladies' faces complete with finery, and severe bodices painted on a yellow-ochre ground. Protruding from it at an angle is a lantern with similar pictures on its glass panes. The whole is like the facade of a fantasy-brothel. Another house, likewise not far from the harbour, has sugar-sacks and coal in grey and black relief on a grey wall. Somewhere else shoes rain from horns of plenty. Ironmongery is painted in detail, hammers, cogs, pliers and the tiniest screws on one board that looks like a page from an outmoded child's painting-book. With such pictures the town is permeated. Between them, however, rise tall, fortress-like desolate buildings evoking all the terrors of Tsarism.

Not for sale.—A mechanical cabinet at the fair at Lucca. The exhibition is accommodated in a long symmetrically-divided tent. A few steps lead up to it. The signboard shows a table with a few motionless puppets. You enter the tent by the right-hand opening and leave it by the left. In the bright interior two tables extend towards the back. They touch with their inner edges so that only a narrow space is left to walk round them. Both tables are low and glass-covered. On them stand the puppets (twenty to twenty-five centimetres high on average), while in their lower concealed part the clockwork that drives them ticks audibly. A narrow raised board for children runs along the sides of the tables. There are distorting mirrors on the walls.—Next to the entrance princely personages are to be seen. Each of them makes a particular gesture: one a spacious, inviting movement with the right or left arm, another a swivelling of his glassy eyes; some roll their eyes and move their arms at the same time. Franz Joseph stands there, Pius IX, enthroned and flanked by two cardinals, Queen Elena of Italy, the Sultaness, Wilhelm I on horseback, a small Napoleon III and an even smaller Victor Emmanuel as Crown Prince. Biblical figurines follow, then the Passion. Herod orders the slaughter of the infants with manifold movements of the head. He opens his mouth wide while nodding, extends and lets fall his arm. Two executioners stand before him, one free-wheeling with a cutting sword, a decapitated child under his arm, the other, on the point of stabbing, stands motionless but for his rolling eyes. And two mothers are there: one endlessly and gently shaking her head like a depressive, the other raising her arms slowly, beseechingly.—The nailing to the cross. It lies on the ground. The hirelings hammer in the nails. Christ nods.—Christ crucified, slaked by the sponge of vinegar, which a soldier offers him in slow jerks and then instantly withdraws. Each time the Saviour slightly raises his chin. From behind an angel bends over the cross with a chalice for blood, holds it in front of the body and then, as if it were filled, removes it.—The other table shows genre pictures. Gargantua with dumplings. In front of a plate he shovels them into his mouth with both hands, alternately lifting his left arm and his right. Each hand holds a fork on which a dumpling is impaled.—An Alpine maiden spinning.—Two monkeys playing violins.—A magician has two barrel-like containers in front of him. The one on the right opens, and the top half of a lady's body emerges. The one on the left opens: from it rises half-length a man's body. Again the right-hand container opens and now a ram's skull appears with the lady's face between its horns. Then on the left a monkey presents itself instead of the man. Then it all starts again from the beginning.—Another magician: he has a table in front of him on which he holds beakers upside-down in each hand. Under them, as he alternately lifts one then the other, appears now a loaf or an apple, now a flower or a die.—The magic well: a farm-boy stands head-shaking at a well. A girl draws water and the unfaltering thick stream of glass runs from the well-mouth.—The enchanted lovers: a golden bush or a golden flame parts in two wings. Within are seen two puppets. They turn their faces towards each other and then away, as if looking at each other in confused astonishment.—Below each figure a small label. The whole dating back to 1862.

Polyclinic

The author lays his idea on the marble table of the café. Lengthy meditation, for he makes use of the time before the arrival of his glass, the lens through which he examines the patient. Then, deliberately, he unpacks his instruments: fountain pens, pencil, and pipe. The numerous clientele, arranged as in an amphitheatre, make up his clinical audience. Coffee, carefully poured and consumed, puts the idea under chloroform. What this idea may be has no more connection with the matter at hand than the dream of an anaesthetized patient with the surgical intervention. With the cautious lineaments of handwriting the operator makes incisions, displaces internal accents, cauterizes proliferations of words, inserts a foreign term as a silver rib. At last the whole is finely stitched together with punctuation, and he pays the waiter, his assistant, in cash.

This Space for Rent

Fools lament the decay of criticism. For its day is long past. Criticism is a matter of correct distancing. It was at home in a world where perspectives and prospects counted and where it was still possible to take a standpoint. Now things press too closely on human society. The 'unclouded', 'innocent' eye has become a lie, perhaps the whole naive mode of expression sheer incompetence. Today the most real, the mercantile gaze into the heart of things is the advertisement. It abolishes the space where contemplation moved and all but hits us between the eyes with things as a car, growing to gigantic proportions, careens at us out of a film screen. And just as the film does not present furniture and façades in completed forms for critical inspection, their insistent, jerky nearness alone being sensational, the genuine advertisement hurtles things at us with the tempo of a good film. Thereby 'matter-of-factness' is finally dispatched, and in face of the huge images across the walls of houses, where toothpaste and cosmetics lie handy for giants, sentimentality is restored to health and liberated in American style, just as people whom nothing moves or touches any longer are taught to cry again by films. For the man in the street, however, it is money that affects him in this way, brings him into perceived contact with things. And the paid critic, manipulating paintings in the dealer's exhibition room, knows more important if not better things about them than the art lover viewing them in the showroom window. The warmth of the subject is communicated to him, stirs sentient springs. What, in the end, makes advertisements so superior to criticism? Not what the moving red neon sign says—but the fiery pool reflecting it in the asphalt.

Office Equipment

The boss's room bristles with weapons. The apparent comfort that disarms those entering is in reality a hidden arsenal. A telephone on the desk shrills at every moment. It interrupts you at the most important point and gives your opponent time to contrive an answer. Meanwhile snatches of conversation show how many matters are dealt with here that are more important than the one under discussion. You think this to yourself, and slowly start to retreat from your position. You begin to wonder who it is they are talking about, and hear with a fright that your interlocutor is leaving tomorrow for Brazil; soon you are so much at one with the firm that you regret the migraine he complains of on the telephone as a disturbance of business (rather than welcoming it as an opportunity). Summoned or unsummoned the secretary enters. She is very pretty. And if her employer is either proof against her charms or else has long clarified his position as her admirer, the newcomer will glance over at her more than once; and she knows how to turn this to advantage with her boss. His personnel are in motion producing card-indexes in which the visitor knows himself to be entered under various rubrics. He starts to tire. The other, with the light behind him, reads this off the dazzlingly illuminated face with satisfaction. The armchair too does its work; you sit in it tilted as far back as at the dentist's, and so finally accept this discomfiting procedure as the legitimate state of affairs. This treatment, too, is followed sooner or later by a liquidation.

Mixed Cargo: Carriage and Packing

In the early morning I drove through Marseilles to the station, and as I passed familiar places on my way, and then new, unfamiliar ones or others that I remembered only vaguely, the city became a book in my hands, into which I hurriedly glanced a few last times before it passed from my sight for who knows how long into a warehouse crate.

Closed for Alterations

In a dream I took my life with a gun. When it went off I did not wake up but saw myself for a while lying. Only then did I wake.

'Augeas' Self-Service Restaurant

This is the weightiest objection to the mode of life of the confirmed bachelor: he eats by himself. Taking food alone tends to make one hard and coarse. Those accustomed to it must lead a Spartan life if they are not to go downhill. Hermits have observed, if for only this reason, a frugal diet. For it is only in company that eating is done justice; food must be divided and distributed if it is to be well received. No matter by whom: formerly a beggar at the table enriched each banquet. The splitting up and giving are all-important, not sociable conversation. What is surprising, on the other hand, is that without food conviviality grows precarious. Playing host levels differences, binds together. The Count of Saint-Germain fasted before loaded tables, and by this alone dominated conversation. When all abstain, however, rivalries and conflict ensue.

Stamp Shop

To someone looking through piles of old letters a stamp that has long been out of circulation on a torn envelope often says more than a reading of dozens of pages. Sometimes you come across them on postcards and are unsure whether you should detach them or keep the card as it is, like a page by

an old master that has different but equally precious drawings on both sides. There are also, in the glass-cases of cafés,
letters with a charge on them, pilloried before all eyes. Or
have they been deported, and have to wait in this case for
years, languishing on a glass Salas y Gomez? Letters that
remain long unopened take on a brutal look; they are disinherited, and malignantly plot revenge for long days of
suffering. Many of them later figure in the windows of stamp
dealers, as entires branded over and over with postmarks.

As is known, there are collectors who concern themselves
only with post-marked stamps, and it would not be difficult to believe them the only ones who have penetrated the
secret. They confine themselves to the occult part of the
stamp: the postmark. For the postmark is the dark side of
stamps. There are ceremonious ones that place a halo about
the head of Queen Victoria, and prophetic ones that give
Humbert a martyr's crown. But no sadistic fantasy can equal
the black practice that covers faces with weals, and cleaves
the land of entire continents like an earthquake. And the perverse pleasure in contrasting this violated stamp-body with
its white lace-garnished tulle dress: the serrated border. The
pursuer of postmarks must possess like a detective information on the most notorious post offices, like an archaeologist
the art of reconstructing the torsos of the most foreign
place-names, and like a cabbalist an inventory of dates for
an entire century. Stamps bristle with tiny numbers, minute
letters, diminutive leaves and eyes. They are graphic cellular tissue. All this swarms about and, like lower animals,
lives on even when mutilated. This is why such powerful
pictures can be made of pieces of stamp stuck together. But
in them life bears always a hint of corruption to signify that

it is composed of dead matter. Their portraits and obscene groups are littered with bones and riddled with worms.

Do the colour sequences of the long sets perhaps refract the light of a strange sun? Did the postal ministries of the Vatican or Ecuador capture rays unknown to us? And why are we not shown the stamps of the superior planets? The thousand gradations of fire-red that are in circulation on Venus, and the four great grey shades of Mars and the unnumbered stamps of Saturn?

Countries and oceans on stamps are only the provinces, kings only the hirelings of numbers that steep them in their colours at will. Stamp-albums are magic reference-books, the numbers of monarchs and palaces, of animals and allegories and states are recorded in them. Postal traffic depends on their harmony as the motions of the planets depend on the harmony of the celestial numbers.

Old *Groschen*-stamps showing only one or two large figures in an oval. They look like those first photos from which, in black-lacquered frames, relations we never knew look down on us: figure-shaped great-aunts or forefathers. Thurn and Taxis too has the big figures on its stamps; there they are like the bewitched numbers of taximeters. One would not be surprised, one evening, to see the light of a candle shining through them from behind. But then there are small stamps without perforations, without indication of currency or country. In a tightly-woven spider's web they bear only a number. These are perhaps fate's true lottery tickets.

Script on Turkish piastre-stamps is like the slanted, altogether too dandyish, too gleaming breast-pin in the tie of a sly, only half-Europeanized merchant from Constantinople.

They number among the postal parvenus, the large, badly perforated, garish formats of Nicaragua or Colombia, which deck themselves out like banknotes.

Extra-postage stamps are the spirits among stamps. They are unaltering. The changes of monarchs and forms of government pass over them without trace, as over phantoms.

The child looks towards far-off Liberia through an inverted opera-glass: there it lies behind its little strip of sea with its palms, just as the stamps show it. With Vasco da Gama he sails around a triangle as isoscelean as hope and whose colours change with the weather. A travel brochure for the Cape of Good Hope. When he sees the swan on Australian stamps, it is always, even on the blue, green and brown issues, the black swan that is found only in Australia and here glides on the waters of a pool as on the most pacific ocean.

Stamps are the visiting-cards that the great states leave in a child's room.

Like Gulliver the child travels among the lands and peoples of his postage stamps. The geography and history of the Lilliputians, the whole science of the little nation with all its figures and names, is instilled in him in sleep. He takes part in their transactions, attends their purple assemblies, watches the launching of their little ships and celebrates with their crowned heads, enthroned behind hedges, jubilees.

There is, it is known, a stamp-language that is to flower-language what the morse alphabet is to the written one. But for how long will the flowers continue to bloom between the telegraph poles? Are not the great artistic stamps of the post-war years, with their full colours, already the autumnal asters and dahlias of this flora? Stephan, a German and not by chance a contemporary of Jean Paul, planted this seed in the summery middle of the nineteenth century. It will not survive the twentieth.

Si Parla Italiano

I sat at night in violent pain on a bench. Opposite me on another two girls sat down. They seemed to want to discuss something in confidence and began to whisper. Nobody except me was nearby and I should not have understood their Italian however loud it had been. But now I could not resist the feeling, in face of this unmotivated whispering in a language inaccessible to me, that a cool dressing was being applied to the painful place.

Technical Aid

Nothing is poorer than a truth expressed as it was thought. Committed to writing in such a case, it is not even a bad photograph. And the truth refuses (like a child or a woman who does not love us), facing the lens of writing while we crouch under the black cloth, to keep still and look amiable. Truth wants to be startled abruptly, at one stroke, from her self-immersion, whether by uproar, music or cries for help. Who could count the alarm signals with which the inner world of the true writer is equipped? And to 'write' is nothing other than to set them jangling. Then the sweet odalisque rises with a start, snatches whatever first comes to hand in the *mêlée* of her boudoir, our cranium, wraps it around her and flees us, almost unrecognizable, to other people. But how well-constituted she must be, how healthily built, to step in such manner among them, contorted, rattled, and yet victorious, captivating.

Hardware

Quotations in my work are like wayside robbers who leap out armed and relieve the stroller of his conviction.

The killing of a criminal can be moral—but never its legitimation.

The provider for all mankind is God, and the state His deputy.

The expressions of people moving about a picture-gallery show ill-concealed disappointment that only pictures hang there.

Tax Advice

Beyond doubt: a secret connection exists between the measure of goods and the measure of life, which is to say, between money and time. The more trivial the content of a lifetime, the more fragmented, multifarious, and disparate are its moments, while the grand period characterizes a superior existence. Very aptly, Lichtenberg suggests that time whiled away should be seen as made smaller, rather than shorter, and he also observes: 'a few dozen million minutes make up a life of forty-five years, and something more'. When a currency is in use a few million units of which are insignificant, life will have to be counted in seconds, rather than years, if it is to appear a respectable sum. And it will be frittered away like a bundle of bank notes: Austria cannot break the habit of thinking in florins.

Money and rain belong together. The weather itself is an index of the state of this world. Bliss is cloudless, knows no weather. There also comes a cloudless realm of perfect goods, on which no money falls.

A descriptive analysis of bank notes is needed. The unlimited satirical force of such a book would be equalled only by its objectivity. For nowhere more naively than in these documents does capitalism display itself in solemn earnest. The innocent cupids frolicking about numbers, the goddesses holding tablets of the law, the stalwart heroes sheathing their swords before monetary units, are a world of their own: ornamenting the façade of hell. If Lichtenberg had found paper money in circulation, the plan of this work would not have escaped him.

Legal Protection for the Needy

Publisher: My expectations have been most rudely disappointed. Your work makes no impression on the public; you do not have the slightest pulling power. And I have not spared expenses. I have incurred advertising costs. You know how highly I think of you, despite all this. But you cannot hold it against me if even I now have to listen to my commercial conscience. If there is anyone who does what he can for authors, I am he. But, after all, I also have a wife and children to look after. I do not mean, of course, that I hold you accountable for the losses of the past years. But a bitter feeling of disappointment will remain. I regret that I am at present absolutely unable to support you further.

Author: Sir, why did you become a publisher? We shall have the answer by return mail. But permit me to say one thing in advance. I figure in your archive as number 27. You have published five of my books; in other words, you have put your money five times on number 27. I am sorry that number 27 did not prove a winner. Incidentally, you only took coupled bets. Only because I come next to your lucky number 28. Now you know why you became a publisher. You might just as well have entered an honest profession, like your esteemed father. But never a thought for the morrow—such is youth. Continue to indulge your habits. But avoid posing as an honest businessman. Do not feign innocence when you have gambled everything away; do not talk about your eight-hour working day, or the night when you hardly get any rest, either. 'Truth and fidelity before all else, my child.' And don't start making scenes with your numbers! Otherwise you will be bounced.

Doctor's Night-Bell

Sexual fulfilment delivers the man from his secret, which does not consist in sexuality but which in its fulfilment, and perhaps in it alone, is severed—not solved. This secret is comparable to the fetter that binds him to life. The woman cuts it, the man is free to die, because his life has lost its secret. Thereby he attains rebirth, and as his beloved frees him from the mother's spell, the woman literally detaches him from Mother Earth—a midwife who cuts that umbilical cord which is woven of nature's mystery.

Madame Ariane—Second Courtyard on the Left

He who asks fortune-tellers the future unwittingly forfeits an inner intimation of coming events that is a thousand times more exact than anything they may say. He is impelled by inertia, rather than curiosity, and nothing is more unlike the submissive apathy with which he hears his fate revealed than the alert dexterity with which the man of courage lays hands on the future. For presence of mind is an extract of the future, and precise awareness of the present moment more decisive than foreknowledge of the most distant events. Omens, presentiments, signals pass day and night through our organism like wave impulses. To interpret them or to use them, that is the question. The two are irreconcilable. Cowardice and apathy counsel the former, lucidity and freedom the latter. For before such prophecy or warning has been mediated by word or image it has lost its vitality, the power to strike at our centre and force us, we scarcely know how, to act accordingly. If we neglect to do so, and only then, the message is deciphered. We read it. But it is now too late. Hence, when you are taken unawares by an outbreak of fire or the news of a death, there is in the first mute shock a feeling of guilt, the indistinct reproach: did you really not know of this? Did not the dead person's name, the last time you uttered it, sound differently in your mouth? Do you not see in the flames a sign from yesterday evening, in a language you only now understand? And if an object dear to you has been lost, was there not, hours, days before, an aura of mockery or mourning about it that gave the secret away? Like ultraviolet rays memory shows to each man in the book of life a script that invisibly and prophetically glosses the text. But it is not with impunity that these intentions are exchanged, that unlived life is handed over to cards, spirits, stars, to be in an instant squandered, misused, and returned to us disfigured; we do not go unpunished for cheating the body of its power to meet the fates on its own ground and triumph. The moment is the Caudine Yoke beneath which fate must bow to the body. To turn the threatening future into a fulfilled now, the only desirable telepathic miracle, is a work of bodily presence of mind. Primitive epochs, when such demeanour was part of man's daily husbandry, provided him, in the naked body, with the most reliable instrument of divination. Even the ancients knew of this true practice, and Scipio, stumbling as he set foot on Carthaginian soil, cried out, spreading his arms wide as he fell, the watchword of victory, '*Teneo te, terra Africana!*' What would have become a portent of disaster he binds bodily to the moment, making himself the factotum of his body. In just such mastery the ancient ascetic exercises of fasting, chastity, and vigil have for all time celebrated their greatest victories. Each morning the day lies like a fresh shirt on our bed; this incomparably fine, incomparably tightly woven tissue of pure prediction fits us perfectly. The happiness of the next twenty-four hours depends on our ability, on waking, to pick it up.

Costume Wardrobe

A bearer of news of death appears to himself as very important. His feeling—even against all reason—makes him a messenger from the realm of the dead. For the community of all the dead is so immense that even he who only reports death is aware of it. *Ad plures ire* was the Latins' expression for dying.

At Bellinzona I noticed three priests in the station waiting room. They were sitting on a bench diagonally opposite mine. In rapt attention I observed the gestures of the one seated in the middle, who was distinguished from his brothers by a red skullcap. While he speaks to them, his hands are folded in his lap, and only now and then is one or the other very slightly raised and moved. I think to myself: his right hand must always know what the left is doing.

Is there anyone who has not once been stunned, emerging from the Métro into the open air, to step into brilliant sunlight? And yet the sun shone a few minutes earlier, when he went down, just as brightly. So quickly has he forgotten the weather of the upper world. And as quickly the world in its turn will forget him. For who can say more of his own existence than that it has passed through the lives of two or three others as gently and closely as the weather?

Again and again, in Shakespeare, in Calderon, battles fill the last act, and kings, princes, attendants and followers 'enter, fleeing'. The moment in which they become visible to spectators brings them to a standstill. The flight of the *dramatis personae* is arrested by the stage. Their entry into the visual field of nonparticipating and truly impartial persons allows the harassed to draw breath, bathes them in new air. The appearance on stage of those who enter 'fleeing' takes from this its hidden meaning. Our reading of this formula is imbued with expectation of a place, a light, a footlight glare, in which our flight through life may be likewise sheltered in the presence of onlooking strangers.

Betting Office

Bourgeois existence is the regime of private affairs. The more important the nature and implications of a mode of behaviour, the further removed it is from observation here. Political conviction, financial situation, religion—all these seek hideouts, and the family is the rotten, dismal edifice in whose closets and crannies the most ignominious instincts are deposited. Mundane life proclaims the total subjugation of eroticism to privacy. So wooing becomes a silent, dead-serious transaction between two persons alone, and this thoroughly private wooing, severed from all responsibility, is what is really new in 'flirting'. In contrast, the proletarian and the feudal type of men resemble each other in that in wooing it is much less the woman than their competitors that they overcome. In this they respect the woman far more deeply than in her freedom, being at her command without cross-examining her. The shift of erotic emphasis to the public sphere is both feudal and proletarian. To be seen with a woman on such-and-such an occasion can mean more than to sleep with her. Thus in marriage, too, value does not lie in the sterile 'harmony' of the partners: it is as the eccentric offshoot of their struggles and rivalries enacted elsewhere that, like the child, the spiritual force of marriage is manifest.

Stand-Up Beer Hall

Sailors seldom come ashore; service on the high seas is a holiday by comparison with the labour in harbours, where loading and unloading must often be done day and night.

When a gang is then given a few hours' shore-leave it is already dark. At best the cathedral looms like a dark promontory on the way to the tavern. The ale-house is the key to every town; to know where German beer can be drunk is geography and ethnology enough. The German seamen's bar unrolls the nocturnal plan of the city: to find the way from there to the brothel, to the other bars is not difficult. Their names have criss-crossed the mealtime conversations for days. For when a harbour has been left behind, one sailor after another hoists like little pennants the nicknames of bars and dance-halls, beautiful women and national dishes from the next. But who knows whether he will go ashore this time? For this reason, no sooner is the ship declared and moored than tradesmen come aboard with souvenirs: chains and picture-postcards, oil-paintings, knives and little marble figures. The city sights are not seen but bought. In the sailors' chests the leather belt from Hong Kong is juxtaposed to a panorama of Palermo and a girl's photo from Stettin. And their real habitat is exactly the same. They know nothing of the hazy distances in which, for the bourgeois, foreign lands are enshrouded. What first asserts itself in every city is, first, service on board, and then German beer, English shaving-soap and Dutch tobacco. Imbued to the marrow with the international norm of industry, they are not the dupes of palms and icebergs. The seaman is sated with close-ups, and only the most exact nuances speak to him. He can distinguish countries better by the preparation of their fish than by their building-styles or landscapes. He is so much at home in detail that the ocean routes where he cuts close to other ships (greeting those of his own firm with howls from the siren) become noisy thoroughfares where you have to give way to traffic. He lives on the open sea in a city where, on the Marseilles Cannebière, a Port Said bar stands diagonally opposite a Hamburg brothel, and the Neapolitan Castel del Ovo is to be found on Barcelona's Plaza Cataluña. For officers their native town still holds pride of place. But for the ordinary sailor, or the stoker, the people whose transported labour-power maintains contact with the commodities in the hull of the ship, the interlaced harbours are no longer even a homeland, but a cradle. And listening to them one realizes what mendacity resides in tourism.

No Vagrants

All religions have honoured the beggar. For he proves that in a matter at the same time as prosaic and holy, banal and regenerating as the giving of alms, intellect and morality, consistency and principles are miserably inadequate.

We deplore the beggars in the South, forgetting that their persistence in front of our noses is as justified as a scholar's before a difficult text. No shadow of hesitation, no slightest wish or deliberation in our faces escapes their notice. The telepathy of the coachman who, by accosting us, makes known to us our previously unsuspected inclination to board his vehicle, and of the shopkeeper who extracts from his junk the single chain or cameo that could delight us, is of the same order.

To the Planetarium

If one had to expound the doctrine of antiquity with utmost brevity while standing on one leg, as did Hillel that of the

Jews, it could only be in this sentence: 'They alone shall possess the earth who live from the powers of the cosmos.' Nothing distinguishes the ancient from the modern man so much as the former's absorption in a cosmic experience scarcely known to later periods. Its waning is marked by the flowering of astronomy at the beginning of the modern age. Kepler, Copernicus, and Tycho Brahe were certainly not driven by scientific impulses alone. All the same, the exclusive emphasis on an optical connection to the universe, to which astronomy very quickly led, contained a portent of what was to come. The ancients' intercourse with the cosmos had been different: the ecstatic trance. For it is in this experience alone that we gain certain knowledge of what is nearest to us and what is remotest to us, and never of one without the other. This means, however, that man can be in ecstatic contact with the cosmos only communally. It is the dangerous error of modern men to regard this experience as unimportant and avoidable, and to consign it to the individual as the poetic rapture of starry nights. It is not; its hour strikes again and again, and then neither nations nor generations can escape it, as was made terribly clear by the last war, which was an attempt at new and unprecedented commingling with the cosmic powers. Human multitudes, gases, electrical forces were hurled into the open country, high-frequency currents coursed through the landscape, new constellations rose in the sky, aerial space and ocean depths thundered with propellers, and everywhere sacrificial shafts were dug in Mother Earth. This immense wooing of the cosmos was enacted for the first time on a planetary scale, that is, in the spirit of technology. But because the lust for profit of the ruling class sought satisfaction through it, technology betrayed man and turned the bridal bed into a bloodbath. The mastery of nature, so the imperialists teach, is the purpose of all technology. But who would trust a cane wielder who proclaimed the mastery of children by adults to be the purpose of education? Is not education above all the indispensable ordering of the relationship between generations and therefore mastery, if we are to use this term, of that relationship and not of children? And likewise technology is not the mastery of nature but of the relation between nature and man. Men as a species completed their development thousands of years ago; but mankind as a species is just beginning his. In technology a *physis* is being organized through which mankind's contact with the cosmos takes a new and different form from that which it had in nations and families. One need recall only the experience of velocities by virtue of which mankind is now preparing to embark on incalculable journeys into the interior of time, to encounter there rhythms from which the sick shall draw strength as they did earlier on high mountains or at Southern seas. The 'Lunaparks' are a prefiguration of sanatoria. The paroxysm of genuine cosmic experience is not tied to that tiny fragment of nature that we are accustomed to call 'Nature'. In the nights of annihilation of the last war the frame of mankind was shaken by a feeling that resembled the bliss of the epileptic. And the revolts that followed it were the first attempt of mankind to bring the new body under its control. The power of the proletariat is the measure of its convalescence. If it is not gripped to the very marrow by the discipline of this power, no pacifist polemics will save it. Living substance conquers the frenzy of destruction only in the ecstasy of procreation.

1925–26

II

On Language as Such and on the Language of Man

Every expression of human mental life can be understood as a kind of language, and this understanding, in the manner of a true method, everywhere raises new questions. It is possible to talk about a language of music and of sculpture, about a language of justice that has nothing directly to do with those in which German or English legal judgments are couched, about a language of technology that is not the specialized language of technicians. Language in such contexts means the tendency inherent in the subjects concerned—technology, art, justice, or religion—toward the communication of mental meanings. To sum up: all communication of mental meanings is language, communication in words being only a particular case of human language and of the justice, poetry, or whatever underlying it or founded on it. The existence of language, however, is not only coextensive with all the areas of human mental expression in which language is always in one sense or another inherent, but with absolutely everything. There is no event

or thing in either animate or inanimate nature that does not
in some way partake of language, for it is in the nature of
all to communicate their mental meanings. This use of the
word 'language' is in no way metaphorical. For to think that
we cannot imagine anything that does not communicate its
mental nature in its expression is entirely meaningful; the
greater or lesser degree of consciousness that is apparently
(or really) involved in such communication cannot alter the
fact that we cannot imagine a total absence of language in
anything. An existence entirely without relationship to language is an idea; but this idea can bear no fruit even within
that realm of Ideas whose circumference defines the idea
of God.

All that is asserted here is that all expression, insofar as
it is a communication of mental meaning, is to be classed as
language. And expression, by its whole innermost nature,
is certainly to be understood only as *language*; on the other
hand, to understand a linguistic entity it is always necessary
to ask of which mental entity it is the direct expression. That
is to say: the German language, for example, is by no means
the expression of everything that we could—theoretically
—express *through* it, but is the direct expression of that
which communicates *itself* in it. This 'itself' is a mental
entity. It is therefore obvious at once that the mental entity
that communicates itself in language is not language itself
but something to be distinguished from it. The view that the
mental essence of a thing consists precisely in its language—
this view, taken as a hypothesis, is the great abyss into which
all linguistic theory threatens to fall, and to survive suspended precisely over this abyss is its task. The distinction
between a mental entity and the linguistic entity in which

it communicates is the first stage of any study of linguistic theory, and this distinction seems so unquestionable that it is, rather, the frequently asserted identity between mental and linguistic being that constitutes a deep and incomprehensible paradox, the expression of which is found in the ambiguity of the word *logos*. Nevertheless, this paradox has a place, as a solution, at the centre of linguistic theory, but remains a paradox, and insoluble, if placed at the beginning.

What does language communicate? It communicates the mental being corresponding to it. It is fundamental that this mental being communicates itself *in* language and not *through* language. Languages therefore have no speaker, if this means someone who communicates *through* these languages. Mental being communicates itself in, not through, a language, which means: it is not outwardly identical with linguistic being. Mental is identical with linguistic being only insofar as it is capable of communication. What is communicable in a mental entity is its linguistic entity. Language therefore communicates the particular linguistic being of things, but their mental being only insofar as this is directly included in their linguistic being, insofar as it is capable of being communicated.

Language communicates the linguistic being of things. The clearest manifestation of this being, however, is language itself. The answer to the question '*What* does language communicate?' is therefore 'All language communicates itself.' The language of this lamp, for example, does not communicate the lamp (for the mental being of the lamp, insofar as it is *communicable*, is by no means the lamp itself), but: the language-lamp, the lamp in communication, the lamp in expression. For in language the situation is this: *the linguistic being of all things is their language.* The understanding of linguistic theory depends on giving this proposition a clarity that annihilates even the appearance of tautology. This proposition is untautological, for it means: that which in a mental entity is communicable *is* its language. On this 'is' (equivalent to 'is immediately') everything depends. Not that which *appears* most clearly in its language is communicable in a mental entity, as was just said by way of transition, but this *capacity* for communication is language itself. Or: the language of a mental entity is directly that which is communicable in it. What is communicable *of* a mental entity, in this it communicates itself. Which signifies: all language communicates itself. Or more precisely: all language communicates itself *in* itself; it is in the purest sense the 'medium' of the communication. Mediation, which is the immediacy of all mental communication, is the fundamental problem of linguistic theory, and if one chooses to call this immediacy magic, then the primary problem of language is its magic. At the same time, the notion of the magic of language points to something else: its infiniteness. This is conditional on its immediacy. For just because nothing is communicated *through* language, what is communicated *in* language cannot be externally limited or measured, and therefore all language contains its own incommensurable, uniquely constituted infinity. Its linguistic being, not its verbal meanings, defines its frontier.

The linguistic being of things is their language; this proposition, applied to man, means: the linguistic being of man is his language. Which signifies: man communicates his own mental being *in* his language. However, the language of man speaks in words. Man therefore communicates his own mental being (insofar as it is communicable) by *naming* all other things. But do we know any other languages that name things? It should not be accepted that we know of no languages other than that of man, for this is untrue. We only know of no *naming* language other than that of man; to identify naming language with language as such is to rob linguistic theory of its deepest insights. *It is therefore the linguistic being of man to name things*.

Why name them? To whom does man communicate himself? But is this question, as applied to man, other than as applied to other communications (languages)? To whom does the lamp communicate itself? The mountain? The fox? But here the answer is: to man. This is not anthropomorphism. The truth of this answer is shown in knowledge and perhaps also in art. Furthermore, if the lamp and the mountain and the fox did not communicate themselves to man, how should he be able to name them? And he names them; *he* communicates himself by naming *them*. To whom does he communicate himself?

Before this question can be answered we must again inquire: how does man communicate himself? A profound distinction is to be made, a choice presented, in face of which an intrinsically false understanding of language is certain to give itself away. Does man communicate his mental being *by* the names that he gives things? Or *in* them? In the paradoxical nature of these questions lies their answer. Anyone who believes that man communicates his mental being *by* names cannot also assume that it is his mental being that he communicates, for this does not happen through the names of things, that is, through the words by which he denotes a thing. And, equally, the advocate of such a view can only assume that man is communicating factual subject matter to other men, for that does happen through the word by which he denotes a thing. This view is the bourgeois conception of language, the invalidity and emptiness of which will become increasingly clear in what follows. It holds that the means of communication is the word, its object factual, its addressee a human being. The other conception of language, in contrast, knows no means, no object, and no addressee of communication. It means: *in naming the mental being of man communicates itself to God*.

Naming, in the realm of language, has as its sole purpose and its incomparably high meaning that it is the innermost nature of language itself. Naming is that by which nothing beyond it is communicated, and *in* which language itself communicates itself absolutely. In naming the mental entity that communicates itself is *language*. Where mental being in its communication is language itself in its absolute wholeness, only there is the name, and only the name is there. Name as the heritage of human language therefore vouches for the fact that language as such is the mental being of man; and only for this reason is the mental being of man, alone among all mental entities, communicable without residue. On this is founded the difference between human language and the language of things. But because the mental being of man is language itself, he cannot communicate himself by it but only in it. The quintessence of this intensive totality of language as the mental being of man is naming. Man is the namer, by this we recognize that through him pure language speaks. All nature, insofar as it communicates itself, communicates itself in language, and so finally in man. Hence he is the lord of nature and can give names to things. Only through the linguistic being of things can he gain knowledge of them from within himself—in name. God's creation is completed when things receive their names from man, from whom in name language alone speaks. Man can call name the language of language (if the genitive refers to the relationship not of a means but of a medium) and in this sense certainly, because he speaks in name, man is the speaker of language, and for this very reason its only speaker. In terming man the speaker (which, however, according to the Bible, for example, clearly means the name giver: 'As man should name all kinds of living creatures, so should they be *called*'), many languages imply this metaphysical truth.

Name, however, is not only the last utterance of language but also the true call of it. Thus in name appears the essential law of language, according to which to express oneself and to address everything else amounts to the same. Language —and in it a mental entity—only expresses itself purely where it speaks in name, that is, in its universal naming. So in name culminate both the intensive totality of language, as the absolutely communicable mental entity, and the extensive totality of language, as the universally communicating (naming) entity. By virtue of its communicating nature, its universality, language is incomplete where the mental entity that speaks from it is not in its whole structure linguistic, that is, communicable. *Man alone has a language that is complete both in its universality and in its intensiveness*.

In the light of this, a question may now be asked without the risk of confusion, a question that, though of the highest metaphysical importance, can be clearly posed first of all as one of terminology. It is whether mental being—not only of man (for that is necessary) but also of things, and thus mental being as such—can from the point of view of linguistic theory be described as of linguistic nature. If mental being is identical with linguistic, then a thing, by virtue of its mental being, is a medium of communication, and what is communicated in it is—in accordance with its mediating relationship—precisely this medium (language) itself. Language is thus the mental being of things. Mental being is therefore postulated at the outset as communicable, or, rather, is situated *within* the communicable, and the thesis that the linguistic being of things is identical with the mental, insofar as the latter is communicable, becomes in its 'insofar' a tautology. *There is no such thing as a meaning of language; as communication, language communicates a mental entity, i.e., something communicable per se.* The differences between languages are those of media that are distinguished as it were by their density, that is, gradually; and this with regard to the density both of the communicating (naming) and of the communicable (name) aspects of communication. These two spheres, which are clearly distinguished yet united only in the name language of man, are naturally constantly interrelated.

For the metaphysics of language the equation of mental with linguistic being, which knows only gradual differences, produces a graduation of all mental being in degrees. This graduation, which takes place within mental being itself, can no longer be embraced by any higher category and so leads to the graduation of all being, both mental and linguistic, by degrees of existence or being, such as was already familiar to scholasticism with regard to mental being. However, the equation of mental and linguistic being is of great metaphysical moment to linguistic theory because it leads to the concept that has again and again, as if of its own accord, elevated itself to the centre of linguistic philosophy and constituted its most intimate connection with the philosophy of religion. This is the concept of revelation. Within all linguistic formation a conflict is waged between what is expressed and expressible and what is inexpressible and unexpressed. On considering this conflict one sees, in the perspective of the inexpressible, at the same time the last mental entity. Now it is clear that in the equation of mental and linguistic being the notion of an inverse proportionality between the two is disputed. For this latter thesis runs: the deeper, i.e., the more existent and real the mind, the more it is inexpressible and unexpressed, whereas it is consistent with the equation proposed above to make the relation between mind and language thoroughly unambiguous, so that the expression that is linguistically most existent (i.e., most fixed) is linguistically the most rounded and definitive; in a word, the most expressed is at the same time the purely mental. Exactly this, however, is meant by the concept of revelation, if it takes the inviolability of the word as the only and sufficient condition and characteristic of the divinity of the mental being that is expressed in it. The highest mental region of religion is (in the concept of revelation) at the same time the only one that does not know the inexpressible. For it is addressed in name and expresses itself as revelation. In this, however, notice is given that only the highest mental being, as it appears in religion, rests solely on man and on the language in him, whereas all art, not excluding poetry, does not rest on the ultimate essence of language-mind, but on language-mind confined to things, even if in consummate beauty. '*Language, the mother* of reason and *revelation*, its alpha and omega', says Hamann.

Language itself is not perfectly expressed in things themselves. This proposition has a double meaning in its metaphorical and literal senses: the languages of things are imperfect, and they are dumb. Things are denied the pure formal principle of language—sound. They can only communicate to one another through a more or less material community. This community is immediate and infinite, like every linguistic communication; it is magical (for there is also a magic of matter). The incomparable feature of human language is that its magical community with things is immaterial and purely mental, and the symbol of this is sound. The Bible expresses this symbolic fact when it says that God breathes his breath into man: this is at once life and mind and language.

If in what follows the nature of language is considered on the basis of the first chapter of Genesis, the object is neither biblical interpretation, nor subjection of the Bible to objective consideration as revealed truth, but the discovery of what emerges of itself from the biblical text with regard to the nature of language; and the Bible is only *initially* indispensable for this purpose because the present argument broadly follows it in presupposing language as an ultimate reality, perceptible only in its manifestation, inexplicable and mystical. The Bible, in regarding itself as a revelation, must necessarily evolve the fundamental linguistic facts. The second version of the story of the Creation, which tells of the breathing of God's breath into man, also reports that man was made from earth. This is, in the whole story of the Creation, the only reference to the material in which the Creator expresses his will, which is doubtless otherwise thought of as creation without mediation. In this second story of the Creation the making of man did not take place through the word: God spoke—and there was—but this man, who is not created from the word, is now invested with the *gift* of language and is elevated above nature.

This curious revolution in the act of creation, where it concerns man, is no less clearly recorded, however, in the first story of the Creation, and in an entirely different context it vouches, with the same certainty, for a special relationship between man and language resulting from the act of creation. The manifold rhythm of the act of creation in the first chapter establishes a kind of basic form from which the act that creates man diverges significantly. Admittedly this passage nowhere expressly refers to a relationship either of man or of nature to the material from which they were created; and the question whether the words 'He made' envisages a creation out of material must here be left open, but the rhythm by which the creation of nature (in Genesis 1) is accomplished is: Let there be—He made (created)— He named. In individual acts of creation (1:3; 1:11) only the words 'Let there be' occur. In this 'Let there be' and in the words 'He named' at the beginning and end of the act, the deep and clear relation of the creative act to language appears each time. With the creative omnipotence of language it begins, and at the end language as it were assimilates the created, names it. Language is therefore both creative and the finished creation, it is word and name. In God name is creative because it is word, and God's word is cognizant because it is name. 'And he saw that it was good'; that is: He had cognized it through name. The absolute relation of name to knowledge exists only in God, only there is name, because it is inwardly identical with the creative word, the pure medium of knowledge. That means: God made things knowable in their names. Man, however, names them according to knowledge.

In the creation of man the threefold rhythm of the creation of nature has given way to an entirely different order. In it, therefore, language has a different meaning: the trinity of the act is here preserved, but in this very parallelism the divergence is all the more striking: in the threefold 'He created' of 1:27. God did not create man from the word, and he did not name him. He did not wish to subject him to language, but in man God set language, which had served *Him* as medium of creation, free. God rested when he had left his creative power to itself in man. This creativity, relieved of its divine actuality, became knowledge. Man is the knower in the same language in which God is creator. God created him in his image, he created the knower in the image of the creator. Therefore the proposition that the mental being of man is language needs explanation. His mental being is the language in which creation took place. In the word creation took place, and God's linguistic being is the word. All human language is only reflection of the word in name. Name is no closer to the word than knowledge to creation. The infinity of all human language always remains limited and analytical in nature in comparison to the absolutely unlimited and creative infinity of the divine word.

The deepest images of this divine word and the point where human language participates most intimately in the divine infinity of the pure word, the point at which it cannot become finite word and knowledge, are the human name. The theory of proper names is the theory of the frontier between finite and infinite language. Of all beings man is the only one who himself names his own kind, as he is the only one whom God did not name. It is perhaps bold, but scarcely impossible, to mention the second part of 2:20 in this context: that man named all beings, '*but* for man there was not found a helper fit for him'. Accordingly, Adam names his wife as soon as he receives her (woman in the second chapter, Eve in the third). By giving names, parents dedicate their children to God; the names they give do not correspond—in a metaphysical, not etymological sense— to any knowledge, for they name newborn children. In a strict sense, no name ought (in its etymological meaning) to correspond to any person, for the proper name is the word of God in human sounds. By it each man is guaranteed his creation by God, and in this sense he is himself creative, as is expressed by mythological wisdom in the idea (which doubtless not infrequently comes true) that a man's name is his fate. The proper name is the communion of man with the *creative* word of God. (Not the only one, however; man knows a further linguistic communion with God's word.) Through the word man is bound to the language of things. The human word is the name of things. Hence it is no longer conceivable, as the bourgeois view of language maintains, that the word has an accidental relation to its object, that it is a sign for things (or knowledge of them) agreed by some convention. Language never gives *mere* signs. However, the rejection of bourgeois by mystical linguistic theory equally rests on a misunderstanding. For according to mystical theory the word is simply the essence of the thing. That is incorrect, because the thing in itself has no word, being created from God's word and known in its name by a human word. This knowledge of the thing, however, is not spontaneous creation, it does not emerge from language in the absolutely unlimited and infinite manner of creation; rather, the name that man gives to language depends on how language is communicated to him. In name the word of God has not remained creative; it has become in one part receptive, even if receptive to language. Thus fertilized, it aims to give birth to the language of things themselves, from which in turn, soundlessly, in the mute magic of nature, the word of God shines forth.

For conception and spontaneity together, which are found in this unique union only in the linguistic realm, language has its own word, and this word applies also to that conception which is enacted by the nameless in names. It is the translation of the language of things into that of man. It is necessary to found the concept of translation at the deepest level of linguistic theory, for it is much too far-reaching and powerful to be treated in any way as an afterthought, as has happened occasionally. Translation attains its full meaning in the realization that every evolved language (with the exception of the word of God) can be considered as a translation of all the others. By the relation, mentioned earlier, of languages as between media of varying densities, the translatability of languages into one another is established. Translation is removal from one language into another through a continuum of transformations. Translation passes through continua of transformation, not abstract areas of identity and similarity.

The translation of the language of things into that of man is not only a translation of the mute into the sonic; it is also the translation of the nameless into name. It is therefore the translation of an imperfect language into a more perfect one, and cannot but add something to it, namely knowledge. The objectivity of this translation is, however, guaranteed by God. For God created things; the creative word in them is the germ of the cognizing name, just as God, too, finally named each thing after it was created. But obviously this naming is only an expression of the identity of the creative word and the cognizing name in God, not the prior solution of the task that God expressly assigns to man himself: that of naming things. In receiving the unspoken nameless language of things and converting it by name into sounds, man performs this task. It would be insoluble were not the name-language of man and the nameless one of things related in God and released from the same creative word, which in things became the communication of matter in magic communion, and in man the language of knowledge and name in blissful mind. Hamann says: 'Everything that man heard in the beginning, saw with his eyes, and felt with his hands was the living word; for God was the word. With this word in his mouth and in his heart, the origin of language was as natural, as close, and as easy as a child's game.' Friedrich Müller, in his poem 'Adam's Awakening and First Blissful Nights', has God summon man to name-giving in these words: 'Man of the earth step near, in gazing grow more perfect, more perfect through the word.' By this combination of contemplation and naming is implied the communicating muteness of things (animals) toward the word language of man, which receives them in name. In the same chapter of the poem, the poet expresses the realization that only the word from which things are created permits man to name them, by communicating itself in the manifold languages of animals, even if mutely, in the image: God gives each beast in turn a sign, whereupon they step before man to be named. In an almost sublime way the linguistic community of mute creation with God is thus conveyed in the image of the sign.

As the unspoken word in the existence of things falls infinitely short of the naming word in the knowledge of man, and as the latter in turn must fall short of the creative word of God, there is reason for the multiplicity of human languages. The language of things can pass into the language of knowledge and name only through translation—as many translations, so many languages—once man has fallen from the paradisiac state that knew only one language. (According to the Bible, this consequence of the expulsion from paradise admittedly came about only later.) The paradisiac language of man must have been one of perfect knowledge; whereas later all knowledge is again infinitely differentiated in the multiplicity of language, was indeed forced to differentiate itself on a lower level as creation in name. For that the language of paradise was fully cognizant, even the existence of the tree of knowledge cannot conceal. Its apples were supposed to impart knowledge of good and evil. But on the seventh day, God had already cognized with the words of creation. And God saw that it was good. The knowledge to which the snake seduces, that of good and evil, is nameless. It is vain in the deepest sense, and this very knowledge is itself the only evil known to the paradisiac state. Knowledge of good and evil abandons name, it is a knowledge from outside, the uncreated imitation of the creative word. Name steps outside itself in this knowledge: the Fall marks the birth of the *human word*, in which name no longer lives intact, and which has stepped out of name language, the language of knowledge, from what we may call its own immanent magic, in order to become expressly, as it were externally, magic. The word must communicate *something* (other than itself). That is really the Fall of language-mind. The word as something externally communicating, as it were a parody by the expressly mediate word of the expressly immediate, the creative word of God, and the decay of the blissful, Adamite language-mind that stand between them. For in reality there exists a fundamental identity between the word that, after the promise of the snake, knows good and evil, and the externally communicating word. The knowledge of things resides in name, whereas that of good and evil is, in the profound sense in which Kierkegaard uses the word, 'prattle', and knows only one purification and elevation, to which the prattling man, the sinner, was therefore submitted: judgment. Admittedly, the judging word has direct knowledge of good and evil. Its magic is different from that of name, but equally magical. This judging word expels the first human beings from paradise; they themselves have aroused it in accordance with the immutable law by which this judging word punishes—and expects—its own awakening as the only, the deepest guilt. In the Fall, since the eternal purity of names was violated, the sterner purity of the judging word arose. For the essential composition of language the Fall has a threefold significance (without mentioning its other meanings). In stepping outside the purer language of name, man makes language a means (that is, a knowledge inappropriate to him), and therefore also, in one part at any rate, a *mere* sign; and this later results in the plurality of languages. The second meaning is that from the Fall, in exchange for the immediacy of name damaged by it, a new immediacy arises, the magic of judgment, which no longer rests blissfully in itself. The third meaning that can perhaps be tentatively ventured is that the origin of abstraction, too, as a faculty of language-mind, is to be sought in the Fall. For good and evil, being unnamable, nameless, stand outside the language of names, which man leaves behind precisely in the abyss opened by this question. Name, however, with regard to existing language, offers only the ground in which its concrete elements are rooted. But the abstract elements of language—we may perhaps surmise—are rooted in the word of judgment. The immediacy (which, however, is the linguistic root) of the communicability of abstraction resides in judgment. This immediacy in the communication of abstraction came into being as judgment, when, in the Fall, man abandoned immediacy in the communication of the concrete, name, and fell into the abyss of the mediateness of all communication, of the word as means, of the empty word, into the abyss of prattle. For—it must be said again—the question as to good and evil in the world after creation was empty prattle. The tree of knowledge did not stand in the garden of God in order to dispense information on good and evil, but as an emblem of judgment over the questioner. This immense irony marks the mythical origin of law.

After the Fall, which, in making language mediate, laid the foundation for its multiplicity, it could be only a step to linguistic confusion. Since men had injured the purity of name, the turning away from that contemplation of things in which their language passes into man needed only to be completed in order to deprive men of the common foundation of an already shaken language-mind. *Signs* must

become confused where things are entangled. The enslavement of language in prattle is joined by the enslavement of
things in folly almost as its inevitable consequence. In this
turning away from things, which was enslavement, the plan
for the tower of Babel came into being, and linguistic confusion with it.

The life of man in pure language-mind was blissful.
Nature, however, is mute. True, it can be clearly felt in
the second chapter of Genesis how this muteness, named
by man, itself became bliss, only of lower degree. Friedrich Müller has Adam say to the animals that leave him after
he has named them, 'And saw by the nobility with which
they leaped away from me that the man had given them a
name.' After the Fall, however, when God's word curses
the ground, the appearance of nature is deeply changed.
Now begins its other muteness, which we mean by the deep
sadness of nature. It is a metaphysical truth that all nature
would begin to lament if it were endowed with language.
(Though to 'endow with language' is more than to 'make
able to speak'.) This proposition has a double meaning. It
means, first: she would lament language itself. Speechlessness: that is the great sorrow of nature (and for the sake of
her redemption the life and language of *man*—not only, as
is supposed, of the poet—are in nature). This proposition
means, secondly: she would lament. Lament, however, is
the most undifferentiated, impotent expression of language;
it contains scarcely more than the sensuous breath; and
even where there is only a rustling of plants, in it there is
always a lament. Because she is mute, nature mourns. Yet
the inversion of this proposition leads even further into the
essence of nature; the sadness of nature makes her mute. In

all mourning there is the deepest inclination to speechlessness, which is infinitely more than inability or disinclination
to communicate. That which mourns feels itself thoroughly
known by the unknowable. To be named—even when the
namer is Godlike and blissful—perhaps always remains an
intimation of mourning. But how much more melancholy
to be named not from the one blessed, paradisiac language
of names, but from the hundred languages of man, in which
name has already withered, yet which, according to God's
pronouncement, have knowledge of things. Things have
no proper names except in God. For in his creative word,
God called them into being, calling them by their proper
names. In the language of men, however, they are over-
named. There is, in the relation of human languages to that
of things, something that can be approximately described as
'over-naming': over-naming as the deepest linguistic reason
for all melancholy and (from the point of view of the thing)
of all deliberate muteness. Overnaming as the linguistic
being of melancholy points to another curious relation of
language: the overprecision that obtains in the tragic relationship between the languages of human speakers.

There is a language of sculpture, of painting, of poetry.
Just as the language of poetry is partly, if not solely, founded
on the name language of man, it is very conceivable that the
language of sculpture or painting is founded on certain kinds
of thing languages, that in them we find a translation of the
language of things into an infinitely higher language, which
may still be of the same sphere. We are concerned here with
nameless, nonacoustic languages, languages issuing from
matter; here we should recall the material community of
things in their communication.

Moreover, the communication of things is certainly communal in a way that grasps the world as such as an undivided whole.

For an understanding of artistic forms it is of value to attempt to grasp them all as languages and to seek their connection with natural languages. An example that is appropriate because it is derived from the acoustic sphere is the kinship between song and the language of birds. On the other hand, it is certain that the language of art can be understood only in the deepest relationship to the doctrine of signs. Without the latter any linguistic philosophy remains entirely fragmentary, because the relationship between language and sign (of which that between human language and writing offers only a very particular example) is original and fundamental.

This provides an opportunity to describe another antithesis that permeates the whole sphere of language and has important relations to the antithesis already mentioned between language in a narrower sense and signs, with which, of course, language by no means necessarily coincides. For language is in every case not only communication of the communicable but also, at the same time, a symbol of the noncommunicable. This symbolic side of language is connected to its relation to signs, but extends more widely, for example, in certain respects, to name and judgment. These have not only a communicating function, but most probably also a closely connected symbolic function, to which, at least explicitly, no reference has here been made.

These considerations therefore leave us a purified concept of language, even though it may still be an imperfect one. The language of an entity is the medium in which its mental being is communicated. The uninterrupted flow of this communication runs through the whole of nature from the lowest forms of existence to man and from man to God. Man communicates himself to God through name, which he gives to nature and (in proper names) to his own kind, and to nature he gives names according to the communication that he receives from her, for the whole of nature, too, is imbued with a nameless, unspoken language, the residue of the creative word of God, which is preserved in man as the cognizing name and above man as the judgment suspended over him. The language of nature is comparable to a secret password that each sentry passes to the next in his own language, but the meaning of the password is the sentry's language itself. All higher language is a translation of those lower, until in ultimate clarity the word of God unfolds, which is the unity of this movement made up of language.

1916

Fate and Character

Fate and character are commonly regarded as causally connected, character being the cause of fate. The idea underlying this is the following: if, on the one hand, the character of a person, the way in which he reacts, were known in all its details, and if, on the other, all the events in the areas entered by that character were known, both what would happen to him and what he would accomplish could be exactly predicted. That is, his fate would be known. Contemporary ideas do not permit immediate logical access to the idea of fate, and therefore modern men accept the idea of reading character from, for example, the physical features of a person, finding knowledge of character as such somehow generally present within themselves, whereas the notion of analogously reading a person's fate from the lines in his hand seems unacceptable. This appears as impossible as 'to predict the future'; for under this category the foretelling of fate is unceremoniously subsumed, while character appears as something existing in the present and the past and therefore as perceptible. It is, however, precisely the

contention of those who profess to predict men's fate from
no matter what signs, that for those able to perceive it (who
find an immediate knowledge of fate as such in themselves)
it is in some way present, or more cautiously stated, accessible. The supposition that some 'accessibility' of future fate
contradicts neither that concept itself nor the human powers
of perception predicting it is not, as can be shown, non-
sensical. Like character, fate, too, can be apprehended only
through signs, not in itself, for even if this or that character
trait, this or that link of fate, is directly in view, it is nevertheless a relationship that is meant by these concepts, never
accessible except through signs because it is situated above
the immediately visible level. The system of characterological signs is generally confined to the body, if we disregard
the characterological significance of those signs investigated
by the horoscope, whereas in the traditional view all the
phenomena of external life, in addition to bodily ones, can
become signs of fate. However, the connection between the
sign and the signified constitutes in both spheres an equally
hermetic and difficult problem, though different in other
respects, because despite all the superficial observation and
false hypostasizing of the signs, they do not in either system
signify character or fate on the basis of causal connections.
A nexus of meaning can never be founded causally, even
though in the present case the existence of the signs may
have been produced causally by fate and character. The
inquiry that follows is not concerned with what such a
system of signs for character and fate is like, but merely
with what it signifies.

It emerges that the traditional conception of the nature
and the relationship of character and fate not only remains

problematic insofar as it is incapable of making the possibility of a prediction of fate rationally comprehensible, but that it is false, because the distinction on which it rests is theoretically untenable. For it is impossible to form an uncontradictory concept of the exterior of an active human being the core of whom is taken to be character. No definition of the external world can disregard the limits set by the concept of the active man. Between the active man and the external world all is interaction, their spheres of action interpenetrate; no matter how different their conceptions may be, their concepts are inseparable. Not only is it impossible to determine in a single case what finally is to be considered a function of character and what a function of fate in a human life (this would make no difference here if the two only merged in experience); the external world that the active man encounters can also in principle be reduced, to any desired degree, to his inner world, and his inner world similarly to his outer world, indeed regarded in principle as one and the same thing. Considered in this way character and fate, far from being theoretically distinct, coincide. Such is the case when Nietzsche says, 'If a man has character, he has an experience that constantly recurs.' That means: if a man has character his fate is essentially constant. Admittedly, it also means: he has no fate—a conclusion drawn by the Stoics.

If a concept of fate is to be attained, therefore, it must be clearly distinguished from that of character, which in turn cannot be achieved until the latter has been more exactly defined. On the basis of this definition the two concepts will become wholly divergent; where there is character there will, with certainty, not be fate, and in the area of fate character will not be found. In addition care must be taken to assign both concepts to spheres in which they do not, as happens in common speech, usurp the rank of higher spheres and concepts. For character is usually placed in an ethical, fate in a religious context. We must banish them from both regions by revealing the error by which they were placed there. This error is caused, as regards the concept of fate, through association with that of guilt. Thus, to mention a typical case, fate-imposed misfortune is seen as the response of God or the gods to a religious offence. Doubts concerning this are aroused, however, by the absence of any corresponding relation of the concept of fate to the concept that necessarily accompanies that of guilt in the ethical sphere, namely that of innocence. In the Greek classical development of the idea of fate, the happiness granted to a man is by no means understood as confirmation of an innocent conduct of life, but as a temptation to the most grievous offence, *hubris*. There is, therefore, no relation of fate to innocence. And—this question strikes even deeper—has fate any reference to good fortune, to happiness? Is happiness, as misfortune doubtless is, an intrinsic category of fate? Happiness is, rather, what releases the fortunate man from the embroilment of the Fates and from the net of his own fate. Hölderlin does not for nothing call the blissful gods 'fateless'. Happiness and bliss are therefore no more part of the sphere of fate than is innocence. But an order the sole intrinsic concepts of which are misfortune and guilt, and within which there is no conceivable path of liberation (for insofar as something is fate, it is misfortune and guilt)—such an order cannot be religious, no matter how the misunderstood concept of guilt appears to suggest the contrary. Another sphere must therefore be sought in which misfortune and guilt alone carry weight, a balance on which bliss and innocence are found too light and float upward. This balance is the scale of law. The laws of fate—misfortune and guilt—are elevated by law to measures of the person; it would be false to assume that only guilt is present in a legal context; it is demonstrable that all legal guilt is nothing other than misfortune. Mistakenly, through confusing itself with the realm of justice, the order of law, which is only a residue of the demonic stage of human existence when legal statutes determined not only men's relationships but also their relation to the gods, has preserved itself long past the time of the victory over the demons. It was not in law but in tragedy that the head of genius lifted itself for the first time from the mist of guilt, for in tragedy demonic fate is breached. But not by having the endless pagan chain of guilt and atonement superseded by the purity of man who has expiated and is with the pure god. Rather, in tragedy pagan man becomes aware that he is better than his god, but the realization robs him of speech, remains unspoken. Without declaring itself, it seeks secretly to gather its forces. Guilt and atonement it does not measure justly in the balance, but mixes indiscriminately. There is no question of the 'moral world order' being restored; instead, the moral hero, still dumb, not yet of age—as such he is called a hero—wishes to raise himself by shaking that tormented world. The paradox of the birth of genius in moral speechlessness, moral infantility, is the sublimity of tragedy. It is probably the basis of all sublimity, in which genius, rather than God, appears. Fate shows itself, therefore, in the view of life, as condemned, as having, at bottom, first been condemned and then become guilty. Goethe summarizes both phrases in the words 'The poor man you let become guilty.' Law condemns, not to punishment but to guilt. Fate is the guilt context of the living. It corresponds to the natural condition of the living, that illusion not yet wholly dispelled from which man is so far removed that, under its rule, he was never wholly immersed in it, but only invisible in his best part. It is not therefore really man who has a fate; rather, the subject of fate is indeterminable. The judge can perceive fate wherever he pleases; with every judgment he must blindly dictate fate. It is never man but only the life in him that it strikes—the part involved in natural guilt and misfortune by virtue of illusion. In the manner of fate, this life can be coupled to cards as to planets, and the clairvoyant makes use of the simple technique of placing it in the context of guilt by means of the first calculable, definite things that come to hand (things unchastely pregnant with certainty). Thereby she discovers in signs something about a natural life in man that she seeks to substitute for the head of genius mentioned earlier; as, on his side, the man who visits her gives way to the guilty life within himself. The guilt context is temporal in a totally inauthentic way, very different in its kind and measure from the time of redemption, or of music, or of truth. On determining the particular nature of time in fate depends the complete elucidation of these matters. The fortune-teller who uses cards and the palmist teach us at least that time can at every moment be made simultaneous with another (not present). It is not an autonomous time, but is parasitically dependent on the time of a higher, less natural life. It has no present, for fateful moments exist only in bad novels, and past and future it knows only in curious variations.

There is therefore a concept of fate—and it is the genuine concept, the only one that embraces equally fate in tragedy and the intentions of the fortune-teller—that is completely independent of that of character, having its foundation in an entirely different sphere. The concept of character must be developed to a similar level. It is no accident that both orders are connected with interpretative practices and that in chiromancy character and fate coincide authentically. Both concern the natural man—or, better, the nature of man, the very being that makes its appearance in signs that either occur spontaneously or are experimentally produced. The foundation of the concept of character will therefore need likewise to be related to a natural sphere and to have no more to do with ethics or morality than fate has with religion. On the other hand, the concept of character will have to be divested of those features that constitute its erroneous connection to that of fate. This connection is effected by the idea of a network that can be tightened by knowledge at will into a dense fabric, for this is how character appears to superficial observation. Along with the broad underlying traits, the trained eye of the connoisseur of men is supposed to perceive finer and closer connections, until what looked like a net is tightened into cloth. In the threads of this weft a weak understanding believes it possesses the moral nature of the character concerned and can distinguish its good and bad qualities. But, as moral philosophy is obliged to demonstrate, only actions and never qualities can be of moral importance. Appearances are admittedly to the contrary. Not just 'thievish', 'extravagant', 'courageous' seem to imply moral valuations (even leaving aside the apparent moral coloration of the concepts), but above all words like 'self-sacrificing', 'malicious', 'vengeful', 'envious' seem to indicate character traits that cannot be abstracted from moral valuation. Nevertheless, such abstraction is in all cases not only possible but necessary in order to grasp the meaning of the concept. This abstraction must be such that valuation itself is fully preserved; only its moral accent is withdrawn, to give way to such conditional evaluations, in either a positive or a negative sense, as are expressed by the morally indifferent descriptions of qualities of the intellect (such as 'clever' or 'stupid').

The true sphere to which these pseudo-moral character descriptions are to be consigned is shown by comedy. At its centre, as the main protagonist in a comedy of character, stands often enough a person whom, if we were confronted by his actions in life instead of by his person on the stage, we would call a scoundrel. On the comic stage, however, his actions take on only the interest shed with the light of character, and the latter is, in classical examples, the subject not of moral condemnation but of high amusement. It is never in themselves, never morally, that the actions of the comic hero affect his public; his deeds are interesting only insofar as they reflect the light of character. Moreover, one notes that the great comic playwright—for example, Molière—does not seek to define his creations by the multiplicity of their character traits. On the contrary, psychological analysis is denied any access to his work. It has nothing to do with the concerns of psychology if miserliness or hypochondria, in *L'avare* or *Le malade imaginaire*, are hypostasized as the foundation of all action. About hypochondria and miserliness these dramas teach nothing; far from making them comprehensible, they depict them with an intensifying crassness; if the object of psychology is the inner life of man understood empirically, Molière's characters are of no use to it even as means of demonstration. Character is unfolded in them like a sun, in the brilliance of its single trait, which allows no other to remain visible in its proximity. The sublimity of character comedy rests on this anonymity of man and his morality, alongside the utmost development of individuality through its exclusive character trait. While fate unfolds the immense complexity of the guilty person, the complications and bonds of his guilt, character gives this mystical enslavement of the person to the guilt context the answer of genius. Complication becomes simplicity, fate freedom. For the character of the comic figure is not the scarecrow of the determinist; it is the beacon in whose beams the freedom of his actions becomes visible. To the dogma of the natural guilt of human life, of original guilt, the irredeemable nature of which constitutes the doctrine, and its occasional redemption the cult, of paganism, genius opposes a vision of the natural innocence of man. This vision remains for its part likewise in the realm of nature, yet moral insights are still at a proximity to its essence that is attained by the opposed idea only in the form of tragedy, which is not its only form. The vision of character, on the other hand, is liberating in all its forms: it is linked to freedom, as cannot be shown here, by way of its affinity to logic. The character trait is not therefore the knot in the net. It is the sun of individuality in the colourless (anonymous) sky of man, which casts the shadow of the comic action. (This places Cohen's profound dictum that every tragic action, however sublimely it strides upon its cothurnus, casts a comic shadow, in its most appropriate context.)

Physiognomic signs, like other mantic symbols, serve for the ancients primarily the exploration of fate, in accordance with the dominance of the pagan belief in guilt. The study of physiognomy, like comedy, was a manifestation of the new age of genius. Modern physiognomics reveals its connection with the old art of divination in the unfruitful, morally evaluative accent of its concepts, as also in the striving for analytical complexity. In precisely this respect the ancient and medieval physiognomists saw things more clearly, in recognizing that character can only be grasped through a small number of morally indifferent basic concepts, like those, for example, that the doctrine of temperaments tried to identify.

1919

Critique of Violence

The task of a critique of violence can be summarized as that of expounding its relation to law and justice. For a cause, however effective, becomes violent, in the precise sense of the word, only when it bears on moral issues. The sphere of these issues is defined by the concepts of law and justice. With regard to the first of these, it is clear that the most elementary relationship within any legal system is that of ends to means, and, further, that violence can first be sought only in the realm of means, not of ends. These observations provide a critique of violence with more—and certainly different—premises than perhaps appears. For if violence is a means, a criterion for criticizing it might seem immediately available. It imposes itself in the question whether violence, in a given case, is a means to a just or an unjust end. A critique of it would then be implied in a system of just ends. This, however, is not so. For what such a system, assuming it to be secure against all doubt, would contain is not a criterion for violence itself as a principle, but, rather, the criterion for cases of its use. The question would remain open whether violence, as a principle, could be a moral means even to just ends. To resolve this question a more exact criterion is needed, which would discriminate within the sphere of means themselves, without regard for the ends they serve.

The exclusion of this more precise critical approach is perhaps the predominant feature of a main current of legal philosophy: natural law. It perceives in the use of violent means to just ends no greater problem than a man sees in his 'right' to move his body in the direction of a desired goal. According to this view (for which the terrorism in the French Revolution provided an ideological foundation), violence is a product of nature, as it were a raw material, the use of which is in no way problematical, unless force is misused for unjust ends. If, according to the theory of state of natural law, people give up all their violence for the sake of the state, this is done on the assumption (which Spinoza, for example, states explicitly in his *Tractatus Theologico-Politicus*) that the individual, before the conclusion of this rational contract, has *de jure* the right to use at will the violence that is *de facto* at his disposal. Perhaps these views have been recently rekindled by Darwin's biology, which, in a thoroughly dogmatic manner, regards violence as the only original means, besides natural selection, appropriate to all the vital ends of nature. Popular Darwinistic philosophy has often shown how short a step it is from this dogma of natural history to the still cruder one of legal philosophy, which holds that the violence that is, almost alone, appropriate to natural ends is thereby also legal.

This thesis of natural law that regards violence as a natural datum is diametrically opposed to that of positive law, which sees violence as a product of history. If natural law can judge all existing law only in criticizing its ends, so positive law can judge all evolving law only in criticizing its means. If justice is the criterion of ends, legality is that of means. Notwithstanding this antithesis, however, both schools meet in their common basic dogma: just ends can be attained by justified means, justified means used for just ends. Natural law attempts, by the justness of the ends, to 'justify' the means, positive law to 'guarantee' the justness of the ends through the justification of the means. This antinomy would prove insoluble if the common dogmatic assumption were false, if justified means on the one hand and just ends on the other were in irreconcilable conflict. No insight into this problem could be gained, however, until the circular argument had been broken, and mutually independent criteria both of just ends and of justified means were established.

The realm of ends, and therefore also the question of a criterion of justness, is excluded for the time being from this study. Instead, the central place is given to the question of the justification of certain means that constitute violence. Principles of natural law cannot decide this question, but can only lead to bottomless casuistry. For if positive law is blind to the absoluteness of ends, natural law is equally so to the contingency of means. On the other hand, the positive theory of law is acceptable as a hypothetical basis at the outset of this study, because it undertakes a fundamental distinction between kinds of violence independently of cases of their application. This distinction is between historically acknowledged, so-called sanctioned violence, and unsanctioned violence. If the following considerations proceed from this it cannot, of course, mean that given forms of violence are classified in terms of whether they are sanctioned or not. For in a critique of violence, a criterion for the latter in positive law cannot concern its uses but only its evaluation. The question that concerns us is, what light is thrown on the nature of violence by the fact that such a criterion or distinction can be applied to it at all, or, in other words, what is the meaning of this distinction? That this distinction supplied by positive law is meaningful, based on the nature of violence, and irreplaceable by any other, will soon enough be shown, but at the same time light will be shed on the sphere in which alone such a distinction can be made. To sum up: if the criterion established by positive law to assess the legality of violence can be analysed with regard to its meaning, then the sphere of its application must be criticized with regard to its value. For this critique a standpoint outside positive legal philosophy but also outside natural law must be found. The extent to which it can only be furnished by a historico-philosophical view of law will emerge.

The meaning of the distinction between legitimate and illegitimate violence is not immediately obvious. The misunderstanding in natural law by which a distinction is drawn between violence used for just and unjust ends must be emphatically rejected. Rather, it has already been indicated that positive law demands of all violence a proof of its historical origin, which under certain conditions is declared legal, sanctioned. Since the acknowledgement of legal violence is most tangibly evident in a deliberate submission to its ends, a hypothetical distinction between kinds of violence must be based on the presence or absence of a general historical acknowledgement of its ends. Ends that lack such acknowledgement may be called natural ends, the other legal ends. The differing function of violence, depending on whether it serves natural or legal ends, can be most clearly traced against a background of specific legal conditions. For the sake of simplicity, the following discussion will relate to contemporary European conditions.

Characteristic of these, as far as the individual as legal subject is concerned, is the tendency not to admit the natural ends of such individuals in all those cases in which such ends could, in a given situation, be usefully pursued by violence. This means: this legal system tries to erect, in all areas where individual ends could be usefully pursued by violence, legal ends that can only be realized by legal power. Indeed, it strives to limit by legal ends even those areas in which natural ends are admitted in principle within wide boundaries, like that of education, as soon as these natural ends are pursued with an excessive measure of violence, as in the laws relating to the limits of educational authority to punish. It can be formulated as a general maxim of present-day European legislation that all the natural ends of individuals must collide with legal ends if pursued with a greater or lesser degree of violence. (The contradiction between this and the right of self-defence will be resolved in what follows.) From this maxim it follows that law sees violence in the hands of individuals as a danger undermining the legal system. As a danger nullifying legal ends and the legal executive? Certainly not; for then violence as such would not be condemned, but only that directed to illegal ends. It will be argued that a system of legal ends cannot be maintained if natural ends are anywhere still pursued violently. In the first place, however, this is a mere dogma. To counter it one might perhaps consider the surprising possibility that the law's interest in a monopoly of violence *vis-à-vis* individuals is not explained by the intention of preserving legal ends but, rather, by that of preserving the law itself; that violence, when not in the hands of the law, threatens it not by the ends that it may pursue but by its mere existence outside the law. The same may be more drastically suggested if one reflects how often the figure of the 'great' criminal, however repellent his ends may have been, has aroused the secret admiration of the public. This cannot result from his deed, but only from the violence to which it bears witness. In this case, therefore, the violence of which present-day law is seeking in all areas of activity to deprive the individual appears really threatening, and arouses even in defeat the sympathy of the mass against law. By what function violence can with reason seem so threatening to law, and be so feared by it, must be especially evident where its application, even in the present legal system, is still permissible.

This is above all the case in the class struggle, in the form of the workers' guaranteed right to strike. Organized labour is, apart from the state, probably today the only legal subject entitled to exercise violence. Against this view there is certainly the objection that an omission of actions, a non-action, which a strike really is, cannot be described as violence. Such a consideration doubtless made it easier for a state power to conceive the right to strike, once this was no longer avoidable. But its truth is not unconditional, and therefore not unrestricted. It is true that the omission of an action, or service, where it amounts simply to a 'severing of relations', can be an entirely non-violent, pure means. And as in the view of the state, or the law, the right to strike conceded to labour is certainly not a right to exercise violence but, rather, to escape from a violence indirectly exercised by the employer, strikes conforming to this may undoubtedly occur from time to time and involve only a 'withdrawal' or 'estrangement' from the employer. The moment of violence, however, is necessarily introduced, in the form of extortion, into such an omission, if it takes place in the context of a conscious readiness to resume the suspended action under certain circumstances that either have nothing whatever to do with this action or only super-ficially modify it. Understood in this way, the right to strike constitutes in the view of labour, which is opposed to that of the state, the right to use force in attaining certain ends. The antithesis between the two conceptions emerges in all its bitterness in face of a revolutionary general strike. In this, labour will always appeal to its right to strike, and the state will call this appeal an abuse, since the right to strike was not 'so intended', and take emergency measures. For the state retains the right to declare that a simultaneous use of strike in all industries is illegal, since the specific reasons for strike admitted by legislation cannot be prevalent in every workshop. In this difference of interpretation is expressed the objective contradiction in the legal situation, whereby the state acknowledges a violence whose ends, as natural ends, it sometimes regards with indifference, but in a crisis (the revolutionary general strike) confronts inimically. For, however paradoxical this may appear at first sight, even conduct involving the exercise of a right can nevertheless, under certain circumstances, be described as violent. More specifically, such conduct, when active, may be called violent if it exercises a right in order to overthrow the legal system that has conferred it; when passive, it is nevertheless to be so described if it constitutes extortion in the sense explained above. It therefore reveals an objective contradiction in the legal situation, but not a logical contradiction in the law, if under certain circumstances the law meets the strikers, as perpetrators of violence, with violence. For in a strike the state fears above all else that function which it is the object of this study to identify as the only secure foundation of its critique. For if violence were, as first appears, merely the means to secure directly whatever happens to be sought, it could fulfil its end as predatory violence. It would be entirely unsuitable as a basis for, or a modification to, relatively stable conditions. The strike shows, however, that it can be so, that it is able to found and modify legal conditions, however offended the sense of justice may find itself thereby. It will be objected that such a function of violence is fortuitous and isolated. This can be rebutted by a consideration of military violence.

The possibility of military law rests on exactly the same objective contradiction in the legal situation as does that of strike law, that is to say, on the fact that legal subjects sanction violence whose ends remain for the sanctioners natural ends, and can therefore in a crisis come into conflict with their own legal or natural ends. Admittedly, military violence is in the first place used quite directly, as predatory violence, toward its ends. Yet it is very striking that even—or, rather, precisely—in primitive conditions that know hardly the beginnings of constitutional relations, and even in cases where the victor has established himself in invulnerable possession, a peace ceremony is entirely necessary. Indeed, the word 'peace', in the sense in which it is the correlative to the word 'war' (for there is also a quite different meaning, similarly unmetaphorical and political, the one used by Kant in talking of 'Eternal Peace'), denotes this a priori, necessary sanctioning, regardless of all other legal conditions, of every victory. This sanction consists precisely in recognizing the new conditions as a new 'law', quite regardless of whether they need *de facto* any guarantee of their continuation. If, therefore, conclusions can be drawn from military violence, as being primordial and paradigmatic of all violence used for natural ends, there is inherent in all such violence a law-making character. We shall return later to the implications of this insight. It explains the above-mentioned tendency of modern law to divest the individual, at least as a legal subject, of all violence, even that directed only to natural ends. In the great criminal this violence confronts the law with the threat of declaring a new law, a threat that even today, despite its impotence, in important instances horrifies the public as it did in primeval times. The state, however, fears this violence simply for its law-making character, being obliged to acknowledge it as law-making whenever external powers force it to concede them the right to conduct warfare, and classes the right to strike.

If in the last war the critique of military violence was the starting point for a passionate critique of violence in general—which taught at least one thing, that violence is no longer exercised and tolerated naïvely—nevertheless, violence was not only subject to criticism for its law-making character, but was also judged, perhaps more annihilatingly, for another of its functions. For a duality in the function of violence is characteristic of militarism, which could only come into being through general conscription. Militarism is the compulsory, universal use of violence as a means to the ends of the state. This compulsory use of violence has recently been scrutinized as closely as, or still more closely than, the use of violence itself. In it violence shows itself in a function quite different from its simple application for natural ends. It consists in the use of violence as a means of legal ends. For the subordination of citizens to laws—in the present case, to the law of general conscription—is a legal end. If that first function of violence is called the law-making function, this second will be called the law-preserving function. Since conscription is a case of law-preserving violence that is not in principle distinguished from others, a really effective critique of it is far less easy than the declamations of pacifists and activists suggest. Rather, such a critique coincides with the critique of all legal violence—that is, with the critique of legal or executive force—and cannot be performed by any lesser programme. Nor, of course—unless one is prepared to proclaim a quite childish anarchism—is it achieved by refusing to acknowledge any constraint toward persons and declaring 'What pleases is permitted.' Such a maxim merely excludes reflection on the moral and historical spheres, and thereby on any meaning in action, and beyond this on any meaning in reality itself, which cannot be constituted if 'action' is removed from its sphere. More important is the fact that even the appeal, so frequently attempted, to the categorical imperative, with its doubtless incontestable minimum programme—act in such a way that at all times you use humanity both in your person and in the person of all others as an end, and never merely as a means-is in itself inadequate for such a critique.[1] For positive law, if conscious of its roots, will certainly claim to acknowledge and promote the interest of mankind˙ in the person of each individual. It sees this interest in the representation and preservation of an order imposed by fate. While this view, which claims to preserve law in its very basis, cannot escape criticism, nevertheless all attacks that are made merely in the name of a formless 'freedom' without being able to specify this higher order of freedom, remain impotent against it. And most impotent of all when, instead of attacking the legal system root and branch, they impugn particular laws or legal practices that the law, of course, takes under the protection of its power, which resides in the fact that there is only one fate and that what exists, and in particular what threatens, belongs inviolably to its order. For law-preserving violence is a threatening violence. And its threat is not intended as the deterrent that uninformed liberal theorists interpret it to be. A deterrent in the exact sense would require a certainty that contradicts the nature of a threat and is not attained by any law, since there is always hope of eluding its arm. This makes it all the more threatening, like fate, on which depends whether the criminal is apprehended. The deepest purpose of the uncertainty of the legal threat will emerge from the later consideration of the sphere of fate in which it originates. There is a useful pointer to it in the sphere of punishments. Among them, since the validity of positive law has been called into question, capital punishment has provoked more criticism than all others. However superficial the arguments may in most cases have been, their motives were and are rooted in principle. The opponent of these critics felt, perhaps without knowing why and probably involuntarily, that an attack on capital punishment assails, not legal measure, not laws, but law itself in its origin. For if violence, violence crowned by fate, is the origin of law, then it may be readily supposed that where the highest violence, that over life and death, occurs in the legal system, the origins of law jut manifestly and fearsomely into existence. In agreement with this is the fact that the death penalty in primitive legal systems is imposed even for such crimes as offences against property, to which it seems quite out of 'proportion'. Its purpose is not to punish the infringement of law but to establish new law. For in the exercise of violence over life and death more than in any other legal act, law reaffirms itself. But in this very violence something rotten in law is revealed, above all to a finer sensibility, because the latter knows itself to be infinitely remote from conditions in which fate might imperiously have shown itself in such a sentence. Reason must, however, attempt to approach such conditions all the more resolutely, if it is to bring to a conclusion its critique of both lawmaking and law-preserving violence.

In a far more unnatural combination than in the death penalty, in a kind of spectral mixture, these two forms of violence are present in another institution of the modern state, the police. True, this is violence for legal ends (in the right of disposition), but with the simultaneous authority to decide these ends itself within wide limits (in the right of decree). The ignominy of such an authority, which is felt by few simply because its ordinances suffice only seldom for the crudest acts, but are therefore allowed to rampage all the more blindly in the most vulnerable areas and against thinkers, from whom the state is not protected by law—this ignominy lies in the fact that in this authority the separation of lawmaking and law-preserving violence is suspended. If the first is required to prove its worth in victory, the second is subject to the restriction that it may not set itself new ends. Police violence is emancipated from both conditions. It is law-making, for its characteristic function is not the promulgation of laws but the assertion of legal claims for any decree, and law-preserving, because it is at the disposal of these ends. The assertion that the ends of police violence are always identical or even connected to those of general law is entirely untrue. Rather, the 'law' of the police really marks the point at which the state, whether from impotence or because of the immanent connections within any legal system, can no longer guarantee through the legal system the empirical ends that it desires at any price to attain. Therefore the police intervene 'for security reasons' in countless cases where no clear legal situation exists, when they are not merely, without the slightest relation to legal ends, accompanying the citizen as a brutal encumbrance through a life regulated by ordinances, or simply supervising him. Unlike law, which acknowledges in the 'decision' determined by place and time a metaphysical category that gives it a claim to critical evaluation, a consideration of the police institution encounters nothing essential at all. Its power is formless, like its nowhere tangible, all-pervasive, ghostly presence in the life of civilized states. And though the police may, in particulars, everywhere appear the same, it cannot finally be denied that their spirit is less devastating where they represent, in absolute monarchy, the power of a ruler in which legislative and executive supremacy are united, than in democracies where their existence, elevated by no such relation, bears witness to the greatest conceivable degeneration of violence.

All violence as a means is either law-making or law-preserving. If it lays claim to neither of these predicates, it forfeits all validity. It follows, however, that all violence as a means, even in the most favourable case, is implicated in the problematic nature of law itself And if the importance of these problems cannot be assessed with certainty at this stage of the investigation, law nevertheless appears, from what has been said, in so ambiguous a moral light that the question poses itself whether there are no other than violent means for regulating conflicting human interests. We are above all obligated to note that a totally non-violent resolution of conflicts can never lead to a legal contract. For the latter, however peacefully it may have been entered into by the parties, leads finally to possible violence. It confers on both parties the right to take recourse to violence in some form against the other, should he break the agreement. Not only that; like the outcome, the origin of every contract also points toward violence. It need not be directly present in it as law-making violence, but is represented in it insofar as the power that guarantees a legal contract is in turn of violent origin even if violence is not introduced into the contract itself. When the consciousness of the latent presence of violence in a legal institution disappears, the institution falls into decay. In our time, parliaments provide an example of this. They offer the familiar, woeful spectacle because they have not remained conscious of the revolutionary forces to which they owe their existence. Accordingly, in Germany in particular, the last manifestation of such forces bore no fruit for parliaments. They lack the sense that a law-making violence is represented by themselves; no wonder that they cannot achieve decrees worthy of this violence, but cultivate in compromise a supposedly non-violent manner of dealing with political affairs. This remains, however, a 'product situated within the mentality of violence, no matter how it may disdain all open violence, because the effort toward compromise is motivated not internally but from outside, by the opposing effort, because no compromise, however freely accepted, is conceivable without a compulsive character. "It would be better otherwise" is the underlying feeling in every compromise.'[2] Significantly, the decay of parliaments has perhaps alienated as many minds from the ideal of a non-violent resolution of political conflicts as were attracted to it by the war. The pacifists are confronted by the Bolsheviks and Syndicalists. These have effected an annihilating and on the whole apt critique of present-day parliaments. Nevertheless, however desirable and gratifying a flourishing parliament might be by comparison, a discussion of means of political agreement that are in principle non-violent cannot be concerned with parliamentarianism. For what parliament achieves in vital affairs can only be those legal decrees that in their origin and outcome are attended by violence.

Is any non-violent resolution of conflict possible? Without doubt. The relationships of private persons are full of examples of this. Non-violent agreement is possible wherever a civilized outlook allows the use of unalloyed means of agreement. Legal and illegal means of every kind that are all the same violent may be confronted with non-violent ones as unalloyed means. Courtesy, sympathy, peaceableness, trust, and whatever else might here be mentioned, are their subjective preconditions. Their objective manifestation, however, is determined by the law (the enormous scope of which cannot be discussed here) that unalloyed means are never those of direct, but always those of indirect solutions. They therefore never apply directly to the resolution of conflict between man and man, but only to matters concerning objects. The sphere of non-violent means opens up in the realm of human conflicts relating to goods. For this reason technique in the broadest sense of the word is their most particular area. Its profoundest example is perhaps the conference, considered as a technique of civil agreement. For in it not only is nonviolent agreement possible, but also the exclusion of violence in principle is quite explicitly demonstrable by one significant factor: there is no sanction for lying. Probably no legislation on earth originally stipulated such a sanction. This makes clear that there is a sphere of human agreement that is nonviolent to the extent that it is wholly inaccessible to violence: the proper sphere of 'understanding', language. Only late and in a peculiar process of decay has it been penetrated by legal violence in the penalty placed on fraud. For whereas the legal system at its origin, trusting to its victorious power, is content to defeat lawbreaking wherever it happens to show itself; and deception, having itself no trace of power about it, was, on the principle *ius civile vigilantibus scriptum est*, exempt from punishment in Roman and ancient Germanic law, the law of a later period, lacking confidence in its own violence, no longer felt itself a match for that of all others. Rather, fear of the latter and mistrust of itself indicate its declining vitality. It begins to set itself ends, with the intention of sparing law-preserving violence more taxing manifestations. It turns to fraud, therefore, not out of moral considerations, but for fear of the violence that it might unleash in the defrauded party. Since such fear conflicts with the violent nature of law derived from its origins, such ends are inappropriate to the justified means of law. They reflect not only the decay of its own sphere, but also a diminution of pure means. For, in prohibiting fraud, law restricts the use of wholly nonviolent means because they could produce reactive violence. This tendency of law has also played a part in the concession of the right to strike, which contradicts the interests of the state. It grants this right because it forestalls violent actions the state is afraid to oppose. Did not workers previously resort at once to sabotage and set fire to factories? To induce men to reconcile their interests peacefully without involving the legal system, there is, in the end, apart from all virtues, one effective motive that often puts into the most reluctant hands pure instead of violent means; it is the fear of mutual disadvantages that threaten to arise from violent confrontation, whatever the outcome might be. Such motives are clearly visible in countless cases of conflict of interests between private persons. It is different when classes and nations are in conflict, since the higher orders that threaten to overwhelm equally victor and vanquished are hidden from the feelings of most, and from the intelligence of almost all. Space does not here permit me to trace such higher orders and the common interests corresponding to them, which constitute the most enduring motive for a policy of pure means.[3] We can therefore only point to pure means in politics as analogous to those which govern peaceful intercourse between private persons.

As regards class struggles, in them strike must under certain conditions be seen as a pure means. Two essentially different kinds of strike, the possibilities of which have already been considered, must now be more fully characterized. Sorel has the credit—from political, rather than purely theoretical, considerations—of having first distinguished them. He contrasts them as the political and the proletarian general strike. They are also antithetical in their relation to violence. Of the partisans of the former he says: 'The strengthening of state power is the basis of their conceptions; in their present organizations the politicians (viz. the moderate socialists) are already preparing the ground for a strong centralized and disciplined power that will be impervious to criticism from the opposition, capable of imposing silence, and of issuing its mendacious decrees.'⁴ 'The political general strike demonstrates how the state will lose none of its strength, how power is transferred from the privileged to the privileged, how the mass of producers will change their masters.' In contrast to this political general strike (which incidentally seems to have been summed up by the abortive German revolution), the proletarian general strike sets itself the sole task of destroying state power. It 'nullifies all the ideological consequences of every possible social policy; its partisans see even the most popular reforms as bourgeois.' 'This general strike clearly announces its indifference toward material gain through conquest by declaring its intention to abolish the state; the state was really ... the basis of the existence of the ruling group, who in all their enterprising benefit from the burdens borne by the public.' While the first form of interruption of work is violent since it causes only an external modification of labour conditions, the second, as a pure means, is non-violent. For it takes place not in readiness to resume work following external concessions and this or that modification to working conditions, but in the determination to resume only a wholly transformed work, no longer enforced by the state, an upheaval that this kind of strike not so much causes as consummates. For this reason, the first of these under-takings is lawmaking but the second anarchistic. Taking up occasional statements by Marx, Sorel rejects every kind of programme, of utopia—in a word, of law-making—for the revolutionary movement: 'With the general strike all these fine things disappear; the revolution appears as a clear, simple revolt, and no place is reserved either for the sociologists or for the elegant amateurs of social reforms or for the intellectuals who have made it their profession to think for the proletariat.' Against this deep, moral, and genuinely revolutionary conception, no objection can stand that seeks, on grounds of its possibly catastrophic conse-quences, to brand such a general strike as violent. Even if it can rightly be said that the modern economy, seen as a whole, resembles much less a machine that stands idle when abandoned by its stoker than a beast that goes berserk as soon as its tamer turns his back, nevertheless the violence of an action can be assessed no more from its effects than from its ends, but only from the law of its means. State power, of course, which has eyes only for effects, opposes precisely this kind of strike for its alleged violence, as distinct from partial strikes which are for the most part actually extortion-ate. The extent to which such a rigorous conception of the general strike as such is capable of diminishing the incidence of actual violence in revolutions, Sorel has explained with highly ingenious arguments. By contrast, an outstanding example of violent omission, more immoral and cruder than the political general strike, akin to a blockade, is the strike by doctors, such as several German cities have seen.

In this is revealed at its most repellent an unscrupulous use of violence that is positively depraved in a professional class that for years, without the slightest attempts at resistance, 'secured death its prey', and then at the first opportunity abandoned life of its own free will. More clearly than in recent class struggles, the means of non-violent agreement have developed in thousands of years of the history of states. Only occasionally does the task of diplomats in their transactions consist of modifications to legal systems. Fundamentally they have, entirely on the analogy of agreement between private persons, to resolve conflicts case by case, in the names of their states, peacefully and without contracts. A delicate task that is more robustly performed by referees, but a method of solution that in principle is above that of the referee because it is beyond all legal systems, and therefore beyond violence. Accordingly, like the intercourse of private persons, that of diplomats has engendered its own forms and virtues, which were not always mere formalities, even though they have become so.

Among all the forms of violence permitted by both natural law and positive law there is not one that is free of the gravely problematic nature, already indicated, of all legal violence. Since, however, every conceivable solution to human problems, not to speak of deliverance from the confines of all the world-historical conditions of existence obtaining hitherto, remains impossible if violence is totally excluded in principle, the question necessarily arises as to other kinds of violence than all those envisaged by legal theory. It is at the same time the question of the truth of the basic dogma common to both theories: just ends can be attained by justified means, justified means used for just ends. How would it be, therefore, if all the violence imposed by fate, using justified means, were of itself in irreconcilable conflict with just ends, and if at the same time a different kind of violence came into view that certainly could be either the justified or the unjustified means to those ends, but was not related to them as means at all but in some different way? This would throw light on the curious and at first discouraging discovery of the ultimate insolubility of all legal problems (which in its hopelessness is perhaps comparable only to the possibility of conclusive pronouncements on 'right' and 'wrong' in evolving languages). For it is never reason that decides on the justification of means and the justness of ends, but fate-imposed violence on the former and God on the latter. An insight that is uncommon only because of the stubborn prevailing habit of conceiving those just ends as ends of a possible law, that is, not only as generally valid (which follows analytically from the nature of justice), but also as capable of generalization, which, as could be shown, contradicts the nature of justice. For ends that for one situation are just, universally acceptable, and valid, are so for no other situation, no matter how similar it may be in other respects. The non-mediate function of violence at issue here is illustrated by everyday experience. As regards man, he is impelled by anger, for example, to the most visible outbursts of a violence that is not related as a means to a preconceived end. It is not a means but a manifestation. Moreover, this violence has thoroughly objective manifestations in which it can be subjected to criticism. These are to be found, most significantly, above all in myth.

Mythical violence in its archetypal form is a mere manifestation of the gods. Not a means to their ends, scarcely a manifestation of their will, but first of all a manifestation of their existence. The legend of Niobe contains an outstanding example of this. True, it might appear that the action of Apollo and Artemis is only a punishment. But their violence establishes a law far more than it punishes for the infringement of one already existing. Niobe's arrogance calls down fate upon itself not because her arrogance offends against the law but because it challenges fate—to a fight in which fate must triumph, and can bring to light a law only in its triumph. How little such divine violence was to the ancients the law-preserving violence of punishment is shown by the heroic legends in which the hero—for example, Prometheus—challenges fate with dignified courage, fights it with varying fortunes, and is not left by the legend without hope of one day bringing a new law to men. It is really this hero and the legal violence of the myth native to him that the public tries to picture even now in admiring the miscreant. Violence therefore bursts upon Niobe from the uncertain, ambiguous sphere of fate. It is not actually destructive. Although it brings a cruel death to Niobe's children, it stops short of the life of their mother, whom it leaves behind, more guilty than before through the death of the children, both as an eternally mute bearer of guilt and as a boundary stone on the frontier between men and gods. If this immediate violence in mythical manifestations proves closely related, indeed identical to lawmaking violence, it reflects a problematic light on law-making violence, insofar as the latter was characterized above, in the account of military violence, as merely a mediate violence. At the same time this connection promises further to illuminate fate, which in all cases underlies legal violence, and to conclude in broad outline the critique of the latter. For the function of violence in law-making is twofold, in the sense that law-making pursues as its end, with violence as the means, *what* is to be established as law, but at the moment of instatement does not dismiss violence; rather, at this very moment of law-making, it specifically establishes as law not an end unalloyed by violence, but one necessarily and intimately bound to it, under the title of power. Law-making is power-making, and, to that extent, an immediate manifestation of violence. Justice is the principle of all divine end-making, power the principle of all mythical law-making.

An application of the latter that has immense consequences is to be found in constitutional law. For in this sphere the establishing of frontiers, the task of 'peace' after all the wars of the mythical age, is the primal phenomenon of all law-making violence. Here we see most clearly that power, more than the most extravagant gain in property, is what is guaranteed by all law-making violence. Where frontiers are decided the adversary is not simply annihilated; indeed, he is accorded rights even when the victor's superiority in power is complete. And these are, in a demonically ambiguous way, 'equal' rights: for both parties to the treaty it is the same line that may not be crossed. Here appears, in a terribly primitive form, the same mythical ambiguity of laws that may not be 'infringed' to which Anatole France refers satirically when he says, 'Poor and rich are equally forbidden to spend the night under the bridges.' It also appears that Sorel touches not merely on a cultural-historical but also on a metaphysical truth in surmising that in the beginning all right was the prerogative of the kings or the nobles—in short, of the mighty; and that, *mutatis mutandis*, it will remain so as long as it exists. For from the point of view of violence, which alone can guarantee law, there is no equality, but at the most equally great violence. The act of fixing frontiers, however, is also significant for an understanding of law in another respect. Laws and unmarked frontiers remain, at least in primeval times, unwritten laws. A man can unwittingly infringe upon them and thus incur retribution. For each intervention of law that is provoked by an offence against the unwritten and unknown law is called, in contradistinction to punishment, retribution. But however unluckily it may befall its unsuspecting victim, its occurrence is, in the understanding of the law, not chance, but fate showing itself once again in its deliberate ambiguity. Hermann Cohen, in a brief reflection on the ancients' conception of fate, has spoken of the 'inescapable realization' that it is 'fate's orders themselves that seem to cause and bring about this infringement, this offence'.[5] To this spirit of law even the modern principle that ignorance of a law is not protection against punishment testifies, just as the struggle over written law in the early period of the ancient Greek communities is to be understood as a rebellion against the spirit of mythical statutes.

Far from inaugurating a purer sphere, the mythical manifestation of immediate violence shows itself fundamentally identical with all legal violence, and turns suspicion concerning the latter into certainty of the perniciousness of its historical function, the destruction of which thus becomes obligatory. This very task of destruction poses again, in the last resort, the question of a pure immediate violence that might be able to call a halt to mythical violence. Just as in all spheres God opposes myth, mythical violence is confronted by the divine. And the latter constitutes its antithesis in all respects. If mythical violence is law-making, divine violence is law-destroying; if the former sets boundaries, the latter boundlessly destroys them; if mythical violence brings at once guilt and retribution, divine power only expiates; if the former threatens, the latter strikes; if the former is bloody, the latter is lethal without spilling blood. The legend of Niobe may be confronted, as an example of this violence, with God's judgment on the company of Korah. It strikes privileged Levites, strikes them without warning, without threat, and does not stop short of annihilation. But in annihilating it also expiates, and a deep connection between the lack of bloodshed and the expiatory character of this violence is unmistakable. For blood is the symbol of mere life. The dissolution of legal violence stems, as cannot be shown in detail here, from the guilt of more natural life, which consigns the living, innocent and unhappy, to a retribution that 'expiates' the guilt of mere life—and doubtless also purifies the guilty, not of guilt, however, but of law. For with mere life the rule of law over the living ceases. Mythical violence is bloody power over mere life for its own sake, divine violence pure power over all life for the sake of the living. The first demands sacrifice, the second accepts it.

This divine power is attested not only by religious tradition but is also found in present-day life in at least one sanctioned manifestation. The educative power, which in its perfected form stands outside the law, is one of its manifestations. These are defined, therefore, not by miracles directly performed by God, but by the expiating moment in them that strikes without bloodshed and, finally, by the absence of all law-making. To this extent it is justifiable to call this violence, too, annihilating; but it is so only relatively, with regard to goods, right, life, and suchlike, never absolutely, with regard to the soul of the living. The premise of such an extension of pure or divine power is sure to provoke, particularly today, the most violent reactions, and to be countered by the argument that taken to its logical conclusion it confers on men even lethal power against one another. This, however, cannot be conceded. For the question 'May I kill?' meets its irreducible answer in the commandment 'Thou shalt not kill.' This commandment precedes the deed, just as God was 'preventing' the deed. But just as it may not be fear of punishment that enforces obedience, the injunction becomes inapplicable, incommensurable once the deed is accomplished. No judgment of the deed can be derived from the commandment. And so neither the divine judgment, nor the grounds for this judgment, can be known in advance. Those who base a condemnation of all violent killing of one person by another on the commandment are therefore mistaken. It exists not as a criterion of judgment, but as a guideline for the actions of persons or communities who have to wrestle with it in solitude and, in exceptional cases, to take on themselves the responsibility of ignoring it. Thus it was understood by Judaism, which expressly rejected the condemnation of killing in self-defence. But those thinkers who take the opposed view refer to a more distant theorem, on which they possibly propose to base even the commandment itself. This is the doctrine of the sanctity of life, which they either apply to all animal or even vegetable life, or limit to human life. Their argumentation, exemplified in an extreme case by the revolutionary killing of the oppressor, runs as follows: 'If I do not kill I shall never establish the world dominion of

justice ... that is the argument of the intelligent terrorist. ...
We, however, profess that higher even than the happiness
and justice of existence stands existence itself.'[6] As certainly
as this last proposition is false, indeed ignoble, it shows the
necessity of seeking the reason for the commandment no
longer in what the deed does to the victim, but in what it
does to God and the doer. The proposition that existence
stands higher than a just existence is false and ignominious,
if existence is to mean nothing other than mere life—and it
has this meaning in the argument referred to. It contains a
mighty truth, however, if existence, or, better, life (words
whose ambiguity is readily dispelled, analogously to that of
freedom, when they are referred to two distinct spheres),
means the irreducible, total condition that is 'man'; if the
proposition is intended to mean that the nonexistence of
man is something more terrible than the (admittedly subordinate) not yet-attained condition of the just man. To this
ambiguity the proposition quoted above owes its plausibility. Man cannot, at any price, be said to coincide with the
mere life in him, no more than with any other of his conditions and qualities, not even with the uniqueness of his
bodily person. However sacred man is (or that life in him
that is identically present in earthly life, death, and after-
life), there is no sacredness in his condition, in his bodily
life vulnerable to injury by his fellow men. What, then, distinguishes it essentially from the life of animals and plants?
And even if these were sacred, they could not be so by virtue
only of being alive, of being in life. It might be well worth
while to track down the origin of the dogma of the sacredness of life. Perhaps, indeed probably, it is relatively recent,
the last mistaken attempt of the weakened Western tradition

to seek the saint it has lost in cosmological impenetrability. (The antiquity of all religious commandments against murder is no counter-argument, because these are based on other ideas than the modern theorem.) Finally, this idea of man's sacredness gives grounds for reflection that what is here pronounced sacred was according to ancient mythical thought the marked bearer of guilt: life itself.

The critique of violence is the philosophy of its history—the 'philosophy' of this history, because only the idea of its development makes possible a critical, discriminating, and decisive approach to its temporal data. A gaze directed only at what is close at hand can at most perceive a dialectical rising and falling in the law-making and law-preserving formations of violence. The law governing their oscillation rests on the circumstance that all law-preserving violence, in its duration, indirectly weakens the lawmaking violence represented by it, through the suppression of hostile counter-violence. (Various symptoms of this have been referred to in the course of this study.) This lasts until either new forces or those earlier suppressed triumph over the hitherto law-making violence and thus found a new law, destined in its turn to decay. On the breaking of this cycle maintained by mythical forms of law, on the suspension of law with all the forces on which it depends as they depend on it, finally therefore on the abolition of state power, a new historical epoch is founded. If the rule of myth is broken occasionally in the present age, the coming age is not so unimaginably remote that an attack on law is altogether futile. But if the existence of violence outside the law, as pure immediate violence, is assured, this furnishes the proof that revolutionary violence, the highest manifestation of unalloyed violence by man, is possible, and by what means. Less possible and also less urgent for humankind, however, is to decide when unalloyed violence has been realized in particular cases. For only mythical violence, not divine, will be recognizable as such with certainty, unless it be in incomparable effects, because the expiatory power of violence is not visible to men. Once again all the eternal forms are open to pure divine violence, which myth bastardized with law. It may manifest itself in a true war exactly as in the divine judgment of the multitude on a criminal. But all mythical, law-making violence, which we may call executive, is pernicious. Pernicious, too, is the law-preserving, administrative violence that serves it. Divine violence, which is the sign and seal but never the means of sacred execution, may be called sovereign violence.

1921

Theologico-Political Fragment

Only the Messiah himself consummates all history, in the sense that he alone redeems, completes, creates its relation to the Messianic. For this reason nothing historical can relate itself on its own account to anything Messianic. Therefore the Kingdom of God is not the *telos* of the historical dynamic; it cannot be set as a goal. From the standpoint of history it is not the goal, but the end. Therefore the order of the profane cannot be built up on the idea of the Divine Kingdom, and therefore theocracy has no political, but only a religious meaning. To have repudiated with utmost vehemence the political significance of theocracy is the cardinal merit of Bloch's *Spirit of Utopia*.

The order of the profane should be erected on the idea of happiness. The relation of this order to the Messianic is one of the essential teachings of the philosophy of history. It is the precondition of a mystical conception of history, containing a problem that can be represented figuratively. If one arrow points to the goal toward which the profane dynamic acts, and another marks the direction of Messianic intensity, then certainly the quest of free humanity for happiness runs counter to the Messianic direction; but just as a force can, through acting, increase another that is acting in the opposite direction, so the order of the profane assists, through being profane, the coming of the Messianic Kingdom. The profane, therefore, although not itself a category of this Kingdom, is a decisive category of its quietest approach. For in happiness all that is earthly seeks its downfall, and only in good fortune is its downfall destined to find it. Whereas, admittedly, the immediate Messianic intensity of the heart, of the inner man in isolation, passes through misfortune, as suffering. To the spiritual *restitutio in integrum*, which introduces immortality, corresponds a worldly restitution that leads to the eternity of downfall, and the rhythm of this eternally transient worldly existence, transient in its totality, in its spatial but also in its temporal totality, the rhythm of Messianic nature, is happiness. For nature is Messianic by reason of its eternal and total passing away.

To strive after such passing, even for those stages of man that are nature, is the task of world politics, whose method must be called nihilism.

1920–21

The Destructive Character

It could happen to someone looking back over his life that he realized that almost all the deeper obligations he had endured in its course originated in people on whose 'destructive character' everyone was agreed. He would stumble on this fact one day, perhaps by chance, and the heavier the blow it dealt him, the better his chances of picturing the destructive character.

The destructive character knows only one watchword: make room; only one activity: clearing away. His need for fresh air and open space is stronger than any hatred.

The destructive character is young and cheerful. For destroying rejuvenates in clearing away the traces of our own age; it cheers because everything cleared away means to the destroyer a complete reduction, indeed eradication, of his own condition. But what contributes most of all to this Apollonian image of the destroyer is the realization of how immensely the world is simplified when tested for its worthiness of destruction. This is the great bond embracing and unifying all that exists. It is a sight that affords the destructive character a spectacle of deepest harmony.

The destructive character is always blithely at work. It is nature that dictates his tempo, indirectly at least, for he must forestall her. Otherwise she will take over the destruction herself.

No vision inspires the destructive character. He has few needs, and the least of them is to know what will replace what has been destroyed. First of all, for a moment at least, empty space, the place where the thing stood or the victim lived. Someone is sure to be found who needs this space without its being filled.

The destructive character does his work, the only work he avoids is being creative. Just as the creator seeks solitude, the destroyer must be constantly surrounded by people, witnesses to his efficacy.

The destructive character is a signal. Just as a trigonometric sign is exposed on all sides to the wind, so is he to rumour. To protect him from it is pointless.

The destructive character has no interest in being understood. Attempts in this direction he regards as superficial. Being misunderstood cannot harm him. On the contrary he provokes it, just as oracles, those destructive institutions of the state, provoked it. The most petty bourgeois of all phenomena, gossip, comes about only because people do not wish to be misunderstood. The destructive character tolerates misunderstanding; he does not promote gossip.

The destructive character is the enemy of the etui-man. The etui-man looks for comfort, and the case is its quintessence. The inside of the case is the velvet-lined track that he has imprinted on the world. The destructive character obliterates even the traces of destruction.

The destructive character stands in the front line of the traditionalists. Some pass things down to posterity, by making them untouchable and thus conserving them, others pass on situations, by making them practicable and thus liquidating them. The latter are called the destructive.

The destructive character has the consciousness of historical man, whose deepest emotion is an insuperable mistrust of the course of things and a readiness at all times to recognize that everything can go wrong. Therefore the destructive character is reliability itself.

The destructive character sees nothing permanent. But for this very reason he sees ways everywhere. Where others encounter walls or mountains, there, too, he sees a way. But because he sees a way everywhere, he has to clear things from it everywhere. Not always by brute force; sometimes by the most refined. Because he sees ways everywhere, he always positions himself at crossroads. No moment can know what the next will bring. What exists he reduces to rubble, not for the sake of the rubble, but for that of the way leading through it.

The destructive character lives from the feeling, not that life is worth living, but that suicide is not worth the trouble.

1931

On the Mimetic Faculty

Nature creates similarities. One need only think of mimicry. The highest capacity for producing similarities, however, is man's. His gift of seeing resemblances is nothing other than a rudiment of the powerful compulsion in former times to become and behave like something else. Perhaps there is none of his higher functions in which his mimetic faculty does not play a decisive role.

This faculty has a history, however, in both the phylogenetic and the ontogenetic sense. As regards the latter, play is for many its school. Children's play is everywhere permeated by mimetic modes of behaviour, and its realm is by no means limited to what one person can imitate in another. The child plays at being not only a shopkeeper or teacher but also a windmill and a train. Of what use to him is this schooling of his mimetic faculty?

The answer presupposes an understanding of the phylogenetic significance of the mimetic faculty. Here it is not enough to think of what we understand today by the concept of similarity. As is known, the sphere of life that formerly seemed to be governed by the law of similarity was comprehensive; it ruled both microcosm and macrocosm. But

these natural correspondences are given their true importance only if seen as stimulating and awakening the mimetic
faculty in man. It must be borne in mind that neither mimetic
powers nor mimetic objects remain the same in the course
of thousands of years. Rather, we must suppose that the gift
of producing similarities—for example, in dances, whose
oldest function this was—and therefore also the gift of recognizing them, have changed with historical development.

The direction of this change seems definable as the increasing decay of the mimetic faculty. For clearly the observable
world of modern man contains only minimal residues of the
magical correspondences and analogies that were familiar to
ancient peoples. The question is whether we are concerned
with the decay of this faculty or with its transformation. Of
the direction in which the latter might lie some indications
may be derived, even if indirectly, from astrology.

We must assume in principle that in the remote past the processes considered imitable included those in the sky. In dance,
on other cultic occasions, such imitation could be produced,
such similarity manipulated. But if the mimetic genius was
really a life-determining force for the ancients, it is not difficult
to imagine that the newborn child was thought to be in full possession of this gift, and in particular to be perfectly moulded on
the structure of cosmic being.

Allusion to the astrological sphere may supply a first reference point for an understanding of the concept of non-sensuous
similarity. True, our existence no longer includes what once
made it possible to speak of this kind of similarity: above all,
the ability to produce it. Nevertheless we, too, possess a canon
according to which the meaning of non-sensuous similarity can
be at least partly clarified. And this canon is language.

From time immemorial the mimetic faculty has been

conceded some influence on language. Yet this was done without foundation: without consideration of a further meaning, still less a history, of the mimetic faculty. But above all such notions remained closely tied to the commonplace, sensuous area of similarity. All the same, imitative behaviour in language formation was acknowledged under the name of onomatopoeia. Now if language, as is evident, is not an agreed system of signs, we shall be constantly obliged to have recourse to the kind of thoughts that appear in their most primitive form as the onomatopoeic mode of explanation. The question is whether this can be developed and adapted to improved understanding.

'Every word—and the whole of language', it has been asserted, 'is onomatopoeic.' It is difficult to conceive in any detail the programme that might be implied by this proposition. However, the concept of non-sensuous similarity is of some relevance. For if words meaning the same thing in different languages are arranged about that thing as their centre, we have to inquire how they all—while often possessing not the slightest similarity to one another—are similar to what they signify at their centre. Yet this kind of similarity may be explained not only by the relationships between words meaning the same thing in different languages, just as, in general, our reflections cannot be restricted to the spoken word. They are equally concerned with the written word. And here it is noteworthy that the latter—in some cases perhaps more vividly than the spoken word—illuminates, by the relation of its written form to what it signifies, the nature of non-sensuous similarity. In brief, it is non-sensuous similarity that establishes the ties not only between the spoken and the signified but also between the written and the signified, and equally between the spoken and the written.

Graphology has taught us to recognize in handwriting images that the unconscious of the writer conceals in it. It may be supposed that the mimetic process that expresses itself in this way in the activity of the writer was, in the very distant times in which script originated, of utmost importance for writing. Script has thus become, like language, an archive of non-sensuous similarities, of non-sensuous correspondences.

This aspect of language as script, however, does not develop in isolation from its other, semiotic aspect. Rather, the mimetic element in language can, like a flame, manifest itself only through a kind of bearer. This bearer is the semiotic element. Thus the coherence of words or sentences is the bearer through which, like a flash, similarity appears. For its production by man—like its perception by him—is in many cases, and particularly the most important, limited to flashes. It flits past. It is not improbable that the rapidity of writing and reading heightens the fusion of the semiotic and the mimetic in the sphere of language.

'To read what was never written.' Such reading is the most ancient: reading before all languages, from the entrails, the stars, or dances. Later the mediating link of a new kind of reading, of runes and hieroglyphs, came into use. It seems fair to suppose that these were the stages by which the mimetic gift, which was once the foundation of occult practices, gained admittance to writing and language. In this way language may be seen as the highest level of mimetic behaviour and the most complete archive of non-sensuous similarity: a medium into which the earlier powers of mimetic production and comprehension have passed without residue, to the point where they have liquidated those of magic.

1933

III

Naples

Walter Benjamin and Asja Lacis

Some years ago a priest was drawn on a cart through the streets of Naples for indecent offences. He was followed by a crowd hurling maledictions. At a corner a wedding procession appeared. The priest stands up and makes the sign of a blessing, and the cart's pursuers fall on their knees. So absolutely, in this city, does Catholicism strive to reassert itself in every situation. Should it disappear from the face of the earth, its last foothold would perhaps not be Rome, but Naples.

Nowhere can this people live out its rich barbarism, which has its source in the heart of the city itself, more securely than in the lap of the Church. It needs Catholicism, for even its excesses are then legalized by a legend, the feast day of a martyr. Here Alfonso de Liguori was born, the saint who made the practice of the Catholic Church supple enough to accommodate the trade of the swindler and the whore, in order to control it with more or less rigorous penances in the confessional, for which he wrote a three-volume compendium. Confession alone, not the police, is a match for the self-administration of the criminal world, the *camorra*.

So it does not occur to an injured party to call the police if he is anxious to seek redress. Through civic or clerical mediators, if not personally, he approaches a *camorrista*. Through him he agrees on a ransom. From Naples to Castellamare, the length of the proletarian suburbs, run the headquarters of the mainland *camorra*. For these criminals avoid quarters in which they would be at the disposal of the police. They are dispersed over the city and the suburbs. That makes them dangerous. The travelling citizen who gropes his way as far as Rome from one work of art to the next, as along a stockade, loses his nerve in Naples.

No more grotesque demonstration of this could be provided than in the convocation of an international congress of philosophers. It disintegrated without trace in the fiery haze of this city, while the seventh-centennial celebration of the university, part of whose tinny halo it was intended to be, unfolded amid the uproar of a popular festival. Complaining guests, who had been instantly relieved of their money and identification papers, appeared at the secretariat. But the banal tourist fares no better. Even Baedeker cannot propitiate him. Here the churches cannot be found, the starred sculpture always stands in the locked wing of the museum, and the word 'mannerism' warns against the work of the native painters.

Nothing is enjoyable except the famous drinking water. Poverty and misery seem as contagious as they are pictured to be to children, and the foolish fear of being cheated is only a scanty rationalization for this feeling. If it is true, as Péladan said, that the nineteenth century inverted the medieval, the natural order of the vital needs of the poor, making shelter and clothing obligatory at the expense of food, such conventions have here been abolished. A beggar lies in the road propped against the sidewalk, waving his empty hat like a leave-taker at a station. Here poverty leads downward, as two thousand years ago it led down to the crypt: even today the way to the catacombs passes through a 'garden of agony'; in it, even today, the disinherited are the leaders. At the hospital San Gennaro dei Poveri the entrance is through a white complex of buildings that one passes via two courtyards. On either side of the road stand the benches for the invalids, who follow those going out with glances that do not reveal whether they are clinging to their garments to be liberated or to satisfy unimaginable desires. In the second courtyard the doorways of the chambers have gratings; behind them cripples put their deformities on show, and the shock given to day-dreaming passers-by is their joy.

One of the old men leads and holds the lantern close to a fragment of early Christian fresco. Now he utters the centuries-old magic word 'Pompeii'. Everything that the foreigner desires, admires, and pays for is 'Pompeii'. 'Pompeii' makes the plaster imitation of the temple ruins, the lava necklace, and the louse-ridden person of the guide irresistible. This fetish is all the more miraculous as only a small minority of those whom it sustains have ever seen it. It is understandable that the miracle-working Madonna enthroned there is receiving a brand-new, expensive church for pilgrims. In this building and not in that of the Vettii, Pompeii lives for the Neapolitans. And to it, again and again, swindling and wretchedness finally come home.

Fantastic reports by travellers have touched up the city. In reality it is grey: a grey-red or ochre, a grey-white. And entirely grey against sky and sea. It is this, not least, that disheartens the tourist. For anyone who is blind to forms sees little here. The city is craggy. Seen from a height not reached by the cries from below, from the Castell San Martino, it lies deserted in the dusk, grown into the rock. Only a strip of shore runs level; behind it buildings rise in tiers. Tenement blocks of six or seven stories, with staircases climbing their foundations, appear against the villas as skyscrapers. At the base of the cliff itself, where it touches the shore, caves have been hewn. As in the hermit pictures of the *Trecento*, a door is seen here and there in the rock. If it is open one can see into large cellars, which are at the same time sleeping places and storehouses. Farther on steps lead down to the sea, to fishermen's taverns installed in natural grottoes. Dim light and thin music come up from them in the evening.

As porous as this stone is the architecture. Building and action interpenetrate in the courtyards, arcades, and stairways. In everything they preserve the scope to become a theatre of new, unforeseen constellations. The stamp of the definitive is avoided. No situation appears intended forever, no figure asserts its 'thus and not otherwise'. This is how architecture, the most binding part of the communal rhythm, comes into being here: civilized, private, and ordered only in the great hotel and warehouse buildings on the quays; anarchical, embroiled, village-like in the centre, into which large networks of streets were hacked only forty years ago. And only in these streets is the house, in the Nordic sense, the cell of the city's architecture. In contrast, within the tenement blocks, it seems held together at the corners, as if by iron clamps, by the murals of the Madonna.

No one orients himself by house numbers. Shops, wells, and churches are the reference points—and not always simple ones. For the typical Neapolitan church does not ostentatiously occupy a vast square, visible from afar, with transepts, gallery, and dome. It is hidden, built in; high domes are often to be seen only from a few places, and even then it is not easy to find one's way to them, impossible to distinguish the mass of the church from that of the neighbouring secular buildings. The stranger passes it by. The inconspicuous door, often only a curtain, is the secret gate for the initiate. A single step takes him from the humble of dirty courtyards into the pure solitude of a tall, whitewashed church interior. His private existence is the baroque opening of a heightened public sphere. For here his private self is not taken up by the four walls, among wife and children, but by devotion or by despair. Side alleys give glimpses of dirty stairs leading down to taverns, where three or four men, at intervals, hidden behind barrels as if behind church pillars, sit drinking.

In such corners one can scarcely discern where building is still in progress and where dilapidation has already set in. For nothing is included. Porosity results not only from the indolence of the Southern artisan, but also, above all, from the passion for improvisation, which demands that space and opportunity be at any price preserved. Buildings are used as a popular stage. They are all divided into innumerable, simultaneously animated theatres. Balcony, courtyard, window, gateway, staircase, roof are at the same time stage and boxes. Even the most wretched pauper is sovereign in the dim, dual awareness of participating, in all his destitution, in one of the pictures of Neapolitan street life that will never return, and of enjoying in all his poverty the leisure to follow the great panorama. What is enacted on the staircases is a high school of stage management. The stairs, never entirely exposed, but still less enclosed in the gloomy box of the Nordic house, erupt fragmentarily from the buildings, make an angular turn, and disappear, only to burst out again.

In their materials, too, the street decorations are closely related to those of the theatre. Paper plays the main part. Red, blue, and yellow fly-catchers, altars of coloured glossy paper on the walls, paper rosettes on the raw chunks of meat. Then the virtuosity of the variety show. Someone kneels on the asphalt, a little box beside him, and it is one of the busiest streets. With coloured chalk he draws the figure of Christ on the stone, below it perhaps the head of the Madonna. Meanwhile a circle has formed around him, the artist gets up, and while he waits beside his work for fifteen minutes or half an hour, sparse, counted-out coins fall from the onlookers onto the limbs, head, and trunk of his portrait. Until he gathers them up, everyone disperses, and in a few moments the picture is erased by feet.

Not the least example of such virtuosity is the art of eating macaroni with the hands. This is demonstrated to foreigners for remuneration. Other things are paid for according to tariffs. Vendors give a fixed price for the cigarette butts that, after a café closes, are culled from the chinks in the floor. (Earlier they were sought by candlelight.) Alongside the leavings from restaurants, boiled cat skulls, and fish shells, they are sold at stalls in the harbour district. Music parades about: not mournful music for the courtyards, but brilliant sounds for the street. The broad cart, a kind of xylophone, is colourfully hung with song texts. Here they can be bought. One of the musicians turns the organ while the other, beside it, appears with his plate before anyone who stops dreamily to listen. So everything joyful is mobile: music, toys, ice cream circulate through the streets.

This music is both a residue of the last and a prelude to the next feast day. Irresistibly the festival penetrates each and every working day. Porosity is the inexhaustible law of the life of this city, reappearing everywhere. A grain of Sunday is hidden in each weekday, and how much weekday in this Sunday!

Nevertheless no city can fade, in the few hours of Sunday rest, more rapidly than Naples. It is crammed full of festal motifs nestling in the most inconspicuous places. When the blinds are taken down before a window, it is similar to flags being raised elsewhere. Brightly dressed boys fish in deep-blue streams and look up at rouged church steeples. High above the streets, wash-lines run, with garments suspended on them like rows of pennants. Faint suns shine from glass vats of iced drinks. Day and night the pavilions glow with the pale, aromatic juices that teach even the tongue what porosity can be.

If politics or the calendar offers the slightest pretext, however, this secret, scattered world condenses into a noisy feast. And regularly it is crowned with a fireworks display over the sea. From July to September, an unbroken band of fire runs, in the evenings, along the coast between Naples and Salerno. Now over Sorrento, now over Minori or Praiano, but always over Naples, stand fiery balls. Here fire is substance and shadow. It is subject to fashion and artifice.

Each parish has to outdo the festival of its neighbour with new lighting effects.

In these festivals the oldest element of their Chinese origin, weather magic in the form of the rockets that spread like kites, proves far superior to terrestrial splendours: the earthbound suns and the crucifix surrounded by the glow of Saint Elmo's fire. At the beach the stone pines of the Giardino Pubblico form a cloister. Riding under them on a festival night, you see a rain of fire in every treetop. But here, too, nothing is dreamy. Only explosions win an apotheosis popular favour. At Piedigrotta, the Neapolitans' main holiday, this childish joy in tumult puts on a wild face. During the night of September 7, bands of men, up to a hundred strong, roam through every street. They blow on gigantic paper comets, the orifice disguised with grotesque masks. Violently if necessary, one is encircled, and from countless pipes the hollow sound clamours in the ears. Whole trades are based on the spectacle. Newspaper boys drag out the names of their wares, *Roma* and the *Corriere di Napoli*, as though they were sticks of gum. Their trumpeting is part of urban manufacture.

Trade, deeply rooted in Naples, borders on a game of chance and adheres closely to the holiday. The well-known list of the seven deadly sins located pride in Genoa, avarice in Florence (the old Germans were of a different opinion and called what is known as Greek love *Florenzen*), voluptuousness in Venice, anger in Bologna, greed in Milan, envy in Rome, and indolence in Naples. Lotto, alluring and consuming as nowhere else in Italy, remains the archetype of business life. Every Saturday at four o'clock, crowds form in front of the house where the numbers are drawn. Naples is one of the few cities with its own draw. With the pawn-shop and lotto the state holds the proletariat in a vice: what it advances to them in one it takes back in the other. The more discreet and liberal intoxication of Hazard, in which the whole family takes part, replaces that of alcohol.

And business life is assimilated to it. A man stands in an unharnessed carriage on a street corner. People crowd around him. The lid of the coachman's box is open, and from it the vendor takes something, singing its praises all the while. It disappears before one has caught sight of it into a piece of pink or green paper. When it is thus wrapped, he holds it aloft, and in a trice it is sold for a few *soldi*. With the same mysterious gesture he disposes of one article after another. Are there lots in this paper? Cakes with a coin in every tenth one? What makes the people so covetous and the man as inscrutable as Mograby? He is selling toothpaste.

A priceless example of such business manners is the auction. When, at eight in the morning, the street vendor has begun unpacking his goods—umbrellas, shirt material, shawls—presenting each item singly to his public, mis-trustfully, as if he had first to test it himself; when, growing heated, he asks fantastic prices, and, while serenely folding up the large cloth that he has spread out for five hundred lire, drops the price at every fold, and finally, when it lies diminished on his arm, is ready to part with it for fifty, he has been true to the most ancient fairground practices. There are delightful stories of the Neapolitan's playful love of trade. In a busy piazza a fat lady drops her fan. She looks around help-lessly; she is too unshapely to pick it up herself. A cavalier appears and is prepared to perform his service for fifty lire. They negotiate, and the lady receives her fan for ten.

Blissful confusion in the storehouses! For here they are still one with the vendor's stalls: they are bazaars. The long gangway is favoured. In a glass-roofed one there is a toyshop (in which perfume and liqueur glasses are also on sale) that would hold its own beside fairy-tale galleries. Like a gallery, too, is the main street of Naples, the Toledo. Its traffic is among the busiest on earth. On either side of this narrow alley all that has come together in the harbour city lies insolently, crudely, seductively displayed. Only in fairy tales are lanes so long that one must pass through without looking to left or right if one is not to fall prey to the devil. There is a department store, in other cities the rich, magnetic centre of purchasing. Here it is devoid of charm, outdone by the tightly packed multiplicity. But with a tiny offshoot—rubber balls, soap, chocolates—it re-emerges somewhere else among the small traders stalls.

Similarly dispersed, porous, and commingled is private life. What distinguishes Naples from other large cities is something it has in common with the African kraal; each private attitude or act is permeated by streams of communal life. To exist, for the Northern European the most private of affairs, is here, as in the kraal, a collective matter.

So the house is far less the refuge into which people retreat than the inexhaustible reservoir from which they flood out. Life bursts not only from doors, not only into front yards, where people on chairs do their work (for they have the faculty of making their bodies tables). Housekeeping utensils hang from balconies like potted plants. From the windows of the top floors come baskets on ropes for mail, fruit, and cabbage.

Just as the living room reappears on the street, with chairs, hearth, and altar, so, only much more loudly, the street migrates into the living room. Even the poorest one is as full of wax candles, biscuit saints, sheaves of photos on the wall, and iron bedsteads, as the street is of carts, people, and lights. Poverty has brought about a stretching of frontiers that mirrors the most radiant freedom of thought. There is no hour, often no place, for sleeping and eating.

The poorer the quarter, the more numerous the eating houses. From stoves in the open street, those who can do so fetch what they need. The same foods taste different at each stall; things are not done randomly but by proven recipes. In the way that, in the window of the smallest trattoria, fish and meat lie heaped up for inspection, there is a nuance that goes beyond the requirements of the connoisseur. In the fish market this seafaring people has created a marine sanctuary as grandiose as those of the Netherlands. Starfish, crayfish, cuttlefish from the gulf waters, which teem with creatures, cover the benches and are often devoured raw with a little lemon. Even the banal beasts of dry land become fantastic. In the fourth or fifth stories of these tenement blocks cows are kept. The animals never walk on the street, and their hoofs have become so long that they can no longer stand.

How could anyone sleep in such rooms? To be sure, there are beds, as many as the room will hold. But even if there are six or seven, there are often more than twice as many occupants. For this reason one sees children late at night—at twelve, even at two—still in the streets. At midday they then lie sleeping behind a shop counter or on a stairway. This sleep, which men and women also snatch in shady corners, is therefore not the protected Northern sleep. Here, too, there is interpenetration of day and night, noise and peace, outer light and inner darkness, street and home.

This extends even into toys. With the pale, watery colours of the Munich *Kindl*, the Madonna stands on the walls of the houses. The child that she holds away from her like a sceptre is to be found, just as stiff, wrapped and without arms or legs, as a wooden doll in the poorest shops of Santa Lucia. With these toys the urchins can hit whatever they like. A sceptre and a magic wand even in *their* fists; the Byzantine saviour still asserts himself today. Bare wood at the back; only the front is painted. A blue garment, white spots, red hem, and red cheeks.

But the demon of profligacy has entered some of these dolls that lie beneath cheap notepaper, clothespins, and tin sheep. In the overpopulated quarters children are also quickly acquainted with sex. But if their increase becomes devastating, if the father of a family dies or the mother wastes away, close or distant relatives are not needed. A neighbour takes a child to her table for a shorter or longer period, and thus families interpenetrate in relationships that can resemble adoption. True laboratories of this great process of intermingling are the cafés. Life is unable to sit down and stagnate in them. They are sober, open rooms resembling the political People's Café, and the opposite of everything Viennese, of the confined bourgeois, literary world. Neapolitan cafés are bluntly to the point. A prolonged stay is scarcely possible. A cup of excessively hot *cafe espresso*—in hot drinks this city is as unrivalled as in sherbets, spumoni, and ice cream— ushers the visitor out. The tables have a coppery shine, they are small and round, and a companion who is less than stalwart turns hesitantly on his heel in the doorway. Only a few people sit down briefly here. Three quick movements of the hand, and they have placed their order.

The language of gestures goes further here than any-where else in Italy. The conversation is impenetrable to anyone from outside. Ears, nose, eyes, breast, and shoul-ders are signalling stations activated by the fingers. These configurations return in their fastidiously specialized eroticism. Helping gestures and impatient touches attract the stranger's attention through a regularity that excludes chance. Yes, here his cause would be hopelessly lost, but the Neapolitan benevolently sends him away, sends him a few kilometres farther on to Mori. '*Vedere Napoli e poi Mori,*' he says, repeating an old pun. 'See Naples and die,' says the foreigner after him.

1924

MOSCOW

1

More quickly than Moscow itself, one gets to know Berlin
through Moscow. For someone returning home from Russia
the city seems freshly washed. There is no dirt, but no
snow, either. The streets seem in reality as desolately clean
and swept as in the drawings of Grosz. And how true-to-
life his types are has become more obvious. What is true
of the image of the city and its people applies also to the
intellectual situation: a new perspective of this is the most
undoubted gain from a stay in Russia. However little one
may know Russia, what one learns is to observe and judge
Europe with the conscious knowledge of what is going on
in Russia. This is the first benefit to the intelligent European
in Russia. But, equally, this is why the stay is so exact a
touchstone for foreigners. It obliges everyone to choose his
standpoint. Admittedly, the only real guarantee of a correct
understanding is to have chosen your position before you
came. In Russia above all, you can only see if you have
already decided. At the turning point in historical events

that is indicated, if not constituted, by the fact of 'Soviet Russia', the question at issue is not which reality is better, or which has greater potential. It is only: which reality is inwardly convergent with truth? Which truth is inwardly preparing itself to converge with the real? Only he who clearly answers these questions is 'objective'. Not toward his contemporaries (which is unimportant) but toward events (which is decisive). Only he who, by decision, has made his dialectical peace with the world can grasp the concrete. But someone who wishes to decide 'on the basis of facts' will find no basis in the facts. Returning home, he will discover above all that Berlin is a deserted city. People and groups moving in its streets have solitude about them. Berlin's luxury seems unspeakable. And it begins on the asphalt, for the breadth of the pavements is princely. They make of the poorest wretch a *grand seigneur* promenading on the terrace of his mansion. Princely solitude, princely desolation hang over the streets of Berlin. Not only in the West End. In Moscow there are three or four places where it is possible to make headway without that strategy of shoving and weaving that one learns in the first week (at the same time, therefore, as the technique of achieving locomotion on sheet ice). Stepping onto the Stolechnikov one breathes again: here at last one may stop without compunction in front of shopwindows and go on one's way without partaking in the loitering, serpentine gait to which the narrow pavements have accustomed most people. But what fullness has this street that overflows not only with people, and how deserted and empty is Berlin! In Moscow goods burst everywhere from the houses, they hang on fences, lean against railings, lie on pavements. Every fifty steps

stand women with cigarettes, women with fruit, women
with sweets. They have their wares in a laundry basket next
to them, sometimes a little sleigh as well. A brightly coloured woollen cloth protects apples or oranges from the
cold, with two prize examples lying on top. Next to them
are sugar figures, nuts, candy. One thinks: before leaving
her house a grandmother must have looked around to see
what she could take to surprise her grandchildren. Now she
had stopped on the way to have a short rest in the street.
Berlin streets know no such places with sleighs, sacks, little
carts, and baskets. Compared to those of Moscow, they are
like a freshly swept, empty racecourse on which a field of
six-day cyclists hastens comfortlessly on.

2

The city seems to deliver itself at the outset, at the station.
Kiosks, arc lamps, buildings crystallize into figures that
are never to return. Yet this is dispelled as soon as I seek
words. I must be on my way.... At first there is nothing to
be seen but snow, the dirty snow that has already installed
itself and the clean snow moving up behind. The instant
one arrives, the childhood stage begins. On the thick sheet
ice of the streets walking has to be relearned. The jungle
of houses is so impenetrable that only brilliance strikes the
eye. A transparency with the inscription '*Kefir*' glows in the
evening. I notice it as if the Tverskaia, the old road to Tver
on which I now am, were really still the open road, with
nothing to be seen far and wide except the plain. Before I
discovered Moscow's real landscape, its real river, found its
real heights, each thoroughfare became for me a contested

river, each house number a trigonometric signal, and each of its gigantic squares a lake. For every step one takes here is on named ground. And where one of these names is heard, in a flash imagination builds a whole quarter about the sound. This will long defy the later reality and remain brittly embedded in it like glass masonry. In the first phase the city still has barriers at a hundred frontiers. Yet one day the gate, the church that were the boundary of a district become without warning its centre. Now the city turns into a labyrinth for the newcomer. Streets that he had located far apart are yoked together by a corner like a pair of horses in a coachman's fist. The whole exciting sequence of topographical dummies that deceives him could only be shown by a film: the city is on its guard against him, masks itself, flees, intrigues, lures him to wander its circles to the point of exhaustion. (This could be approached in a very practical way; during the tourist season in great cities, 'orientation films' would run for foreigners.) But in the end, maps and plans are victorious: in bed at night, imagination juggles with real buildings, parks, and streets.

3

Moscow in winter is a quiet city. The immense bustle on the streets takes place softly. This is because of the snow, but also because of the backwardness of the traffic. Car horns dominate the orchestra of cities. But in Moscow there are only a few cars. They are used only for weddings and funerals and for accelerated government. True, in the evening they switch on brighter lights than are permitted in any other great city. And the cones of light they project are so

dazzling that anyone caught in them stands helplessly rooted
to the spot. In the blinding light before the Kremlin gate the
guards stand in their brazen ochre furs. Above them shines
the red signal that regulates the traffic passing through the
gate. All the colours of Moscow converge prismatically
here, at the centre of Russian power. Beams of excessive
brilliance from the car headlights race through the darkness.
The horses of the cavalry, who have a large drill ground in
the Kremlin, shy in their light. Pedestrians force their way
between cars and unruly horses. Long rows of sleighs transport snow away. Single horsemen. Silent swarms of ravens
have settled in the snow. The eye is infinitely busier than
the ear. The colours do their utmost against the white. The
smallest coloured rag glows out of doors. Picture books lie
in the snow; Chinese sell artfully made paper fans, and still
more frequently, paper kites in the form of exotic deep-sea
fish. Day in, day out, children's festivals are provided for.
There are men with baskets full of wooden toys, carts and
spades; the carts are yellow and red, yellow or red the children's shovels. All these carved wooden utensils are more
simply and solidly made than in Germany, their peasant
origin being clearly visible. One morning, at the side of the
road stand tiny houses that have never been seen before,
each with shining windows and a fence around the front
garden: wooden toys from the Vladimir government. That
is to say, a new consignment of goods has arrived. Serious,
sober utensils become audacious in street trading. A basket
seller with all kinds of brightly coloured wares, such as
can be bought everywhere in Capri, two-handled baskets
with plain square patterns, carries at the end of his pole
glazed-paper cages with glazed-paper birds inside them.

But a real parrot, too, a white ara can sometimes be seen. In the Miasnitskaia stands a woman with linen goods, the bird perching on her tray or shoulder. A picturesque background for such animals must be sought elsewhere, at the photographer's stand. Under the bare trees of the boulevards are screens showing palms, marble staircases, and southern seas. And something else, too, reminds one of the South. It is the wild variety of the street trade. Shoe polish and writing materials, handkerchiefs, dolls' sleighs, swings for children, ladies' underwear, stuffed birds, clotheshangers—all this sprawls on the open street, as if it were not twenty-five degrees below zero but high Neapolitan summer. I was for a long time mystified by a man who had in front of him a densely lettered board. I wanted to see a soothsayer in him. At last I succeeded in watching him at work: I saw him sell two of his letters and fix them as initials to his customer's galoshes. Then the wide sleighs with three compartments for peanuts, hazelnuts, and *semitchky* (sunflower seeds, which now, according to a ruling of the Soviet, may no longer be chewed in public places). Cookshop owners gather in the neighbourhood of the labour exchange. They have hot cakes to sell, and sausage fried in slices. But all this goes on silently; calls like those of every trader in the South are unknown. Rather, the people address the passer-by with words, measured if not whispered words, in which there is something of the humility of beggars. Only one caste parades noisily through the streets here, the rag-and-bone men with sacks on their backs; their melancholy cry rings one or more times a week in every quarter. Street trading is in part illegal and therefore avoids attracting attention. Women, each with a piece of meat, a chicken, or a leg of pork resting on a layer of straw in her open hand, stand offering it to passers-by. These are vendors without permits. They are too poor to pay the duty for a stall and have no time to stand in line many hours at an office for a weekly concession. When a member of the militia approaches, they simply run away. The street trade culminates in the large markets, on the Smolenskaia and the Arbat. And on the Sucharevskaia. This, the most famous of all, is situated at the foot of a church that rises with blue domes above the booths. First one passes the quarter of the scrap-iron dealers. The people simply have their wares lying in the snow. One finds old locks, metre rulers, hand tools, kitchen utensils, electrical goods. Repairs are carried out on the spot; I saw someone soldering over a pointed flame. There are no seats anywhere, everyone stands up, gossiping or trading. At this market the architectonic function of wares is perceptible: cloth and fabric form buttresses and columns; shoes, *valenki*, hanging threaded on strings across the counters, become the roof of the booth; large *garmoshkas* (accordions) form sounding walls, therefore in a sense Memnos walls. Whether, at the few stalls with pictures of saints, one can still secretly buy those strange icons that it was already punishable under tsarism to sell, I do not know. There was the Mother of God with three hands. She is half naked. From her navel rises a strong, well-formed hand. At right and left the two others spread in the gesture of blessing. This threesome of hands is deemed a symbol of the Holy Trinity. There was another devotional picture of the Mother of God that shows her with open belly; clouds come from it instead of entrails; in their midst dances the Christ child holding a violin in his hand. Since the sale of icons is considered a branch of the paper and picture trade, these booths with pictures of saints stand next to those with paper goods, so that they are always flanked by portraits of Lenin, like a prisoner between two policemen. The street life does not cease entirely even at night. In dark gateways you stumble against furs built like houses. Night watchmen huddle inside on chairs, from time to time bestirring themselves ponderously.

4

In the street scene of any proletarian quarter the children are important. They are more numerous there than in other districts, and move more purposefully and busily. Moscow swarms with children everywhere. Even among them there is a Communist hierarchy. The 'Komsomoltsy', as the eldest, are at the top. They have their clubs in every town and are really trained as the next generation of the Party. The younger children become—at six-'Pioneers'. They, too, are united in clubs, and wear a red tie as a proud distinction. '*Oktiabr*' ('Octobrists'), lastly—or 'Wolves'—is the name given to little babies from the moment they are able to point to the picture of Lenin. But even now one also comes across the derelict, unspeakably melancholy *besprizornye*, war orphans. By day they are usually seen alone; each one on his own warpath. But in the evening they join up before the lurid façades of movie houses to form gangs, and foreigners are warned against meeting such bands alone when walking home. The only way for the educator to understand these thoroughly savage, mistrustful, embittered people was to go out on the street himself. In each of Moscow's districts, children's centres have been installed for years already. They are supervised by a female state employee who seldom has more than one assistant. Her task is, in one way or another, to make contact with the children of her district. Food is distributed, games are played. To begin with, twenty or thirty children come to the centre, but if a superintendent does her work properly, it may be filled with hundreds of children after two weeks. Needless to say, traditional pedagogical methods never made much impression on these infantile masses. To get through to them at all, to be heard, one has to relate as directly and clearly as possible to the catchwords of the street itself, of the whole collective life. Politics, in the organization of crowds of such children, is not tendentious, but as natural a subject, as obvious a visual aid, as the toy shop or doll-house for middle-class children. If one also bears in mind that a superintendent has to look after the children, to occupy and feed them, and in addition to keep a record of all expenses for milk, bread, and materials, that she is responsible for all this, it must become drastically clear how much room such work leaves for the private life of the person performing it. But amid all the images of childhood destitution that is still far from having been overcome, an attentive observer will perceive one thing: how the liberated pride of the proletariat is matched by the emancipated bearing of the children. Nothing is more pleasantly surprising on a visit to Moscow's museums than to see how, singly or in groups, sometimes around a guide, children and workers move easily through these rooms. Nothing is to be seen of the forlornness of the few proletarians who dare to show themselves to the other visitors in our museums. In Russia the proletariat has really begun to take possession of bourgeois culture, whereas on such occasions in our country they have the appearance of planning a burglary. Admittedly, there are collections in Moscow in which workers and children can quickly feel themselves at home. There is the Polytechnic Museum, with its many thousands of experiments, pieces of apparatus, documents, and models relating to the history of primary production and manufacturing industry. There is the admirably run toy museum, which under its director, Bartram, has brought together a precious, instructive collection of Russian toys, and serves the scholar as much as the children who walk about for hours in these rooms (about midday there is also a big, free puppet show, as fine as any in Luxembourg). There is the famous Tretiakov Gallery in which one understands for the first time what genre painting means and how especially appropriate it is to the Russians. Here the proletarian finds subjects from the history of his movement: *A Conspirator Surprised by the Police*, *The Return from Exile in Siberia*, *The Poor Governess Enters Service in a Rich Merchant's House*. And the fact that such scenes are still painted entirely in the spirit of bourgeois art not only does no harm—it actually brings them closer to this public. For education in art (as Proust explains very well from time to time) is not best promoted by the contemplation of 'masterpieces'. Rather, the child or the proletarian who is educating himself rightly acknowledges very different works as masterpieces from those selected by the collector. Such pictures have for him a very transitory but solid meaning, and a strict criterion is necessary only with regard to the topical works that relate to him, his work, and his class.

5

Begging is not aggressive as in the South, where the importunity of the ragamuffin still betrays some remnant of vitality. Here it is a corporation of the dying. The street corners of some quarters are covered with bundles of rags—beds in the vast open-air hospital called Moscow. Long, beseeching speeches are addressed to people. There is one beggar who always begins, at the approach of a promising-looking passer-by, to emit a soft, drawn-out howling; this is directed at foreigners who cannot speak Russian. Another has the exact posture of the pauper for whom Saint Martin, in old pictures, cuts his cloak in two with his sword: he kneels with both arms outstretched. Shortly before Christmas, two children sat day after day in the snow against the wall of the Museum of the Revolution, covered with a scrap of material, and whimpering. (But outside the English Club, the most genteel in Moscow, to which this building earlier belonged, even that would not have been possible.) One ought to know Moscow as such beggar children know it. They know of a corner beside the door of a certain shop where, at a particular time, they are allowed to warm themselves for ten minutes, they know where one day each week at a certain hour they can fetch themselves crusts, and where a sleeping place among stacked sewage pipes is free. They have developed begging to a high art with a hundred schematisms and variations. They watch the customers of a pastry-cook on a busy street corner, approach one, and accompany him, whining and pleading, until he has relinquished to them a piece of his hot pie. Others keep station at a streetcar terminus, board a vehicle, sing a song, and collect kopecks. And there are places, admittedly only a few, where even street trading has the appearance of begging. A few Mongols stand against the wall of Kitai Gorod. One stands no more than five paces from the next, selling leather briefcases, each with exactly the same article as his neighbour. There must be some agreement behind this, for they cannot seriously intend such hopeless competition. Probably in their homeland the winter is no less harsh and their ragged furs are no worse than those of the natives. Nevertheless they are the only people in Moscow whom one pities on account of the climate. Even priests who go begging for their churches are still to be seen. But one very seldom sees anyone give. Begging has lost its strongest foundation, the bad social conscience, which opens purses so much wider than does pity. Beyond this it appears as an expression of the unchanging wretchedness of these beggars; perhaps, too, it is only the result of judicious organization that, of all the institutions of Moscow, they alone are dependable, remaining unchanged in their place while everything around them shifts.

6

Each thought, each day, each life lies here as on a laboratory table. And as if it were a metal from which an unknown substance is by every means to be extracted, it must endure experimentation to the point of exhaustion. No organism, no organization, can escape this process. Employees in their factories, offices in buildings, pieces of furniture in the apartments are rearranged, transferred, and shoved about. New ceremonies for christening and marriage are presented in the clubs as at research institutes. Regulations are changed from day to day, but streetcar stops migrate, too, shops turn into restaurants and a few weeks later into offices. This astonishing experimentation—it is here called *remonte*—affects not only Moscow, it is Russian. In this ruling passion there is as much naïve desire for improvement as there is boundless curiosity and playfulness. Few things are shaping Russia more powerfully today. The country is mobilized day and night, most of all, of course, the Party. Indeed, what distinguished the Bolshevik, the Russian Communist, from his Western comrade is this unconditional readiness for mobilization. The material basis of his existence is so slender that he is prepared, year in, year out, to decamp. He would not otherwise be a match for this life. Where else is it conceivable that a distinguished military leader should one day be made director of a great state theatre? The present director of the Theatre of the Revolution is a former general. True: he was a man of letters before he became a victorious commander. Or in which other country can one hear stories like those told me by the commissionaire of my hotel? Until 1924 he was employed in in the Kremlin. Then one day he was afflicted by severe sciatica. The Party had him treated by their best doctors, sent him to the Crimea, had him take mud baths and try radiation treatment. When all proved in vain he was told, 'You need a job in which you can look after yourself, keep warm, and not move!' The next day he was a hotel porter. When he is cured he will go back to the Kremlin. Ultimately, even the health of comrades is a prized possession of the Party, which, against the person's wishes if necessary, takes such measures as are needed to conserve it. So it is presented, at any rate, in an excellent novella by Boris Pilniak. Against his will a high official undergoes an operation that has a fatal outcome. (A very famous name is mentioned here among the dead of the last few years.) There is no knowledge and no faculty that are not somehow appropriated by collective life and made to serve it. The specialist is a spearhead of this increasingly practical approach and the only citizen who, outside the political sphere, has any status. At times the respect for this type verges on fetishism. Thus the red Military Academy employed as a teacher a general who is notorious for his part in the civil war. He had every captured Bolshevik unceremoniously hanged. For Europeans such a point of view, which intransigently subordinates the prestige of ideology to practical demands, is barely comprehensible. But this incident is also characteristic of the opposing side. For it is not only the military of the tsarist empire who, as is known, placed themselves at the service of the Bolsheviks. Intellectuals, too, return in time as specialists to the posts they sabotaged during the civil war. Opposition, as we should like to imagine it in the West—intellectuals holding themselves aloof and languishing under the yoke—does not exist, or, better, no longer exists. It has—with whatever reservations-accepted the truce with the Bolsheviks, or it has been annihilated. There is in Russia-particularly outside the Party-only the most loyal opposition. For this new life weighs on no one more heavily than on the outsider observing from a distance. To endure this existence in idleness is impossible because, in each smallest detail, it becomes beautiful and comprehensible only through work. To the integration of personal thoughts with the pre-existing field of forces, with the mandate, however virtual, for organized, guaranteed contact with comrades—to this, life here is so tightly bound that anyone who abstains or cannot achieve it degenerates intellectually as if through years of solitary confinement.

7

Bolshevism has abolished private life. The bureaucracy, political activity, the press are so powerful that no time remains for interests that do not converge with them. Nor any space. Apartments that earlier accommodated single families in their five to eight rooms now often lodge eight. Through the hall door one step into a little town. More often still, an army camp. Even in the lobby one can encounter beds. Indoors one only camps, and usually the scanty inventory is only a residue of petty-bourgeois possessions that have a far more depressing effect because the room is so sparsely furnished. An essential feature of the petty-bourgeois interior, however, was completeness: pictures must cover the walls, cushions the sofa, covers the cushions, ornaments fill the mantelpiece, coloured glass the windows. (Such petty-bourgeois rooms are battlefields over which the attack of commodity capital has advanced victoriously; nothing human can flourish there again.) Of all that, only a part here or there has been indiscriminately preserved. Weekly the furniture in the bare rooms is rearranged—that is the only luxury indulged in with them, and at the same time a radical means of expelling 'cosiness', along with the melancholy with which it is paid for, from the house. People can bear to exist in it because they are estranged from it by their way of life. Their dwelling place is the office, the club, the street. Of the mobile army of officials only the baggage train is to be found here. Curtains and partitions, often only half the height of the walls, have had to multiply the number of rooms. For each citizen is entitled by law to only thirteen square metres of living space. For his accommodations he pays according to his income. The state—all house ownership is nationalized—charges the unemployed one ruble monthly for the same area for which the better-off pay sixty or more. Anyone who lays claim to more than this prescribed area must, if he cannot justify his claim professionally, make manifold amends. Every step away from the preordained path meets with an immeasurable bureaucratic apparatus and with impossible costs. The member of a trade union who produces a certificate of illness and goes through the prescribed channels can be admitted to the most modern sanatorium, sent to health resorts in the Crimea, can enjoy expensive radiation treatment, without paying a penny for it. The outsider can go begging and sink into penury if he is not in a position, as a member of the new bourgeoisie, to buy all this for thousands of rubles. Anything that cannot be based on the collective framework demands a disproportionate expenditure of effort. For this reason there is no 'homeliness'. But nor are there any cafés. Free trade and the free intellect have been abolished. The cafés are thereby deprived of their public. There remain, therefore, even for private affairs, only the office and the club. Here, however, transactions are under the aegis of the new *byt*—the new environment for which nothing counts except the function of the producer in the collective. The new Russians call *milieu* the only reliable educator.

8

For each citizen of Moscow the days are full to the brim. Meetings, committees are fixed at all hours in offices, clubs, factories, and often have no site of their own, being held in corners of noisy editorial rooms, at the cleared table of a canteen. There is a kind of natural selection and a struggle for existence between these meetings. Society projects them to some extent, plans them, they are convened. But how often must this be repeated until finally one of the many is successful, proves viable, is adapted, takes place. That nothing turns out as was intended and expected—this banal expression of the reality of life here asserts itself in each individual case so inviolably and intensely that Russian fatalism becomes comprehensible. If civilizing calculation slowly establishes itself in the collective, this will, in the first place, only complicate matters. (One is better provided for in a house that has only candles than where electric light is installed but the supply of current is interrupted hourly.) A feeling for the value of time, notwithstanding all 'rationalization', is not met with even in the capital of Russia. 'Trud', the trade-union institute for the study of work, under its director, Gastiev, launched a poster campaign for punctuality. From earliest times a large number of clockmakers have been settled in Moscow. They are crowded, in the manner of medieval guilds, in particular streets, on the Kuznetsky Bridge, on Ulitsa Gertsena. One wonders who actually needs them. 'Time is money'—for this astonishing statement posters claim the authority of Lenin, so alien is the idea to the Russians. They fritter everything away. (One is tempted to say that minutes are a cheap liquor of which they can never get enough, that they are tipsy with time.) If on the street a scene is being shot for a film, they forget where they are going and why, and follow the camera for hours, arriving at the office distraught. In his use of time, therefore, the Russian will remain 'Asiatic' longest of all. Once I needed to be wakened at seven in the morning: 'Please knock tomorrow at seven.' This elicited from the hotel porter the following Shakespearean monologue: 'If we think of it we shall wake you, but if we do not think of it we shall not wake you. Actually we usually do think of it, and then we wake people. But to be sure, we also forget sometimes when we do not think of it. Then we do not wake people. We are under no obligation, of course, but if it crosses our mind, we do it. When do you want to be wakened? At seven? Then we shall write that down. You see, I am putting the message there where he will find it. Of course, if he does not find it, then he will not wake you. But usually we do wake people.' The real unit of time is the *seichas*. That means 'at once'. You can hear it ten, twenty, thirty times, and wait hours, days, or weeks until the promise is carried out. Just as you seldom hear the answer 'no'. Negative replies are left to time. Time catastrophes, time collisions are therefore as much the order of the day as the *remonte*. They make each hour superabundant, each day exhausting, each life a moment.

9

Travel by streetcar in Moscow is above all a tactical experience. Here the newcomer learns perhaps most quickly of all to adapt himself to the curious tempo of this city and to the rhythm of its peasant population. And the complete interpenetration of technological and primitive modes of life, this world-historical experiment in the new Russia, is illustrated in miniature by a streetcar ride. The conductresses stand fur-wrapped at their places like Samoyed women on a sleigh. A tenacious shoving and barging during the boarding of a vehicle usually overloaded to the point of bursting takes place without a sound and with great cordiality. (I have never heard an angry word on these occasions.) Once everyone is inside, the migration begins in earnest. Through the ice-covered windows you can never make out where the vehicle has just stopped. If you do find out, it is of little avail. The way to the exit is blocked by a human wedge. Since you must board at the rear but alight at the front, you have to thread your way through this mass. However, conveyance usually occurs in batches; at important stops the vehicle is almost completely emptied. Thus even the traffic in Moscow is to a large extent a mass phenomenon. So one can encounter whole caravans of sleighs blocking the streets on a long row because loads that require a truck are being stacked on five or six large sleighs. The sleighs here take the horse into consideration first and then the passenger. They do not know the slightest superfluity. A feeding sack for the nags, a blanket for the passenger—and that is all. There is room for not more than two on the narrow bench, and as it has no back (unless you are willing so to describe a low rail), you must keep a good balance on sharp corners. Everything is based on the assumption of the highest velocity; long journeys in the cold are hard to bear and distances in this gigantic village immeasurable. The *izvozshchik* drives his vehicle close to the sidewalk. The passenger is not enthroned high up; he looks out on the same level as everyone else and brushes the passers-by with his sleeve. Even this is an incomparable experience for the sense of touch. Where Europeans, on their rapid journeys, enjoy superiority, dominance over the masses, the Muscovite in the little sleigh is closely mingled with people and things. If he has a box, a child, or a basket to take with him—for all this the sleigh is the cheapest means of transport—he is truly wedged into the street bustle. No condescending gaze: a tender, swift brushing along stones, people, and horses. You feel like a child gliding through the house on its little chair.

10

Christmas is a feast of the Russian forest. With pines, candles, tree decorations, it settles for many weeks in the streets, for the advent of Greek Orthodox Christians over-laps the Christmas of those Russians who celebrate the feast by the Western, that is the new, official calendar. Nowhere does one see Christmas trees more beautifully decorated. Little boats, birds, fishes, houses, and fruit crowd the street stalls and shops, and every year about this time the Kustarny Museum for Regional Art holds a kind of trade fair for all this. At a crossroads I found a woman selling tree decorations. The glass balls, yellow and red, glinted in the sun; it was like an enchanted apple basket in which red and yellow were divided among different fruit. Pines are drawn through the streets on slow sleighs. The smaller ones are trimmed only with silk bows; little pines with blue, pink, and green ribbons stand on the corners. But to the children the Christmas toys, even without a Santa Claus, tell how they come from deep in the forests of Russia. It is as if only under Russian hands does wood put forth such luxuriant greenness. It turns green—and then reddens and puts on a coat of gold, flares sky-blue and petrifies black. 'Red' and 'beautiful' are in [old] Russian *one* word. Certainly the glowing logs in the stove are the most magical metamorphosis of the Russian forest. Nowhere does the hearth seem to glow with such splendour as here. But radiance is captured in all the wood that the peasant carves and paints. And when varnished, it is fire frozen in all colours. Yellow and red on the balalaika, black and green on the little *garmoshka* for children, and every shade in the thirty-six eggs that fit one inside another. But forest night, too, lives in the wood. There are the heavy little boxes with scarlet interiors: on the outside, on a gleaming-black background, a picture. Under the tsars this industry was on the point of extinction. Now, besides new miniatures, the old, gold-embellished images are again emerging from peasant life. A *troika* with its three horses races through the night, or a girl in a sea-blue dress stands at night beside green flaring bushes, waiting for her lover. No night of terror is as dark as this durable lacquer night in whose womb all that appears in it is enfolded. I saw a box with a picture of a seated woman selling cigarettes. Beside her stands a child who wants to take one. Pitch-black night here, too. But on the right a stone and on the left a leafless tree are discernible. On the woman's apron is the word *Mossel'prom*. She is the Soviet 'Madonna with the Cigarettes'.

11

Green is the supreme luxury of the Moscow winter. But it shines from the shop in the Petrovka not half as beautifully as the paper bunches of artificial carnations, roses, lilies on the street. In markets they are the only wares to have no fixed stall and appear now among groceries, now among textile goods and crockery stalls. But they outshine everything, raw meat, coloured wool, and gleaming dishes. Other bouquets are seen at New Year's. On the Strasnaia Square I saw as I passed long twigs with red, white, blue, green blooms stuck to them, each stalk of a different colour. When talking of Moscow flowers one must not forget the heroic Christmas roses, nor the gigantically tall hollyhock made of lampshades that the trader carries through the streets. Or the glass cases full of flowers with the heads of saints looking out among them. Nor what the frost here inspires, the peasant cloths with patterns, embroidered in blue wool, imitating ice ferns on windows. Finally, the glistening candy-icing flower beds on cakes. The Pastry Cook from children's fairy tales seems to have survived only in Moscow. Only here are there structures made of nothing but spun sugar, sweet icicles with which the tongue indemnifies itself against the bitter cold. Most intimately of all, snow and flowers are united in candy icing; there at last the marzipan flora seems to have fulfilled entirely Moscow's dream, to bloom out of whiteness.

12

Under capitalism power and money have become commensurable qualities. Any given amount of money may be converted into a specific power, and the market value of all power can be calculated. So things stand on a large scale. We can only speak of corruption where the process is handled too hastily. It has in the smooth interplay of press, boards, and trusts a switchgear within the limits of which it remains entirely legal. The Soviet state has severed this communication between money and power. It reserves power for the Party, and leaves money to the NEP man. In the eyes of any Party functionary, even the highest, to put something aside, to secure the 'future', even if only 'for the children', is quite unthinkable. To its members the Communist Party guarantees the bare minimum for material existence—it does so practically, without actual obligation. On the other hand, it controls their further earnings and sets an upper limit of two hundred and fifty rubles on their monthly income. This can be increased solely through literary activity alongside one's profession. To such discipline the life of the ruling class is subjected. However, the power of the ruling authorities is by no means identical with their possessions. Russia is today not only a class but also a caste state. Caste state— that means that the social status of a citizen is determined not by the visible exterior of his existence—his clothes or living place—but exclusively by his relations to the Party. This is also decisive for those who do not directly belong to it. To them, too, jobs are open to the extent that they do not overtly repudiate the regime. Between them, too, the most precise distinctions are made. But however exaggerated-or obsolete—the European conception of the official suppression of nonconformists in Russia may on the one hand be, on the other, no one living abroad has any idea of the terrible social ostracism to which the NEP man is here subjected. The silence, the mistrust, perceptible not only between strangers, could not otherwise be explained. If you ask a superficial acquaintance here about his impressions of however unimportant a play, however trivial a film, you may expect stock phrases in reply: 'We say here ...' or 'The conviction is prevalent here ...' A judgment is weighed innumerable times before being uttered to more distant contacts. For at any time the Party can casually, unobtrusively change its line in *Pravda*, and no one likes to see himself disavowed. Because a reliable political outlook, if not the only good, is for most people the only guarantee of other goods, everyone uses his name and his voice so cautiously that the citizen with a democratic turn of mind cannot understand him. Two close acquaintances are having a conversation. In the course of it one of them says: 'That fellow Mikhailovich was in my office yesterday looking for a job. He said he knew you.' 'He is an excellent comrade, punctual and hard-working.' They change the subject. But as they part the first says, 'Would you be kind enough to give me a few words on that Mikhailovich in writing?' Class rule had adopted symbols that serve to characterize the opposing class. And of them jazz is perhaps the most popular. That people also enjoy listening to it in Russia is not surprising. But dancing to it is forbidden. It is kept behind glass, as it were, like a brightly coloured, poisonous reptile, and so appears as an attraction in revues. Yet always a symbol of the 'bourgeois'. It is one of the crude stage sets with the aid of which, for propaganda purposes, a grotesque image of the bourgeois type is constructed. In reality the image is often merely ridiculous, the discipline and competence of the adversary being overlooked. In this distorted view of the bourgeois a nationalistic moment is present. Russia was the possession of the tsar (indeed, anyone walking past the endlessly piled-up valuables in the Kremlin collections is tempted to say, '*a* possession'). The people, however, have become overnight his immeasurably wealthy heirs. They now set about drawing up a grand inventory of their human and territorial wealth. And they undertake this work in the consciousness of having already performed unimaginably difficult tasks, and built up, against the hostility of half the world, the new system of power. In admiration for this national achievement all Russians are united. It is this reversal of the power structure that makes life here so heavy with content. It is as complete in itself and rich in events, as poor, and in the same breath as full of prospects, as a gold digger's life on the Klondike. From early till late people dig for power. All the combinations of our leading figures are meagre in comparison to the countless constellations that here confront the individual in the course of a month. True, a certain intoxication can result, so that a life without meetings and committees, debates, resolutions, and votes (and all these are wars or at least manoeuvres of the will to power) can no longer be imagined. What does it matter—Russia's next generation will be adjusted to this existence. Its health, however, is subject to one indispensable condition: that never (as one day happened even to the Church) should a black market of power be opened. Should the European correlation of power and money penetrate Russia, too, then perhaps not the country, perhaps not even the Party, but Communism in Russia would be lost. People here have not yet developed European consumer concepts and consumer needs. The reasons for this are above all economic.

Yet it is possible that in addition an astute Party stratagem is involved: to equal the level of consumption in Western Europe, the trial by fire of the Bolshevik bureaucracy, at a freely chosen moment, steeled and with the absolute certainty of victory.

13

In the Red Army Club at the Kremlin, a map of Europe hangs on the wall. Beside it is a handle. When this handle is turned, the following is seen: one after the other, at all the places through which Lenin passed in the course of his life, little electric lights flash. At Simbirsk, where he was born, at Kazan, Petersburg, Geneva, Paris, Cracow, Zurich, Moscow, up to the place of his death, Gorki. Other towns are not marked. The contours of this wooden relief map are rectilinear, angular, schematic. On it Lenin's life resembles a campaign of colonial conquest across Europe. Russia is beginning to take shape for the man of the people. On the street, the snow, lie maps of the SFSR[1], piled up by street vendors who offer them for sale. Meyerhold uses a map in *D.E. (Here with Europe!)*—on it the West is a complicated system of little Russian peninsulas. The map is almost as close to becoming the centre of the new Russian iconic cult as Lenin's portrait. Quite certainly the strong national feeling that Bolshevism has given all Russians without distinction has conferred a new reality on the map of Europe. They want to measure, compare, and perhaps enjoy that intoxication with grandeur which is induced by the mere sight of Russia; citizens can only be urgently advised to look at their country on the map of neighbouring states, to study

Germany on a map of Poland, France, or even Denmark; but all Europeans ought to see, on a map of Russia, their little land as a frayed, nervous territory far out to the west.

14

What figure does the man of letters cut in a country where his employer is the proletariat? The theoreticians of Bolshevism stress how widely the situation of the proletariat in Russia after this successful revolution differs from that of the bourgeoisie in 1789. At that time the victorious class, before it attained power, had secured for itself in struggles lasting decades the control of the cultural apparatus. Intellectual organization, education, had long been pervaded by the ideas of the third estate, and the mental struggle for emancipation was fought out before the political. In present-day Russia it is quite different. For millions upon millions of illiterates, the foundations of a general education have yet to be laid. This is a national, Russian task. Pre-revolutionary education in Russia was, however, entirely unspecific, European. The European moment in higher education, and the national on the elementary level, are in Russia seeking an accommodation. That is one side of the educational question. On the other the victory of the Revolution has in many areas accelerated the process of Europeanization. There are writers like Pilniak who see in Bolshevism the crowning of the work of Peter the Great. In the technical area this tendency, despite all the adventures of its earliest years, is presumably sure of victory sooner or later. Not so in the intellectual and scientific areas. It is now apparent in Russia that European values are being popularized in just the distorted, desolating form that they owe finally to imperialism. The second academic theatre— a state-supported institution—is putting on a performance of the *Oresteia* in which a dusty antiquity struts about the stage as untruthfully as in a German Court theatre. And as the marble-stiff gesture is not only corrupt in itself, but also a copy of Court acting in revolutionary Moscow, it has a still more melancholy effect than in Stuttgart or Anhalt. The Russian Academy of Science has for its part made a man like Walzel—an average specimen of the modern academic *bel esprit*—a member. Probably the only cultural conditions in the West for which Russia has a lively enough understanding for disagreement with it to be profitable, are those of America. In contrast, cultural *rapprochement* as such (without the foundation of the most concrete economic and political community) is an interest of the pacifist variety of imperialism, benefits only gossiping busy-bodies, and is for Russia a symptom of restoration. The country is isolated from the West less by frontiers and censorship than by the intensity of an existence that is beyond all comparison with the European. Stated more precisely: contact with the outside world is through the Party and primarily concerns political questions. The old bourgeoisie has been annihilated; the new is neither materially nor intellectually in a position to establish external relations. Undoubtedly Russians know far less about the outside world than foreigners (with the possible exception of the Romantic countries) know about Russia. If an influential Russian mentions Proust and Bronnen in the same breath as authors who take their subject matter from the area of sexual problems, this shows clearly the foreshortened perspective in which European matters appear from here. But if one of Russia's leading authors, in conversation, quotes Shakespeare as one of the great poets who wrote before the invention of printing, such a lack of training can only be understood from the completely changed conditions affecting Russian writing as a whole. Theses and dogmas that in Europe—admittedly only for the last two centuries—have been regarded as alien to art and beneath discussion by men of letters are decisive in literary criticism and production in the new Russia. Message and subject matter are declared of primary importance. Formal controversies still played a not inconsiderable part at the time of the civil war. Now they have fallen silent. Today it is official doctrine that subject matter, not form, decides the revolutionary or counter-revolutionary attitude of a work. Such doctrines cut the ground from under the writer's feet just as irrevocably as the economy has done on the material plane. In this Russia is ahead of Western developments —but not as far ahead as is believed. For sooner or later, with the middle classes who are being ground to pieces by the struggle between capital and labour, the 'freelance' writer must also disappear. In Russia the process is complete: the intellectual is above all a functionary, working in the departments of censorship, justice, finance, and, if he survives, participating in work—which, however, in Russia means power. He is a member of the ruling class. Of his various organizations the most prominent is the general association of proletarian writers in Russia. It supports the notion of dictatorship even in the field of intellectual creation. In this it takes account of Russian reality. The transfer of the mental means of production into public ownership can be distinguished only fictitiously from that of the material means. To begin with, the proletarian can be trained in the use of both only under the protection of dictatorship.

15

Now and again one comes across streetcars painted all over with pictures of factories, mass meetings, red regiments, Communist agitators. These are gifts from the personnel of a factory to the Moscow Soviet. These vehicles carry the only political posters still to be seen in Moscow, but they are by far the most interesting. For nowhere are more naïve commercial posters to be seen than here. The wretched level of pictorial advertising is the only similarity between Paris and Moscow. Countless walls around churches and monasteries offer on all sides the finest surfaces for posters. But the constructivists, suprematists, abstractivists who under wartime Communism put their graphic propaganda at the service of the Revolution have long since been dismissed. Today only banal clarity is demanded. Most of these posters repel the Westerner. But Moscow shops are inviting; they have something of the tavern about them. The shop signs point at right angles into the street, as otherwise only old inn signs do, or golden barbers' basins, or a top hat before a hatter's. Also, the last charming, unspoiled motifs that remain are most likely to be found here. Shoes falling out of a basket; a Pomeranian running away with a sandal in his mouth. Pendants before the entrance of a Turkish kitchen: gentlemen, each with a fez adorning his head and each at his own little table. Catering to a primitive taste, advertising is still tied to narrative, example, or anecdote. In contrast, the Western advertisement convinces first and foremost by the expense of which it shows the firm capable. Here almost every ad also specifies the commodity in question. The grand, showy device is alien to commerce. The city, so inventive in abbreviations of all kinds, does not yet possess the simplest—brand names. Often Moscow's evening sky glows in frightening blue: one has unwittingly looked at it through one of the gigantic pairs of blue spectacles that project from opticians' shops like signposts. From the gateways, on the frames of front doors, in black, blue, yellow, and red letters of varying sizes-as an arrow, a picture of boots or freshly-ironed washing, a worn step or a solid staircase-a silently determined, contentious life accosts the passer-by. One must ride through the streets on the streetcar to perceive how this struggle is continued upward through the various stories, finally to reach its decisive phase on the roof. That height only the strongest, youngest slogans and signs attain. Only from an airplane does one have a view of the industrial élite of the city, the film and automobile industries. Mostly, however, the roofs of Moscow are a lifeless wasteland, having neither the dazzling electric signs of Berlin, nor the forest of chimneys of Paris, nor the sunny solitude of the rooftops of great cities in the South.

16

Anyone entering a Russian classroom for the first time will stop short in surprise. The walls are crammed with pictures, drawings, and pasteboard models. They are temple walls to which the children daily donate their own work as gifts to the collective. Red predominates; they are pervaded by Soviet emblems and heads of Lenin. Something similar is to be seen in many clubs. Wall newspapers are for grownups schemata of the same collective form of expression. They came into being under the pressure of the civil war, when in many places neither newspaper nor printing ink was available. Today they are an obligatory part of the public life of factories. Every Lenin niche has its wall newspaper, which varies its style among factories and authors. The only thing common to all is the naïve cheerfulness: colourful pictures interspersed with prose and verses. The newspaper is the chronicle of the collective. It gives statistical reports but also jocular criticism of comrades mingled with suggestions for improving the factory or appeals for communal aid. Notices, warning signs, and didactic pictures cover the walls of the Lenin niche elsewhere, too. Even inside a factory everyone is as if surrounded by coloured posters all exorcising the terrors of the machine. One worker is portrayed with his arm forced between the spokes of a driving wheel, another, drunk, causing an explosion with a short circuit, a third with his knee caught between two pistons. In the lending room of the Red Army bookshop hangs a notice, its short text clarified by many charming drawings, showing how many ways there are of ruining a book. In hundreds of thousands of copies a poster introducing the weights and measures normal in Europe is disseminated throughout the whole of Russia. Metres, litres, kilogrammes, etc., must be stuck up in every pub. In the reading room of the peasant club on Trubnaia Square the walls are covered with visual aids. The village chronicle, agricultural development, production technique, cultural institutions are graphically recorded in lines of development, along with components of tools, machine parts, retorts containing chemicals displayed everywhere on the walls. Out of curiosity I went up to a shelf from which two Negro faces grimaced at me. But as I came nearer, they turned out to be gas masks. Earlier, the building occupied by this club was one of the leading restaurants in Moscow. The erstwhile *séparées* are today bedrooms for the peasants of both sexes who have received a *komandirovka* to visit the city. There they are conducted through collections and barracks, and attend courses and educational evenings. From time to time there is also pedagogical theatre in the form of 'legal proceedings'. About three hundred people, sitting and standing, fill the red-draped room to its farthest corners. In a niche a bust of Lenin. The proceedings take place on a stage in front of which, on the right and the left, painted proletarian types—a peasant and an industrial worker—symbolize the *smychka*, the clasping together of town and country. The hearing of evidence has just finished, an expert is called on to speak. He and his assistant have one table, opposite him is the table of the defence, both facing sideways to the public. In the background, frontally, the judge's table. Before it, dressed in black, with a thick branch in her hand, sits the defendant, a peasant woman. She is accused of medical incompetence with fatal results. Through incorrect treatment she caused the death of a woman in childbirth. The argumentation now circles around this case in monotonous, simple trains of thought. The expert gives his report: to blame for the mother's death was the incorrect treatment. The defence counsel, however, pleads against harshness; in the country there is a lack of sanitary aid and hygienic instruction. The final word of the defendant: *nichevo*, people have always died in childbirth. The prosecution demands the death penalty. Then the presiding judge turns to the assembly: Are there any questions? But only a Komsomol appears on the stage, to demand severe punishment. The court retires to deliberate. After a short pause comes the judgment, for which everyone stands up: two years' imprisonment with recognition of mitigating circumstances. Solitary confinement is thus ruled out. In conclusion, the president points to the necessity of establishing centres of hygiene and instruction in rural areas. Such demonstrations are carefully prepared; there can be no question of improvisation. For mobilizing the public on questions of Bolshevik morality in accordance with Party wishes there can be no more effective means. On one occasion, alcoholism will be disposed of in this way, on others fraud, prostitution, hooliganism. The austere forms of such educational work are entirely appropriate to Soviet life, being precipitates of an existence that requires that a stand be taken a hundred times each day.

17

In the streets of Moscow there is a curious state of affairs: the Russian village is playing hide-and-seek in them. If you step through one of the high gateways—they often have wrought-iron gates, but I never found them closed—you stand on the threshold of a spacious settlement. Opening before you, broad and expansive, is a farmyard or a village, the ground is uneven, children ride about in sleighs, sheds for wood and tools fill the corners, trees stand here and there, wooden staircases give the backs of houses, which look like city buildings from the front, the appearance of Russian farmhouses. Frequently churches stand in these yards, just as on a large village green. So the street is augmented by the dimension of landscape. Nor is there any Western city that, in its vast squares, looks so rurally formless and perpetually sodden from bad weather, thawing snow or rain. Scarcely one of these broad spaces bears a monument. (In contrast, there is hardly one in Europe whose secret structure was not profaned and destroyed by a monument in the nineteenth century.) Like every other city, Moscow builds up with names a little world within itself. There is a casino called Alcazar, a hotel named Liverpool, a Tirol boardinghouse. From there it still takes half an hour to reach the centres of urban winter sport. True, skaters and skiers are encountered throughout the city, but the toboggan track is closer to the centre. There sleighs of the most diverse construction are used: from a board that runs at the front on sleigh rails and at the back drags in the snow, to the most comfortable bobsleds. Nowhere does Moscow look like the city itself; at the most it resembles its outskirts. The wet ground, the wooden booths, long convoys carrying raw materials, cattle being driven to the slaughterhouse, and indigent taverns are found in the busiest parts. The city is still interspersed with little wooden buildings in exactly the same Slavonic style as those found everywhere in the surroundings of Berlin. What looks so desolate in Brandenburg stone attracts here with the lovely colours of warm wood. In the suburban streets leading off the broad avenues, peasant huts alternate with *art nouveau* villas or with the sober façades of eight-story blocks. Snow lies deep, and if all of a sudden silence falls, one can believe oneself in a village in midwinter, deep in the Russian interior. Nostalgia for Moscow is engendered not only by the snow, with its starry lustre by night and its flowerlike crystals by day, but also by the sky. For between low roofs the horizon of the broad plains is constantly entering the city. Only toward evening does it become invisible. But then the shortage of housing in Moscow produces its most astonishing effect. If you wander the streets in the dusk you see in the large and small houses almost every window brightly lit. If the light coming from them were not so unsteady, you would believe you had a festive illumination before your eyes.

18

The churches are almost mute. The city is as good as free of the chimes that on Sundays spread such deep melancholy over our cities. But there is still perhaps not a single spot in Moscow from which at least *one* church is not visible. More exactly: at which one is not watched by at least *one* church. The subject of the tsars was surrounded in this city by more than four hundred chapels and churches, which is to say by two thousand domes, which hide in the corners everywhere, cover one another, spy over walls. An architectural *okhrana* was around him. All these churches preserve their incognito. Nowhere do high towers jut into the sky. Only with time does one become accustomed to putting together the long walls and crowds of low domes into complexes of monastery churches. It then also becomes clear why in many places Moscow looks as tightly sealed as a fortress. The monasteries still bear traces today of their old defensive purpose. Here Byzantium with its thousand domes is not the wonder that the European dreams it to be. Most of the churches are built on an insipid, sickly-sweet pattern:

their blue, green, and golden domes are a candied Orient.
If you enter one of these churches you first find a spacious
anteroom with a few sparse portraits of saints. It is gloomy,
the half-light lending itself to conspiracy. In such rooms
one can discuss the most dubious business, even pogroms if
the occasion demands. Adjoining the anteroom is the only
room for worship. In the background it had a few small steps
leading to a narrow, low platform along which one advances
past pictures of saints to the iconostasis. At short intervals,
altar succeeds altar, a glimmering red light denoting each.
The side walls are occupied by large pictures of saints. All
parts of the wall that are not thus covered with pictures are
lined with shining gold-coloured tin plate. From the trash-
ily painted ceiling hangs a crystal chandelier. Nevertheless
the room is always lit only by candles, a drawing room with
sanctified walls against which the ceremony unrolls. The
large pictures are greeted by making the sign of the cross
and kneeling down to touch the ground with the forehead;
then, with renewed signs of the cross, the worshipper,
praying or doing penance, goes on to the next. Before small,
glass-covered pictures lying in rows or singly on desks the
genuflection is omitted. One bends over them and kisses the
glass. On such desks, beside the most precious old icons,
series of the gaudiest oil paintings are displayed. Many pictures of saints have taken up positions outside on the facade
and look down from the highest cornices under the tinny
eaves like birds sheltering there. From their inclined, retort-
shaped heads affliction speaks. Byzantium seems to have no
church-window form of its own. A magical but uncanny
impression: the profane, drab windows looking out onto the
street from the assembly rooms and towers of the church as

if from a living room. Behind them the Orthodox priest is ensconced like the Buddhist monk in his pagoda. The lower part of the Basilius Cathedral might be the ground floor of a fine boyar house. However, if you enter Red Square from the west, its domes gradually rise into the sky like a pack of fiery suns. This building always holds something back, and could only be surprised by a gaze coming from an airplane, against which the builders forgot to take precautions. The inside has been not just emptied but eviscerated like a shot deer. (And it could hardly have turned out differently, for even in 1920 people still prayed here with fanatical fervour.) With the removal of all the furniture, the colourful vegetal convolutions that proliferate as murals in all the corridors and vaults are hopelessly exposed, distorting with a sad rococo playfulness the much older decoration that sparingly preserves in the interior the memory of the colourful spirals of the domes. The vaulted passageways are narrow, suddenly broadening into altar niches or circular chapels into which so little light falls from the high windows above that isolated devotional objects that have been left standing are scarcely discernible. Many churches remain as untended and as empty. But the glow that now shines only occasionally from the altars into the snow has been well preserved in the wooden cities of booths. In their snow-covered, narrow alleyways it is quiet. One hears only the soft jargon of the Jewish clothiers in their stalls next to the junk of the paper dealer, who, enthroned in concealment behind silver chains, has drawn tinsel and cotton-wool-tufted Father Christmases across her face like an oriental veil.

19

Even the most laborious Moscow weekday has two coordinates that define each of its moments sensuously as expectation and fulfilment. One is the vertical coordinate of mealtimes, crossed by the evening horizontal of the theatre. One is never very far from either. Moscow is crammed with pubs and theatres. Sentries with sweets patrol the street, many of the large grocery stores do not close until about eleven at night, and on the corners tearooms and beerhouses open. *Chainaia, pivnaia*—but usually both are painted on a background where a dull green from the upper edge gradually and sullenly merges into a dirty yellow. Beer is served with curious condiments: tiny pieces of dried white and black bread baked over with a salt crust, and dried peas in salt water. In certain taverns one can dine in this way and enjoy in addition a primitive *intsenirovka*. This is the term for an epic or lyrical subject that has been adapted for the theatre. It is often a folk song crudely divided for a choir. In the orchestra of such folk music, alongside accordions and violins, abacuses used as instruments are sometimes to be heard. (They can be found in every shop and office. The smallest calculation is unthinkable without them.) The intoxicating warmth that overcomes the guest on entering these taverns, on drinking the hot tea and enjoying the sharp *zakuska*, is Moscow's most secret winter lust. Therefore no one knows the city who has not known it in snow. Or each district must be visited during the season in which its climatic extreme falls, for to this it is primarily adapted, and it can be understood only through this adaptation. In Moscow, life in winter is richer by a dimension. Space literally changes according to whether it is hot or cold. People live on the street as if in a frosty chamber of mirrors, each pause to think is unbelievably difficult. It needs half a day's resolution even to mail an already addressed letter, and despite the severe cold it is a feat of will power to go into a shop and buy something. Yet when you have finally found a restaurant, no matter what is put on the table—vodka (which is here spiced with herbs), cakes, or a cup of tea—warmth makes the passing time itself an intoxicant. It flows into the weary guest like honey.

20

On the anniversary of Lenin's death many wear black arm bands. For at least three days, flags throughout the city are at half-mast. Many of the black-veiled pennants, however, once hanging, are left out for a few weeks. Russia's mourning for a dead leader is certainly not comparable to the attitudes adopted by other peoples on such days. The generation that was active in the civil wars is growing old in vitality if not in years. It is as if stabilization had admitted to their lives the calm, sometimes even the apathy, that is usually brought only by old age. The halt the Party one day called to wartime Communism with the NEP had a terrible backlash, which felled many of the movement's fighters. At that time many returned their membership books to the Party. Cases are known of such total demoralization that trusty pillars of the Party became defrauders within a few weeks. The mourning for Lenin is, for Bolsheviks, also mourning for heroic Communism. The few years since its passing are for Russian consciousness a long time. Lenin's

cellars. It seems to be still awaiting its designated use, but it already has it. For this depot of worn-out alleyways is the prostitutes' quarter. Invisible lines divide the area up into sharp, angular territories like African colonies. The whores are strategically placed, ready at a sign to encircle hesitant visitors, and to bounce the reluctant guest like a ball from one side of the street to the other. If he forfeits nothing else in this game, it is his hat. Has anyone yet probed deeply enough into this refuse heap of houses to reach the innermost place in the gynaeceum, the chamber where the trophies of manhood—boaters, bowlers, hunting hats, trilbies, jockey caps—hang in rows on consoles or in layers on racks? From the interiors of taverns the eye meets the sea. Thus the alleyway passes between rows of innocent houses as if shielded by a bashful hand from the harbour. On this bashful, dripping hand, however, shines a signet ring on a fishwife's hard finger, the old Hôtel de Ville. Here, two hundred years ago, stood patricians' houses. The highbreasted nymphs, the snake-ringed Medusa's heads over their weather-beaten doorframes have only now become unambiguously the signs of a professional guild. Unless, that is, signboards were hung over them as the midwife Bianchamori has hung hers, on which, leaning against a pillar, she turns a defiant face to all the brothel keepers of the quarter, and points unruffled to a sturdy baby in the act of emerging from an egg.

Noises. High in the empty streets of the harbour district they are as densely and loosely clustered as butterflies on a hot flower bed. Every step stirs a song, a quarrel, a flapping of wet linen, a rattling of boards, a baby's bawling, a clatter of buckets. Only you have to have strayed up here alone, if you are to pursue them with a net as they flutter away unsteadily into the stillness. For in these deserted corners all sounds and things still have their own silences, just as, at midday in the mountains, there is a silence of hens, of the axe of the cicadas. But the chase is dangerous, and the net is finally torn when, like a gigantic hornet, a grindstone impales it from behind with its whizzing sting.

Notre Dame de la Garde. The hill from which she looks down is the starry garment of the Mother of God, into which the houses of the Cité Chabas snuggle. At night, the lamps in its velvet lining form constellations that have not yet been named. It has a zipper: the cabin at the foot of the steel band of the rack railway is a jewel, from the coloured bull's-eyes of which the world shines back. A disused fortress is her holy footstool, and about her neck is an oval of waxen, glazed votive wreaths that look like relief profiles of her forebears. Little chains of streamers and sails are her earrings, and from the shady lips of the crypt issues jewellery of ruby-red and golden spheres on which swarms of pilgrims hang like flies.

Cathedral. On the least frequented, sunniest square stands the cathedral. This place is deserted, despite the proximity at its feet of La Joliette, the harbour, to the south, and a proletarian district to the north. As a reloading point for intangible, unfathomable goods, the bleak building stands between quay and warehouse. Nearly forty years were spent on it. But when all was complete, in 1893, place and time had conspired victoriously in this monument against its architects and sponsors, and the wealth of the clergy had given rise to a gigantic railway station that could never be opened to traffic. The facade gives an indication of the waiting rooms within, where passengers of the first to fourth classes (though before God they are all equal), wedged among their spiritual possessions as between cases, sit reading hymnbooks that, with their concordances and cross-references, look very much like international timetables. Extracts from the railway traffic regulations in the form of pastoral letters hang on the walls, tariffs for the discount on special trips in Satan's luxury train are consulted, and cabinets where the long-distance traveller can discreetly wash are kept in readiness as confessionals. This is the Marseilles religion station. Sleeping cars to eternity depart from here at Mass times.

The light from greengroceries that is in the paintings of Monticelli comes from the inner streets of his city, the monotonous residential quarters of the long-standing inhabitants, who know something of the sadness of Marseilles. For childhood is the divining rod of melancholy, and to know the mourning of such radiant, glorious cities one must have been a child in them. The grey houses of the Boulevard de Longchamps, the barred windows of the Cours Puget, and the trees of the Allée de Meilhan give nothing away to the traveller if chance does not lead him to the cubiculum of the city, the Passage de Lorette, the narrow yard where, in the sleepy presence of a few women and men, the whole world shrinks to a single Sunday afternoon. A real-estate company has carved its name on the gateway. Does not this interior correspond exactly to the white mystery ship moored in the harbour, *Nautique*, which never puts to sea, but daily feeds foreigners at white tables with dishes that are much too clean and as if surgically rinsed?

Shellfish and oyster stalls. Unfathomable wetness that swills from the upper tier, in a dirty, cleansing flood over dirty planks and warty mountains of pink shellfish, bubbles between the thighs and bellies of glazed Buddhas, past yellow domes of lemons, into the marshland of cresses and through the woods of French pennants, finally to irrigate the palate as the best sauce for the quivering creatures. *Oursins de l'Estaque, Portugaises, Maremmes, Clovisses, Moules marinières*—all this is incessantly sieved, grouped, counted, cracked open, thrown away, prepared, tasted. And the slow, stupid agent of inland trade, paper, has no place in the unfettered element, the breakers of foaming lips that forever surge against the streaming steps. But over there, on the other quay, stretches the mountain range of 'souvenirs', the mineral hereafter of sea shells. Seismic forces have thrown up this massif of paste jewellery, shell limestone, and enamel, where inkpots, steamers, anchors, mercury columns, and sirens commingle. The pressure of a thousand atmospheres under which this world of imagery writhes, rears, piles up, is the same force that is tested in the hard hands of seamen, after long voyages, on the thighs and breasts of women, and the lust that, on the shell-covered caskets, presses from the mineral world a red or blue velvet heart to be pierced with needles and brooches, is the same that sends tremors through these streets on paydays.

Walls. Admirable, the discipline to which they are subject in this city. The better ones, in the centre, wear livery and are in the pay of the ruling class. They are covered with gaudy patterns and have sold their whole length many hundreds of times to the latest brand of apéritif, to department stores, to the 'Chocolat Menier', or Dolores del Rio. In the poorer quarters they are politically mobilized and post their spacious red letters as the forerunners of red guards in front of dockyards and arsenals.

The down-and-out who, after nightfall, sells his books on the corner of rue de la République and the Vieux Port, awakens bad instincts in the passers-by. They feel tempted to make use of so much fresh misery. And they long to learn more about such nameless misfortune than the mere image of catastrophe that it presents to us. For what extremity must have brought a man to tip such books as he has left on the asphalt before him, and to hope that a passer-by will be seized at this late hour by a desire to read? Or is it all quite different? And does a poor soul here keep vigil, mutely beseeching us to lift the treasure from the ruins? We hasten by. But we shall falter again at every corner, for everywhere the Southern peddler has so pulled his beggar's coat around him that fate looks at us from it with a thousand eyes. How far we are from the sad dignity of our poor, the war-disabled of competition, on whom tags and tins of boot blacking hang like braid and medals.

Suburbs. The farther we emerge from the inner city, the more political the atmosphere becomes. We reach the docks, the inland harbours, the warehouses, the quarters of poverty, the scattered refugees of wretchedness: the outskirts. Outskirts are the state of emergency of a city, the terrain on which incessantly rages the great decisive battle between town and country. It is nowhere more bitter than

between Marseilles and the Provencal landscape. It is the
hand-to-hand fight of telegraph poles against Agaves,
barbed wire against thorny palms, the miasmas of stinking
corridors against the damp gloom under the plane trees in
brooding squares, short-winded outside staircases against
the mighty hills. The long rue de Lyon is the powder conduit
that Marseilles has dug in the landscape in order, in Saint-
Lazare, Saint-Antoine, Arenc, Septèmes, to blow it up,
burying it in the shell splinters of every national and commercial language. Alimentation Moderne, rue de Jamaïque,
Comptoir de la Limite, Savon Abat-Jour, Minoterie de la
Campagne, Bar du Gaz, Bar Facultatif—and over all this
the dust that here conglomerates out of sea salt, chalk, and
mica, and whose bitterness persists longer in the mouths of
those who have pitted themselves against the city than the
splendour of sun and sea in the eyes of its admirers.

1928

Hashish in Marseilles

Preliminary remark: One of the first signs that hashish is beginning to take effect 'is a dull feeling of foreboding; something strange, ineluctable is approaching … images and chains of images, long-submerged memories appear, whole scenes and situations are experienced; at first they arouse interest, now and then enjoyment, and finally, when there is no turning away from them, weariness and torment. By everything that happens, and by what he says and does, the subject is surprised and overwhelmed. His laughter, all his utterances happen to him like outward events. He also attains experiences that approach inspiration, illumination… Space can expand, the ground tilt steeply, atmospheric sensations occur: vapour, an opaque heaviness of the air; colours grow brighter, more luminous; objects more beautiful, or else lumpy and threatening…. All this does not occur in a continuous development; rather, it is typified by a continual alternation of dreaming and waking states, a constant and finally exhausting oscillation between totally different worlds of consciousness; in the middle of a sentence these transitions can take place.... All this the subject reports in a form that usually diverges very widely from the norm. Connections become difficult to perceive, owing to the frequently sudden rupture of all memory of past events, thought is not formed into words, the situation can become so compulsively hilarious that the hashish eater for minutes on end is capable of nothing except laughing.... The memory of the intoxication is surprisingly clear.' 'It is curious that hashish poisoning has not yet been experimentally studied. The most admirable description of the hashish trance is by Baudelaire (*Les paradis artificiels*).' From Joël and Fränkel, 'Der Haschisch-Rausch', *Klinische Wochenschrift*, 1926, vol. 5, p. 37.

Marseilles, July 29. At seven o'clock in the evening, after long hesitation, I took hashish. During the day I had been in Aix. With the absolute certainty, in this city of hundreds of thousands where no one knows me, of not being disturbed, I lie on the bed. And yet I am disturbed, by a little child crying. I think three-quarters of an hour have already passed. But it is only twenty minutes.... So I lie on the bed, reading and smoking. Opposite me always this view of the belly of Marseilles. The street I have so often seen is like a knife cut.

At last I left the hotel, the effects seeming non-existent or so weak that the precaution of staying at home was unnecessary. My first port of call was the café on the corner of the Cannebière and Cours Belsunce. Seen from the harbour, the one on the right, therefore not my usual café. What now? Only a certain benevolence, the expectation of being received kindly by people. The feeling of loneliness is very quickly lost. My walking stick begins to give me a special pleasure. One becomes so tender, fears that a shadow falling on the paper might hurt it. The nausea disappears. One reads the notices on the urinals. It would not surprise me if this or that person came up to me. But when no one does I am not disappointed, either. However, it is too noisy for me here.

Now the hashish eater's demands on time and space come into force. As is known, these are absolutely regal. Versailles, for one who has taken hashish, is not too large, or eternity too long. Against the background of these immense dimensions of inner experience, of absolute duration and immeasurable space, a wonderful, beatific humour dwells all the more fondly on the contingencies of the world of space and time. I feel this humour infinitely when I am told at the Restaurant Basso that the hot kitchen has just been closed, while I have just sat down to feast into eternity. Afterward, despite this, the feeling that all this is indeed bright, frequented, animated, and will remain so. I must note how I found my seat. What mattered to me was the view of the old port that one got from the upper floors. Walking past below, I had spied an empty table on the balcony of the second story. Yet in the end I only reached the first. Most of the window tables were occupied, so I went up to a very large one that had just been vacated. As I was sitting down, however, the disproportion of seating myself at so large a table caused me such shame that I walked across the entire floor to the opposite end to sit at a smaller table that became visible to me only as I reached it.

But the meal came later. First, the little bar on the harbour. I was again just on the point of retreating in confusion, for a concert, indeed a brass band, seemed to be playing there. I only just managed to explain to myself that it was nothing more than the blaring of car horns. On the way to the Vieux Port I already had this wonderful lightness and sureness of step that transformed the stony, unarticulated earth of the great square that I was crossing into the surface of a country road along which I strode at night like an energetic hiker. For at this time I was still avoiding the Cannebière, not yet quite sure of my regulatory functions. In that little harbour bar the hashish then began to exert its canonical magic with a primitive sharpness that I had scarcely felt until then. For it made me into a physiognomist, or at least a contemplator of physiognomies, and I underwent something unique in my experience: I positively fixed my gaze on the faces that I had around me, which were, in part, of remarkable coarseness or ugliness. Faces that I would normally have avoided for a twofold reason: I should neither have wished to attract their gaze nor endured their brutality. It was a very advanced post, this harbour tavern. (I believe it was the farthest accessible to me without danger, a circumstance I had gauged, in the trance, with the same accuracy with which, when utterly weary, one is able to fill a glass exactly to the brim without spilling a drop, as one can never do with sharp senses.) It was still sufficiently far from rue Bouterie, yet no bourgeois sat there; at the most, besides the true port proletariat, a few petty-bourgeois families from the neighbourhood. I now suddenly understood how, to a painter—had it not happened to Rembrandt and many others?—ugliness could appear as the true reservoir of beauty, better than any treasure cask, a jagged mountain with all the inner gold of beauty gleaming from the wrinkles, glances, features. I especially remember a boundlessly animal and vulgar male face in which the 'line of renunciation' struck me with sudden violence. It was above all men's faces that had begun to interest me. Now began the game, to be long maintained, of recognizing someone I knew in every face; often I knew the name, often not; the deception vanished as deceptions vanish in dreams: not in shame and compromised, but peacefully and amiably, like a being who has performed his service. Under these circumstances there was no question of loneliness. Was I my own company? Surely not so undisguisedly. I doubt whether that would have made me so happy. More likely this: I became my own skilful, fond, shameless procurer, gratifying myself with the ambiguous assurance of one who knows from profound study the wishes of his employer. Then it began to take half an eternity until the waiter reappeared. Or, rather, I could not wait for him to appear. I went into the bar-room and paid at the counter. Whether tips are usual in such taverns I do not know. But under other circumstances I should have given something in any case. Under hashish yesterday, however, I was on the stingy side; for fear of attracting attention by extravagance, I succeeded in making myself really conspicuous.

Similarly at Basso's. First I ordered a dozen oysters. The man wanted me to order the next course at the same time. I named some local dish. He came back with the news that none was left. I then pointed to a place in the menu in the vicinity of this dish, and was on the point of ordering each item, one after another, but then the name of the one above it caught my attention, and so on, until I finally reached the top of the list. This was not just from greed, however, but from an extreme politeness toward the dishes that I did not wish to offend by a refusal. In short, I came to a stop at a *pâté de Lyon*. Lion paste, I thought with a witty smile, when it lay clean on a plate before me, and then, contemptuously: this tender rabbit or chicken meat—whatever it may be. To my lionish hunger it would not have seemed inappropriate to satisfy itself on a lion. Moreover, I had tacitly decided that as soon as I had finished at Basso's (it was about half past ten) I should go elsewhere and dine a second time.

But first, back to the walk to Basso's. I strolled along the quay and read one after another the names of the boats tied up there. As I did so an incomprehensible gaiety came over me, and I smiled in turn at all the Christian names of France. The love promised to these boats by their names seemed wonderfully beautiful and touching to me. Only one of them, *Aero II*, which reminded me of aerial warfare, I passed by without cordiality, exactly as, in the bar that I had just left, my gaze had been obliged to pass over certain excessively deformed countenances.

Upstairs at Basso's, when I looked down, the old games began again. The square in front of the harbour was my palette, on which imagination mixed the qualities of the place, trying them out now this way, now that, without concern for the result, like a painter daydreaming on his palette. I hesitated before taking wine. It was a half bottle of Cassis. A piece of ice was floating in the glass. Yet it went excellently with my drug. I had chosen my seat on account of the open window, through which I could look down on the dark square. And as I did so from time to time, I noticed that it had a tendency to change with everyone who stepped onto it, as if it formed a figure about him that, clearly, had nothing to do with the square as he saw it but, rather, with the view that the great portrait painters of the seventeenth century, in accordance with the character of the dignitary whom they placed before a colonnade or a window, threw into a relief by this colonnade, this window. Later I noted as I looked down, 'From century to century things grow more estranged.'

Here I must observe in general: the solitude of such trances has its dark side. To speak only of the physical aspect, there was a moment in the harbour tavern when a violent pressure in the diaphragm sought relief through humming. And there is no doubt that truly beautiful, illuminating visions were not awakened. On the other hand, solitude works in these states as a filter. What one writes down the following day is more than an enumeration of impressions; in the night the trance cuts itself off from everyday reality with fine, prismatic edges; it forms a kind of figure and is more easily memorable. I should like to say: it shrinks and takes on the form of a flower.

To begin to solve the riddle of the ecstasy of trance, one ought to meditate on Ariadne's thread. What joy in the mere act of unrolling a ball of thread. And this joy is very deeply related to the joy of trance, as to that of creation. We go forward; but in so doing we not only discover the twists and turns of the cave, but also enjoy this pleasure of discovery against the background of the other, rhythmical bliss of unwinding the thread. The certainty of unrolling an artfully wound skein—is that not the joy of all productivity, at least in prose? And under hashish we are enraptured prose-beings in the highest power.

A deeply submerged feeling of happiness that came over me afterward, on a square off the Cannebière where rue

Paradis opens onto a park, is more difficult to recall than everything that went before. Fortunately I find on my newspaper the sentence 'One should scoop sameness from reality with a spoon.' Several weeks earlier I had noted another, by Johannes V. Jensen, which appeared to say something similar: 'Richard was a young man with understanding for everything in the world that was of the same kind.' This sentence had pleased me very much. It enabled me now to confront the political, rational sense it had had for me earlier with the individual magical meaning of my experience the day before. Whereas Jensen's sentence amounted, as I had understood it, to saying that things are as we know them to be, thoroughly mechanized and rationalized, the particular being confined today solely to nuances, my new insight was entirely different. For I saw only nuances, yet these were the same. I immersed myself in contemplation of the sidewalk before me, which, through a kind of unguent with which I covered it, could have been, precisely as these very stones, also the sidewalk of Paris. One often speaks of stones instead of bread. These stones were the bread of my imagination, which was suddenly seized by a ravenous hunger to taste what is the same in all places and countries. And yet I thought with immense pride of sitting here in Marseilles in a hashish trance; of who else might be sharing my intoxication this evening, how few. Of how I was incapable of fearing future misfortune, future solitude, for hashish would always remain. The music from a nearby night-club that I had been following played a part in this stage. G. rode past me in a cab. It happened suddenly, exactly as, earlier, from the shadows of the boat, U. had suddenly detached himself in the form of a harbour loafer and pimp. But there were not only known faces. Here, while I was in the state of deepest trance, two figures—citizens, vagrants, what do I know?—passed me as 'Dante and Petrarch'. 'All men are brothers.' So began a train of thought that I am no longer able to pursue. But its last link was certainly much less banal than its first and led on perhaps to images of animals.

'Barnabe', read the sign on a streetcar that stopped briefly at the square where I was sitting. And the sad confused story of Barnabas seemed to me no bad destination for a street-car going into the outskirts of Marseilles. Something very beautiful was going on around the door of the dance hall. Now and then a Chinese in blue silk trousers and a glowing pink silk jacket stepped outside. He was the doorman. Girls displayed themselves in the doorway. My mood was free of all desire. It was amusing to see a young man with a girl in a white dress coming toward me and to be immediately obliged to think: 'She got away from him in there in her shift, and now he is fetching her back. Well, well.' I felt flattered by the thought of sitting here in a centre of dissipation, and by 'here' I did not mean the town but the little, not-very-eventful spot where I found myself. But events took place in such a way that the appearance of things touched me with a magic wand, and I sank into a dream of them. People and things behave at such hours like those little stage sets and people made of elder pith in the glazed tin-foil box, which, when the glass is rubbed, are electrified and fall at every movement into the most unusual relationships.

The music that meanwhile kept rising and falling, I called the rush switches of jazz. I have forgotten on what grounds I permitted myself to mark the beat with my foot. This is against my education, and it did not happen without inner disputation. There were times when the intensity of acoustic impressions blotted out all others. In the little bar, above all, everything was suddenly submerged in the noise of voices, not of streets. What was most peculiar about this din of voices was that it sounded entirely like dialect. The people of Marseilles suddenly did not speak good enough French for me. They were stuck at the level of dialect. The phenomenon of alienation that may be involved in this, which Kraus has formulated in the fine dictum 'The more closely you look at a word the more distantly it looks back' appears to extend to the optical. At any rate I find among my notes the surprised comment 'How things withstand the gaze.'

The trance abated when I crossed the Cannebière and at last turned the corner to have a final ice cream at the little Café des Cours Belsunce. It was not far from the first café of the evening, in which, suddenly, the amorous joy dispensed by the contemplation of some fringes blown by the wind had convinced me that the hashish had begun its work. And when I recall this state I should like to believe that hashish persuades nature to permit us—for less egoistic purposes—that squandering of our own existence that we know in love. For if, when we love, our existence runs through nature's fingers like golden coins that she cannot hold and lets fall to purchase new birth thereby, she now throws us, without hoping or expecting anything, in ample handfuls to existence.

1928

IV

Surrealism

The Last Snapshot of the European Intelligentsia

Intellectual currents can generate a sufficient head of water for the critic to install his power station on them. The necessary gradient, in the case of Surrealism, is produced by the difference in intellectual level between France and Germany. What sprang up in 1919 in France in a small circle of literati—we shall give the most important names at once: Andre Breton, Louis Aragon, Philippe Soupault, Robert Desnos, Paul Eluard—may have been a meagre stream, fed on the damp boredom of post-war Europe and the last trickle of French decadence. The know-alls who even today have not advanced beyond the 'authentic origins' of the movement, and even now have nothing to say about it except that yet another clique of literati is here mystifying the honourable public, are a little like a gathering of experts at a spring who, after lengthy deliberation, arrive at the conviction that this paltry stream will never drive turbines.

The German observer is not standing at the head of the stream. That is his opportunity. He is in the valley. He can gauge the energies of the movement. As a German he is long acquainted with the crisis of the intelligentsia, or, more precisely, with that of the humanistic concept of freedom; and he knows how frantic is the determination that has awakened in the movement to go beyond the stage of eternal discussion and, at any price, to reach a decision; he has had direct experience of its highly exposed position between an anarchistic *fronde* and a revolutionary discipline, and so has no excuse for taking the movement for the 'artistic', 'poetic' one it superficially appears. If it was such at the outset, it was, however, precisely at the outset that Breton declared his intention of breaking with a praxis that presents the public with the literary precipitate of a certain form of existence while withholding that existence itself. Stated more briefly and dialectically, this means that the sphere of poetry was here explored from within by a closely knit circle of people pushing the 'poetic life' to the utmost limits of possibility. And they can be taken at their word when they assert that Rimbaud's *Saison en enfer* no longer had any secrets for them. For this book is indeed the first document of the movement (in recent times; earlier precursors will be discussed later). Can the point at issue be more definitively and incisively presented than by Rimbaud himself in his personal copy of the book? In the margin, beside the passage 'on the silk of the seas and the arctic flowers', he later wrote, 'There's no such thing.'

In just how inconspicuous and peripheral a substance the dialectical kernel that later grew into Surrealism was originally embedded, was shown by Aragon in 1924—at a time when its development could not yet be foreseen—in his *Vague de rêves*. Today it can be foreseen. For there is no doubt that the heroic phase, whose catalogue of heroes Aragon left us in that work, is over. There is always, in such movements, a moment when the original tension of the secret society must either explode in a matter-of-fact, profane struggle for power and domination, or decay as a public demonstration and be transformed. Surrealism is in this phase of transformation at present. But at the time when it broke over its founders as an inspiring dream wave, it seemed the most integral, conclusive, absolute of movements. Everything with which it came into contact was integrated. Life only seemed worth living where the threshold between waking and sleeping was worn away in everyone as by the steps of multitudinous images flooding back and forth, language only seemed itself where sound and image, image and sound interpenetrated with automatic precision and such felicity that no chink was left for the penny-in-the-slot called 'meaning'. Image and language take precedence. Saint-Pol Roux, retiring to bed about daybreak, fixes a notice on his door: 'Poet at work.' Breton notes: 'Quietly. I want to pass where no one yet has passed, quietly!—After you, dearest language.' Language takes precedence.

Not only before meaning. Also before the self. In the world's structure dream loosens individuality like a bad tooth. This loosening of the self by intoxication is, at the same time, precisely the fruitful, living experience that allowed these people to step outside the domain of intoxication. This is not the place to give an exact definition of Surrealist experience. But anyone who has perceived that the writings of this circle are not literature but something else— demonstrations, watchwords, documents, bluffs, forgeries if you will, but at any rate not literature—will also know,

for the same reason, that the writings are concerned literally with experiences, not with theories and still less with
phantasms. And these experiences are by no means limited
to dreams, hours of hashish eating, or opium smoking. It is
a cardinal error to believe that, of 'Surrealist experiences',
we know only the religious ecstasies or the ecstasies of
drugs. The opium of the people, Lenin called religion, and
brought the two things closer together than the Surrealists
could have liked. I shall refer later to the bitter, passionate
revolt against Catholicism in which Rimbaud, Lautréamont,
and Apollinaire brought Surrealism into the world. But the
true, creative overcoming of religious illumination certainly
does not lie in narcotics. It resides in a *profane illumination*, a
materialistic, anthropological inspiration, to which hashish,
opium, or whatever else can give an introductory lesson.
(But a dangerous one; and the religious lesson is stricter.)
This profane illumination did not always find the Surrealists
equal to it, or to themselves, and the very writings that proclaim it most powerfully, Aragon's incomparable *Paysan de
Paris* and Breton's *Nadja*, show very disturbing symptoms
of deficiency. For example, there is in *Nadja* an excellent
passage on the 'delightful days spent looting Paris under
the sign of Sacco and Vanzetti'; Breton adds the assurance
that in those days Boulevard Bonne-Nouvelle fulfilled the
strategic promise of revolt that had always been implicit in
its name. But Madame Sacco also appears, not the wife of
Fuller's victim but a *voyante*, a fortune-teller who lives at
3 rue des Usines and tells Paul Eluard that he can expect no
good from Nadja. Now I concede that the breakneck career
of Surrealism over rooftops, lightning conductors, gutters,
verandas, weathercocks, stucco work—all ornaments are

grist to the cat burglar's mill—may have taken it also into the humid backroom of spiritualism. But I am not pleased to hear it cautiously tapping on the windowpanes to inquire about its future. Who would not wish to see these adoptive children of revolution most rigorously severed from all the goings-on in the conventicles of down-at-heel dowagers, retired majors, and émigré profiteers?

In other respects Breton's book illustrates well a number of the basic characteristics of this 'profane illumination'. He calls *Nadja* 'a book with a banging door'. (In Moscow I lived in a hotel in which almost all the rooms were occupied by Tibetan lamas who had come to Moscow for a congress of Buddhist churches. I was struck by the number of doors in the corridors that were always left ajar. What had at first seemed accidental began to be disturbing. I found out that in these rooms lived members of a sect who had sworn never to occupy closed rooms. The shock I had then must be felt by the reader of *Nadja*.) To live in a glass house is a revolutionary virtue par excellence. It is also an intoxication, a moral exhibitionism, that we badly need. Discretion concerning one's own existence, once an aristocratic virtue, has become more and more an affair of petty-bourgeois parvenus. *Nadja* has achieved the true, creative synthesis between the art novel and the *roman-à-clef*.

Moreover, one need only take love seriously to recognize in it, too—as *Nadja* also indicates—a 'profane illumination'. 'At just that time' (i.e., when he knew Nadja), the author tells us, 'I took a great interest in the epoch of Louis VII, because it was the time of the "courts of love", and I tried to picture with great intensity how people saw life then.' We have from a recent author quite exact information on Provençal love poetry, which comes surprisingly close to the Surrealist conception of love. 'All the poets of the "new style",' Erich Auerbach points out in his excellent *Dante: Poet of the Secular World*, 'possess a mystical beloved, they all have approximately the same very curious experience of love; to them all Amor bestows or withholds gifts that resemble an illumination more than sensual pleasure; all are subject to a kind of secret bond that determines their inner and perhaps also their outer lives'. The dialectics of intoxication are indeed curious. Is not perhaps all ecstasy in one world humiliating sobriety in that complementary to it? What is it that courtly *Minne* seeks—and it, not love, binds Breton to the telepathic girl—if not to make chastity, too, a transport? Into a world that borders not only on tombs of the Sacred Heart or altars to the Virgin, but also on the morning before a battle or after a victory.

The lady, in esoteric love, matters least. So, too, for Breton. He is closer to the things that Nadja is close to than to her. What are these things? Nothing could reveal more about Surrealism than their canon. Where shall I begin? He can boast an extraordinary discovery. He was the first to perceive the revolutionary energies that appear in the 'outmoded', in the first iron constructions, the first factory buildings, the earliest photos, the objects that have begun to be extinct, grand pianos, the dresses of five years ago, fashionable restaurants when the vogue has begun to ebb from them. The relation of these things to revolution—no one can have a more exact concept of it than these authors. No one before these visionaries and augurs perceived how destitution—not only social but architectonic, the poverty of interiors, enslaved and enslaving objects—can be suddenly transformed into revolutionary nihilism. Leaving aside Aragon's *Passage de l'Opéra*, Breton and Nadja are the lovers who convert everything that we have experienced on mournful railway journeys (railways are beginning to age), on Godforsaken Sunday afternoons in the proletarian quarters of the great cities, in the first glance through the rain-blurred window of a new apartment, into revolutionary experience, if not action. They bring the immense forces of 'atmosphere' concealed in these things to the point of explosion. What form do you suppose a life would take that was determined at a decisive moment precisely by the street song last on everyone's lips?

The trick by which this world of things is mastered—it is more proper to speak of a trick than a method—consists in the substitution of a political for a historical view of the past. 'Open, graves, you, the dead of the picture galleries, corpses behind screens, in palaces, castles, and monasteries, here stands the fabulous keeper of keys holding a bunch of the keys to all times, who knows where to press the most artful lock and invites you to step into the midst of the world of today, to mingle with the bearers of burdens, the mechanics whom money ennobles, to make yourself at home in their automobiles, which are beautiful as armour from the age of chivalry, to take your places in the international sleeping cars, and to weld yourself to all the people who today are still proud of their privileges. But civilization will give them short shrift.' This speech was attributed to Apollinaire by his friend Henri Hertz. Apollinaire originated this technique. In his volume of novellas, *L'hérésiarque*, he used it with Machiavellian calculation to blow Catholicism (to which he inwardly clung) to smithereens.

At the centre of this world of things stands the most dreamed-of of their objects, the city of Paris itself. But only revolt completely exposes its Surrealist face (deserted streets in which whistles and shots dictate the outcome). And no face is surrealistic in the same degree as the true face of a city. No picture by de Chirico or Max Ernst can match the sharp elevations of the city's inner strongholds, which one must overrun and occupy in order to master their fate and, in their fate, in the fate of their masses, one's own. Nadja is an exponent of these masses and of what inspires them to revolution: 'The great living, sonorous unconsciousness that inspires my only convincing acts, in the sense that I always want to prove that it commands forever everything that is mine.' Here, therefore, we find the catalogue of these fortifications, from Place Maubert, where as nowhere else dirt has retained all its symbolic power, to the 'Théâtre Moderne', which I am inconsolable not to have known. But in Breton's description of her bar on the upper floor—'it is quite dark, with arbours like impenetrable tunnels—a drawing room on the bottom of a lake'—there is something that brings back to my memory that most uncomprehended room in the old Princess Café. It was the back room on the first floor, with couples in the blue light. We called it the 'anatomy school'; it was the last restaurant designed for love. In such passages in Breton, photography intervenes in a very strange way. It makes the streets, gates, squares of the city into illustrations of a trashy novel, draws off the banal obviousness of this ancient architecture to inject it with the most pristine intensity toward the events described, to which, as in old chambermaids' books, word-for-word quotations with page numbers refer. And all the parts of Paris that appear here are places where what is between these people turns like a revolving door.

The Surrealists' Paris, too, is a 'little universe'. That is to say, in the larger one, the cosmos, things look no different. There, too, are crossroads where ghostly signals flash from the traffic, and inconceivable analogies and connections between events are the order of the day. It is the region from which the lyric poetry of Surrealism reports. And this must be noted if only to counter the obligatory misunderstanding of *l'art pour l'art*. For art's sake was scarcely ever to be taken literally; it was almost always a flag under which sailed a cargo that could not be declared because it still lacked a name. This is the moment to embark on a work that would illuminate as has no other the crisis of the arts that we are witnessing: a history of esoteric poetry. Nor is it by any means fortuitous that no such work yet exists. For written as it demands to be written—that is, not as a collection to which particular 'specialists' all contribute 'what is most worth knowing' from their fields, but as the deeply grounded composition of an individual who, from inner compulsion, portrays less a historical evolution than a constantly renewed, primal upsurge of esoteric poetry—written in such a way it would be one of those scholarly confessions that can be counted in every century. The last page would have to show an X-ray picture of Surrealism. Breton indicates in his *Introduction au discours sur le peu de réalité* how the philosophical realism of the Middle Ages was the basis of poetic experience. This realism, however—that is, the belief in a real, separate existence of concepts whether outside or inside things—has always very quickly crossed over from the logical realm of ideas to the magical realm of words. And

it is as magical experiments with words, not as artistic dab-
bling, that we must understand the passionate phonetic and
graphical transformational games that have run through the
whole literature of the avant-garde for the past fifteen years,
whether it is called Futurism, Dadaism, or Surrealism. How
slogans, magic formulas, and concepts are here intermin-
gled is shown by the following words of Apollinaire's from
his last manifesto, *L'esprit nouveau et les poètes*. He says, in
1918: 'For the speed and simplicity with which we have all
become used to referring by a single word to such complex
entities as a crowd, a nation, the universe, there is no modern
equivalent in literature. But today's writers fill this gap; their
synthetic works create new realities the plastic manifestations of which are just as complex as those referred to by the
words standing for collectives.' If, however, Apollinaire and
Breton advance even more energetically in the same direction and complete the linkage of Surrealism to the outside
world with the declaration, 'The conquests of science rest far
more on a surrealistic than on a logical thinking'—if, in other
words, they make mystification, the culmination of which
Breton sees in poetry (which is defensible), the foundation
of scientific and technical development, too—then such integration is too impetuous. It is very instructive to compare
the movement's over-precipitate embrace of the uncomprehended miracle of machines—'the old fables have for the
most part been realized, now it is the turn of poets to create
new ones that the inventors on their side can then make real'
(Apollinaire)—to compare these overheated fantasies with
the well-ventilated utopias of a Scheerbart.

'The thought of all human activity makes me laugh.'
This utterance of Aragon's shows very clearly the path

Surrealism had to follow from its origins to its politicization. In his excellent essay '*La révolution et les intellectuels*', Pierre Naville, who originally belonged to this group, rightly called this development dialectical. In the transformation of a highly contemplative attitude into revolutionary opposition, the hostility of the bourgeoisie toward every manifestation of radical intellectual freedom played a leading part. This hostility pushed Surrealism to the left. Political events, above all the war in Morocco, accelerated this development. With the manifesto 'Intellectuals Against the Moroccan War', which appeared in *L'Humanité*, a fundamentally different platform was gained from that which was characterized by, for example, the famous scandal at the Saint-Pol Roux banquet. At that time, shortly after the war, when the Surrealists, who deemed the celebration for a poet they worshipped compromised by the presence of nationalistic elements, burst out with the cry 'Long live Germany', they remained within the boundaries of scandal, toward which, as is known, the bourgeoisie is as thick-skinned as it is sensitive to all action. There is remarkable agreement between the ways in which, under such political auspices, Apollinaire and Aragon saw the future of the poet. The chapters 'Persecution' and 'Murder' in Apollinaire's *Poète assassiné* contain the famous description of a pogrom against poets. Publishing houses are stormed, books of poems thrown on the fire, poets lynched. And the same scenes are taking place at the same time all over the world. In Aragon, 'Imagination', in anticipation of such horrors, calls its company to a last crusade.

To understand such prophecies, and to assess strategically the line arrived at by Surrealism, one must investigate the mode of thought widespread among the so-called well-meaning left-wing bourgeois intelligentsia. It manifests itself clearly enough in the present Russian orientation of these circles. We are not of course referring here to Béraud, who pioneered the lie about Russia, or to Fabre-Luce, who trots behind him like a devoted donkey, loaded with every kind of bourgeois ill-will. But how problematic is even the typical mediating book by Duhamel. How difficult to bear is the strained uprightness, the forced animation and sincerity of the Protestant method, dictated by embarrassment and linguistic ignorance, of placing things in some kind of symbolic illumination. How revealing his résumé: 'the true, deeper revolution, which could in some sense transform the substance of the Slavonic soul itself, has not yet taken place'. It is typical of these left-wing French intellectuals—exactly as it is of their Russian counterparts, too—that their positive function derives entirely from a feeling of obligation, not to the Revolution, but to traditional culture. Their collective achievement, as far as it is positive, approximates conservation. But politically and economically they must always be considered a potential source of sabotage.

Characteristic of this whole left-wing bourgeois position is its irremediable coupling of idealistic morality with political practice. Only in contrast to the helpless compromises of 'sentiment' are certain central features of Surrealism, indeed of the Surrealist tradition, to be understood. Little has happened so far to promote this understanding. The seduction was too great to regard the Satanism of a Rimbaud and a Lautréamont as a pendant to art for art's sake in an inventory of snobbery. If, however, one resolves to open up this romantic dummy, one finds something usable inside. One finds the cult of evil as a political device, however romantic, to disinfect and isolate against all moralizing dilettantism. Convinced of this, and coming across the scenario of a horror play by Breton that centres about a violation of children, one might perhaps go back a few decades. Between 1865 and 1875 a number of great anarchists, without knowing of one another, worked on their infernal machines. And the astonishing thing is that independently of one another they set its clock at exactly the same hour, and forty years later in Western Europe the writings of Dostoevsky, Rimbaud, and Lautréamont exploded at the same time. One might, to be more exact, select from Dostoevsky's entire work the one episode that was actually not published until about 1915, 'Stavrogin's Confession' from *The Possessed*. This chapter, which touches very closely on the third canto of the *Chants de Maldoror*, contains a justification of evil in which certain motifs of Surrealism are more powerfully expressed than by any of its present spokesmen. For Stavrogin is a Surrealist *avant la lettre*. No one else understood, as he did, how naïve is the view of the Philistines that goodness, for all the manly virtue of those who practise it, is God-inspired; whereas evil stems entirely from our spontaneity, and in it we are independent and self-sufficient beings. No one else saw inspiration, as he did, in even the most ignoble actions, and precisely in them. He considered vileness itself as something preformed, both in the course of the world and also in ourselves, to which we are disposed if not called, as the bourgeois idealist sees virtue. Dostoyevsky's God created not only heaven and earth and man and beast, but also baseness, vengeance, cruelty. And here, too, he gave the devil no opportunity to meddle in his handiwork. That is why all these vices have a pristine vitality in his work; they are perhaps not 'splendid', but eternally new, 'as on the first day', separated by an infinity from the clichés through which sin is perceived by the Philistine.

The pitch of tension that enabled the poets under discussion to achieve at a distance their astonishing effects is documented quite scurrilously in the letter Isidore Ducasse addressed to his publisher on October 23, 1869, in an attempt to make his poetry look acceptable. He places himself in the line of descent from Mickiewicz, Milton, Southey, Alfred de Musset, Baudelaire, and says: 'Of course, I somewhat swelled the note to bring something new into this literature that, after all, only sings of despair in order to depress the reader and thus make him long all the more intensely for goodness as a remedy. So that in the end one really sings only of goodness, only the method is more philosophical and less naive than that of the old school, of which only Victor Hugo and a few others are still alive.' But if Lautréamont's erratic book has any lineage at all, or, rather, can be assigned one, it is that of insurrection. Soupault's attempt, in his edition of the complete works in 1927, to write a political curriculum vitae for Isidore Ducasse was therefore a quite understandable and not unperceptive venture. Unfortunately, there is no documentation for it, and that adduced by Soupault rests on a confusion. On the other hand, and happily, a similar attempt in the case of Rimbaud was successful, and it is the achievement of Marcel Coulon to have defended the poet's true image against the Catholic usurpation by Claudel and Berrichon. Rimbaud is indeed a Catholic, but he is one, by his own account, in the most wretched part of himself, which he does not tire of denouncing and consigning to his own and everyone's hatred, his own and everyone's contempt: the part that forces him to confess that he does not understand revolt. But that is the concession of a communard dissatisfied with his own contribution who, by the time he turned his back on poetry, had long since—in his earliest work—taken leave of religion. 'Hatred, to you I have entrusted my treasure', he writes in the *Saison en enfer*. This is another dictum around which a poetics of Surrealism might grow like a climbing plant, to sink its roots deeper than the theory of 'surprised' creation originated by Apollinaire, to the depth of the insights of Poe.

Since Bakunin, Europe has lacked a radical concept of freedom. The Surrealists have one. They are the first to liquidate the sclerotic liberal-moral-humanistic ideal of freedom, because they are convinced that 'freedom, which on this earth can only be bought with a thousand of the hardest sacrifices, must be enjoyed unrestrictedly in its fullness without any kind of pragmatic calculation, as long as it lasts'. And this proves to them that 'mankind's struggle for liberation in its simplest revolutionary form (which, however, is liberation in every respect), remains the only cause worth serving'. But are they successful in welding this experience of freedom to the other revolutionary experience that we have to acknowledge because it has been ours, the constructive, dictatorial side of revolution? In short, have they bound revolt to revolution? How are we to imagine an existence oriented solely toward Boulevard Bonne-Nouvelle, in rooms by Le Corbusier and Oud?

To win the energies of intoxication for the revolution—this is the project about which Surrealism circles in all its books and enterprises. This it may call its most particular task.

For them it is not enough that, as we know, an ecstatic component lives in every revolutionary act. This component is identical with the anarchic. But to place the accent exclusively on it would be to subordinate the methodical and disciplinary preparation for revolution entirely to a praxis oscillating between fitness exercises and celebration in advance. Added to this is an inadequate, undialectical conception of the nature of intoxication. The aesthetic of the painter, the poet, *en état de surprise*, of art as the reaction of one surprised, is enmeshed in a number of pernicious romantic prejudices. Any serious exploration of occult, surrealistic, phantasmagoric gifts and phenomena presupposes a dialectical intertwinement to which a romantic turn of mind is impervious. For histrionic or fanatical stress on the mysterious side of the mysterious takes us no further; we penetrate the mystery only to the degree that we recognize it in the everyday world, by virtue of a dialectical optic that perceives the everyday as impenetrable, the impenetrable as everyday. The most passionate investigation of telepathic phenomena, for example, will not teach us half as much about reading (which is an eminently telepathic process), as the profane illumination of reading about telepathic phenomena. And the most passionate investigation of the hashish trance will not teach us half as much about thinking (which is eminently narcotic), as the profane illumination of thinking about the hashish trance. The reader, the thinker, the loiterer, the *flâneur*, are types of illuminati just as much as the opium eater, the dreamer, the ecstatic. And more profane. Not to mention that most terrible drug— ourselves—which we take in solitude.

'To win the energies of intoxication for the revolution' —in other words, poetic politics? 'We have tried that beverage. Anything, rather than that!' Well, it will interest you all the more how much an excursion into poetry clarifies things. For what is the programme of the bourgeois parties? A bad poem on springtime, filled to bursting with metaphors. The socialist sees that 'finer future of our children and grandchildren' in a condition in which all act 'as if they were angels', and everyone has as much 'as if he were rich', and everyone lives 'as if he were free'. Of angels, wealth, freedom, not a trace. These are mere images. And the stock imagery of these poets of the social-democratic associations? Their *gradus ad parnassum?* Optimism. A very different air is breathed in the Naville essay that makes the 'organization of pessimism' the call of the hour. In the name of his literary friends he delivers an ultimatum in face of which this unprincipled, dilettantish optimism must unfailingly show its true colours: where are the conditions for revolution? In the changing of attitudes or of external circumstances? That is the cardinal question that determines the relation of politics to morality and cannot be glossed over. Surrealism has come ever closer to the Communist answer. And that means pessimism all along the line. Absolutely. Mistrust in the fate of literature, mistrust in the fate of freedom, mistrust in the fate of European humanity, but three times mistrust in all reconciliation: between classes, between nations, between individuals. And unlimited trust only in I. G. Farben and the peaceful perfection of the air force. But what now, what next?

Here due weight must be given to the insight that in the *Traité du style*, Aragon's last book, required in distinction between metaphor and image, a happy insight into questions of style that needs extending. Extension: nowhere do these two—metaphor and image—collide so drastically and so irreconcilably as in politics. For to organize pessimism means nothing other than to expel moral metaphor from politics and to discover in political action a sphere reserved one hundred percent for images. This image sphere, however, can no longer be measured out by contemplation. If it is the double task of the revolutionary intelligentsia to overthrow the intellectual predominance of the bourgeoisie and to make contact with the proletarian masses, the intelligentsia has failed almost entirely in the second part of this task because it can no longer be performed contemplatively. And yet this has hindered hardly anybody from approaching it again and again as if it could, and calling for proletarian poets, thinkers, and artists. To counter this, Trotsky had to point out—as early as *Literature and Revolution*—that such artists would only emerge from a victorious revolution. In reality it is far less a matter of making the artist of bourgeois origin into a master of 'proletarian art' than of deploying him, even at the expense of his artistic activity, at important points in this sphere of imagery. Indeed, might not perhaps the interruption of his 'artistic career' be an essential part of his new function?

The jokes he tells are the better for it. And he tells them better. For in the joke, too, in invective, in misunderstanding, in all cases where an action puts forth its own image and exists, absorbing and consuming it, where nearness looks with its own eyes, the long-sought image sphere is opened, the world of universal and integral actualities, where the 'best room' is missing—the sphere, in a word, in which political materialism and physical nature share the inner man, the psyche, the individual, or whatever else we wish to throw to them, with dialectical justice, so that no limb remains unrent. Nevertheless—indeed, precisely after such dialectical annihilation—this will still be a sphere of images and, more concretely, of bodies. For it must in the end be admitted: metaphysical materialism, of the brand of Vogt and Bukharin, as is attested by the experience of the Surrealists, and earlier of Hebel, Georg Büchner, Nietzsche, and Rimbaud, cannot lead without rupture to anthropological materialism. There is a residue. The collective is a body, too. And the *physis* that is being organized for it in technology can, through all its political and factual reality, only be produced in that image sphere to which profane illumination initiates us. Only when in technology body and image so interpenetrate that all revolutionary tension becomes bodily collective innervation, and all the bodily innervations of the collective become revolutionary discharge, has reality transcended itself to the extent demanded by the *Communist Manifesto*. For the moment, only the Surrealists have understood its present commands. They exchange, to a man, the play of human features for the face of an alarm clock that in each minute rings for sixty seconds.

1929

A Small History of Photography

The fog that surrounds the beginnings of photography is
not as thick as that which shrouds the early days of printing; more obviously than in the case of the printing press,
perhaps, the time was ripe for the invention, and was sensed
by more than one—by men who strove independently for
the same objective: to capture the images in the camera
obscura, which had been known at least since Leonardo's
time. When, after about five years of effort, both Niepce and
Daguerre simultaneously succeeded in doing this, the state,
aided by the patent difficulties encountered by the inventors, assumed control of the enterprise and made it public,
with compensation to the pioneers. This paved the way for
a rapid ongoing development which long precluded any
backward glance. Thus it is that the historical or, if you like,
philosophical questions suggested by the rise and fall of photography have gone unheeded for decades. And if people are
starting to be aware of them today, there is a definite reason
for it. The latest writings on the subject point up the fact
that the flowering of photography—the work of Hill and

Cameron, Hugo and Nadar—came in its first decade. But this was the decade which preceded its industrialization. Not that hucksters and charlatans did not appropriate the new techniques for gain, even in that early period; indeed, they did so *en masse*. But that was closer to the arts of the fairground, where photography is at home to this day, than to industry. Industry made its first real inroads with the visiting card picture, whose first manufacturer significantly became a millionaire. It would not be surprising if the photographic methods which today, for the first time, are harking back to the pre-industrial heyday of photography had an underground connection with the crisis of capitalist industry. But that does not make it any easier to use the charm of old photographs, available in fine recent publications,[1] for real insights into their nature. Attempts at theoretical mastery of the subject have so far been entirely rudimentary. And no matter how extensively it may have been debated in the last century, basically the discussion never got away from the ludicrous stereotype which a chauvinistic rag, the *Leipziger Stadtanzeiger*, felt it must offer in timely opposition to this black art from France. 'To try to capture fleeting mirror images', it said, 'is not just an impossible undertaking, as has been established after thorough German investigation; the very wish to do such a thing is blasphemous. Man is made in the image of God, and God's image cannot be captured by any machine of human devising. The utmost the artist may venture, borne on the wings of divine inspiration, is to reproduce man's God-given features without the help of any machine, in the moment of highest dedication, at the higher bidding of his genius.' Here we have the philistine notion of *art* in all its overweening obtuseness, a stranger to all technical considerations, which feels that its end is nigh with the alarming appearance of the new technology. Nevertheless, it was this fetishistic and fundamentally anti-technical concept of art with which the theoreticians of photography sought to grapple for almost a hundred years, naturally without the smallest success. For they undertook nothing less than to legitimize the photographer before the very tribunal he was in the process of overturning. Far different is the tone of the address which the physicist Arago, speaking on behalf of Daguerre's invention, gave in the Chamber of Deputies on 3 July 1839. The beautiful thing about this speech is the connections it makes with all aspects of human activity. The panorama it sketches is broad enough not only to make the dubious project of authenticating photography in terms of painting—which it does anyway—seem beside the point; more important, it offers an insight into the real scope of the invention. 'When inventors of a new instrument', says Arago, 'apply it to the observation of nature, what they expect of it always turns out to be a trifle compared with the succession of subsequent discoveries of which the instrument was the origin.' In a great arc Arago's speech spans the field of new technologies, from astrophysics to philology: alongside the prospects for stellar photography we find the idea of establishing a photographic record of the Egyptian hieroglyphs.

Daguerre's photographs were iodized silver plates exposed in the camera obscura, which had to be turned this way and that until, in the proper light, a pale grey image could be discerned. They were one of a kind; in 1839 a plate cost an average of 25 gold francs. They were not infrequently kept in a case, like jewellery. In the hands of

many a painter, though, they became a technical adjunct.
Just as 70 years later Utrillo painted his fascinating views
of Paris not from life but from picture postcards, so did the
highly regarded English portrait painter David Octavius
Hill base his fresco of the first general synod of the Church
of Scotland in 1843 on a long series of portrait photographs.
But these pictures he took himself. And it is they, unpreten-
tious makeshifts meant for internal use, that gave his name
a place in history, while as a painter he is forgotten. Admittedly a number of his studies lead even deeper into the new
technology than this series of portraits: anonymous images,
not posed subjects. Such figures had long been known in
painting. Where the painting remained in the possession of
a particular family, now and then someone would ask after
the originals. But after two or three generations this interest fades; the pictures, if they last, do so only as testimony
to the art of the painter. With photography, however, we
encounter something new and strange: in Hill's Newhaven
fishwife, her eyes cast down in such indolent, seductive
modesty, there remains something that goes beyond testimony to the photographer's art, something that cannot be
silenced, that fills you with an unruly desire to know what
her name was, the woman who was alive there, who even
now is still real and will never consent to be wholly absorbed
in art. 'And I ask: how did the beauty of that hair, those
eyes, beguile our forebears: how did that mouth kiss, to
which desire curls up senseless as smoke without fire.' Or
you turn up the picture of Dauthendey the photographer,
the father of the poet, from the time of his engagement to
that woman whom he then found one day, shortly after the
birth of her sixth child, lying in the bedroom of his Moscow

house with her arteries severed. Here she can be seen with
him, he seems to be holding her; but her gaze passes him by,
absorbed in an ominous distance. Immerse yourself in such
a picture long enough and you will recognize how alive the
contradictions are, here too: the most precise technology can
give its products a magical value, such as a painted picture
can never again have for us. No matter how artful the photographer, no matter how carefully posed his subject, the
beholder feels an irresistible urge to search such a picture
for the tiny spark of contingency, of the Here and Now,
with which reality has so to speak seared the subject, to
find the inconspicuous spot where in the immediacy of that
long-forgotten moment the future subsists so eloquently
that we, looking back, may rediscover it. For it is another
nature that speaks to the camera than to the eye: other in the
sense that a space informed by human consciousness gives
way to a space informed by the unconscious. Whereas it is
a commonplace that, for example, we have some idea what
is involved in the act of walking, if only in general terms,
we have no idea at all what happens during the fraction of
a second when a person *steps out*. Photography, with its
devices of slow motion and enlargement, reveals the secret.
It is through photography that we first discover the existence of this optical unconscious, just as we discover the
instinctual unconscious through psychoanalysis. Details of
structure, cellular tissue, with which technology and medi-
cine are normally concerned—all this is in its origins more
native to the camera than the atmospheric landscape or the
soulful portrait. Yet at the same time photography reveals
in this material the physiognomic aspects of visual worlds
which dwell in the smallest things, meaningful yet covert

enough to find a hiding place in waking dreams, but which, enlarged and capable of formulation, make the difference between technology and magic visible as a thoroughly historical variable. Thus Blossfeldt with his astonishing plant photographs[2] reveals the forms of ancient columns in horse willow, a bishop's crosier in the ostrich fern, totem poles in tenfold enlargements of chestnut and maple shoots, and gothic tracery in the fuller's thistle. Hill's subjects, too, were probably not far from the truth when they described 'the phenomenon of photography' as still being 'a great and mysterious experience'; even if for them this was no more than the consciousness of 'standing before a device which in the briefest time could produce a picture of the visible environment that seemed as real and alive as nature itself'. It has been said of Hill's camera that it kept a discreet distance. But his subjects, for their part, are no less reserved; they maintain a certain shyness before the camera, and the watchword of a later photographer from the heyday of the art, 'Don't look at the camera', could be derived from their attitude. But that did not mean the 'they're looking at you' of animals, people and babies, that so distastefully implicates the buyer and to which there is no better counter than the way old Dauthendey talks about daguerrotypes: 'We didn't trust ourselves at first', so he reported, 'to look long at the first pictures he developed. We were abashed by the distinctness of these human images, and believed that the little tiny faces in the picture could see *us*, so powerfully was everyone affected by the unaccustomed clarity and the unaccustomed truth to nature of the first daguerrotypes.'

The first people to be reproduced entered the visual space of photography with their innocence intact, uncompromised by captions. Newspapers were still a luxury item, which people seldom bought, preferring to consult them in the coffee house; photography had not yet become a journalistic tool, and ordinary people had yet to see their names in print. The human countenance had a silence about it in which the gaze rested. In short, the portraiture of this period owes its effect to the absence of contact between actuality and photography. Many of Hill's portraits were made in the Edinburgh Greyfriars cemetery—nothing is more characteristic of this early period than the way his subjects were at home there. And indeed the cemetery itself, in one of Hill's pictures, looks like an interior, a separate closed-off space where the gravestones propped against gable walls rise up from the grass, hollowed out like chimney-pieces, with inscriptions inside instead of flames. But this setting could never have been so effective if it had not been chosen on technical grounds. The low light-sensitivity of the early plates made prolonged exposure outdoors a necessity. This in turn made it desirable to take the subject to some out-of-the-way spot where there was no obstacle to quiet concentration. 'The expressive coherence due to the length of time the subject had to remain still', says Orlik of early photography, 'is the main reason why these photographs, apart from their simplicity, resemble well drawn or painted pictures and produce a more vivid and lasting impression on the beholder than more recent photographs.' The procedure itself caused the subject to focus his life in the moment rather than hurrying on past it; during the considerable period of the exposure, the subject as it were grew into the picture, in the sharpest contrast with appearances in a snap-shot—which is appropriate to that changed environment where, as Kracauer has aptly noted, the split second of the exposure determines 'whether a sportsman becomes so famous that photographers start taking his picture for the illustrated papers'. Everything about these early pictures was built to last; not only the incomparable groups in which people came together—and whose disappearance was surely one of the most telling symptoms of what was happening in society in the second half of the century—but the very creases in people's clothes have an air of permanence. Just consider Schelling's coat; its immortality, too, rests assured; the shape it has borrowed from its wearer is not unworthy of the creases in his face. In short, everything suggests that Bernhard von Brentano was right in his view 'that a photographer of 1850 was on a par with his instrument'—for the first time, and for a long while the last.

To appreciate the full impact made by the daguerrotype in the age of its discovery, one should also bear in mind that entirely new vistas were then being opened up in landscape painting by the most advanced painters. Conscious that in this very area photography had to take over where painting left off, even Arago, in his historical review of the early attempts of Giovanni Battista Porta, explicitly commented: 'As regards the effect produced by the imperfect transparency of our atmosphere (which has been loosely termed "degradation"), not even experienced painters expect the camera obscura'—i.e. the copying of images appearing in it—'to help them to render it accurately.' At the moment when Daguerre succeeded in fixing the images of the camera obscura, the painters parted company on this point with the technician. The real victim of photography, however, was not landscape painting, but the portrait miniature. Things developed so rapidly that by 1840 most of the innumerable miniaturists had already become professional photographers, at first only as a sideline, but before long exclusively. Here the experience of their original livelihood stood them in good stead, and it is not their artistic background so much as their training as craftsmen that we have to thank for the high level of their photographic achievement. This transitional generation disappeared very gradually; indeed, there seems to have been a kind of Biblical blessing on those first photographers: the Nadars, Stelzners, Piersons, Bayards all lived well into their eighties and nineties. In the end, though, businessmen invaded professional photography from every side, and when later on the retouched negative, which was the bad painter's revenge on photography, became ubiquitous, a sharp decline in taste set it. This was the time photograph albums came into vogue. They were most at home in the chilliest spots, on occasional tables or little stands in the drawing room: leather-bound tomes with ugly metal hasps and those gilt-edged pages as thick as your finger, where foolishly draped or corseted figures were displayed: Uncle Alex and Aunt Riekchen, little Trudi when she was still a baby, Papa in his first term at university ... and finally, to make our shame complete, we ourselves: as a parlour Tyrolean, yodelling, waving our hat against a painted snowscape, or as a smartly turned-out sailor, standing leg and trailing leg, as is proper, leaning against a polished door jamb. The accessories used in these portraits, the pedestals and balustrades and little oval tables, are still reminiscent of the period when because of the long exposure time the subjects had to be given supports so that they wouldn't move. And if at first *head-holders* or *knee-braces*

were felt to be sufficient, further impedimenta were soon
added, such as were to be seen in famous paintings and must
therefore be *artistic*. First it was pillars, or curtains. The most
capable started resisting this nonsense as early as the sixties.
As an English trade journal of the time put it, 'in painting
the pillar has some plausibility, but the way it is used in photography is absurd, since it usually stands on a carpet. But
anyone can see that pillars of marble or stone are not erected
on a foundation of carpeting.' This was the period of those
studios, with their draperies and palm trees, their tapestries
and easels, which occupied so ambiguous a place between
execution and representation, between torture chamber and
throne room, and to which an early portrait of Kafka bears
pathetic witness. There the boy stands, perhaps six years
old, dressed up in a humiliatingly tight child's suit overloaded with trimming, in a sort of conservatory landscape.
The background is thick with palm fronds. And as if to make
these upholstered tropics even stuffier and more oppressive,
the subject holds in his left hand an inordinately large broad-
brimmed hat, such as Spaniards wear. He would surely be
lost in this setting were it not for the immensely sad eyes,
which dominate this landscape predestined for them.

This picture in its infinite sadness forms a pendant to
the early photographs in which people did not yet look out
at the world in so excluded and god-forsaken a manner as
this boy. There was an aura about them, an atmospheric
medium, that lent fullness and security to their gaze even
as it penetrated that medium. And once again the technical
equivalent is obvious; it consists in the absolute continuum from brightest light to darkest shadow. Here too we
see in operation the law that new advances are prefigured

in older techniques, for the earlier art of portrait painting had produced the strange flower of the mezzotint before its disappearance. The mezzotint process was of course a technique of reproduction, which was only later combined with the new photographic reproduction. The way light struggles out of darkness in the work of a Hill is reminiscent of mezzotint: Orlik talks about the 'coherent illumination' brought about by the long exposure times, which 'gives these early photographs their greatness'. And among the invention's contemporaries, Delaroche already noted the 'unprecedented and exquisite' general impression, 'in which nothing disturbs the tranquillity of the composition'. So much for the technical considerations behind the atmospheric appearances. Many group photos in particular still preserve an air of animated conviviality for a brief space on the plate, before being ruined by the print. It was this atmosphere that was sometimes captured with delicacy and depth by the now old-fashioned oval frame. That is why it would be a misreading of these incunabula of photography to make too much of their *artistic perfection* or their *taste*. These pictures were made in rooms where every client was confronted, in the photographer, with a technician of the latest school; whereas the photographer was confronted, in every client, with a member of a rising class equipped with an aura that had seeped into the very folds of the man's frock coat or floppy cravat. For that aura was by no means the mere product of a primitive camera. Rather, in that early period subject and technique were as exactly congruent as they become incongruent in the period of decline that immediately followed. For soon advances in optics made instruments available that put darkness entirely to flight and recorded appearances as faithfully as any mirror. After 1880, though, photographers made it their business to simulate with all the arts of retouching, especially the so-called rubber print, the aura which had been banished from the picture with the rout of darkness through faster lenses, exactly as it was banished from reality by the deepening degeneration of the imperialist bourgeoisie. Thus, especially in *Jugendstil*, a penumbral tone, interrupted by artificial highlights, came into vogue; notwithstanding this fashionable twilight, however, a pose was more and more clearly in evidence, whose rigidity betrayed the impotence of that generation in the face of technical progress.

And yet, what is again and again decisive for photography is the photographer's attitude to his techniques. Camille Recht has found an apt metaphor: 'The violinist', he says, 'must first produce the note, must seek it out, find it in an instant; the pianist strikes the key and the note rings out. The painter and the photographer both have an instrument at their disposal. Drawing and colouring, for the painter, correspond to the violinist's production of sound; the photographer, like the pianist, has the advantage of a mechanical device that is subject to restrictive laws, while the violinist is under no such restraint. No Paderewski will ever reap the fame, ever cast the almost fabulous spell, that Paganini did.' There is, however—to continue the metaphor—a Busoni of photography, and that is Atget. Both were virtuosi, but at the same time precursors. The combination of unparalleled absorption in their work and extreme precision is common to both. There was even a facial resemblance. Atget was an actor who, disgusted with the profession, wiped off the mask and then set about removing the make-up from reality too.

He lived in Paris poor and unknown, selling his pictures for a trifle to photographic enthusiasts scarcely less eccentric than himself; he died recently, leaving behind an *oeuvre* of more than 4,000 pictures. Berenice Abbot from New York has gathered these together, and a selection has just appeared in an exceptionally beautiful volume published by Camille Recht.[3] The contemporary journals 'knew nothing of the man who for the most part hawked his pictures round the studios, sold them off for next to nothing, often for the price of one of those picture postcards which, around 1900, showed such pretty town views, bathed in midnight blue, complete with touched-up moon. He reached the pole of utmost mastery; but with the bitter mastery of a great craftsman who always lives in the shadows, he neglected to plant his flag there. Therefore many are able to flatter themselves that they have discovered the pole, when Atget was there before them.' Indeed, Atget's Paris photos are the forerunners of surrealist photography; an advance party of the only really broad column surrealism managed to set in motion. He was the first to disinfect the stifling atmosphere generated by conventional portrait photography in the age of decline. He cleanses this atmosphere, indeed he dispels it altogether: he initiates the emancipation of object from aura which is the most signal achievement of the latest school of photography. When avant-garde periodicals like *Bifur* or *Variété* publish pictures captioned *Westminster*, *Lille*, *Antwerp* or *Breslau* but showing only details, here a piece of balustrade, there a tree-top whose bare branches criss-cross a gas lamp, or a gable wall, or a lamp-post with a lifebuoy bearing the name of the town—this is nothing but a literary refinement of themes that Atget discovered. He looked for what was unremarked, forgotten, cast adrift, and thus such pictures too work against the exotic, romantically sonorous names of the cities; they pump the aura out of reality like water from a sinking ship. What is aura, actually? A strange weave of space and time: the unique appearance or semblance of distance, no matter how close the object may be. While resting on a summer's noon, to trace a range of mountains on the horizon, or a branch that throws its shadow on the observer, until the moment or the hour become part of their appearance—that is what it means to breathe the aura of those mountains, that branch. Now, to bring things *closer* to us, or rather to the masses, is just as passionate an inclination in our day as the overcoming of whatever is unique in every situation by means of its reproduction. Every day the need to possess the object in close-up in the form of a picture, or rather a copy, becomes more imperative. And the difference between the copy, which illustrated papers and newsreels keep in readiness, and the picture is unmistakable. Uniqueness and duration are as intimately conjoined in the latter as are transience and reproducibility in the former. The stripping bare of the object, the destruction of the aura, is the mark of a perception whose sense of the sameness of things has grown to the point where even the singular, the unique, is divested of its uniqueness—by means of its reproduction. Atget almost always passed by the 'great sights and the so-called landmarks'; what he did not pass by was a long row of boot lasts; or the Paris courtyards, where from night to morning the hand-carts stand in serried ranks; or the tables after people have finished eating and left, the dishes not yet cleared away—as they exist in their hundreds of thousands at the same hour; or the brothel at Rue ... No 5, whose street number appears, gigantic, at four different places on the building's façade. Remarkably, however, almost all these pictures are empty. Empty the Porte d'Arceuil by the Fortifications, empty the triumphal steps, empty the courtyards, empty, as it should be, the Place du Tertre. They are not lonely, merely without mood; the city in these pictures looks cleared out, like a lodging that has not yet found a new tenant. It is in these achievements that surrealist photography sets the scene for a salutary estrangement between man and his surroundings. It gives free play to the politically educated eye, under whose gaze all intimacies are sacrificed to the illumination of detail.

It is obvious that this new way of seeing stands to gain least in an area where there was the greatest self-indulgence: commercial portrait photography. On the other hand, to do without people is for photography the most impossible of renunciations. And anyone who did not know it was taught by the best of the Russian films that milieu and landscape, too, reveal themselves most readily to those photographers who succeed in capturing their anonymous physiognomy, as it were presenting them at face value. Whether this is possible, however, depends very much on the subject. The generation that was not obsessed with going down to posterity in photographs, rather shyly drawing back into their private space in the face of such proceedings—the way Schopenhauer withdrew into the depths of his chair in the Frankfurt picture, taken about 1850—for that very reason allowed that space, the space where they lived, to get onto the plate with them. That generation did not pass on its virtues. So the Russian feature film was the first opportunity in decades to put people before the camera who had no use for their photographs. And immediately the human face appeared on film with new and immeasurable significance. But it was no longer a portrait. What was it? It is the outstanding service of a German photographer to have answered this question. August Sander[4] has compiled a series of faces that is in no way inferior to the tremendous physiognomic gallery mounted by an Eisenstein or a Pudovkin, and he has done it from a scientific viewpoint. 'His complete work comprises seven groups which correspond to the existing social order, and is to be published in some 45 folios containing 12 photographs each.' So far we have a sample volume containing 60 reproductions, which offer inexhaustible material for study. 'Sander starts off with the peasant, the earth-bound man, takes the observer through every social stratum and every walk of life up to the highest representatives of civilization, and then back down all the way to the idiot.' The author did not approach this enormous undertaking as a scholar, or with the advice of ethnographers and sociologists, but, as the publisher says, 'from direct observation'. It was assuredly a very impartial, indeed bold sort of observation, but delicate too, very much in the spirit of Goethe's remark: 'There is a delicate empiricism which so intimately involves itself with the object that it becomes true theory.' So it was quite in order for an observer like Döblin to have hit on precisely the scientific aspects of this work, commenting: 'Just as there is comparative anatomy, which helps us to understand the nature and history of organs, so this photographer is doing comparative photography, adopting a scientific standpoint superior to the photographer of detail.' It would be a pity if economic considerations should prevent the continuing publication of this extraordinary body of work. Apart from this basic encouragement, there is a more specific incentive one might offer the publisher. Work like Sander's could overnight assume unlooked-for topicality. Sudden shifts of power such as are now overdue in our society can make the ability to read facial types a matter of vital importance. Whether one is of the left or right, one will have to get used to being looked at in terms of one's provenance. And one will have to look at others the same way. Sander's work is more than a picture book. It is a training manual.

'In our age there is no work of art that is looked at so closely as a photograph of oneself, one's closest relatives and friends, one's sweetheart', wrote Lichtwark back in 1907, thereby moving the inquiry out of the realm of aesthetic distinctions into that of social functions. Only from this vantage point can it be carried further. It is indeed significant that the debate has raged most fiercely around the aesthetics of *photography as art*, whereas the far less questionable social fact of art *as photography* was given scarcely a glance. And yet the impact of the photographic reproduction of art works is of very much greater importance for the function of art than the greater or lesser artistry of a photography that regards all experience as fair game for the camera. The amateur who returns home with great piles of artistic shots is in fact no more appealing a figure than the hunter who comes back with quantities of game of no use to anyone but the dealer. And the day does indeed seem to be at hand when there will be more illustrated magazines than game merchants. So much for the *snapshot*. But the emphasis changes completely if we turn from photography-as-art to art-as-photography. Everyone will have noticed how much easier it is to get hold of a picture, more particularly a piece of sculpture, not to mention architecture, in a photograph than in reality. It is all too tempting to blame this squarely on the decline of artistic appreciation, on a failure of contemporary sensibility. But one is brought up short by the way the understanding of great works was transformed at about the same time the techniques of reproduction were being developed. They can no longer be regarded as the work of individuals; they have become a collective creation, a corpus so vast it can be assimilated only through miniaturization. In the final analysis, mechanical reproduction is a technique of diminution that helps men to achieve a control over works of art without whose aid they could no longer be used.

If one thing typifies present-day relations between art and photography, it is the unresolved tension between the two introduced by the photography of works of art. Many of those who, as photographers, determine the present face of this technology started out as painters. They turned their back on painting after attempts to bring its expressive resources into a living and unequivocal relationship with modern life. The keener their feel for the temper of the times, the more problematic their starting point became for them. For once again, as eighty years before, photography was taking over from painting. 'The creative potential of the new', says Moholy-Nagy, 'is for the most part slowly revealed through old forms, old instruments and areas of design that in their essence have already been superseded by the new, but which under pressure from the new as it takes shape are driven to a euphoric efflorescence. Thus, for example, futurist (structural) painting brought forth the clearly defined *Problematik* of the simultaneity of motion, the representation of the instant, which was later to destroy it—and this at a time when film was already known but far from being understood … Similarly, some of the painters (neoclassicists and verists) today using representational-objective methods can be regarded—with caution—as forerunners of a new representational optical form which will soon be making use only of mechanical, technical methods.' And Tristan Tzara, 1922: 'When everything that called itself art was stricken with palsy, the photographer switched on his thousand candle-power lamp and gradually the light-sensitive paper absorbed the darkness of a few everyday objects. He had discovered what could be done by a pure and sensitive flash of light that was more important than all the constellations arranged for the eye's pleasure.' The photographers who went over from figurative art to photography not on opportunistic grounds, not by chance, not out of sheer laziness, today constitute the avant-garde among their colleagues, because they are to some extent protected by their background against the greatest danger facing photography today, the touch of the commercial artist. 'Photography as art', says Sasha Stone, 'is a very dangerous field.'

Where photography takes itself out of context, severing the connections illustrated by Sander, Blossfeldt or Germaine Krull, where it frees itself from physiognomic, political and scientific interest, then it becomes *creative*. The lens now looks for interesting juxtapositions; photography turns into a sort of arty journalism. 'The spirit that overcomes mechanics translates exact findings into parables of life.' The more far-reaching the crisis of the present social order, the more rigidly its individual components are locked together in their death struggle, the more has the creative—in its deepest essence a sport, by contradiction out of imitation—become a fetish, whose lineaments live only in the fitful illumination of changing fashion. The creative in photography is its capitulation to fashion. *The world is beautiful*—that is its watchword. Therein is unmasked the posture of a photography that can endow any soup can with cosmic significance but cannot grasp a single one of the human connexions in which it exists, even where most far-fetched subjects are more concerned with saleability than with insight. But because the true face of this kind of photographic creativity is the advertisement or association, its logical counterpart is the act of unmasking or construction. As Brecht says: 'the situation is complicated by the fact that less than ever does the mere reflection of reality reveal anything about reality. A photograph of the Krupp works or the A.E.G. tells us next to nothing about these institutions. Actual reality has slipped into the functional. The reification of human relations—the factory, say— means that they are no longer explicit. So something must in fact be *built up*, something artificial, posed.' We owe it to the surrealists that they trained the pioneers of such a constructivist photography. A further stage in this contest between creative and constructivist photography is typified by the Russian film. It is not too much to say that the great achievements of the Russian directors were only possible in a country where photography does not set out to charm or persuade, but to experiment and instruct. In this sense, and in this only, there is still some meaning in the grandiloquent salute offered to photography in 1855 by the uncouth painter of ideas, Antoine Wiertz. 'For some years now the glory of our age has been a machine which daily amazes the mind and startles the eye. Before another century is out, this machine will be the brush, the palette, the colours, the craft, the experience, the patience, the dexterity, the sureness of touch, the atmosphere, the lustre, the exemplar, the perfection, the very essence of painting ... Let no one suppose that daguerrotype photography will be the death of art ... When the daguerrotype, that infant prodigy, has grown to its full stature, when all its art and its strength have been revealed, then will Genius seize it by the scruff of the neck and shout: Come with me, you are mine now! We shall work together!' How sober, indeed pessimistic by contrast are the words in which Baudelaire announced the new technology to his readers, two years later, in the *Salon of 1857.* Like the preceding quotation, they can be read today only with a subtle shift of emphasis. But as a counterpart to the above, they still make sense as a violent reaction to the encroachments of artistic photography. 'In these sorry days a new industry has arisen that has done not a little to strengthen the asinine belief ... that art is and can be nothing other than the accurate reflection of nature ... A vengeful god has hearkened to the voice of this multitude. Daguerre is his Messiah.' And: 'If photography is permitted to supplement some of art's functions, they will forthwith be usurped and corrupted by it, thanks to photography's natural alliance with the mob. It must therefore revert to its proper duty, which is to serve as the handmaiden of science and the arts.'

One thing, however, both Wiertz and Baudelaire failed to grasp: the lessons inherent in the authenticity of the photograph. These cannot be forever circumvented by a commentary whose clichés merely establish verbal associations in the viewer. The camera is getting smaller and smaller, ever readier to capture fleeting and secret moments whose images paralyse the associative mechanisms in the beholder. This is where the caption comes in, whereby photography turns all life's relationships into literature, and without which all constructivist photography must remain arrested in the approximate. Not for nothing have Atget's photographs been likened to those of the scene of a crime. But is not every square inch of our cities the scene of a crime? Every passer-by a culprit? Is it not the task of the photographer —descendant of the augurs and haruspices—to reveal guilt and to point out the guilty in his pictures? 'The illiteracy of the future', someone has said, 'will be ignorance not of reading or writing, but of photography.' But must not a photographer who cannot read his own pictures be no less accounted an illiterate? Will not the caption become the most important part of the photograph? Such are the questions in which the interval of ninety years that separate us from the age of the daguerrotype discharges its historical tension. It is in the illumination of these sparks that the first photographs emerge, beautiful and unapproachable, from the darkness of our grandfathers' day.

1931

Karl Kraus

Dedicated to Gustav Glück

I. Cosmic Man

> How noisy everything grows.
> —*Words in Verse II*

In old engravings there is a messenger who rushes toward us crying aloud, his hair on end, brandishing a sheet of paper in his hands, a sheet full of war and pestilence, of cries of murder and pain, of danger from fire and flood, spreading everywhere the 'latest news'. News in this sense, in the sense that the word has in Shakespeare, is disseminated by *Die Fackel* [*The Torch*].[1] Full of betrayal, earthquakes, poison, and fire from the *mundus intelligibilis*. The hatred with which it pursues the tribe of journalists that swarms into infinity is not only a moral but a vital one, such as is hurled by an ancestor upon a race of degenerate and dwarfish rascals that has sprung from his seed. The very term 'public opinion' outrages him. Opinions are a private matter. The public has an interest only in judgments. Either it is a judging public, or it is none. But it is precisely the purpose of the public opinion generated by the press to make the public incapable of judging, to insinuate into it the attitude of someone irresponsible, uninformed. Indeed, what is even the most precise information in the daily newspapers in comparison to the hair-raising meticulousness observed by *Die Fackel* in the presentation of legal, linguistic, and political facts? *Die Fackel* need not trouble itself about public opinion, for the blood-steeped novelties of this 'newspaper' demand a passing of judgment. And on nothing more impetuously, urgently, than on the press itself.

A hatred such as that which Kraus has heaped on journalists can never be founded simply on what they do—however obnoxious this may be; this hatred must have its reason in their very nature, whether it be antithetical or akin to his own. In fact, it is both. His most recent portrait characterizes the journalist in the first sentence as 'a person who has little interest either in himself and his own existence, or in the mere existence of things, but who feels things only in their relationships, above all where these meet in events—and only in this moment become united, substantial, and alive'. What we have in this sentence is nothing other than the negative of an image of Kraus. Indeed, who could have shown a more burning interest in himself and his own existence than the writer who is never finished with this subject; who a more attentive concern for the mere existence of things, their origin; whom does that coincidence of the event with the date, the witness, or the camera cast into deeper despair than him? In the end he brought together all his energies in the struggle against the empty phrase, which is the linguistic expression of the despotism with which, in journalism, topicality sets up its dominion over things.

This side of his struggle against the press is illuminated most vividly by the life's work of his comrade-in-arms, Adolf Loos. Loos found his providential adversaries in the arts-and-crafts mongers and architects who, in the ambit of the 'Vienna Workshops', were striving to give birth to a new art industry. He sent out his rallying cry in numerous essays, particularly, in its enduring formulation, in the article 'Ornamentation and Crime', which appeared in 1908 in the *Frankfurter Zeitung*. The lightning flash ignited by this essay described a curiously zigzag course. 'On reading the words with which Goethe censures the way the Philistine, and thus many an art connoisseur, run their fingers over engravings and reliefs, the revelation came to him that what may be touched cannot be a work of art, and that a work of art must be out of reach.' It was therefore Loos's first concern to separate the work of art from the article of use, as it was that of Kraus to keep apart information and the work of art. The hack journalist is in his heart at one with the ornamentalist. Kraus did not tire of denouncing Heine as an ornamentalist, as one who blurred the boundary between journalism and literature, as the creator of the *feuilleton* in poetry and prose; indeed, he later placed even Nietzsche beside Heine as the betrayer of the aphorism to the impression. 'It is my opinion', he said of the latter, 'that to the mixture of elements ... in the decomposing European style of the last half century, he added psychology, and that the new level of language that he created is the level of essayism, as Heine's was that of feuilletonism.' Both forms appear as symptoms of the chronic sickness of which all attitudes and standpoints merely mark the temperature curve: inauthenticity. It is from the unmasking of the inauthentic that this battle against the press arose. 'Who was it that brought into the world this great excuse: I can do what I am not?'

The empty phrase. It, however, is an abortion of technology. 'The newspaper industry, like a factory, demands separate areas for working and selling. At certain times of day—twice, three times in the bigger newspapers—a particular quantity of work has to have been procured and prepared for the machine. And not from just any material: everything that has happened in the meantime, anywhere, in any region of life, politics, economics, art, etc., must by now have been reached and journalistically processed.' Or, as Kraus so splendidly sums it up: 'He ought to throw light on the way in which technology, while unable to coin new platitudes, leaves the spirit of mankind in the state of being unable to do without old ones. In this duality of a changed life dragging on in unchanged forms, the world's ills grow and prosper.' In these words Kraus deftly tied the knot binding technology to the empty phrase. True, its untying would have to follow a different pattern, journalism being clearly seen as the expression of the changed function of language in the world of high capitalism. The empty phrase of the kind so relentlessly pursued by Kraus is the label that makes a thought marketable, the way flowery language, as ornament, gives it value for the connoisseur. But for this very reason the liberation of language has become identical with that of the empty phrase—its transformation from reproduction to productive instrument. *Die Fackel* itself contains models of this, even if not the theory: its formulae are of the kind that tie up, never that untie. The combination of biblical magniloquence with stiff-necked fixation on the indecencies of Viennese life—that is its way of approaching

phenomena. It is not content to call on the world as witness
to the misdemeanours of a cashier; it must summon the
dead from their graves. Rightly so, For the shabby, obtrusive abundance of these Viennese coffee-houses, press, and
society scandals is only a minor manifestation of a foreknowledge that then, more swiftly than any could perceive,
suddenly arrived at its true and original subject; two months
after the outbreak of war, he called this subject by its name
in the speech 'In This Great Age', with which all the demons
that had populated this possessed man passed into the herd
of the swine who were his contemporaries.

'In these great times, which I knew when they were small,
which will again be small if they still have time, and which,
because in the field of organic growth such transformations
are not possible, we prefer to address as fat times and truly
also as hard times; in these times, when precisely what is
happening could not be imagined, and when what must
happen can no longer be *imagined*, and if it could it would
not happen; in these grave times that have laughed themselves to death at the possibility of growing serious and,
overtaken by their own tragedy, long for distraction and
then, catching themselves in the act, seek words; in these
loud times, booming with the fearful symphony of deeds
that engender reports, and of reports that bear the blame for
deeds; in these unspeakable times, you can expect no word
of my own from me. None except this, which just preserves
silence from misinterpretation. Too deeply am I awed by
the unalterable, is language subordinate to misfortune. In
the empires bereft of imagination, where man is dying of
spiritual starvation while not feeling spiritual hunger, where
pens are dipped in blood and swords in ink, that which is

not thought must be done, but that which is only thought is inexpressible. Expect from me no word of my own. Nor should I be capable of saying anything new; for in the room where someone writes the noise is so great, and whether it comes from animals, from children, or merely from mortars shall not be decided now. He who addresses deeds violates both word and deed and is twice despicable. This profession is not extinct. Those who now have nothing to say because it is the turn of deeds to speak, talk on. Let him who has something to say step forward and be silent!'

Everything Kraus wrote is like that: a silence turned inside out, a silence that catches the storm of events in its black folds, billows, its livid lining turned outward. Notwithstanding their abundance, each of the instances of this silence seems to have broken upon it with the suddenness of a gust of wind. Immediately, a precise apparatus of control is brought into play: through a meshing of oral and written forms the polemical possibilities of every situation are totally exhausted. With what precautions this is surrounded can be seen from the barbed wire of editorial pronouncements that encircles each edition of *Die Fackel*, as from the razor-sharp definitions and provisos in the programmes and lectures accompanying his readings from his own work. The trinity of silence, knowledge, and alertness constitutes the figure of Kraus the polemicist. His silence is a dam before which the reflecting basin of his knowledge is constantly deepened. His alertness permits no one to ask it questions, forever unwilling to conform to principles proffered to it. Its first principle is, rather, to dismantle the situation, to discover the true question the situation poses, and to present this in place of any other to his opponents. If in Johann Peter

Hebel we find, developed to the utmost, the constructive, creative side of tact, in Kraus we see its most destructive and critical face. But for both, tact is moral alertness—Stössl calls it 'conviction refined into dialectics'—and the expression of an unknown convention more important than the acknowledged one. Kraus lived in a world in which the most shameful act was still the *faux pas*; he distinguishes between degrees of the monstrous, and does so precisely because his criterion is never that of bourgeois respectability, which once above the threshold of trivial misdemeanour becomes so quickly short of breath that it can form no conception of villainy on a world-historical scale.

Kraus knew this criterion from the first, and moreover there is no other criterion for true tact. It is a theological criterion. For tact is now—as narrow minds imagine it—the gift of allotting to each, on consideration of all relationships, what is socially befitting. On the contrary, tact is the capacity to treat social relationships, though not departing from them, as natural, even as paradisiac relationships, and so not only to approach the king as if he had been born with the crown on his brow, but the lackey like an Adam in livery. Hebel possessed this *noblesse* in his priestly bearing, Kraus in armour. His concept of creation contains the theological inheritance of speculations that last possessed contemporary validity for the whole of Europe in the seventeenth century. At the theological core of this concept, however, a transformation has taken place that has caused it, quite without constraint, to coincide with the cosmopolitan credo of Austrian worldliness, which made creation into a church in which nothing remained to recall the rite except an occasional whiff of incense in the mists. Stifter gave this creed its most authentic stamp, and his echo is heard wherever Kraus concerns himself with animals, plants, children.

'The stirring of the air,' Stifter writes, 'the rippling of water, the growing of corn, the tossing of the sea, the verdure of the earth, the shining of the sky, the twinkling of the stars I hold great: the thunderstorm approaching in splendour, the lightning flash that cleaves houses, the storm driving the surf, the mountains spewing fire, the earthquake laying waste to countries, I do not hold greater than the former phenomena; indeed, I believe them smaller, because they are only effects of far higher laws. … When man was in his infancy, his spiritual eye not yet touched by science, he was seized by what was close at hand and obtrusive, and was moved to fear and admiration; but when his mind was opened, when his gaze began to be directed at the connections between things particular phenomena sank from sight and the law rose even higher, miracles ceased, and wonder increased…. Just as in nature the general laws act silently and incessantly, and conspicuous events are only single manifestations of these laws, so the moral law acts silently, animating the soul through the infinite intercourse of human beings, and the miracles of the moment when deeds are performed are only small signs of this general power.' Tacitly, in these famous sentences, the holy has given place to the modest yet questionable concept of law. But this nature of Stifter's and his moral universe are transparent enough to escape any confusion with Kant, and to be still recognizable in their core as creation. This insolently secularized thunder and lightning, storms, surf, and earthquakes—cosmic man has won them back for creation by making them its world-historical answer to the criminal existence of men. Only the span between Creation and the Last Judgment here finds no redemptive fulfilment, let alone a historical resolution. For as the landscape of Austria fills unbroken the captivating expanse of Stifter's prose, so for him, Kraus, the terrible years of his life are not history, but nature, a river condemned to meander through a landscape of hell. It is a landscape in which every day fifty thousand tree trunks are felled for sixty newspapers. Kraus imparted this information under the title 'The End'. For that mankind is losing the fight against the creaturely world is to him just as certain as that technology, once deployed against creation, will not stop short of its master, either. His defeatism is of a supranational, that is, planetary kind, and history for him is merely the wilderness dividing his face from creation, whose last act is world conflagration. As a deserter to the camp of animal creation—so he measures out this wilderness. 'And only the animal that is conquered by humanity is the hero of life': never was Adalbert Stifter's patriarchal credo given so lugubrious and heraldic a formulation.

It is in the name of animal creation that Kraus again and again bends toward the animal and toward 'the heart of all hearts, that of the dog', for him creation's true mirror virtue, in which fidelity, purity, gratitude smile from times lost and remote. How lamentable that people usurp its place! These are his followers. More numerously and eagerly than about their master they throng with unlovely sniffings about the mortally wounded opponent. Certainly the dog is not for nothing the emblematic beast of this author: the dog, the ideal example of the follower, who is nothing except devoted creaturely life. And the more personal and unfounded this devotion, the better. Kraus is right to put it to the hardest test. But if anything makes plain what is infinitely questionable in these creatures, it is that they are recruited solely from those whom Kraus himself first called intellectually to life, whom he conceived and convinced in one and the same act. His word can be decisive only for those whom it did not beget.

It is entirely logical when the impoverished, reduced human being of our days, the contemporary, can only seek sanctuary in the temple of living things in that most withered form, as a private individual. How much renunciation and how much irony lie in the curious struggle for the 'nerves', the last root fibres of the Viennese to which Kraus could still find Mother Earth adhering. 'Kraus', writes Robert Scheu, 'had discovered a great subject that had never before set in motion the pen of a publicist: the rights of the nerves. He found that they were just as worthy an object of impassioned defence as were property, house and home, party, and constitution. He became the advocate of the nerves and took up the fight against the petty, everyday imitations, but the subject grew under his hands, became the problem of private life. To defend this against police, press, morality, and concepts, finally against neighbours in every form, constantly to find new enemies, became his profession.' Here, if anywhere, is manifest the strange interplay between reactionary theory and revolutionary practice that is met everywhere in Kraus. Indeed, to secure private life against morality and concepts in a society that perpetrates the political radioscopy of sexuality and family, of economic and physical existence, in a society that is in the process of building houses with glass walls, and patios extending far into the drawing rooms that are no longer drawing rooms—such a watchword would be the most reactionary of all were not the private life that Kraus had made it his business to defend precisely that which, unlike the bourgeois form, is in strict accordance with this social upheaval; in other words, the private life that is dismantling itself, openly shaping itself, that of the poor, from whose ranks came Peter Altenberg, the agitator, and Adolf Loos. In this fight—and only in it—his followers also have their use, since it is they who most sublimely ignore the anonymity with which the satirist has tried to surround his private existence, and nothing holds them in check except Kraus's decision to step in person before his threshold and pay homage to the ruins in which he is a 'private individual'.

As decisively as he makes his own existence a public issue when the fight demands it, he has always just as ruthlessly opposed the distinction between personal and objective criticism with the aid of which polemics are discredited, and which is a chief instrument of corruption in our literary and political affairs. That Kraus attacks people less for what they are than for what they do, more for what they say than for what they write, and least of all for their books, is the precondition of his polemical authority, which is able to lift the intellectual universe of an author—all the more surely the more worthless it is, in confidence of a truly prestabilized, reconciling harmony—whole and intact from a single fragment of sentence, a single word, a single intonation. But the coincidence of personal and objective elements not only in his opponents but above all in himself is best demonstrated by the fact that he never puts forward an opinion. For opinion is false objectivity that can be separated from the person and incorporated in the circulation of commodities.

Kraus never offered an argument that had not engaged his whole person. Thus he embodies the secret of authority: never to disappoint. Authority has no other end than this: it dies or disappoints. It is not in the last undermined by what others must avoid: its own despotism, injustice, inconsistency. On the contrary, it would be disappointing to observe how it arrived at its pronouncements—by fairness, for example, or even self-consistency. 'For the man,' Kraus once said, 'being right is not an erotic matter, and he gladly prefers others' being right to his being wrong.' To prove his manhood in this way is denied to Kraus; his existence demands that at most the self-righteousness of others is opposed to his wrongness, and how right he then is to cling to this. 'Many will be right one day. But it will be a rightness resulting from my wrongness today.' That is the language of true authority. Insight into its operations can discover only one thing: that it is binding, mercilessly binding toward itself in the same degree as toward others; that it does not tire of trembling before itself, though never before others; that it never does enough to satisfy itself, to fulfil its responsibility toward itself, and that this sense of responsibility never allows him to accept arguments derived from his private constitution or even from the limits of human capacity, but always only from the matter at hand, however unjust, from a private point of view, it may be.

The characteristic of such unlimited authority has for all time been the union of legislative and executive power. But it was never a more intimate union than in the theory of language. This is therefore the most decisive expression of Kraus's authority. Incognito like Haroun al-Rashid, he passes by night among the sentence constructions of the journals, and, from behind the petrified facades of phrases, he peers into the interior, discovers in the orgies of 'black magic' the violation, the martyrdom of words: 'Is the press a messenger? No: the event. Is it speech? No: life. It not only claims that the true events are its news of events, but it also brings about a sinister identification that constantly creates the illusion that deeds are reported before they are carried out, and frequently also the possibility of a situation, which in any case exists, that while war correspondents are not allowed to witness events, soldiers become reporters. I therefore welcome the charge that all my life I have overestimated the press. It is not a servant—how could a servant demand and receive so much—it is the event. Once again the instrument has run away with us. We have placed the person who is supposed to report outbreaks of fire, and who ought doubtless to play the most subordinate role in the state, in power over the world, over fire and over the house, over fact and over our fantasy.' Authority and word against corruption and magic—these are the catchwords distributed in this struggle. It is not idle to prognosticate its outcome. No one, Kraus least of all, can leave the utopia of an 'objective' newspaper, the chimera of an 'impartial transmission of news', to its own devices. The newspaper is an instrument of power. It can derive its value only from the character of the power it serves; not only in what it represents, but also in what it does, it is the expression of this power. If, however, high capitalism defiles not only the ends but also the means of journalism, then a new blossoming of paradisiac, cosmic humanity can no more be expected of a power that defeats it than a second blooming of the language of Goethe or Claudius. From that now prevailing it will distinguish itself first of all by putting out of circulation ideals that debase the former. This is enough to give a measure of how little Kraus would have to win or lose in such a struggle, of how unerringly *Die Fackel* would illuminate it. To the ever-repeated sensations with which the daily press serves its public he opposes the eternally fresh 'news' of the history of creation: the eternally renewed, the uninterrupted lament.

II. Demon

> Have I slept? I am just falling asleep.
> —*Words in Verse IV*

It is deeply rooted in Kraus's nature, and it is the stigma of every debate concerning him, that all apologetic arguments miss their mark. The great work of Leopold Liegler springs from an apologetic posture. To certify Kraus as an 'ethical personality' is his first objective. That cannot be done. The dark background from which his image detaches itself is not formed by his contemporaries, but is the primeval world or the world of the demon. The light of the first day falls on him—thus he emerges from this darkness. But not in all parts; others remain that are more deeply immersed in it than one suspects. An eye that cannot adjust to this darkness will never perceive the outline of this figure. On it will be wasted all the gestures that Kraus tirelessly makes in his unconquerable need to be perceived. For, as in the fairy tale, the demon in Kraus has made vanity the expression of his being. The demon's solitude, too, is felt by him who gesticulates wildly on the hidden hill: 'Thank God nobody

knows my name is Rumpelstiltskin.' Just as this dancing
demon is never still, in Kraus eccentric reflection is in continuous uproar. 'The patient of his gifts', Viertel called him.
In fact, his capacities are maladies, and over and above the
real ones, his vanity makes him a hypochondriac.

If he does not see his reflection in himself, he sees it
in the adversary at his feet. His polemics have been from
the first the most intimate intermingling of a technique of
unmasking that works with the most advanced means, and
a self-expressive art operating with the most archaic. In this
zone, too, however, ambiguity, the demon, is manifest: self-
expression and unmasking merge in it as self-unmasking.
Kraus has said, 'Anti-Semitism is the mentality ... that means
seriously a tenth part of the jibes that the stock-exchange
wit holds ready for his own blood'; he thereby indicates the
nature of the relationship of his own opponents to himself.
There is no reproach to him, no vilification of his person,
that could not find its most legitimate formulation in his own
writings, in those passages where self-reflection is raised to
self-admiration. He will pay any price to get himself talked
about, and is always justified by the success of these speculations. If style is the power to move freely in the length and
breadth of linguistic thinking without falling into banality, it
is attained chiefly by the cardiac strength of great thoughts,
which drives the blood of language through the capillaries
of syntax into the remotest limbs. While such thoughts are
quite unmistakable in Kraus, the powerful heart of his style is
nevertheless the image he bears of himself in his own breast
and exposes in the most merciless manner. Yes, he is vain.
As such he has been described by Karin Michaelis, crossing a
room with swift, restless bounds to reach the lecture podium.

And if he then offers a sacrifice to his vanity, he would not be the demon that he is were it not finally himself, his life and his suffering, that he exposes with all its wounds, all its nakedness. In this way his style comes into being, and with it the typical reader of *Die Fackel*, for whom in a subordinate clause, in a particle, indeed in a comma, fibres and nerves quiver; from the obscurest and driest fact a piece of his mutilated flesh hangs. Idiosyncrasy as the highest critical organ—that is the hidden logic of this self-reflection and the hellish state known only to a writer for whom every act of gratification becomes at the same time a station of his martyrdom, a state that was experienced, apart from Kraus, by no one as deeply as by Kierkegaard.

'I am', Kraus has said, 'perhaps the first instance of a writer who simultaneously writes and acts his writing', and thus he shows his vanity its most legitimate place: in mime. His mimetic genius, imitating while it glosses, pulling faces in the midst of polemics, is festively unleashed in the readings of dramas whose authors do not for nothing occupy a peculiarly intermediate position: Shakespeare and Nestroy, dramatists and actors; Offenbach, composer and conductor. It is as if the demon in the man sought the tumultuous atmosphere of these dramas, shot through with all the lightning flashes of improvisation, because it alone offered him the thousand opportunities to break out, teasing, tormenting, threatening. In them his own voice tries out the abundance of *personae* inhabiting the performer—*persona*: that through which sound passes—and about his fingertips dart the gestures of the figures populating his voice. But in his polemics, too, mimesis plays a decisive role. He imitates his subjects in order to insert the crowbar of his hate into the finest joints of their posture. This quibbler, probing between syllables, digs out the grubs of humbug. The grubs of venality and garrulity, ignominy and bonhomie, childishness and covetousness, gluttony and dishonesty. Indeed, the exposure of inauthenticity—more difficult than that of wickedness—is here performed behaviouristically. The quotations in *Die Fackel* are more than documentary proof: they are masks stripped off mimetically by the quoter. Admittedly, what emerges in just this connection is how closely the cruelty of the satirist is linked to the ambiguous modesty of the interpreter, which in his public readings is heightened beyond comprehension. To creep—so is termed, not without cause, the lowest kind of flattery; and Kraus creeps into those he impersonates, in order to annihilate them. Has courtesy here become the camouflage of hate, hate the camouflage of courtesy? However that may be, both have attained perfection, the Chinese pitch. 'Torment', of which there is so much talk in Kraus in such opaque allusions, here has its seat. His protests against letters, printed matter, documents are nothing but the defensive reaction of a man who is himself implicated. But what implicates him so deeply is more than the deeds and misdeeds; it is the language of his fellow men. His passion for imitating them is at the same time the expression of and the struggle against this implication, and also the cause and the result of that ever-watchful guilty conscience in which the demon has his habitat.

The economy of his errors and weaknesses—a fantastic edifice, rather than the totality of his gifts—is so delicately and precisely organized that all outward confirmation only disrupts it. Well it may, if this man is to be certified as the 'pattern of a harmoniously and perfectly formed human type', if he is to appear—in a term as absurd stylistically as semantically—as a philanthropist, so that anyone listening to his 'hardness' with 'the ears of the soul' would find the reason for it in compassion. No! This incorruptible, piercing, resolute assurance does not spring from the noble poetic or humane disposition that his followers are so fond of attributing to him. How utterly banal, and at the same time how fundamentally wrong, is their derivation of his hatred from love, when it is obvious how much more elemental are the forces here at work: a humanity that is only an alternation of malice and sophistry, sophistry and malice, a nature that is the highest school of aversion to mankind and a pity that is alive only when mingled with vengeance. 'Oh, had I only been left the choice / to carve the dog or the butcher, / I should have chosen.' Nothing is more perverse than to try to fashion him after the image of what he loves. Rightly, Kraus the 'timeless world-disturber' has been confronted with the 'eternal world-improver' on whom benign glances not infrequently fall.

'When the age laid hands upon itself, he was the hands,' Brecht said. Few insights can stand beside this, and certainly not the comment of his friend Adolf Loos. 'Kraus', he declares, 'stands on the frontier of a new age.' Alas, by no means. For he stands on the threshold of the Last Judgment. As in the most opulent example of baroque altar painting, saints hard-pressed against the frame extend defensive hands toward the breathtakingly foreshortened extremities of the angels, the blessed, and the damned floating before them, so the whole of world history presses in on Kraus in the extremities of a single item of local news, a single phrase, a single advertisement. This is the inheritance that has come down to him from the sermon of Abraham a Santa Clara. Thence the overwhelming immediacy, the ready wit of the wholly uncontemplative moment, and the inversion that allows his will only theoretical, his knowledge only practical expression. Kraus is no historic genius. He does not stand on the frontier of a new age. If he ever turns his back on creation, if he breaks off in lamentation, it is only to file a complaint at the Last Judgment.

Nothing is understood about this man until it has been perceived that, of necessity and without exception, everything—language and fact—falls for him within the sphere of justice. All his fire-eating, sword-swallowing philology in the newspapers pursues justice just as much as language. It is to misunderstand his theory of language to see it as other than a contribution to the linguistic rules of court, the word of someone else in his mouth as other than a *corpus delicti*, and his own as other than a judging word. Kraus knows no system. Each thought has its own cell. But each cell can in an instant, and apparently almost without cause, become a chamber, a legal chamber over which language presides. It has been said of Kraus that he has to 'suppress the Jewishness in himself', even that he 'travels the road from Jewishness to freedom'; nothing better refutes this than the fact that, for him, too, justice and language remain founded in each other. To worship the image of divine justice in language—even in the German language—that is the genuinely Jewish somersault by which he tries to break the spell of the demon. For this is the last official act of this zealot: to place the legal system itself under accusation. And not in a petty-bourgeois revolt against the enslavement of the 'free individual' by 'dead formulae'. Still less in the

posture of those radicals who storm paragraphs without
ever for a moment having taken thought of justice. Kraus
accuses the law in its substance, not in its effect. His charge
is the betrayal of justice by law. More exactly, of the word
by the concept, which derives its existence from the word:
the premeditated murder of imagination, which dies of the
absence of a single letter and for which, in his 'Elegy on the
Death of a Sound', he has sung the most moving lament.
For over jurisdiction, right-saying, stands orthography,
right-spelling, and woe to the former if the latter should
be wanting. Here, too, therefore, he confronts the press;
indeed, in this charmed circle he holds his fondest rendezvous with the lemures. He has seen through law as have few
others. If he nevertheless invokes it, he does so precisely
because his own demon is drawn so powerfully by the abyss
it represents. By the abyss that, not without reason, he finds
most gaping where mind and sexuality meet—in the trial for
sexual offences—and he has sounded in these famous words:
'A sexual trial is the deliberate development from an individual to a general immorality, against which dark background
the proven guilt of the accused stands out luminously.'

Mind and sexuality move in this sphere with a solidarity
whose law is ambiguity. The possession of demonic sexuality is that of the ego that, surrounded by sweet feminine
mirages 'such as the bitter earth does not harbour', enjoys
itself. And no different is the loveless and self-gratifying
trope of possessed mind: the joke. Neither reaches its object,
the ego women no more than the joke words. Decomposition
has taken the place of procreation, stridency that of secrecy.
Now, however, they shimmer in the most winsome nuances:
in the repartee lust comes into its own, and in onanism, the

joke. Kraus portrayed himself as hopelessly subjugated to the demon; in the pandemonium of the age he reserved for himself the most melancholy place in the icy wilderness lit by reflected flames. There he stands on the 'Last Day of Mankind'—the 'grumbler' who has described the preceding days. 'I have taken the tragedy, which is divided into the scenes of decaying humanity, on myself; so that it might be heard by the spirit who takes pity on the victims, even though he may have renounced for all time his connection with a human ear. May he receive the keynote of this age, the echo of my bloodstained madness, through which I share the guilt for these noises. May he accept it as redemption!'

'I share the guilt ...' Because this has the ring of the manifestoes of an intelligentsia seeking to call to mind the memory of an epoch that seemed to be turning away from it, there is something to be said about this guilt feeling in which private and historical consciousness so vividly meet. This guilt will always lead to Expressionism, from which his mature work was nourished by roots that cracked open their soil. The slogans are well known—with what scorn did not Kraus himself register them: '*geballt*', '*gestuft*', '*gesteilt*' [clenched, stepped, steeped], stage sets, sentences, paintings were composed. Unmistakable—and the Expressionists themselves proclaim it—is the influence of early medieval miniatures on the world of their imagination. But anyone who examines their figures—for example, in the Vienna Genesis—is struck by something very mysterious, not only in their wide-open eyes, not only in the unfathomable folds of their garments, but also in their whole expression. As if falling sickness had overtaken them thus, in their running that is always precipitous, they lean toward one another.

'Inclination' may be seen, before all else, as the deep human affect tremulously pervading the world of these miniatures, as it does the manifestoes of that generation of poets. But only one, as it were inwardly curved, aspect is revealed by the front of these figures. The same phenomenon appears quite different to someone who looks at their backs. These backs are piled—in the saints of the adorations, in the servants of the Gethsemane scene, in the witnesses of the entrance into Jerusalem—into terraces of human necks, of human shoulders that, really clenched in steep steps, lead less toward heaven than downward, to and even under the earth. It is impossible to find for their emotional impact an expression that ignores the fact that they could be climbed like heaped rocks or rough-hewn steps. Whatever powers may have fought out their spiritual battles on these shoulders, one of them, from our experience of the condition of the defeated masses immediately after the end of the war, we are able to call by its name. What finally remained of Expressionism, in which an originally human impulse was converted almost without residue into a fashion, was the experience and the name of that nameless power toward which the backs of people bent: guilt. 'That an obedient mass is led into danger not by an unknown will but by an unknown guilt, makes them pitiable', Kraus wrote as early as 1912. As a 'grumbler' he participates in their lot in order to denounce them, and denounces them in order to participate. To meet them through sacrifice he one day threw himself into the arms of the Catholic Church.

In those biting minuets that Kraus whistled to the *chassé-croisé* of Justitia and Venus, the leitmotif—that the Philistine knows nothing of love—is articulated with a sharpness and persistence that have a counterpart only in the corresponding attitude of *décadence*, in the proclamation of art for art's sake. For it was precisely art for art's sake, which for the decadent movement applies to love as well, that linked expertise as closely as possible to craftsmanship, to technique, and allowed poetry to shine at its brightest only against the foil of hack writing, as it made love stand out against perversion. 'Penury can turn every man into a journalist, but not every woman into a prostitute.' In this formulation Kraus betrayed the false bottom of his polemic against journalism. It is much less the philanthropist, the enlightened friend of man and nature, who unleashed this implacable struggle, than the literary expert, artiste, indeed the dandy who has his forebear in Baudelaire. Only Baudelaire hated as Kraus did the satiety of healthy common sense, and the compromise that intellectuals made with it in order to find shelter in journalism. Journalism is betrayal of the literary life, of mind, of the demon. Idle chatter is its true substance, and every *feuilleton* poses anew the insoluble question of the relationship between the forces of stupidity and malice, whose expression is gossip. It is, fundamentally, the complete agreement of two forms of existence—life under the aegis of mere mind or of mere sexuality—in which is founded that solidarity of the man of letters with the whore to which Baudelaire's existence is once again the most inviolable testimony. So Kraus can call by their name the laws of his own craft, entwined with those of sexuality, as he did in the *Wall of China*. The man 'has wrestled a thousand times with the other, who perhaps does not live, but whose victory over him is certain. Not because he has superior qualities but because he is the other, the late-comer, who brings the woman the joy of variety and will triumph as the last in the sequence. But they rub it from her brow like a bad dream, and want to be the first.' Now if language—this we read between the lines—is a woman, how far is the author removed, by an unerring instinct, from those who hasten to be the first with her, how multifariously he forms his thought, which incites her with intuition, rather than slake her with knowledge, how he lets hatred, contempt, malice ensnare one another, how he slows his step and seeks the detour of followership, in order finally to end her joy in variety with the last thrust that Jack holds in readiness for Lulu.

The life of letters is existence under the aegis of mere mind, as prostitution is existence under the aegis of mere sexuality. The demon, however, who leads the whore to the street exiles the man of letters to the courtroom. This is therefore for Kraus the forum that it has always been for the great journalist—for a Carrel, a Paul-Louis Courier, a Lassalle. Evasion of the genuine and demonic function of mere mind, to be a disturber of the peace; abstention from attacking the whore from behind—Kraus sees this double omission as defining the journalist. Robert Scheu rightly perceived that for Kraus prostitution was a natural form, not a social deformation, of female sexuality. Yet it is only the entanglement of sexual with commercial intercourse that constitutes the character of prostitution. It is a natural phenomenon as much in terms of its natural economic aspect, as a manifestation of commodity exchange, as in terms of its natural sexuality. 'Contempt for prostitution? / Harlots worse than thieves? / Learn this: not only is love paid, / but payment, too, wins love!' This ambiguity—this double nature as twofold naturalness—makes prostitution demonic.

But Kraus 'enlists with the power of nature'. That the socio-logical area never becomes transparent to him—no more in his attack on the press than in his defence of prostitution —is connected to this attachment to nature. That to him the fit state of man appears not as the destiny and fulfilment of nature liberated through revolutionary change, but as an element of nature per se, of an archaic nature without history, in its pristine, primeval state, throws uncertain, disquieting reflections even on his idea of freedom and of humanity. It is not removed from the realm of guilt that he has traversed from pole to pole: from mind to sexuality.

In face of this reality, however, to which Kraus exposed himself more harrowingly than any other, the 'pure mind' that his followers worship in the master's activity is revealed as a worthless chimera. For this reason, none of the motives for his development is more important than the continu-ous curbing and checking of mind. *By Night*, he entitles the logbook of this control. For night is the mechanism by which mere mind is converted into mere sexuality, mere sexuality into mere mind, and where these two abstractions hostile to life find rest in recognizing each other. 'I work day and night. So I have a lot of free time. To ask a picture in the room how it likes work, to ask the clock whether it is tired and the night how it has slept.' These questions are sacrificial gifts that he throws to the demon while working. His night, however, is not maternal, or a moonlit, romantic night: it is the hour between sleeping and waking, the night watch, the centrepiece of his threefold solitude: that of the coffeehouse where he is alone with his enemy, of the noc-turnal room where he is alone with his demon, of the lecture hall where he is alone with his work.

III. Monster

> Already the snow falls.
>
> —*Words in Verse III*

Satire is the only legitimate form of regional art. This, however, was not what people meant by calling Kraus a Viennese satirist. Rather, they were attempting to shunt him for as long as possible into this siding where his work could be assimilated in the great store of literary consumer goods. The presentation of Kraus as a satirist can thus yield the deepest insight both into what he is and into his most melancholy caricature. For this reason, he was at pains from the first to distinguish the genuine satirist from the scribblers who make a trade of mockery and in their invectives have little more in mind than giving the public something to laugh about. In contrast, the great type of the satirist never had firmer ground under his feet than amid a generation about to board tanks and put on gas masks, a mankind that has run out of tears but not of laughter. In him civilization prepares to survive, if it must, and communicates with him in the true mystery of satire, which consists in the devouring of the adversary. The satirist is the figure in whom the cannibal was received into civilization. His recollection of his origin is not without filial piety, so that the proposal to eat people has become an essential constituent of his inspiration, from Swift's pertinent project concerning the use of the children of the less wealthy classes, to Léon Bloy's suggestion that landlords of insolvent lodgers be conceded a right to the sale of their flesh. In such directives the great satirists have taken the measure of the humanity of their fellow men. 'Humanity, culture, and freedom are precious things

that cannot be bought dearly enough with blood, understanding, and human dignity'—thus Kraus concludes the
dispute between the cannibal and human rights. It should be
compared to Marx's treatment of the 'Jewish question', in
order to judge how totally this playful reaction of 1909—the
reaction against the classical ideal of humanity—was likely
to become a confession of materialist humanism at the first
opportunity. Admittedly, one would need to understand *Die
Fackel* from the first number on literally word for word to
predict that this aesthetically oriented journalism, without
sacrificing or gaining a single motif, was destined to become
the political prose of 1930. For that it had to thank its partner,
the press, which disposed of humanity in the way to which
Kraus alludes in these words: 'Human rights are the fragile
toy that grownups like to trample on and so will not give
up.' Thus drawing the frontier between the private and
public spheres, which in 1789 was supposed to inaugurate
freedom, became a mockery. 'Through the newspaper,' says
Kierkegaard, 'the distinction between public and private
affairs is abolished in private-public prattle.'

To open a dialectical debate between the public and
private zones that commingle demonically in prattle, to lead
materialist humanity to victory, that is 'the Purpose of the
operetta' that Kraus discovered and in Offenbach[2] raised to
its most expressive level. Just as prattle seals the enslavement
of language with stupidity, so operetta transfigures stupidity
through music. To fail to recognize the beauty of feminine
stupidity was for Kraus always the blackest Philistinism.
Before its radiance the chimeras of progress evaporate.
And in Offenbach's operetta the bourgeois trinity of true,
beautiful, and good is brought together, freshly rehearsed

and with musical accompaniment, in its star turn on the trapeze of stupidity. Nonsense is true, stupidity beautiful, weakness good. This is Offenbach's secret: how in the deep nonsense of public discipline—whether it be of the upper ten thousand, a dance floor, or a military state—the deep sense of private licentiousness opens a dreamy eye. And what as language might have been judicial strictness, renunciation, discrimination, becomes cunning and evasion, obstruction and postponement, as music. Music as the preserver of the moral order? Music as the police of a world of pleasure? Yes, that is the splendour that falls on the old Paris ballrooms, on the Grande Chaumière, the Clôserie des Lilas in his performance of *La Vie Parisienne*. 'And the inimitable duplicity of this music, which simultaneously puts a plus and a minus sign before everything it says, betraying idyll to parody, mockery to lyricism; the abundance of musical devices ready to perform all duties, uniting pain and pleasure—this gift is here developed to its purest pitch.' Anarchy as the only international constitution that is moral and worthy of man becomes the true music of these operettas. The voice of Kraus speaks, rather than sings, this inner music. It whistles bitingly about the peaks of dizzying stupidity, reverberates shatteringly from the abyss of the absurd, and in Frescata's lines it hums, like the wind in the chimney, a requiem to the generation of our grandfathers. Offenbach's work is touched by the pangs of death. It contracts, rids itself of everything superfluous, passes through the dangerous span of this existence and re-emerges saved, more real than before. For where this fickle voice is heard, the lightning flashes of the advertisements and the thunder of the Métro cleave the Paris of the omnibuses and the gas flames. And the work gives him all this in return. For at moments it is transformed into a curtain, and with the wild gestures of a fairground showman with which he accompanies the whole performance, Kraus tears aside this curtain and suddenly reveals the interior of his cabinet of horrors. There they stand: Schober, Bekessy, Kerr, and the other skits, no longer enemies but curiosities, heirlooms from the world of Offenbach or Nestroy, no, older, rarer still, lares of the troglodytes, household gods of stupidity from prehistoric times. Kraus, in his recitals, does not speak the words of Offenbach or Nestroy: they speak from him. And now and then a breathtaking, half-blank, half-glittering whoremonger's glance falls on the crowd before him, inviting them to the unholy marriage with the masks in which they do not recognize themselves, and for the last time invokes his evil privilege of ambiguity.

It is only now that the satirist's true face, or rather true mask, is revealed. It is the mask of Timon, the misanthrope. 'Shakespeare had foreknowledge of everything'—yes. But above all of Kraus. Shakespeare portrays inhuman figures—and Timon as the most inhuman of them—and says: Nature would produce such a creature if she wished to create something befitting the world as your kind have fashioned it, something worthy of it. Such a creature is Timon; such is Kraus. Neither has, or wants, anything in common with men. 'An animal feud is on, and so we renounce humanity'; from a remote village in the Swiss mountains Kraus throws down this challenge to mankind, and Timon wants only the sea to weep at his grave. Like Timon's verse, Kraus's poetry stands opposite the colon of the *dramatis persona*, of the role. A fool, a Caliban, a Timon—no more thoughtful, no more dignified or better—but, nevertheless, his own Shakespeare.

All the figures thronging about him should be seen as originating in Shakespeare. Always he is the model, whether Kraus speaks with Weininger about man or with Altenberg about women, with Wedekind about the stage or with Loos about food, with Else Lasker-Schüler about the Jews or with Theodor Haecker about the Christians. The power of the demon ends in this realm. His demi- or sub-human traits are conquered by a truly inhuman being, a monster. Kraus hinted at this in the words 'In me a capacity for psychology is united with the greater capacity to ignore the psychological.' It is the inhuman quality of the actor that he pre-empts in these words: the cannibal quality. For in each of his roles the actor assimilates bodily a human being, and in Shakespeare's baroque tirades—when the cannibal is unmasked as the better man, the hero as an actor, when Timon plays the rich man, Hamlet the madman—it is as if his lips dripped blood. So Kraus, following Shakespeare's example, wrote himself parts that let him taste blood. The endurance of his convictions is persistence in a role, in its stereotypes, its cues. His experiences are in their entirety nothing but this: cues. This is why he insists on them, demanding them of existence like an actor who never forgives a partner for denying him his cue.

The Offenbach readings, the recital of couplets from Nestroy, are bereft of all musical means. The word never gives way to the instrument; but by extending its boundaries further and further it finally enfeebles itself, dissolving into a merely animal voice: a humming that is to the word what his smile is to the joke is the holy of holies of this performer's art. In this smile, this humming in which, as in a crater lake amid the most monstrous crags and cinders, the world is peacefully and contentedly mirrored, irrupts the deep complicity with his listeners and models that Kraus has never allowed to enter his words. His service to the world permits no compromise. But as soon as he turns his back on it, he is ready for a good many. Then is felt the tormenting, inexhaustible charm of these recitals: that of seeing the distinction between like and unlike minds annulled, and the homogeneous mass of false friends created, that sets the tone of these performances. Kraus confronts a world of enemies, seeks to coerce them to love and yet coerces them to nothing but hypocrisy. His defencelessness before the latter has a precise connection to the subversive dilettantism that is particularly predominant in the Offenbach performances. Here Kraus confines music to limits narrower than were ever dreamed of in the manifestoes of the George school. This cannot, of course, obscure the antithesis between the linguistic gestures of both men. Rather, an exact correlation exists between the factors that give Kraus access to the two poles of linguistic expression —the enfeebled pole of humming and the armed pole of pathos—and those which forbid his sanctification of the word to take on the forms of the Georgean cult of language. To the cosmic rising and falling that for George 'deifies the body and embodies the divine', language is only the Jacob's ladder with its ten thousand word-rungs. Kraus's language, by contrast, has done away with all hieratic moments. It is the medium neither of clairvoyance nor of domination. It is the theatre of a sanctification of the name—with the Jewish certainty it sets itself against the theurgy of the 'word-body'. Very late, with a decisiveness that must have matured in years of silence, Kraus entered the lists against the great partner whose work had arisen at the same time as his own, beneath the threshold of the century. George's

first published book and the first volume of *Die Fackel* are
dated 1899. And only retrospectively, 'After Thirty Years',
in 1929, did Kraus issue the challenge. There, as the zealot,
he confronts George, the object of worship,

> who in the temple dwells from which
> he never had to drive the traders and the lenders,
> nor yet the pharisees and scribes
> who, therefore, camped about the place, describe it.
> *Profanum vulgus* praises this renouncer
> who never told it what it ought to hate.
> And he who found the goal before the way
> did not come from the source.

'You came from the source—the source is the goal' is
received by the 'Dying Man' as God's comfort and promise.
To this Kraus alludes here, as does Viertel when, in the same
way as Kraus, he calls the world a 'wrong, deviating, circu-
itous way back to paradise'. 'And so,' he continues in this
most important passage of his essay on Kraus, 'I attempt
to interpret the development of this remarkable talent:
intellectuality as a deviation ... leading back to immediacy; publicity—a false trail back to language; satire—a
detour to poetry.' This 'source'—the phenomenon's seal of
authenticity—is the subject of a discovery that has a curious
element of rediscovery. The theatre of this philosophical
recognition scene in Kraus's work is poetry, and its language
rhyme: 'A word that never lies at source' and that, just as
blessedness has its source at the end of time, has its at the
end of the line. Rhyme—two *putti* bearing the demon to its
grave. It died at its source because it came into the world as a

hybrid of mind and sexuality. Its sword and shield—concept and guilt—have fallen from its hands to become emblems beneath the feet of the angel that killed it. This is a poetic, martial angel with a foil in his hand, as only Baudelaire knew him: 'practising alone fantastic swordsmanship',

> *Flairant dans tous les coins les hasards de la rime,*
> *Trébuchant sur les mots comme sur les pavés,*
> *Heurtant parfois des vers depuis longtemps rêvés.*
> (Scenting rhyme's hazards in every corner,
> Stumbling on words as on uneven pavements,
> Jostling now and then long-dreamed-of lines.)

Also a licentious angel, to be sure, 'here chasing a metaphor that has just turned the corner, there coupling words like a procurer, perverting phrases, infatuated with similarities, blissfully abusing chiastic embraces, always on the look-out for adventure, impatient and hesitant to consummate in joy and torment.' So finally the hedonistic moment of the work finds its purest expression in this melancholy and fantastic relationship to existence in which Kraus, in the Viennese tradition of Raimund and Girardi, arrives at a conception of happiness that is as resigned as it is sensual. This must be borne in mind if one is to understand the urgency with which he opposed the dancing pose affected by Nietzsche— not to mention the wrath with which the monster was bound to greet the Superman.

The child recognizes by rhyme that it has reached the summit of language, from which it can hear at their source the rushing of all springs. Up there creaturely existence is at home; after so much dumbness in the animal and so much lying in the whore, it has found its tongue in the child. 'A good brain must be capable of imagining each fibre of child-hood with all its phenomena so intensely that temperature is raised'—in statements such as this Kraus aims further than it appears. He himself, at any rate, satisfied this requirement to the extent that he never envisaged the child as the object of education but, in an image from his own youth, as the antagonist of education who is educated by this antagonism, not by the educator. 'Not the cane was to be abolished, but the teacher who uses it badly.' Kraus wants to be nothing except the teacher who uses it better. The limit of his philan-thropy, his pity, is marked by the cane, which he first felt in the same class at school to which he owes his best poems.

'I am only one of the late followers'—Kraus is a late fol-lower of the school anthologies. 'The German Boy's Table Grace', 'Siegfried's Sword', 'The Grave in the Busento', 'Kaiser Karl Inspects a School'—these were his models, poetically recreated by the attentive pupil who learned them. So the 'Steeds of Gravelotte' became the poem 'To Eternal Peace', and even the most incandescent of his hate poems were ignited by Hölty's 'Forest Fire', the glow of which pervaded the anthologies of our school days. And if on the last day not only the graves but the school anthologies open, to the tune of 'How the trumpets blow, Hussars away', the true Pegasus of the little folk will burst from them and, a shrivelled mummy, a puppet of cloth or yellowish ivory, hanging dead and dried up over the shoulders of his horse, this unparalleled fashioner of verses will go careening off; but the two-edged sabre in his hand, polished as his rhymes and incisive as on the First Day, will belabour the green woods, and blooms of style bestrew the ground.

Language has never been more perfectly distinguished from mind, never more intimately bound to Eros, than by Kraus in the observation 'The more closely you look at a word the more distantly it looks back.' This is a Platonic love of language. The only closeness from which the word cannot escape, however, is rhyme. So the primal erotic relationship between closeness and distance is given voice in his language: as rhyme and name. As rhyme, language rises up from the creaturely world; as name, it draws all creation up to it. In 'The Forsaken' the most ardent interpenetration of language and Eros, as Kraus experienced them, expresses itself with an innocent grandeur that recalls the perfect Greek epigrams and vase pictures. 'The Forsaken' are forsaken by each other. But—this is their great solace—also with each other. On the threshold between dying and rebirth they pause. With head turned back, joy 'in unheard-of fashion' takes her eternal leave; turned from her the soul 'in unwanted fashion' silently sets foot in an alien world. Thus forsaken with each other are joy and soul, but also language and Eros, also rhyme and name. To 'The Forsaken' the fifth volume of *Words in Verse* is dedicated. Only the dedication now reaches them, which is nothing other than avowal of Platonic love, which does not satisfy its desire in what it loves, but possesses and holds it in name. This self-obsessed man knows no other self-renunciation than giving thanks. His love is not possession, but gratitude. Thanking and dedicating—for to thank is to put feelings under a name. How the beloved grows distant and lustrous, how her minuteness and her glow withdraw into name, that is the only experience of love known to *Words in Verse*. And, therefore, 'To live without women, how easy—to have lived without women, how hard.'

From within the linguistic compass of the man, and only from within it, can we discern Kraus's basic polemical procedure: quotation. To quote a word is to call it by its name. So Kraus's achievement exhausts itself at its highest level by making even the newspaper quotable. He transports it to his own sphere, and the empty phrase is suddenly forced to recognize that even in the deepest dregs of the journals it is not safe from the voice that swoops on the wings of the word to drag it from its darkness. How wonderful, if this voice approaches not to punish but to save, as it does on the Shakespearean wings of the lines in which, before Arras, someone sends word home of how in the early morning, on the last blasted tree before the fortifications, a lark began to sing. A single line, and not even one of his, is enough to enable Kraus to descend, as saviour, into *this* inferno, a single italicization: 'It was a nightingale and not a lark which sat there on the pome*granate* tree and sang.'[3] In the quotation that both saves and chastises, language proves the matrix of justice. It summons the word by its Lame, wrenches it destructively from its context, but precisely thereby calls it back to its origin. It appears, now with rhyme and reason, sonorously, congruously in the structure of a new text. As rhyme it gathers the similar into its aura; as name it stands alone and expressionless. In quotation the two realms—of origin and destruction—justify themselves before language. And conversely, only where they interpenetrate—in quotation —is language consummated. In it is mirrored the angelic tongue in which all words, startled from the idyllic context of meaning, have become mottoes in the book of Creation.

From its two poles—classical and materialist humanism —the whole world of this man's culture is embraced by

quotation. Schiller, admittedly unnamed, stands beside
Shakespeare: 'There is also a moral nobility. Mean natures
pay / With that which they do, noble with that which they
are'—this classical distich characterizes, in the convergence
of manorial *noblesse* and cosmopolitan rectitude, the utopian
vanishing point where Weimar humanism was at home, and
which was finally fixed by Stifter. It is decisive for Kraus
that he locates origin at exactly this vanishing point. It is
his programme to reverse the development of bourgeois-
capitalist affairs to a condition that was never theirs. But he is
nonetheless the last bourgeois to claim his justification from
Being, and Expressionism was portentous for him because
in it this attitude had for the first time to prove its worth
in face of a revolutionary situation. It was precisely the
attempt to do justice to this situation not by actions but by
Being that led Expressionism to its clenched ensteepments.
So it became the last historical refuge of personality. The
guilt that bowed it and the purity it proclaimed—both are
part of the phantom of the unpolitical or 'natural' man who
emerges at the end of that regression and was unmasked by
Marx. 'Man as member of bourgeois society,' writes Marx,
'the unpolitical man, necessarily appears as the natural man.
... Political revolution dissolves bourgeois life into its component parts without revolutionizing or criticizing these
components themselves. It stands to bourgeois society, to
the world of needs, work, private interests, private right, in
the same relation as to the foundation of its existence ... and
therefore to its natural basis. ... The real man is acknowledged only in the form of the egoistical individual, the true
man only in the form of the abstract *citoyen*. ... Only when
the really individual man takes back into himself the abstract

citizen and, as an individual man, has become in his empirical
life, in his individual work, in his individual circumstances
a species-being ... and therefore no longer separates social
power from himself in the form of political power, only then
is human emancipation complete.' The materialist humanism which Marx here opposes to its classical counterpart
manifests itself for Kraus in the child, and the developing human being raises his face against the idols of ideal
man—the romantic child of nature as much as the dutiful
citizen. For the sake of such development Kraus revised
the school anthology, investigated German education,
and found it tossing helplessly on the waves of journalistic caprice. Hence the 'Lyric of the Germans': 'He who
can is their man and not he who must, / they strayed from
being to seeming. / Their lyrical case was not Claudius /
but Heine.' The fact, however, that the developing man
actually takes form not within the natural sphere but in that
of mankind, in the struggle for liberation, and that he is recognized by the posture that the fight with exploitation and
poverty stamp upon him, that there is no idealistic but only a
materialistic deliverance from myth, and that at the origin of
creation stands not purity but purification—all this did not
leave its trace on Kraus's materialist humanism until very
late. Only in despair did he discover in quotation the power
not to preserve but to purify, to tear from context, to destroy;
the only power in which hope still resides that something
might survive this age—because it was wrenched from it.

Here we find confirmation that all the martial energies
of this man are innate civic virtues; only in the *melée* did
they take on their combative aspect. But already no one
recognizes them any more; no one can grasp the necessity

that compelled this great bourgeois character to become a comedian, this guardian of Goethean linguistic values a polemicist, or why this irreproachably honourable man went berserk. This, however, was bound to happen, since he thought fit to begin changing the world with his own class, in his own home, in Vienna. And when, recognizing the futility of his enterprise, he abruptly broke it off, he placed the matter back in the hands of nature—this time destructive, not creative nature:

> Let time stand still! Sun, be consummate!
> Make great the end! Announce eternity!
> Rise up with menace, let your light boom thunder,
> That our strident death be silenced.
> You golden bell, melt in your own heat,
> Make yourself a gun against the cosmic foe!
> Shoot firebrands in his face! Had I but Joshua's power,
> I tell you, Gibeon would be again!

On this unfettered nature Kraus's later political credo is founded, though in antithesis to Stifter's patriarchal code; it is a confession that is in every respect astonishing, but incomprehensible only in the fact that it has not been preserved in *Die Fackel's* largest type, and that this most powerful of post-war bourgeois prose must be sought in a vanished edition of the issue of November 1920:

'What I mean is—and now for once I shall speak plainly to this dehumanized brood of owners of property and blood, and all their followers, because they do not understand German and from my "contradictions" are incapable of deducing my true intention ... —what I mean is:

Communism as a reality is only the obverse of their own life-violating ideology, admittedly by the grace of a purer ideal origin, a deranged remedy with a purer ideal purpose—the devil take its practice, but God preserve it as a constant threat over the heads of those who have property and would like to compel all others to preserve it, driving them, with the consolation that worldly goods are not the highest, to the fronts of hunger and patriotic honour. God preserve it, so that this rabble who are beside themselves with brazenness do not grow more brazen still, and so that the society of those exclusively entitled to enjoyment, who believe it is loving subordinate humanity enough if they give it syphilis, may at least go to bed with a nightmare! So that at least they may lose their appetite for preaching morality to their victims, take less delight in ridiculing them!'

A human, natural, noble language—particularly in the light of a noteworthy declaration by Loos: 'If human work consists only of destruction, it is truly human, natural, noble work.' For far too long the accent was placed on creativity. People are only creative to the extent that they avoid tasks and supervision. Work as a supervised task—its model: political and technical work—is attended by dirt and detritus, intrudes destructively into matter, is abrasive to what is already achieved, critical toward its conditions, and is in all this opposite to that of the dilettante luxuriating in creation. His work is innocent and pure, consuming and purifying masterliness. And therefore the monster stands among us as the messenger of a more real humanism. He is the conqueror of the empty phrase. He feels solidarity not with the slender pine but with the plane that devours it, not with the precious ore but with the blast furnace that purifies it. The average European has not succeeded in uniting his life with technology, because he has clung to the fetish of creative existence. One must have followed Loos in his struggle with the dragon 'ornament', heard the stellar Esperanto of Scheerbart's creations, or seen Klee's *New Angel*, who preferred to free men by taking from them, rather than make them happy by giving to them, to understand a humanity that proves itself by destruction.

Justice, therefore, is destructive in opposing the constructive ambiguities of law, and destructively Kraus did justice to his own work: 'All my errors stay behind to lead.' This is a sober language that bases its dominance on permanence, and the writings of Kraus have already begun to last, so that he might furnish them with an epigraph from Lichtenberg, who dedicated one of his most profound works to 'Your Majesty Forgetfulness'. So his modesty now appears— bolder than his former self-assertion, which dissolved in demonic self-reflection. Neither purity nor sacrifice mastered the demon; but where origin and destruction come together, his rule is over. Like a creature sprung from the child and the cannibal his conqueror stands before him: not a new man; a monster, a new angel. Perhaps one of those who, according to the Talmud, are at each moment created anew in countless throngs, and who, once they have raised their voices before God, cease and pass into nothingness. Lamenting, chastising, or rejoicing? No matter—on this evanescent voice the ephemeral work of Kraus is modelled. Angelus—that is the messenger in the old engravings.

1930–31

V

A Berlin Chronicle

For my dear Stefan

Now let me call back those who introduced me to the city. For although the child, in his solitary games, grows up at closest quarters to the city, he needs and seeks guides to its wider expanses, and the first of these—for a son of wealthy middle-class parents like me—are sure to have been nurse-maids. With them I went to the Zoo—although I recall it only from much later, with blaring military bands and 'Scandal Avenue' (as the adherents of *art nouveau* dubbed this promenade)—or, if not to the Zoo, to the Tiergarten. I believe the first 'street' that I discovered in this way that no longer had anything habitable or hospitable about it, emanating forlornness between the shopfronts and even danger at the crossings, was Schillstrasse; I like to imagine that it has altered less than others in the West End and could now accommodate a scene rising irresistibly from the mist: the saving of the life of 'little brother'. The way to the Tiergarten led over the Herkules Bridge, the gently sloping embankment of which must have been the first hillside the child encountered—accentuated by the fine stone flanks of the lion rising above. At the end of Bendlerstrasse, however, began the labyrinth, not without its Ariadne: the maze surrounding Frederick William III and Queen Louise, who, rising sheer from the flower beds on their illustrated, Empire-style plinths, seemed as if petrified by the signs that a little rivulet inscribed in the sand. Rather than the figures, my eyes sought the plinths, since the events taking place on them, if less clear in their ramifications, were closer in space. But that a particular significance attaches to this Hohenzollern labyrinth I find confirmed even now by the utterly unconcerned, banal appearance of the forecourt on Tiergartenstrasse, where nothing suggests that you stand but a few yards from the strangest place in the city. At that time, it is true, it must have corresponded more than closely to what was waiting behind it, for here, or not far away, were the haunts of that Ariadne in whose proximity I learned for the first time (and was never entirely to forget) something that was to make instantly comprehensible a word that at scarcely three I cannot have known: love. Here the nurse-maid supervenes, a cold shadow driving away what I loved. It is likely that no one ever masters anything in which he has not known impotence; and if you agree, you will also see that this impotence comes not at the beginning of or before the struggle with the subject, but in the heart of it. Which brings me to the middle period of my life in Berlin, extend-ing from the whole of my later childhood to my entrance to the university: a period of impotence before the city. This had two sources. First was a very poor sense of direction; but if it was thirty years before the distinction between left and right had become visceral to me, and before I had acquired the art of reading a street map, I was far from appreciating the extent of my ineptitude; and if anything was capable of increasing my disinclination to perceive this fact, it was the insistence with which my mother thrust it under my nose. On her I lay the blame for my inability even today to make a cup of coffee; to her propensity for turning the most insignificant items of conduct into tests of my aptitude for practical life I owe the dreamy recalcitrance with which I accompanied her as we walked through the streets, rarely frequented by me, of the city centre. But to this resistance in turn is due who knows how much that underlies my present intercourse with the city's streets. Above all, a gaze that appears to see not a third of what it takes in. I remember, too, how nothing was more intolerable to my mother than the pedantic care with which, on these walks, I always kept half a step behind her. My habit of seeming slower, more maladroit, more stupid than I am, had its origin in such walks, and has the great attendant danger of making me think myself quicker, more dexterous, and shrewder than I am.

I have long, indeed for years, played with the idea of setting out the sphere of life—bios—graphically on a map. First I envisaged an ordinary map, but now I would incline to a general stall's map of a city centre, if such a thing existed. Doubtless it does not, because of ignorance of the theatre of future wars. I have evolved a system of signs, and on the grey background of such maps they would make a colourful show if I clearly marked in the houses of my friends and girl friends, the assembly halls of various collectives, from the 'debating chambers' of the Youth Movement to the gathering places of the Communist youth, the hotel and brothel rooms that I knew for one night, the decisive benches in the Tiergarten, the ways to different schools and the graves that I saw filled, the sites of prestigious cafes whose long-forgotten names daily crossed our lips, the tennis courts where empty apartment blocks stand today, and the halls emblazoned with gold and stucco that the terrors of dancing classes made almost the equal of gymnasiums. And even without this map, I still have the encouragement provided by an illustrious precursor, the Frenchman Léon Daudet, exemplary at least in the title of his work, which exactly encompasses the best that I might achieve here: *Paris vécu*. 'Lived Berlin' does not sound so good but is as real. And it is not just this title that concerns me here; Paris itself is the fourth in the series of voluntary or involuntary guides that began with my nursemaids. If I had to put in one word what I owe to Paris for these reflections, it would be 'caution'; I should scarcely be able to abandon myself to the shifting currents of these memories of my earliest city life, had not Paris set before me, strictly circumscribed, the two forms in which alone this can legitimately—that is, with a guarantee of permanence—be done; and had I not forsworn the attempt to equal the first as firmly as I hope one day to realize the second. The first form was created in the work of Marcel Proust, and the renunciation of any dalliance with related possibilities could scarcely be more bindingly embodied than in the translation of it that I have produced. Related possibilities—do they really exist? They would certainly permit no dalliance. What Proust began so playfully became awesomely serious. He who has once begun to open the fan of memory never comes to the end of its segments; no image satisfies him, for he has seen that it can be unfolded, and only in its folds does the truth reside; that image, that taste, that touch for whose sake all this has been unfurled and dissected; and now remembrance advances from small to smallest details, from the smallest to the infinitesimal, while that which it encounters in these microcosms grows ever mightier. Such is the deadly game that Proust began so dilettantishly, in which he will hardly find more successors than he needed companions.

How totally unlike this (the music at the Zoo) was some other park music that had begun to reach my ears at an earlier time. It came from Rousseau Island and drove the skaters looping and whirling on New Lake. I was among them long before I had any conception of the source of the island's name, not to mention the difficulty of his style. Through its position this ice rink was comparable to no other, and still more by virtue of its life through the seasons: for what did summer make of the rest? Tennis courts. But here, under the overhanging branches of the trees along the bank, stretched a lake connected to labyrinthine waterways, and now one skated under the little arched bridges where in summer one had leaned on balustrades, or on chains held by lions' mouths, watching the boats gliding in the dark water. There were serpentine paths near the lake and, above all, the tender retreats of lonely old men, benches for 'adults only' at the edge of the sand pit with its ditches, where toddlers dig or stand sunk in thought until bumped by a playmate or roused by the voice of a nursemaid from the bench of command; there she sits, stern and studious, reading her novel and keeping the child in check while hardly raising an eyelid until, her labour done, she changes places with the nurse at the other end of the bench, who is holding the baby between

her knees and knitting. Old, solitary men found their way
here, paying due honour, amid these scatterbrained women-
folk, among the shrieking children, to the serious side of life:
the newspaper. Even if the girl I loved, after tarrying long on
the paths of this garden, had left at last, there was nowhere I
liked staying to think of her better than on a backless bench
in one of those playgrounds, and I never swept the sand
from where I was going to sit down. All these pictures I
have preserved. But none would bring back New Lake and
a few hours of my childhood so vividly as to hear once more
the bars of music to which my feet, heavy with their skates
after a lone excursion across the bustling ice, touched the
familiar planks and stumbled past the chocolate-dispensing
slot machines, and past the more splendid one with a hen
laying candy-filled eggs, through the doorway behind which
glowed the anthracite stove, to the bench where you now
savoured for a while the weight of the iron rails on your
feet, which did not yet reach the ground, before resolving
to unbuckle them. If you then slowly rested one calf on the
other knee and unscrewed the skate, it was as if in its place
you had suddenly grown wings, and you went out with steps
that nodded to the frozen ground.

And then my fifth guide: Franz Hessel. I do not mean
his book *On Foot in Berlin*, which was written later, but the
Celebration that our walks together in Paris received in our
native city, as if we were returning to harbour, the jetty still
rising and falling as on waves under the feet of strolling
seamen. The centrepiece of this *Celebration*, however, was
the 'Green Meadow'—a bed that still stands high above
the couches spreading all around, on which we composed a
small, complaisant, orientally pallid epilogue to those great,

sleeping feasts with which, a few years earlier in Paris, the Surrealists had unwittingly inaugurated their reactionary career, thus fulfilling the text that the Lord giveth unto his own in sleep. On this meadow we spread out such women as still amused us at home, but they were few. From beneath lowered lids our gaze often met, better than on drafty stairways, the palms, caryatids, windows, and niches from which the 'Tiergarten mythology' was evolving as the first chapter of a science of this city. It prospered, for we had been astute enough to gather to us girls from the most latinate quarter and in general to observe the Parisian custom of residing in the *quartier*. True, the *quartier* in Berlin is unfortunately an affair of the well-to-do, and neither Wedding nor Reinickendorf nor Tegel bears comparison on this account with Ménilmontant, Auteuil, or Neuilly.

All the more gratifying, therefore, were marauding Sunday-afternoon excursions on which we discovered an arcade in the Moabit quarter, the Stettin tunnel, or liberty in front of the Wallner Theatre. A girl photographer was with us. And it seems to me, as I think of Berlin, that only the side of the city that we explored at that time is truly receptive to photography. For the closer we come to its present-day, fluid, functional existence, the narrower draws the circle of what can be photographed; it has been rightly observed that photography records practically nothing of the essence of, for example, a modern factory. Such pictures can perhaps be compared to railway stations, which, in this age when railways are beginning to be out of date, are no longer, generally speaking, the true 'gateways' through which the city unrolls its outskirts as it does along the approach roads for motorists. A station gives the order, as it were, for a surprise attack, but it is an outdated manoeuvre that confronts us with the archaic, and the same is true of photography, even the snapshot. Only film commands optical approaches to the essence of the city, such as conducting the motorist into the new centre.

The fourth guide.[1] Not to find one's way in a city may well be uninteresting and banal. It requires ignorance— nothing more. But to lose oneself in a city—as one loses oneself in a forest—that calls for quite a different school- ing. Then, signboards and street names, passers-by, roofs, kiosks, or bars must speak to the wanderer like a cracking twig under his feet in the forest, like the startling call of a bittern in the distance, like the sudden stillness of a clearing with a lily standing erect at its centre. Paris taught me this art of straying; it fulfilled a dream that had shown its first traces in the labyrinths on the blotting pages of my school exercise books. Nor is it to be denied that I penetrated to its innermost place, the Minotaur's chamber, with the only difference being that *this* mythological monster had three heads: those of the occupants of the small brothel on rue de la Harpe, in which, summoning my last reserves of strength (and not entirely without an Ariadne's thread), I set my foot. But if Paris thus answered my most uneasy expecta- tions, from another side it surpassed my graphic fantasies. The city, as it disclosed itself to me in the footsteps of a hermetic tradition that I can trace back at least as far as Rilke and whose guardian at that time was Franz Hessel, was a maze not only of paths but also of tunnels. I cannot think of the underworld of the Métro and the North-South line opening their hundreds of shafts all over the city, without recalling my endless *flâneries*.

The most remarkable of all the street images from my early childhood, however—more so even than the arrival of the bears, which I witnessed at the side of a nursemaid, or it may have been my French governess-more remarkable than the racecourse that passed Schillstrasse or ended there, is—it must have been about 1900—a completely deserted stretch of road upon which ponderous torrents of water continuously thundered down. I had been caught up in a local flood disaster, but in other ways, too, the idea of extraordinary events is inseparable from that day; possibly we had been sent home from school. In any case, this situation left behind an alarm signal; my strength must have been failing, and in the *midst* of the asphalt streets of the city I felt exposed to the powers of nature; in a primeval forest I should not have been more abandoned than here on Kurfürstenstrasse, between the columns of water. How I reached the bronze lions' mouths on our front door with their rings that were now life belts, I cannot remember.

Rides to the station in the rattling taxi, skirting the Landwehr Canal while, among the dirty cushions, the weekly evening gathering in the drawing room or the living room of my parents' apartment, which had just neared its end, for a week at least, was revived with stricken violence. And so it was not what impended that weighed so terrifyingly upon me, or even the parting from what had been, but that which still continued, persisted, asserting itself even in this first stage of the journey. The destination of such rides would usually have been the Anhalt Station—where you took the train to Suderode or Hahnenklee, to Bad Salzschlirf or in the later years—to Freudenstadt. But now and again it was Arendsee, too, or Heiligendamm, and then you went by the Stettin Station. I believe it is since that time that the dunes of the Baltic landscape have appeared to me like a *fata morgana* here on Chausseestrasse, supported only by the yellow, sandy colours of the station building and the boundless horizon opening in my imagination behind its walls.

But this vista would indeed be delusive if it did not make visible the medium in which alone such images take form, assuming a transparency in which, however mistily, the contours of what is to come are delineated like mountain peaks. The present in which the writer lives is this medium. And in it he now cuts another section through the sequence of his experiences. He detects in them a new and disturbing articulation. First, his early childhood, enclosing him in the district where he lived—the old or the new West End, where the class that had pronounced him one of its number resided in a posture compounded of self-satisfaction and resentment that turned it into something like a ghetto held on lease. In any case, he was confined to this affluent quarter without knowing of any other. The poor? For rich children of his generation they lived at the back of beyond. And if at this early age he could picture the poor, it was, without his knowing either name or origin, in the image of the tramp who is actually a rich man, though without money, since he stands—far removed from the process of production and the exploitation not yet abstracted from it—in the same contemplative relation to his destitution as the rich man to his wealth. The child's first excursion into the exotic world of abject poverty characteristically took written form (only by chance, perhaps, one of his first excursions to do so), being the depiction of a sandwich man and his humiliation at the hands of the public, who did not trouble even to take the leaflets he held out to them, so that the wretched man—thus the story ended—secretly jettisoned his entire consignment. Certainly a wholly unfruitful solution to the problem, already announcing the flight into sabotage and anarchism that later makes it so difficult for the intellectual to see things clearly. Perhaps the same sabotage of real social existence is to be found even later in my manner, already described, of walking in the city, in the stubborn refusal under any circumstances to form a united front, be it even with my own mother. There is no doubt, at any rate, that a feeling of crossing the threshold of one's class for the first time had a part in the almost unequalled fascination of publicly accosting a whore in the street. At the beginning, however, this was a crossing of frontiers not only social but topographical, in the sense that whole networks of streets were opened up under the auspices of prostitution. But is it really a crossing, is it not, rather, an obstinate and voluptuous hovering on the brink, a hesitation that has its most cogent motive in the circumstance that beyond this frontier lies nothingness? But the places are countless in the great cities where one stands on the edge of the void, and the whores in the doorways of tenement blocks and on the less sonorous asphalt of railway platforms are like the household goddesses of this cult of nothingness. So on these erring paths the stations became my especial habitat, each with its outskirts like a city: the Silesian, Stettin, Görlitz stations, and Friedrichstrasse.

Just as there are, for children, fairy tales in which a witch or even a fairy holds a whole forest in thrall, as a child I knew a street that was ruled and occupied entirely by a woman, even though she was always enthroned in her bay window, one minute's walk from the house in which I was born: Aunt Lehmann. The stairs rose steeply to her room from just behind the hall door; it was dark on them, until the door opened and the brittle voice bid us a thin 'good-morning' and directed us to place before us on the table the glass rhombus containing the mine, in which little men pushed wheelbarrows, laboured with pickaxes, and shone lanterns into the shafts in which buckets were winched perpetually up and down. On account of this aunt and her mine, Steglitzer Strasse could henceforth, for me, never be named after Steglitz. A goldfinch [*Stieglitz*] in its cage bore greater resemblance to this street harbouring the aunt at her window than the Berlin suburb that meant nothing to me. Where it joins Genthiner Strasse, it is one of the streets least touched by the changes of the last thirty years. In the back rooms and attics, as guardians of the past, numerous prostitutes have established themselves here, who, during the inflation period, brought the district the reputation of being a theatre of the most squalid diversions. Needless to say, no one could ever determine on which stories the impoverished opened their drawing rooms, and their daughters their skirts, to rich Americans.

Climbing the stairs in this fashion,[2] with nothing before me but boots and calves, and the scraping of hundreds of feet in my ears, I was often seized—I seem to remember—by revulsion at being hemmed in by this multitude, and again, as on those walks in the city with my mother, solitude appeared to me as the only fit state of man. Very understandably, for such a mob of school children is among the most formless and ignoble of all masses, and betrays its bourgeois origin in representing, like every assembly of that class, the most rudimentary organizational form that its individual members can give their reciprocal relationships. The corridors, and the classrooms that finally came into view, are among the horrors that have embedded themselves most ineradicably in me, that is to say, in my dreams; and these have taken revenge on the monotony, the cold torpor that overcame me at each crossing of the classroom thresholds, by turning themselves into the arena of the most extravagant events. The backdrop was often the fear of having to take the *Abitur* again (under more unfavourable conditions), a position in which I had been placed by my own recklessness and folly. Undoubtedly, these rooms lend themselves to dreamlike representation; there is something nightmarish even in the sober recollection of the damp odour of sweat secreted by the stone steps that I had to hasten up five times or more each day. The school, outwardly in good repair, was in its architecture and situation among the most desolate. It matched its emblem, a plaster statue of the Emperor Frederick, which had been deposited in a remote corner of the playground (admittedly one favoured by hordes engaged in martial games), puny and pitiful against a fire wall. According to a school legend it was, if I am not mistaken, a donation. This monument, unlike the classrooms, was never washed, and had acquired in the course of years an admirable coat of dirt and soot. It still stands today in its appointed place. But soot descends upon it daily from the passing municipal railway. It is far from impossible that my uncommon aversion to this railway dates from this time, since all the people sitting at their windows seemed enviable to me. They could afford to ignore the school clock that held sway above our heads, and quite unawares they cut through the invisible bars of our timetable cage. They could only be seen, incidentally, during

the breaks, for the lower panes of the classroom windows
were of frosted glass. 'Vagabond clouds, sailors of the skies'
had for us the absolute precision that the verse holds for
prisoners. Moreover, little about the actual classrooms has
remained in my memory except these exact emblems of
imprisonment: the frosted windows and the infamous carved
wooden battlements over the doors. It would not surprise
me to hear that the cupboards, too, were crowned with such
adornments, not to mention the pictures of the Kaiser on
the walls. Heraldic and chivalrous obtuseness shone forth
wherever possible. In the great hall, however, it was most
ceremoniously united with *art nouveau*. A crude, extravagant
ornament stretched with stiff grey-green limbs across the
panelling of the walls. References to objects were no more
to be found in it than references to history; nowhere did it
offer the eye the slightest refuge, while the ear was helplessly
abandoned to the clatter of idiotic harangues. All the same,
one of these occasions is perhaps noteworthy for the effect
it had on me for years afterward. It was the leave-taking
ceremony for those who had graduated. Here, as in several
other places, I find in my memory rigidly fixed words,
expressions, verses that, like a malleable mass that has later
cooled and hardened, preserve in me the imprint of the col-
lision between a larger collective and myself. Just as a certain
kind of significant dream survives awakening in the form of
words when all the rest of the dream content has vanished,
here isolated words have remained in place as marks of catastrophic encounters. Among them is one in which for me
the whole atmosphere of the school is condensed; I heard it
when, having hitherto received only private tutoring, I was
sent for my first morning, on a trial basis, to what was later

to become the Kaiser Friedrich School, but at that time was
still situated on Passauerstrasse. This word that still adheres
in my mind to a phlegmatic, fat, unbecoming figure of a boy
is the following: ringleader. Nothing else is left of this earliest school experience. It was re-enacted in similar form,
however, some six years later, when I spent my first day in
alien and threatening circumstances in Haubinda and was
asked by a tall, hostile-seeming lout who played a prominent
part in the class whether my 'old man' had already left. This
common piece of schoolboy parlance was entirely unfamiliar
to me. An abyss opened before me, which I sought to bridge
with a laconic protest. Here in the great hall it was the verses
with which the school choir began the farewell song to the
leavers—'Brother now may we / your companions be / in
the world so wide'—followed by something containing the
words 'loyally by your side'; at any rate these were the verses
that enabled me year by year to take the measure of my
own weakness. For no matter how palpably the abominable
goings-on at school were daily before my eyes, the melody
of this song seemed to surround the departure from this hell
with infinite melancholy. But by the time it was addressed
to me and my class it must have made little impression, for
I remember nothing of it. More remarkable are some other
verses that I heard once in the gymnasium dressing room
after the lesson, and never forgot. Why? Perhaps because
'Schulze'—as the imprudent boy who knew the lines was
called—was rather pretty, perhaps because I thought them
true, but most probably because the situation in which they
were spoken, one of frenetic, military hyper-activity, was so
utterly appropriate. 'Loitering at the rear / you never need
fear / neurasthenia.'

If I write better German than most writers of my generation, it is thanks largely to twenty years' observance of one little rule: never use the word 'I' except in letters. The exceptions to this precept that I have permitted myself could be counted. Now this has had a curious consequence that is intimately connected to these notes. For when one day it was suggested that I should write, from day to day in a loosely subjective form, a series of glosses on everything that seemed noteworthy in Berlin—and when I agreed— it became suddenly clear that this subject, accustomed for years to waiting in the wings, would not so easily be summoned to the limelight. But far from protesting, it relied on ruse, so successfully that I believed a retrospective glance at what Berlin had become for me in the course of years would be an appropriate 'preface' to such glosses. If the preface has now far exceeded the space originally allotted to the glosses, this is not only the mysterious work of remembrance— which is really the capacity for endless interpolations into what has been—but also, at the same time, the precaution of the subject represented by the 'I', which is entitled not to be sold cheap. Now there is one district of Berlin with which this subject is more closely connected than any other that it has consciously experienced. To be sure, there are parts of the city in which it was destined to have equally deep and harrowing experiences, but in none of them was the place itself so much a part of the event. The district I am talking of is the Tiergarten quarter. There, in a back wing of one of the houses standing nearest the municipal railway viaduct, was the 'Meeting House'. It was a small apartment that I had rented jointly with the student Ernst Joël. How we had agreed on this I no longer remember; it can hardly have been simple, for the student 'Group for Social Work' led by Joël was, during the term in which I was president of the Berlin Free Students' Union, a chief target of my attacks, and it was precisely as leader of this group that Joël had signed the lease, while my contribution secured the rights of the 'debating chamber' to the Meeting House. The distribution of the rooms between the two groups—whether of a spatial or a temporal character—was very sharply defined, and in any case, for me at that time only the debating group mattered.

My co-signatory, Ernst Joël, and I were on less than cordial terms, and I had no inkling of the magical aspect of the city that this same Joël, fifteen years later, was to reveal to me. So his image appears in me at this stage only as an answer to the question whether forty is not too young an age at which to evoke the most important memories of one's life. For this image is already now that of a dead man, and who knows how he might have been able to help me cross this threshold, with memories of even the most external and superficial things? To the other threshold he had no access, and of all those who once had it I alone remain. I should never have thought that I should seek him by this topographical route. But if I call to mind the first trial run I made in this direction, more than ten years ago now, the earlier and more modest essay has the better of the comparison. It was in Heidelberg, during what was undoubtedly self-forgetful work, that I tried to summon up, in a meditation on the nature of the lyric, the figure of my friend Fritz Heinle, around whom all the happenings in the Meeting House arrange themselves and with whom they vanish. Fritz Heinle was a poet, and the only one of them all whom I met not 'in real life' but in his work. He died at nineteen, and could be known in no other way. All the same, this first attempt to evoke the sphere of his life through that of poetry was unsuccessful, and the immediacy of the experience that gave rise to my lecture asserted itself irresistibly in the incomprehension and snobbery of the audience, who came to hear it at the house of Marianne Weber. No matter how much memory has subsequently paled, or how indistinctly I can now give an account of the rooms in the Meeting House, it nevertheless seems to me today more legitimate to attempt to delineate the outward space the dead man inhabited, indeed the room where he was 'announced', than the inner space in which he created. But perhaps that is only because, in this last and most crucial year of his life, he traversed the space in which I was born. Heinle's Berlin was the Berlin of the Meeting House. He lived at this period in closest proximity to it, in a fourth-floor room on Klopstockstrasse. I once visited him there. It was after a long separation resulting from a serious dissension between us. But even today I remember the smile that lifted the whole weight of these weeks of separation, that turned a probably insignificant phrase into a magic formula that healed the wound. Later, after the morning when an express letter awoke me with the words 'You will find us lying in the Meeting House'—when Heinle and his girl friend were dead—this district remained for a period the central meeting place of the living. Today, however, when I recall its old-fashioned apartment houses, its many trees dust-covered in summer, the cumbersome iron-and-stone constructions of the municipal railway cutting through it, the sparse streetcars spaced at great intervals, the sluggish water of the Landwehr Canal

that marked the district off from the proletarian quarters of
Moabit, the splendid but wholly unfrequented cluster of
trees in the Schlosspark Bellevue, and the unspeakably cruel
hunting groups flanking its approach at the star-shaped
intersection of roads—today this point in space where we
chanced then to open our Meeting House is for me the strictest pictorial expression of the point in history occupied by
this last true élite of bourgeois Berlin. It was as close to the
abyss of the Great War as the Meeting House was to the
steep slope down to the Landwehr Canal, it was as sharply
divided from proletarian youth as the houses of this *rentiers'*
quarter were from those of Moabit, and the houses were the
last of their line just as the occupants of those apartments
were the last who could appease the clamorous shades of the
dispossessed with philanthropic ceremonies. In spite—or
perhaps because—of this, there is no doubt that the city of
Berlin was never again to impinge so forcefully on my existence as it did in that epoch when we believed we could leave
it untouched, only improving its schools, only breaking the
inhumanity of their inmates' parents, only making a place in
it for the words of Hölderlin or George. It was a final, heroic
attempt to change the attitudes of people without changing
their circumstances. We did not know that it was bound to
fail, but there was hardly one of us whose resolve such
knowledge could have altered. And today, as clearly as at
that time, even if on the basis of entirely different reasoning,
I understand that the 'language of youth' had to stand at the
centre of our associations. Nor do I know today of any truer
expression of our impotence than the struggle that seemed
the pinnacle of our strength and our exuberance, even if the
shadow of downfall, cast by the incomprehension of the

audience, was seldom more palpable than on that evening. I think here of an altercation between Heinle and myself on an evening at the *Aktion*.[3] Originally only a speech by me entitled 'Youth' had been on the agenda. I took it for granted that its text should be known to our closest circle before it was delivered. Scarcely had this happened, however, when Heinle raised objections. Whether he wanted to speak himself, or to impose alterations on me that I refused —the upshot was an ugly quarrel into which, as always happens on such occasions, the whole existence of each participant was drawn—Heinle's side being taken by the youngest of the three sisters around whom the most import-ant events used to gravitate,[4] as if the fact that a Jewish widow was living with her three daughters represented, for a group seriously intent upon the abolition of the family, an appropriate base from which to launch an attack. In short, the girl reinforced her friend's demands. But I was not pre-pared to yield, either. So it happened that on that evening at the *Aktion*, before an astonished but less-than-captivated audience, two speeches with the same title and almost exactly identical texts were delivered, and in truth the lati-tude within which the 'Youth Movement' had to manoeuvre was no larger than the area bounded by the nuances of those speeches. Thinking about the two speeches today, I should like to compare them to the clashing islands in the legend of the Argonauts, the Symplegades, between which no ship can pass in safety and where, at that time, a sea of love and hatred tossed. Assemblies of bourgeois intellectuals were then far commoner than nowadays, since they had not yet recognized their limits. We may say, however, that we felt those limits, even if much time was to pass before the realization matured that no one can improve his school or his parental home without first smashing the state that needs bad ones. We felt these limits when we held our discussions, at which the younger among us spoke of the brutalities they had to endure at home, in drawing rooms kindly made available by parents who at bottom thought no differently from those we wished to oppose. We felt them when we older members held our literary evenings in rooms at beerhouses that were never for a moment safe from the serving waiters; we felt them when we were obliged to receive our lady friends in furnished rooms with doors we were not at liberty to lock; we felt them in our dealings with owners of public rooms and with porters, with relations and guardians. And when, finally, after August 8, 1914, the days came when those among us who were closest to the dead couple did not want to part from them until they were buried, we felt the limits in the shame of being able to find refuge only in a seedy railway hotel on Stuttgart Square. Even the graveyard demonstrated the boundaries set by the city to all that filled our hearts: it was impossible to procure for the pair who had died together graves in one and the same cemetery. But those were days that ripened a realization that was to come later, and that planted in me the conviction that the city of Berlin would also not be spared the scars of the struggle for a better order. If I chance today to pass through the streets of the quarter, I set foot in them with the same uneasiness that one feels when entering an attic unvisited for years. Valuable things may be lying around, but nobody remembers where. And in truth this dead quarter with its tall apartment houses is today the junk room of the West End bourgeoisie.

That was the time when the Berlin cafés played a part in our lives. I still remember the first that I took in consciously. This was much earlier, immediately after my graduation. The Viktoria Café, where our first communal jaunt ended at three in the morning, no longer exists. Its place—on the corner of Friedrichstrasse and Unter den Linden—has been taken by one of the noisiest luxury cafés of new Berlin, against which the earlier one, however luxurious it may have been in its day, stands out with all the magic of the age of chandeliers, mirrored walls and plush comfort. This old Viktoria Café was on that occasion our last port of call, and we doubtless reached it a depleted group. It must have been more than half empty—at any rate I can discern, through the veils that mask the image today, no one apart from a few whores, who seemed to have the spacious cafe to themselves. We did not stay long, and I do not know whether I paid the Viktoria Café, which must have disappeared soon after, a second visit. The time had not yet arrived when the frequenting of cafes was a daily need, and it can hardly have been Berlin that fostered this vice in me, however well the vice later adapted itself to the establishments of that city, which leads far too strenuous and conscious a life of pleasure to know real coffeehouses. Our first café, accordingly, was more a strategic quarter than a place of siesta. And I have thus unmistakably revealed its name: as is well known, the headquarters of bohemians until the first war years was the old West End Café. It was in this café that we sat together in those very first August days, choosing among the barracks that were being stormed by the onrush of volunteers. We decided on the cavalry on Belle-Alliance Strasse, where I duly appeared on one of the

following days, no spark of martial fervour in my breast; yet
however reserved I may have been in my thoughts, which
were concerned only with securing a place among friends
in the inevitable conscription, one of the bodies jammed in
front of the barracks gates was mine. Admittedly only for
two days: on August 8 came the event that was to banish
for long after both the city and the war from my mind. I
often saw Heinle in the West End Café. We usually met
there late, about twelve. I cannot say that we had close relations to the literary Bohemia whose days, or nights, were
spent there; we were a self-contained group, the world of
our 'movement' was different from that of the emancipated
people around us, and contacts with them were only fleeting.
A mediator between the two sides for a period was Franz
Pfemfert, editor of *Die Aktion*; our relations with him were
purely Machiavellian. Else Lasker-Schüler once drew me to
her table; Wieland Herzfelde, then a young student, was to
be seen there, and Simon Guttmann, to whom I shall return;
but the list here reaches the boundaries of our narrower
world. I believe we were alien to the café; the feverish concentration induced by concern with so many rival actions,
the organization of the Free Students' Union and the development of the debating chambers, the elaboration of our
speeches in large assemblies of pupils, help for comrades in
need, care for those imperilled by entanglements either of
friendship or of love—all this set us apart from the sated,
self-assured bohemians about us. Heinle was more closely
acquainted with one or another of them, such as the painter
Meidner, who drew him; but this connection remained
unfruitful for us. Then, one day in Switzerland, I read that
the West End Café had been closed. I had never been much

at home in it. At that time I did not yet possess that passion for waiting without which one cannot thoroughly appreciate the charm of a café. And if I see myself waiting one night amid tobacco smoke on the sofa that encircled one of the central columns, it was no doubt in feverish expectation of the outcome of some negotiation at the debating chamber, or of one of the mediators who were brought into play when tensions had once again reached an unbearable pitch. I came to be on much more intimate terms with the neighbouring café, which had its beginning during the period I now refer to. This was the Princess Café. In an attempt to create a 'Physiology of Coffeehouses', one's first and most superficial classification would be into professional and recreational establishments. If, however, one leaves aside the most brazen entertainment places run along industrial lines, it becomes very noticeable that in the development of most hostelries the two functions coincide. A particularly telling example is the history of the Romanische Cafe from exactly the moment when the proprietor of the West End Café evicted his clientele. Very soon the Romanische Café accommodated the bohemians, who, in the years immediately after the war, were able to feel themselves masters of the house. The legendary, now-departed waiter Richard, distributor of newspapers—a hunchback who on account of his bad reputation enjoyed high esteem in these circles-was the symbol of their dominance. When the German economy began to recover, the bohemian contingent visibly lost the threatening nimbus that had surrounded them in the era of the Expressionist revolutionary manifestoes. The bourgeois revised his relationship to the inmates of the Café Megalomania (as the Romanische Café soon came to be called) and found that everything was back to normal. At this moment the physiognomy of the Romanische Café began to change. The 'artists' withdrew into the background, to become more and more a part of the furniture, while the bourgeois, represented by stock-exchange speculators, managers, film and theatre agents, literary-minded clerks, began to occupy the place—as a place of relaxation. For one of the most elementary and indispensable diversions of the citizen of a great metropolis, wedged, day in, day out, in the structure of his office and family amid an infinitely variegated social environment, is to plunge into another world, the more exotic the better. Hence the bars haunted by artists and criminals. The distinction between the two, from this point of view, is slight. The history of the Berlin coffeehouses is largely that of different strata of the public, those who first conquered the floor being obliged to make way for others gradually pressing forward, and thus to ascend the stage.

Such a stage, for Heinle and me, was the Princess Café, which we were in the habit of patronizing as occupants of private boxes. The latter should be taken almost literally, for this café, designed by Lucian Bernhard, an interior decorator and poster artist much in demand at that time, offered its visitors an abundance of snug recesses, standing historically midway between the *chambres séparées* and the coffee parlours. The profession primarily served by this establishment is therefore clear. And when we visited it, indeed made it for a time our regular meeting place, it was certainly on account of the *cocottes*. Heinle wrote 'Princess Café' at that time. 'Doors draw coolness over through the song.' We had no intention of making acquaintances in this café. On the contrary—what attracted us here was being enclosed in an environment that isolated us. Every distinction between us and the literary coteries of the city was welcome to us. This one, to be sure, more so than all others. And that certainly had to do with the *cocottes*. But this leads into a subterranean stratum of the Youth Movement, reached by way of an artist's studio in Halensee, to which we shall return. It is quite possible that S. Guttmann, its occupant, met us here, too, from time to time. I have no recollection of it, just as in general, here more than elsewhere, the human figures recede before the place itself, and *none* of them is as vividly present to me as a forlorn, approximately circular chamber in the upper story, hung with violet drapery and illuminated with a violet glow, in which many seats were always empty, while on others couples took up as little space as possible. I called this amphitheatre the 'anatomy school'. Later, when this epoch was long since closed, I sat long evenings there, close to a jazz band, discreetly consulting sheets and slips of paper, writing my *Origin of German Tragic Drama*. When one day a new 'renovation' set in, turning the Princess Café into Café Stenwyk, I gave up. Today it has sunk to the level of a beerhouse.

Never again has music possessed so dehumanized and shameless a quality as that of the two brass bands that tempered the flood of people surging torpidly along 'Scandal Avenue' between the café restaurants of the Zoo. Today I perceive what gave this flow its elemental force. For the city dweller there was no higher school of flirtation than this, surrounded by the sandy precincts of gnus and zebras, the bare trees and clefts where vultures and condors nested, the stinking enclosures of wolves, and the hatcheries of pelicans and herons. The calls and screeches of these animals mingled with the noise of drums and percussion. This was the air in which the glance of a boy fell for the first time on a passing girl, while he talked all the more zealously to his friend. And such were his efforts to betray himself neither by his eyes nor his voice that he saw nothing of her.

At that time the Zoological Garden still had an entrance by the Lichtenstein Bridge. Of the three gates it was the least frequented, and gave access to the park's most deserted quarter: an avenue that, with the milk-white orbs of its candelabras, resembled some deserted promenade at Wiesbaden or Pyrmont; and before the economic crisis had so depopulated these resorts that they seemed more antique than Roman spas, this dead corner of the Zoological Garden was an image of what was to come, a prophesying place. It must be considered certain that there are such places; indeed, just as there are plants that primitive peoples claim confer the power of clairvoyance, so there are places endowed with such power: they may be deserted promenades, or treetops, particularly in towns, seen against walls, railway level-crossings, and above all the thresholds that mysteriously divide the districts of a town. The Lichtenstein gate was really such a threshold, between the two West End parks. It was as if in both, at the point where they were nearest, life paused. And this daily desertion was the more keenly felt by one who remembered the dazzling approach to be seen on festal nights for a number of years from a doorway of the Adler ballrooms, which has fallen now into just such disuse as has this long-closed gate.

Language shows clearly that memory is not an instrument for exploring the past but its theatre. It is the medium of past experience, as the ground is the medium in which dead cities lie interred. He who seeks to approach his own buried past must conduct himself like a man digging. This confers the tone and bearing of genuine reminiscences. He must not be afraid to return again and again to the same matter; to scatter it as one scatters earth, to turn it over as one turns over soil. For the matter itself is only a deposit, a stratum, which yields only to the most meticulous examination what constitutes the real treasure hidden within the earth: the images, severed from all earlier associations, that stand—like precious fragments or torsos in a collector's gallery—in the prosaic rooms of our later understanding. True, for successful excavations a plan is needed. Yet no less indispensable is the cautious probing of the spade in the dark loam, and it is to cheat oneself of the richest prize to preserve as a record merely the inventory of one's discoveries, and not this dark joy of the place of the finding itself. Fruitless searching is as much a part of this as succeeding, and consequently remembrance must not proceed in the manner of a narrative or still less that of a report, but must, in the strictest epic and rhapsodic manner, assay its spade in ever-new places, and in the old ones delve to ever-deeper layers.

It is true that countless façades of the city stand exactly as they stood in my childhood. Yet I do not encounter my childhood in their contemplation. My gaze has brushed them too often since, too often they have been the *décor* and theatre of my walks and concerns. And the few exceptions to this rule—above all St. Matthew's Church on St. Matthew's Square—are perhaps only apparently so. For did I as a child really frequent the remote corner where it stands, did I even know it? I cannot tell. What it says to me today it owes solely to the edifice itself: the church with the two pointed, gabled roofs over its two side aisles, and the yellow-and-ochre brick of which it is built. It is an old-fashioned church, of which the same is true as of many an old-fashioned building: although they were not young with us and perhaps did not even know us when we were children, they have much knowledge of our childhood, and for this we love them. But I should confront myself at that age in quite a different way had I the courage to enter a certain front door that I have passed thousands upon thousands of times. A front door in the old West End. True, my eyes no longer see it, or the façade of the house. My soles would doubtless be the first to send me word, once I had closed the door behind me, that on this worn staircase they trod in ancient tracks, and if I no longer cross the threshold of that house it is for fear of an encounter with this stairway interior, which has conserved in seclusion the power to recognize me that the façade lost long ago. For with its columned windows it has stayed the same, even if within the living quarters all is changed. Bleak verses filled the intervals between our heartbeats, when we paused exhausted on the landings between floors. They glimmered or shone from panes in which a woman with nut-brown eyebrows floated aloft with a goblet from a niche, and while the straps of my satchel cut into my shoulders I was forced to read, 'Industry adorns the burgher, blessedness is toil's reward.' Outside it may have been raining. One of the coloured windows was open, and to the beat of raindrops the upward march resumed.

Motto: O brown-baked column of victory
With children's sugar from the winter days.

I never slept on the street in Berlin. I saw sunset and dawn, but between the two I found myself a shelter. Only those for whom poverty or vice turns the city into a landscape in which they stray from dark till sunrise know it in a way denied to me. I always found quarters, even though sometimes tardy and also unknown ones that I did not revisit and where I was not alone. If I paused thus late in a doorway, my legs had become entangled in the ribbons of the streets, and it was not the cleanest of hands that freed me.

Reminiscences, even extensive ones, do not always amount to an autobiography. And these quite certainly do not, even for the Berlin years that I am exclusively concerned with here. For autobiography has to do with time, with sequence and what makes up the continuous flow of life. Here, I am talking of a space, of moments and discontinuities. For even if months and years appear here, it is in the form they have at the moment of recollection. This strange form—it may be called fleeting or eternal—is in neither case the stuff that life is made of. And this is shown not so much by the role that my own life plays here, as by that of the people closest to me in Berlin—whoever and whenever they may have been. The atmosphere of the city that is here evoked allots them only a brief, shadowy existence. They steal along its walls like beggars, appear wraithlike at windows, to vanish again, sniff at thresholds like a *genius loci*, and even if they fill whole quarters with their names, it is as a dead man's fills his gravestone. Noisy, matter-of-fact Berlin, the city of work and the metropolis of business, nevertheless has more, rather than less, than some others, of those places and moments when it bears witness to the dead, shows itself full of dead; and the obscure awareness of these moments, these places, perhaps more than anything else, confers on childhood memories a quality that makes them at once as evanescent and as alluringly tormenting as half-forgotten dreams. For childhood, knowing no preconceived opinions, has none about life. It is as dearly attached (though with just as strong reservations) to the realm of the dead, where it juts into that of the living, as to life itself. How far a child has access to the past is difficult to tell, and depends on many things—time, environment, its nature and education. The limitation of my own feeling for the Berlin that is not circumscribed by a few facts about the Stratau Fair and Frederick in 1848—that is, for the topographical tradition representing the connection with the dead of this ground—results entirely from the circumstance that neither of my parents' families were natives of Berlin. That sets a limit to the child's memory—and it is this limit, rather than childhood experience itself, that is manifest in what follows. Wherever this boundary may have been drawn, however, the second half of the nineteenth century certainly lies within it, and to it belong the following images, not in the manner of general representations, but of images that, according to the teaching of Epicurus, constantly detach themselves from things and determine our perception of them.

First of all, let no one think we were talking of a *Markt-Halle* [covered market]. No: it was pronounced '*Mark-Talle*', and just as these words were eroded by the habit of speech until none retained its original 'sense', so by the habit of this walk all the images it offered were worn away, so that none of them conforms to the original concept of buying and selling.

Behind us lay the forecourt, with its dangerous, heavy swing doors on their whiplash springs, and we had now set foot on the flagstones, slippery with fish water or swill, on which you could so easily slip on carrots or lettuce leaves. Behind wire partitions, each bearing a number, were ensconced the ponderous ladies, priestesses of Venal Ceres, purveyors of all the fruits of field and tree, and of all edible birds, fishes, and mammals, procuresses, untouchable wool-clad colossi exchanging vibrant signs from booth to booth with a flash of their large mother-of-pearl buttons or a slap on their booming black aprons or their money-filled pouches. Did it not bubble and seethe below the hems of their skirts, and was this not the truly fertile ground? Did not a god of the market himself cast the gods into their laps: berries, crustaceans, mushrooms, chunks of meat and cabbage, invisibly cohabiting with those who abandoned themselves as they languidly and mutely eyed the unsteady procession of housewives who, laden with baskets and bags, laboriously drove their brood before them along these slippery alleyways of ill repute. But if in winter the gas lamps went on in the early evening, you had at once a feeling of sinking, becoming aware, in this gentle gliding, of the depths of sea below the surface that heaved opaque and sluggish in the glassy waters.

The more frequently I return to these memories, the less fortuitous it seems to me how slight a role is played in them by people: I think of an afternoon in Paris to which I owe insights into my life that came in a flash, with the force of an illumination. It was on this very afternoon that my biographical relationships to people, my friendships and comradeships, my passions and love affairs, were revealed to me in their most vivid and hidden intertwinings. I tell myself it had to be in Paris, where the walls and quays, the places to pause, the collections and the rubbish, the railings and the squares, the arcades and the kiosks, teach a language so singular that our relations to people attain, in the solitude encompassing us in our immersion in that world of things, the depths of a sleep in which the dream image waits to show the people their true faces. I wish to write of this afternoon because it made so apparent what kind of regimen cities keep over imagination, and why the city, where people make the most ruthless demands on one another, where appointments and telephone calls, sessions and visits, flirtations and the struggle for existence grant the individual not a single moment of contemplation, indemnifies itself in memory, and why the veil it has covertly woven out of our lives shows the images of people less than those of the sites of our encounters with others or ourselves. Now on the afternoon in question I was sitting inside the Café des Deux Magots at St.-Germain-des-Prés, where I was waiting—I forget for whom. Suddenly, and with compelling force, I was struck by the idea of drawing a diagram of my life, and knew at the same moment exactly how it was to be done. With a very simple question I interrogated my past life, and the answers were inscribed, as if of their own accord, on a sheet of paper that I had with me. A year or two later, when I lost this sheet, I was inconsolable. I have never since been able to restore it as it arose before me then, resembling a series of family trees. Now, however, reconstructing its outline in thought without directly reproducing it, I should, rather, speak of a labyrinth. I am not concerned here with what is installed in the chamber at its enigmatic centre, ego or fate, but all the more with the many entrances leading into the interior. These entrances I call primal acquaintances; each of them is a graphic symbol of my acquaintance with a person whom I met, not through other people, but through neighbourhood, family relationships, school comradeship, mistaken identity, companionship on travels, or other such—hardly numerous—situations. So many primal relationships, so many entrances to the maze. But since most of them—at least those that remain in our memory—for their part open up new acquaintances, relations to new people, after some time they branch off these corridors (the male may be drawn to the right, female to the left). Whether cross-connections are finally established between these systems also depends on the intertwinements of our path through life. More important, however, are the astonishing insights that a study of this plan provides into the differences among individual lives. What part is played in the primal acquaintanceships of different people's lives by profession and school, family and travel? And above all: is the formation of the many offshoots governed in individual existence by hidden laws? Which ones start early and which late in life? Which are continued to the end of life and which peter out? 'If a man has character,' says Nietzsche, 'he will have the same experience over and over again.' Whether or not this is true on a large scale, on a small one there are perhaps paths that lead us again and again to people who have one and the same function for us: passageways that always, in the most diverse periods of life, guide us to the friend, the betrayer, the beloved, the pupil, or the master. This is what the sketch of my life revealed to me as it took shape before me on that Paris afternoon. Against the background of the city, the people who had

surrounded me closed together to form a figure. It was many
years earlier, I believe at the beginning of the war, that in
Berlin, against the background of the people then closest to
me, the world of things contracted to a symbol similarly
profound. It was an emblem of four rings. This takes me to
one of the old Berlin houses on the Kupfergraben. With
their plain, genteel façades and their wide hallways they may
have stemmed from the Schinkel period. In one of them
lived at that time a prominent antique dealer. He had no
display window. You had to go into his apartment to admire,
in a number of showcases, a selection of prehistoric brooches
and clasps, Lombard earrings, late Roman neck chains,
medieval coins, and many similar valuables. How my friend
A. C.[5] had tracked him down I do not know. But I remember
distinctly the engrossment with which, under the impression
of Alois Riegl's *Late Roman Art Industry*, which I had
recently studied, I contemplated the breastplates made from
sheet gold and garnet-adorned bracelets. There were, if I
am not mistaken, three of us: my friend, his fiancée at that
time or Frau Dorothea J., and me. C. asked to see rings—
Greek and Renaissance cameos, rings from the imperial
period, usually work carved in semi-precious stone. Each of
the four that he finally purchased is imprinted unforgettably
on my mind. Except for one that I have lost sight of, they
are still today with those for whom they were intended that
morning. One, a bright-yellow smoky topaz, was chosen by
Dorothea J. The workmanship was Grecian and depicted in
a tiny space Leda receiving the swan between her parted
thighs. It was most graceful. I was less able to admire the
amethyst that the donor, Ernst S[choen], selected for our
mutual friend: a fifteenth- or sixteenth-century Italian had

carved a profile in it which Lederer claimed to be that of Pompey. I was quite differently affected, however, by the last two rings. One was intended for me, but only as a very temporary owner; it was really destined to reach, through me, my then fiancée, Grete R[adt]. It was the most fascinating ring I have ever seen. Cut in a dark, solid garnet, it portrayed a Medusa's head. It was a work of the Roman imperial period. The proustite mounting was not the original. Worn on the finger, the ring seemed merely the most perfect of signet rings. You only entered its secret by taking it off and contemplating the head against the light. As the different strata of the garnet were unequally translucent, and the thinnest so transparent that it glowed with rose hues, the sombre bodies of the snakes seemed to rise above the two deep, glowing eyes, which looked out from a face that, in the purple-black portions of the cheeks, receded once more into the night. Later I tried more than once to seal with this stone, but it proved easy to crack and in need of the utmost care. Shortly after giving it away, I broke off my relationship with its new owner. My heart had already gone with the last of the four rings, which the giver had reserved for his sister. And certainly this girl was the true centre of the circle's fate, though years were to elapse before we realized it. For apart from her beauty—itself not dazzling, but inconspicuous and without lustre—she had nothing that seemed to destine her for the centre of the stage. And in fact she never was the centre of people but, in the strictest sense, of fates, as if her plantlike passivity and inertia had arranged the latter— which, of all human things, seem the most subject to vegetal laws—concentrically about her. Many years were needed before what at that time was in part beginning to unfold in its seed, and in part still dormant, emerged in its ramifications to the light of day: the fate by virtue of which she, who stood in a relation to her brother that by its tenderness filled to the very edge the limits of sisterly love, was to form a liaison with her brother's two closest friends—with the recipient of the ring with the head of Pompey and with me—to find her husband finally in the brother of the woman who married her own brother as her second husband[6]—and she it was, on the day I am speaking of, who received from me the ring with the Medusa's head. It cannot have been many days later that I sent after the lapis lazuli with the lute wreathed in foliage engraved in it—after the fourth ring and to its wearer—this sonnet: To your finger constantly encircled.[7]

The treasure-dispensing giant in the green pine forest or the fairy who grants one wish—they appear to each of us at least once in a lifetime.[8] But only Sunday's children remember the wish they made, and so it is only a few who recognize its fulfilment in their own lives. I know of such a wish that was fulfilled for me, and would not claim it to be wiser than those of children in fairy tales. It goes back to my early childhood, and arose in me in connection with the lamp that on dark winter mornings at half past six was carried through my doorway and cast the shadow of our nursemaid on the ceiling. The fire was lit in the stove and soon, amid reddish reflections, the grating was marked out on the bare floor. When the temperature—the nightly warmth from my bed and the morning warmth from the fire—had made me doubly drowsy, it was time to get up. Then I had no other wish than to finish my sleep. This wish accompanied me throughout the whole of my school days.

Its inseparable attendant, however, was fear of being late. I can still feel today, when I pass the Savignyplatz, the dread with which, stepping into Carmerstrasse, where I lived, I read my judgment in the spellbound space between the ten and the twelve on the repulsive clockface. The wish that animated me on such winter days, and even later, when, in an extremity of fatigue, I rose from the couch in the afternoon because of a gymnastics class, had been fulfilled. Only I did not always recognize this fulfilment when yet another of my attempts to find a place of work, in the bourgeois sense of the word, had come to grief.

There is one other sound that, thanks to the decades in which it neither passed my lips nor reached my ears, has preserved the unfathomable mystery that certain words from the language of adults possess for children. It was not long ago that I rediscovered it, and indeed a number of indivisible finds of this nature have played a large part in my decision to write down these memories. My parents being wealthy, we moved every year, before I went to school and perhaps later, too, notwithstanding other occasional summer trips, into summer residences not far from home. First it was Potsdam, later Neubabelsberg. Whereas the latter period still survives in a number of images, of which I may perhaps have more to tell—the night of the great burglary when my parents locked themselves in my room, the hours I stood fishing beside my father on the bank of Lake Griebnitz, the visit to Peacock Island that brought the first great disappointment of my life, because I could not find the peacock feathers in the grass as I had been promised—by contrast, the summer months in Potsdam have wholly vanished, unless I may situate the asparagus cutting—my first and only agricultural

passion—as far back as the garden on the Brauhausberg.
And I have thus divulged the word in which, like countless rose petals in a drop of Rose Malmaison, hundreds of
summer days, forfeiting their form, their colour, and their
multiplicity, are preserved in their scent. The word is Brauhausberg. To approach what it enfolds is almost impossible.
These words that exist on the frontier between two linguistic
regions, of children and of adults, are comparable to those
of Mallarmes poems, which the conflict between the poetic
and the profane word has as it were consumed and made
evanescent, airy. Likewise the word Brauhausberg has lost
all heaviness, no longer contains a trace of a brewery [*Brau-
haus*], and is at the most a hill swathed in blue that rose up
each summer to give lodging to me and my parents.

The economic basis on which the finances of my parents
rested was, surrounded, long past my childhood and adoles-
cence, by deepest secrecy. Probably not only for me, the
eldest child, but also for my mother. And it is certain that
such a state of affairs was the rule in a Jewish family, and no
doubt in very many Christian ones as well. More curious is
the fact that consumption, too, was wrapped in some of the
mystery that so deeply shrouded income and fortune. I
remember, at any rate, that the mention of certain suppliers
—'sources', as they were called—always took place with
the solemnity befitting an initiation. There are, it is true,
distinctions to be drawn. The purveyors who met the daily
household needs no more belonged to that secret circle than
did the Berlin firms of long-standing repute that my mother
visited when she took me and the younger children 'to
town'. On such occasions it was as certain that our suits
would be bought at Arnold Müller's, shoes at Stiller's, and

suitcases at Mädler's, as that at the end of these commissions our hot chocolate with whipped cream would be ordered at Hillbrich's. These shopping places were strictly preordained by tradition—quite unlike the connections with traders, which were my father's responsibility. My father possessed at base, along with a number of inhibitions stemming not only from his decency but also from a certain civic worthiness, the entrepreneurial nature of a big businessman. Unfavourable influences brought about his very premature retirement from an enterprise that was probably by no means ill-suited to his capacities, the Lepke art auction, in which he was a partner. When he had relinquished his share in the firm, he concerned himself increasingly with speculative investments of his capital, and it would not surprise me if the interest he took in household transactions was far keener from this time on. What is certain is that the suppliers he henceforth searched out were indirectly connected with his investments. If, therefore, from my mother's shopping excursions, a traditional and as it were official image of the Berlin commercial world emerged, the hints and instructions of my father gave rise to an unknown and slightly sinister one, the prestige of which derived as much from the authoritarian resonance that these names carried at the family table as from the fact that these firms, unlike the others, were never seen by me. At their head, so to speak, was the Lepke auction room itself, with which my father not only had connections but from which, from time to time, he also brought home a purchase. I doubt that this commerce was an altogether happy one, with the exception perhaps of his carpet buying. Shortly before his death he told me that he could distinguish the qualities of a pile with the ball of his foot, if his soles were suitably thin. In my childhood, however, what impressed me most was to imagine the gavel blows with which my father accompanied the auction. Later, when he had withdrawn from Lepke's, this gavel always lay on his desk. Even if I never heard the rap of this gavel, there is another sound that became indissoluble from the image of my father's power and grandeur—or, rather, from those of a man in his profession. It is, implausible as it may seem, the noise made by the knife that my mother used to spread the rolls that my father took to his work in the morning, when it was scraped for the last time, to remove the butter still adhering to it, against the crisp surface of the cut roll. This signal preluding the labour of my father's day was no less exciting to me than, in later years, the sound of the bell that announced the start of a performance at the theatre. Apart from this, the real token of my father's profession in our apartment was a Moor, almost life-size, who stood on a gondola reduced to one-thirtieth of its size, holding with one hand an oar that could be taken out, and lifting on the other a golden bowl. This work of art was made of wood, the Moor black, the gondola and oar glowing in many colours beneath the varnish. The whole, however, was so urgently oriented toward its companion piece that I cannot tell today whether a second Moor, whom I imagine with it, really stood there originally or is a creature of my imagination. So much for Lepke's art auction. There was, besides, a further purveyor of art-works—at least as far as bronzes were concerned; it was the firm of Gladenbeck. Whether the choice was affected here, too, by more intimate commercial ties, I do not know. Such was certainly the case, however, with our supply of mouthwash, hydrogen peroxide obtained in huge bottles from the 'Medicinal Stores', of which my father was a director. Less transparent, on the other hand, was the state of affairs regarding the Stabernack firm, which for years held an uncontested monopoly of installations in our apartment. Here the intermediate party was perhaps a certain company of building contractors, one of whose directors, Herr Altgelt, filled the role of partner in countless telephone conversations with my father, and whose name has stayed in my memory because his son was a member, and one of the most inglorious, of my class. Leaving aside mealtime conversations, it was only the telephone that intimated to us the occult world of business and traders. My father telephoned a great deal. He, whose outward manner seems to have been almost always courteous and pliable, possessed perhaps only on the telephone the bearing and decisiveness corresponding to his sometimes great wealth. In conversations with mediating agencies this energy not infrequently grew vociferous, and the 'serious side of life', which was embodied tangibly in my father's activity, found in the altercations with the telephone operators its true symbol. The telephone first came into use during my childhood. I have therefore known it nailed in some corner of the corridor, whence, shrilling from the darkness, it augmented the terrors of that Berlin apartment with the endless passage leading from the half-lit dining room to the back bedrooms. It became a truly infernal machine when my school friends phoned in the prohibited period between two and four. But not all my father's mysterious transactions were carried out by telephone. From earliest times he had had—like many husbands who do not always find life easy in marriage—a tendency to address himself independently to certain

branches of the domestic economy. Thus he had connections
in the provinces, principally in the vicinity of Hamburg,
which frequently called him away on business. The house
was regularly plied from this source with Holstein butter,
and in autumn with teal. Wine, on the other hand, was
catered for by a Berlin firm, whose share certificates were
also in my father's possession: this was the Central Wine
Distributors, who were trying out new methods of calculation in the wine business. Finally these names became
entwined, in the parental discussions, with others in which
the traditions of the middle-class Berlin of that time converged from both sides: for notarial attestation Oberneck
was consulted, operations were performed by Rinne,
dancing instruction was entrusted to Quaritsch, the family
doctor was Renvers, at least as long as he lived in the same
building,[9] Joseph Goldschmidt was our banker. But as for
me, I was most lastingly affected by a reckless attempt that
my father embarked upon one evening to bring even the
family's amusements into harmony with his business enterprises that he had been able to establish for all its other
needs. For when, about 1910, on Lutherstrasse in the West
End, a consortium erected the building that now houses the
Scala as an 'Ice Palace', my father, with a sizable stake, was
among their number. Now one evening, I do not know
whether it was the opening date or later, my father conceived the idea of taking me there. The Ice Palace, however,
was not only the first artificial ice rink to be seen in Berlin,
but also a thriving nightclub. So it happened that my attention was held far less by the convolutions in the arena than
by the apparitions at the bar, which I was able to survey
at my ease from a box in the circle. Among these was a

prostitute in a very tight-fitting white sailor's suit, who, without my having been able to exchange a word with her, determined my erotic fantasies for years to come.

In those early years I got to know the 'town' only as the theatre of purchases, on which occasions it first became apparent how my father's money could cut a path for us between the shop counters and assistants and mirrors, and the appraising eyes of our mother, whose muff lay on the counter. In the ignominy of a 'new suit' we stood there, our hands peeping from the sleeves like dirty price tags, and it was only in the confectioner's that our spirits rose with the feeling of having escaped the false worship that humiliated our mother before idols bearing the names of Mannheimer, Herzog and Israel, Gerson, Adam, Esders and Mädler, Emma Bette, Bud and Lachmann. An impenetrable chain of mountains, no, caverns of commodities—that was 'the town'.

There are people who think they find the key to their destinies in heredity, others in horoscopes, others again in education. For my part, I believe that I should gain numerous insights into my later life from my collection of picture postcards, if I were able to leaf through it again today. The main contributor to this collection was my maternal grandmother, a decidedly enterprising lady, from whom I believe I have inherited two things: my delight in giving presents and my love of travel. If it is doubtful what the Christmas holidays—which cannot be thought of without the Berlin of my childhood—meant for the first of these passions, it is certain that none of my boys' adventure books kindled my love of travel as did the postcards with which she supplied me in abundance from her far-flung travels. And because the longing we feel for a place determines it as much as does its outward image, I shall say something about these post-cards. And yet—was what they awakened in me longing? Did they not have far too magnetic an attraction to leave room for a wish to travel to the places they showed? For I was there—in Tabarz, Brindisi, Madonna di Campiglio, Westerland, when I gazed, unable to tear myself away, at the wooded slopes of Tabarz covered with glowing red berries, the yellow-and-white-daubed quays at Brindisi, the cupolas of Madonna di Campiglio printed bluish on blue, and the bows of the 'Westerland' slicing high through the waves. Visiting the old lady in her carpeted window alcove, ornamented with a little balustrade and looking out onto the Blumeshof, it was hard to imagine how she had undertaken long sea voyages or even camel rides under the direction of Stangel's Travel Bureau. She was a widow; three of her daughters were already married when I was small. I can tell nothing about the fourth, but a good deal about the room that she occupied in her mother's apartment. But perhaps I must first say something about the apartment as a whole. With what words am I to circumscribe the almost imme-morial feeling of bourgeois security that emanated from these rooms? Paradoxical as it may sound, the idea of that particular protectedness seems to relate most directly to their shortcomings. The inventory that filled these many rooms—twelve or fourteen—could today be accommo-dated without incongruity in the shabbiest of secondhand furniture shops. And if these ephemeral forms were so much more solid than those of the *art nouveau* that superseded them—what made you feel at home, at ease, comfortable, and comforted in them was the nonchalance with which they attached themselves to the sauntering passage of years and days, entrusting their future to the durability of their material alone, and nowhere to rational calculation. Here reigned a species of things that was, no matter how compliantly it bowed to the minor whims of fashion, in the main so wholly convinced of itself and its permanence that it took no account of wear, inheritance, or moves, remaining forever equally near to and far from its ending, which seemed the ending of all things. Poverty could have no place in these rooms where even death had none. They had no space for dying—which is why their owners died in a sanitorium, while the furniture went straight to the secondhand dealer. Death was not provided for in them—that is why they were so cosy by day, and by night the theatre of our most oppressive dreams. It is for this reason that, when I think of this house—it was number 10 or 12 Blumeshof—in which were spent so many of my childhood's happiest hours, such as when I was allowed, to the sound of piano études, to browse in *Darling's Diversions* in an armchair—I am met on its threshold by a nightmare. My waking existence has preserved no image of the staircase. But in my memory it remains today the scene of a haunting dream that I once had in just those happy years. In this dream the stairway seemed under the power of a ghost that awaited me as I mounted, though without barring my way, making its presence felt when I had only a few more stairs to climb. On these last stairs it held me spellbound. The rooms in this apartment on the Blumeshof were not only numerous but also in some cases very large. To reach my grandmother at her window I had to cross the huge dining room and attain the farthest end of the living room. Only feast days, and above all Christmas

Day, could give an idea of the capaciousness of these rooms.
But if, when this day came, it seemed as though it had been
awaited all the year long in the front rooms, there were other
occasions that brought other parts of the apartment to life: a
visit by a married daughter unlocked a long-disused ward-
robe; another back room opened to us children when the
grownups wished to take their afternoon nap at the front
of the house, and another part again was animated by the
piano lessons received by the last daughter to remain at
home. The most important of these remote, less-frequented
rooms, however, was the loggia. Perhaps this was because,
being the least furnished, it was least suited to the sojourn
of adults, or because muted street noises came in, or finally
because it opened onto the back courtyards with children,
domestic servants, hurdy-gurdy men, and porters. But
of these it was more often the voices than the forms that
were to be described from the loggia. Moreover, the courtyards of a residential quarter as genteel as this never really
bustled with activity; something of the composure of the
rich people whose work was being done there seemed to
have permeated this work itself, and everything seemed to
await the Sleeping Beauty slumber that descended here on
Sundays. For this reason Sunday was properly the day of
the loggia—Sunday, which none of the other rooms could
ever quite contain, as if they were damaged. Sunday seeped
out of them; only the loggia, looking out onto the yard with
the carpet rails and the other loggias with their bare walls
of Pompeian red, could hold it, and not a chime of the cargo
of bells with which the churches—the Twelve Apostles, St.
Matthew's, and the Emperor William Memorial Church—
slowly loaded it throughout the afternoon, slipped over

its balustrade; all remained piled high till evening. As I have already indicated, my grandmother did not die in the Blumeshof; nor did the other, who lived opposite her in the same street and was older and more severe, my father's mother. So the Blumeshof has become for me an Elysium, an indefinite realm of the shades of deceased but immortal grandmothers. And just as imagination, having once cast its veil over a district, is apt to adorn its edges with incomprehensible, capricious frills, so, in the course of decades and to this day it made of a long-established grocer's store situated near this house but on Magdeburgerstrasse, to one driving past without ever having set foot inside, a monument to an early-departed grandfather, solely because the first name of its owner, like his, was Georg.

But is not this, too, the city: the strip of light under the bedroom door on evenings when we were 'entertaining'. Did not Berlin itself find its way into the expectant childhood night, as later the world of William Tell or Julius Caesar invaded the night of an audience? The dream ship that came to fetch us on those evenings must have rocked at our bedside on the waves of conversation, or under the spray of clattering plates, and in the early morning it set us down on the ebb of the carpet beating that came in at the window with the moist air on rainy days and engraved itself more indelibly in the child's memory than the voice of the beloved in that of the man, the carpet beating that was the language of the nether world, of servant girls, the real grownups, a language that sometimes took its time, languid and muted under the grey sky, breaking at others into an inexplicable gallop, as if the servants were pursued by phantoms. The courtyard was one of the places where the city opened itself to the child; others, admitting him or letting him go, were railway stations. On departure, their openings were a panorama, the frame of a *fata morgana*. No distance was more remote than the place where the rails converged in the mist. Returning home, however, all was different. For the lamps still burned in us that had shone in isolation from courtyard windows often without curtains, from staircases bristling with filth, from cellar windows hung with rags. These were the back yards that the city showed me as I returned from Hahnenklee or Sylt, only to close upon them once more, never to let me see or enter them. But those five last fearful minutes of the journey before everyone got out have been converted into the gaze of my eyes, and there are those perhaps who look into them as into courtyard windows in damaged walls, in which at early evening a lamp stands.

Among the postcards in my album there are a number of which the written side has lasted better in my memory than the picture. All bear the handsome, legible signature 'Helene Pufahl'. She was my first teacher. Long before I knew of classes at school, I was brought by her into close relationship to the children of my 'class', in the sense of the word that I was to become acquainted with only two decades later. And that it was high on the social scale I can infer from the names of the two girls from the little circle that remain in my memory: Ilse Ullstein and Luise von Landau. What order of nobility these Landaus belonged to I do not know. But their name had an immense attraction for me and—I have grounds to suppose—for my parents. Yet this is hardly the reason why their name has remained undimmed in my mind until today; rather, it is the circumstance that this was the first name on which I consciously heard fall the accent of

death. That was, as far as I know, not long after I had grown
out of the little private circle. Later, each time I passed the
Lützow Ufer, my eyes sought her house, and when, toward
the end of my school days, I wrote my first philosophical
essay, with the title 'Reflections on the Nobility', beside that
of Pindar with which I started, the alluring name of my first
schoolmate stood unuttered. Fraülein Pufahl was succeeded
by Herr Knoche, whom I had to confront quite alone. He
was the pre-school teacher from the school for which my
parents later intended me. His instruction does not appear
to have entirely agreed with me. At any rate, I performed
on occasion magical rites directed against his person, and I
still remember the feeling of omnipotence that came over
me one day on the Herkules Bridge on receiving the news
that Herr Knoche had cancelled the next day's class. At that
time I knew to what I might attribute this, but today, sadly,
I have forgotten the magic formula. More than in his private
appearances, Herr Knoche impressed me in the classroom
lessons I had with him later, when I had started school.
They were enlivened by frequent intermezzi for thrashing.
Herr Knoche was a zealous exponent of the cane. He was
also entrusted with our singing instruction. And it was in a
singing lesson that he showed me one of the shut gates that
we all know from our childhood, behind which, we were
assured, the way to later, real life lay open. We were practising the cuirassier's song from *Wallenstein's Camp*. 'To horse,
trusty friends, to horse and away / to the field of freedom and
valiance, / where a man's worth more than dust and clay /
and the heart's still weighed in the balance.' Herr Knoche
wanted the class to tell him what these last words actually
meant. No one, of course, could give an answer. It was one

of those artful questions that make children obtuse. Our dis-
comfiture seemed most agreeable to Herr Knoche, who said
pointedly, 'You'll understand that when you are grown up.'
Now I am grown up; I am today inside the gate that Herr
Knoche showed me; but it is still firmly shut. I was not to
make my entrance through that portal.

As lights on a foggy night have around them gigantic rings, my earliest theatrical impressions emerge from
the mist of my childhood with great aureoles. At the very
beginning is a 'monkey theatre' that played perhaps on
Unter den Linden and at which I appeared, as I remember,
heavily escorted, as neither parents nor grandmother was
prepared to forgo witnessing the effect on me of my first theatrical performance. True, the source of the light, the actual
happening on the stage, I can no longer discern in so much
luminous haze. A pinkish-grey cloud of seats, lights, and
faces has obliterated the pranks of the poor little monkeys
on the stage. And while I can recount the sequence of theatrical events in the following six or seven years, I can say
nothing more of them—neither of the *Ladies' Man* I saw at
the Spa Theatre at Suderode; nor of the *William Tell* that,
as is customary, initiated me to the Berlin stage; nor of the
Fiesco, with Matkowsky, that I saw at the Schauspielhaus or
the *Carmen*, with Destinn, at the Opera. The latter two performances my grandmother had taken under her wing; hence
not only the dazzling programme but also the imposing circle
seats. And yet more fondly than to them, my mind goes back
to the *William Tell*, because of the event that preceded it,
the highly hermetic nature of which is still undimmed, while
nothing remains in my memory of the same evening's performance. It must have been in the afternoon that a difference

of opinion arose between myself and my mother. Something was to be done that I did not like. Finally, my mother had recourse to coercion. She threatened that unless I did her bidding I should be left at home in the evening. I obeyed. But the feeling with which I did so, or rather, with which, the threat hardly uttered, I measured the two opposed forces and instantaneously perceived how enormous was the preponderance of the other side, and thus my silent indignation at so crude and brutal a procedure, which put at stake something totally disproportionate to the end—for the end was momentary whereas the stake, the gratitude for the evening that my mother was about to give me, as I know today and anticipated then, was deep and permanent—this feeling of misused and violated trust has outlived in me all that succeeded it that day. Many years afterwards it was proved a second time how much more significant and enduring the anticipation of an event can be than what actually ensues. As a boy I longed for nothing more than to see Kainz. But his guest performances in Berlin were during school time. As the advance bookings in the morning offered the only possibility of procuring seats at prices commensurate with my pocket money, my wish was denied for years. My parents, at any rate, did nothing to advance its fulfilment. One day— whether because the advance bookings were on a Sunday or for another reason—I was able after all to be one of the first at the ticket office, which was already that of the theatre at the Nollendorfplatz. I see myself standing at the box office and—as if memory wanted to prelude the approaching main theme—waiting there, sure enough, but not buying my ticket. At this point memory pauses, and only picks up its thread again when I am mounting the stairs to the circle in the evening, before the performance of *Richard II*. What is it that imposes once again on memory, at the door of the auditorium, a 'so far and no further'? True, I see before me a scene from the drama, but entirely cut off, without my knowing whether it is really from this performance or from another, any more than I know whether I saw Kainz or not; whether his appearance was cancelled or whether the disappointment of finding him less great than I had believed him annulled, with the image of his acting, the whole evening. So I confront uncertainty wherever I follow my earliest theatrical memories, and in the end I can no longer even distinguish dream from reality. This is true of a dark winter evening when I went with my mother to a production of *The Merry Wives of Windsor*. I really saw this opera, in a kind of people's theatre. It was a noisy, cheerful evening, but all the more silent was the journey there, through a snow-covered, unknown Berlin spreading about me in the gaslight. It stood in the same relation to the city I knew as that most jealously guarded of my postcards, the depiction of the Halle Gate in pale blue on a darker blue background. The Belle-Allianceplatz was to be seen with the houses that frame it; the full moon was in the sky. From the moon and the windows in the façades, however, the top layer of card had been removed; their contrasting white disrupted the picture, and one had to hold it against a lamp or a candle to see, by the light of windows and a lunar surface parading in exactly the same illumination, the whole scene regain its composure. Perhaps that evening the opera we were approaching was the source of light that made the city suddenly gleam so differently, but perhaps it was only a dream that I had later of this walk, the memory of which had displaced what previously stood in for reality.

The architect of the Kaiser Friedrich School must have had something on the order of Brandenburg brick Gothic in mind. At any rate, it is constructed in red brick-work and displays a preference of motifs commonly found at Stendal or Tangermünde. The whole, however, gives a narrow-chested, high-shouldered impression. Rising close by the precincts of the municipal railway, the building exudes a sad, spinsterish primness. Even more than to the experiences I had within, it is probably to this exterior that I should attribute the fact that I have not retained a single cheerful memory of it. Nor, since leaving, have I ever had the idea of going back. Of the walk to school I have already spoken. But if the portal had been reached just in time, or there was no longer sufficient time—and the nightmarish things to come did not weigh too heavily—to allow me to buy at the adjoining stationer's another piece of plasticine, a protractor, or, at the very beginning, wafers and the little ribbons used to attach blotting sheets to exercise-book covers—if finally the wrought-iron door, which the janitor was allowed to open only ten minutes before school started, was still closed—how melancholy and oppressed must this wait at the door have been, under the arch of the municipal railway, which crossed Knesebeckstrasse at this point, if nothing of it comes back to me besides the compulsion incessantly to remove my cap, to pay attention to myself, when another of the teachers passed, who were permitted to enter, of course, at any time they pleased.

Only today, it seems to me, am I able to appreciate how much hatefulness and humiliation lay in the obligation to raise my cap to teachers. The necessity of admitting them by this gesture into the sphere of my private existence

seemed presumptuous. I should have had no objection to a
less intimate, and in some way military display of respect.
But to greet a teacher as one would a relation or a friend
seemed inordinately unfitting, as if they had wanted to hold
school in my home. From this alone it can be seen how little
school was ever able to win me over. And if I experienced
the antiquated forms of school discipline—caning, change
of seats, or detention—only in the lower forms, nevertheless the terror and the pall they placed me under in those
years never lifted from me. I find this not only in the importance attached to promotion to the next form and to the
four reports brought home each year, but also in smaller
but more telling details. Above all in the unfathomable
shock or, rather, bewilderment into which I was plunged
by interruptions in the continuity of teaching—such as
excursions to the country, games, and above all the great
annual competition between the schools of Greater Berlin
to decide the best team at prisoner's base. Needless to say,
I never belonged to the school team, which seldom met
with success. But in the mobilization of the whole school
that took place on such occasions, I, too, was involved. The
matches were normally played in May or June, on some field
or drill ground in the vicinity of the Lehrter station. As a
rule, the weather was blazing hot. Nervously I alighted at
the Lehrter station, uncertainly I set off in the direction I
vaguely remembered, and found myself at last, with mixed
feelings of relief and repugnance, amid some alien troop of
schoolboys. From now on bewilderment was uninterrupted:
whether I had to look for my own school party, or sought
a resting place in the shade, whether I had to reach a stall
without crossing the field in order to buy fruit for breakfast,

or congregate, while avoiding any appearance of indifference, around one of the gentlemen who made known the day's results, or finally, although I had not understood these results, exchange with my school fellows during the homeward journey observations on the course of the game. Yet what made these sporting occasions most hated and most repellent of all was not their multitudinous attendance but their site. The broad, unfrequented avenues leading to it were flanked by barracks, barracks bordered the playing field, the field was a parade ground. And on those days the feeling never left me that if for only a moment I relaxed my vigilance, permitted myself only the briefest wellbeing in the shade of a tree or before a sausage vendor's stand, I should fall in ten years' time irredeemably into the power of this place: I should have to become a soldier. The Kaiser Friedrich School stands close by the municipal railway yard at the Savignyplatz. At the Savignyplatz station you can look down into its playground. And because, once liberated from it, I frequently took the opportunity to do this, it now stands before me quite uselessly, similar to one of those Mexican temples that were excavated much too early and inexpertly, their frescoes having been long effaced by rain by the time the excavation of the ceremonial implements and papyri, which might have thrown some light on these images, could at last seriously begin. So I have to make do with what is resurrected only today, isolated pieces of interior that have broken away and yet contain the whole within them, while the whole, standing out there before me, has lost its details without trace. The first fragment to reappear is what was certainly, throughout my whole time at school, the idlest of my perceptions: the moulding, crowned with crenellations, above the classrooms. And perhaps that is not so difficult to explain. For everything else that came within my visual field sooner or later became of use to me, became associated with a thought or a notion that swept it along into the sea of oblivion. Only this narrow moulding, cast out innumerable times by the healthy beat of everyday waves until it was left stranded like a shell on the shore of my daydreaming. And there I now come across it. I pick it up and question it like Hamlet addressing the skull. It is, as I have said, a moulding representing a row of battlements. What is visible between them, therefore, is not empty space but the same wood, only bevelled and notched. The intention was certainly to remind the onlooker of a castle. What he was to do with the recollection was another question. In any event, this moulding reinforced the dense mass divided in the morning behind the closed doors: the class at lessons. Over the doors leading to the arts-and-crafts rooms it became the emblem of a certain guild-like solidity. On the classroom cupboard I encountered it again, but how much more emphasis it had on the identically shaped cupboards standing along the faculty-room wall. In the first, second, and third forms, in the vicinity of the many little coats and caps on their racks, its impact was lost; but in the upper classes it acquired an allusion to the *Abitur* that was soon to crown the labours of their members. Yet never more than a shadow of meaning and reason passed across it in such places, and it remained, with the unspeakable grey-green ornaments adorning the wall of the hall, and with the absurd bosses and scrolls of the cast-iron balustrades, the refuge of all my minutes of terror and my nightmares. Nothing, however, could compare with the moulding, unless it were the bell that shrilly marked the beginning and end of lessons and breaks. The timbre and duration of this signal never varied. And yet how different it sounded at the beginning of the first and at the end of the last period—to circumscribe this difference would be to lift the veil that seven years of school cast ever more tightly over each of the days that composed them. In the winter the lamps were often still on when it rang, but it was bereft of cosiness, offering as little shelter as the light the dentist shines into the mouth on which he is about to operate. Between two peals of the bell lay the break, the second precipitating the shuffling, chattering uproar with which the mass of pupils, streaking through only two doors, surged up the narrow stairway from floor to floor. These staircases I have always hated: hated when forced to climb them in the midst of the herd, a forest of calves and feet before me, defencelessly exposed to the bad odours emanating from all the bodies pressing so closely against mine, hated no less when, arriving late, passing deserted corridors, I hastened up them quite alone to the very top, arriving breathless in the classroom. If that happened before the teacher's hand was on the door handle, even though he might be quite near, you got in unseen. But woe if the door was already shut—however wide open those next to it might still be, and even if above or below some time passed before the bang or a shutting door announced the start of a lesson, and no matter how harmlessly the eye of a strange teacher approaching along the corridor brushed you—the judgment was ineluctable within, once you had plucked up courage to open it.

In one of the streets I passed along on my endless wanderings I was surprised, many years earlier, by the first stirring of my sexual urge, under the oddest circumstances.

It was on the Jewish New Year's Day, and my parents had made arrangements for me to attend some divine celebration. Probably it was a service at the reformed synagogue, which my mother, on grounds of a family tradition, held in some sympathy, whereas my father's upbringing inclined him more to the orthodox rite. However, he had to give way. For this visit to the synagogue I had been entrusted to a relative whom I had to fetch on my way. But whether because I had forgotten his address or because I was unfamiliar with the district, it grew later and later without my drawing nearer to my goal. To make my way independently to the synagogue was out of the question, since I had no idea where it was. This bewilderment, forgetfulness, and embarrassment were doubtless chiefly due to my dislike of the impending service, in its familial no less than its divine aspect. While I was wandering thus, I was suddenly and simultaneously overcome, on the one hand, by the thought 'Too late, time was up long ago, you'll never get there'—and, on the other, by a sense of the insignificance of all this, of the benefits of letting things take what course they would; and these two streams of consciousness converged irresistibly in an immense pleasure that filled me with blasphemous indifference toward the service, but exalted the street in which I stood as if it had already intimated to me the services of procurement it was later to render to my awakened drive.

We had our 'summer residences' first at Potsdam, then at Babelsberg. They were outside, from the point of view of the city; but from that of the summer, inside; we were ensconced within it, and I must disengage my memories of it, like moss that one plucks at random in the dark from the walls of a cave, from its sultry, humid glimmer. There are memories that are especially well preserved because, although not themselves affected, they are isolated by a shock from all that followed. They have not been worn away by contact with their successors and remain detached, self-sufficient. The first such memory appears when I speak of these summer days: it is an evening in my seventh or eighth year. One of our maidservants stands a long while at the wrought-iron gate, which opens onto I know not what tree-lined walk. The big garden, where I have been roaming in overgrown border regions, is already closed to me. It is time to go to bed. Perhaps I have sated myself with my favourite game, shooting with the rubber bolts of my 'Eureka' pistol, somewhere in the bushes by the wire fence, at the wooden birds, which, struck by a bolt, fell backward out of the painted foliage to which they were attached by strings. The whole day I had been keeping a secret to myself: the dream of the previous night. It had been an eerie one. A ghost had appeared to me. The site of its operations did not, in exact truth, really exist, but had nevertheless a very strong resemblance to one known, tantalizing, and inaccessible to me, namely the corner of my parents' bed-chamber that was separated from the rest of the chamber by an arch hung with a heavy, faded-violet curtain, and in which my mother's dressing gowns, house dresses, and shawls were suspended. The darkness behind the curtain was impenetrable, and this corner was the sinister, noctur-nal counterpart of that bright, beatific realm that opened occasionally with my mother's linen cupboard, in which, piled up on the shelves, edged with white trimming and bearing a blue-embroidered text from Schiller's 'The Bell', lay the sheets, tablecloths, napkins, and pillowcases. A sweet lavender scent came from the brightly coloured silk sachets hanging on the inside of the cupboard doors. These were the hell and paradise into which the ancient magic of hearth and home, which had once been lodged in the spinning wheel, had been sundered. Now my dream had risen from the evil world: a ghost busying itself at a trestle draped with a profusion of silken fabrics, one covering another. These silks the ghost was stealing. It did not snatch them up or carry them away, it did nothing with or to them that was actually visible and distinguishable, and yet I knew it stole them, just as in legends people who discover a spirits' banquet know that these dead things are feasting, without seeing them eat or drink. It was this dream that I had kept secret. And in the night that followed it I noticed, half asleep, my mother and father coming quietly into my room at an unusual hour. I did not see them lock themselves in; when I got up next morning there was nothing for breakfast. The house had been stripped of everything. At midday my grandmother arrived from Berlin with the bare necessities. A numerous band of burglars had descended on the house in the night. Fortunately the noise they made gave an indication of their number, so that my mother had succeeded in restraining my father, who, armed only with a pocketknife, had wanted to confront them. The dangerous visit had lasted almost until morning. In vain my parents had stood at the window in the first light, signalling to the outside world: the band had departed at their leisure with the baskets. Much later they were caught, and it emerged that their organizer, a murderer and criminal with many previous convictions, was a deaf-mute. It made me proud that I was questioned about the events of the previous evening—for a complicity was

suspected between the housebreakers and the maidservant
who had stood at the gate. What made me even prouder,
however, was the question why I had kept silent about
my dream, which I now, of course, narrated at length as a
prophecy.

What my first books were to me—to remember this I
should first have to forget all other knowledge of books. It
is certain that all I know of them today rests on the readiness with which I then opened myself to books; but whereas
now content, theme, and subject matter are extraneous to
the book, earlier they were solely and entirely in it, being
no more external or independent of it than are today the
number of its pages or its paper. The world that revealed
itself in the book and the book itself were never, at any price,
to be divided. So with each book its content, too, its world,
was palpably there, at hand. But, equally, this content and
world transfigured every part of the book. They burned
within it, blazed from it; located not merely in its binding
or its pictures, they were enshrined in chapter headings and
opening letters, paragraphs and columns. You did not read
books through; you dwelt, abided between their lines, and,
reopening them after an interval, surprised yourself at the
spot where you had halted. The rapture with which you
received a new book, scarcely venturing a fleeting glance
between its pages, was that of the guest invited for a few
weeks to a mansion and hardly daring to dart a glance of
admiration at the long suites of state rooms through which
he must pass to reach his quarters. He is all the more impatient to be allowed to withdraw. And so each year scarcely
had I found the latest volume of the *New Companion of
German Youth* when I retreated completely behind the

ramparts of its cover, which was adorned with coats of arms, and felt my way into the spy or hunting story in which I was to spend the first night. There was nothing finer than to sniff out, on this first tentative expedition into the labyrinth of stories, the various drafts, scents, brightnesses, and sounds that came from its different chambers and corridors. For in reality the longer stories, interrupted many times to reappear as continuations, extended through the whole like subterranean passages. And what did it matter if the aromas that rose from the tunnels high into the air, where we saw globes or waterwheels glisten, mingled with the smell of the gingerbread, or if a Christmas carol wove its halo around the head of Stephenson glimpsed between two pages like an ancestral portrait through a door crack, or if the smell of the gingerbread joined with that of a Sicilian sulphur mine that suddenly burst upon us in a full-page illustration as in a fresco. But if I had sat for a while immersed in my book and then went back to the table bearing the presents, it no longer stood almost imperiously over me as it had when I first entered the Christmas room; rather, I seemed to be walking on a small platform that led down to it from my fairy castle.

Anyone can observe that the duration for which we are exposed to impressions has no bearing on their fate in memory. Nothing prevents our keeping rooms in which we have spent twenty-four hours more or less clearly in our memory, and forgetting others in which we passed months. It is not, therefore, due to insufficient exposure-time if no image appears on the plate of remembrance. More frequent, perhaps, are the cases when the half-light of habit denies the plate the necessary light for years, until one day from an alien source it flashes as if from burning magnesium powder, and now a snapshot transfixes the room's image on the plate. Nor is this very mysterious, since such moments of sudden illumination are at the same time moments when we are beside ourselves, and while our waking, habitual, everyday self is involved actively or passively in what is happening, our deeper self rests in another place and is touched by the shock, as is the little heap of magnesium powder by the flame of the match. It is to this immolation of our deepest self in shock that our memory owes its most indelible images. So the room in which I slept at the age of six would have been forgotten had not my father come in one night—I was already in bed—with the news of a death. It was not, really, the news itself that so affected me: the deceased was a distant cousin. But in the way in which my father told me, there lay [text breaks off].

With the joy of remembering, however, another is fused: that of possession in memory. Today I can no longer distinguish them: it is as if it were only a part of the gift of the moment I am now relating, that it, too, received the gift of never again being wholly lost to me—even if decades have passed between the seconds in which I think of it.

The first great disappointment of my life reached me one afternoon on Peacock Island. I had been told on the way there that I should find peacock feathers in the grass. Scarcely had I heard this when, with the speed of a spark leaping between two charged systems, a close connection must have been formed in me between the name of these islands and the peacock feathers. It was not that the spark took a roundabout path by way of the image of the peacock. This had no part in the process. And so my reproachful dismay as I scoured the turf so vainly was not directed against the peacocks that I saw strutting up and down, but rather, against the soil of the island itself, which was a peacock island yet bore no peacock earth. Had I found the feather I craved in the grass, I should have felt as if I were expected and welcome at this spot. Now the island seemed to have broken a promise. Certainly the peacocks could not console me. Were they not there for everybody to see? And I was to have had something intended only for me, concealed from all others, to be found in the grass only by me. This disappointment would not have been so great had it not been Mother Earth herself who had inflicted it on me. Similarly, the bliss at having, after much toil, at last learned to ride a bicycle would have been less sweet had not Mother Earth herself let me feel her praise. One learned to ride in those days—it was the heyday of bicycle racing—in large halls specially established for the purpose. These halls did not however, have the snobbish character of the later ice palaces or indoor tennis courts; rather, they resembled skating rinks or gymnasiums, and bespoke a mentality for which sport and open air were not inseparable as they are today. It was the era of 'sporting costumes' that, unlike our present track suits, did not yet seek to adapt the body to immediate needs, but, rather, to define the particular sport as sharply as possible and isolate it from all others, just as those halls cut it off from nature and other exercises. The sport, as it was practised in those halls, still had about it all the eccentricities of its beginnings. On the asphalted floor, moving under the supervision of trainers among the ordinary tricycles for gentlemen, ladies, and children, were constructions with front wheels ten times larger than their small rear wheels, their airy seats probably occupied by artistes rehearsing a number. The orchard at Gleinicke, the broad, ceremonious promenade of Schloss Babelsberg, the narrow, concealed pathways of our summer garden, the shady ways through the foliage leading down to Lake Griebnitz at the places where there were jetties—all this I annexed to my domain, completing in an instant in fantasy the work of countless walks, games, and outings, kneeling in my nuptials with the ground as a dynast conquers endless territories by means of a single felicitous union.

I have talked of the courtyards. Even Christmas was fundamentally a festival of the courtyards. There it began with the barrel organs, which stretched the week before the festival with chorales, and there it ended with the Christmas trees, which, bereft of feet, leaned in the snow or glistened in the rain. But Christmas came, and all at once, before the eyes of the bourgeois child, it divided his city into two mighty camps. These were not the genuine ones, in which the exploited and their rulers lie irreconcilably opposed. No, it was a camp posed and arranged almost as artificially as the cribs composed as paper or wooden figures, but also as old and as honourable: Christmas came and divided the children into those who shuffled past the booths on Potsdam Square and those who, alone, indoors, offered their dolls and farm animals for sale to children of their age. Christmas came and with it a whole, unknown world of wares, [text breaks off].

The *déjà vu* effect has often been described. But I wonder whether the term is actually well chosen, and whether the metaphor appropriate to the process would not be far better taken from the realm of acoustics. One ought to speak of events that reach us like an echo awakened by a call, a sound that seems to have been heard somewhere in the darkness of past life. Accordingly, if we are not mistaken, the shock with which moments enter consciousness as if already lived usually strikes us in the form of a sound. It is a word, tapping, or a rustling that is endowed with the magic power to transport us into the cool tomb of long ago, from the vault of which the present seems to return only as an echo. But has the counterpart of this temporal removal ever been investigated, the shock with which we come across a gesture or a word as we suddenly find in our house a forgotten glove or reticule? And just as they cause us to surmise a stranger who has been there, there are words or gestures from which we infer that invisible stranger, the future, who left them in our keeping. I was perhaps five years old. One evening—I was already in bed—my father appeared, probably to say good night. It was half against his will, I thought, that he told me the news of a relative's death. The deceased was a cousin, a grown man who scarcely concerned me. But my father gave the news with details, took the opportunity to explain, in answer to my question, what a heart attack was, and was communicative. I did not take in much of the explanation. But that evening I must have memorized my room and my bed, as one observes exactly a place where one feels dimly that one will later have to search for something one has forgotten there. Many years afterward I discovered what I had 'forgotten', a part of the news that my father had broken to me in that room: that the illness was called syphilis.

1932

VI

Eduard Fuchs, Collector and Historian

1

The life's work of Eduard Fuchs belongs to the most recent past. A retrospect of this work involves all the difficulties posed by an attempt to render an account of the immediate past—in this case the immediate past of the Marxist theory of art, which does not ease matters. For by contrast with Marxist economics, there is still no history of this theory. Its teachers, Marx and Engels, did no more than indicate a broad field for the materialist dialectic in it. While the first who broached it, a Plekhanov, a Mehring, assimilated the lessons of the masters only indirectly or at any rate belatedly. The tradition that leads from Marx through Wilhelm Liebknecht to Bebel developed the political far more than the scientific side of Marxism. Mehring passed through nationalism and the school of Lassalle; and when he first entered the Social Democratic Party, its theoretical outlook was—according to Kautsky—dominated by a 'more or less vulgar Lassalleanism. Coherent Marxist thought was non-existent, apart from a few isolated personalities'.[1] Mehring

came into contact with Marxism later, in the final years of
Engels's life. Fuchs on the other hand came upon Mehring
quite early. In the relationship between the two a tradition
of cultural investigation for the first time emerged within
historical materialism. But Mehring's field, the history of literature, had few points of contact with that of Fuchs, as both
researchers were aware. The difference in their dispositions
was even more important. Mehring was by temperament a
scholar, Fuchs a collector.

There are many kinds of collector, and in any one there
is a host of impulses at work. Fuchs as a collector is above
all a pioneer: the founder of a unique archive on the history
of caricature, erotic art, and the portrayal of manners. More
important, though, is another and indeed complementary
circumstance: it was as a pioneer that Fuchs became a collector. That is, as a pioneer of the materialist view of art. But
what made this materialist a collector was his more or less
clear feeling for what he saw as his historical situation. This
was the situation of historical materialism itself.

It finds expression in a letter Friedrich Engels sent to
Mehring at a time when Fuchs, in a socialist editorial office,
was winning his first victories as a publicist. The letter is
dated 14 July 1893 and says, among other things: 'It is above
all this semblance of an independent history of state constitutions, of systems of law, of ideological conceptions in
every separate domain, that dazzles most people. If Luther
and Calvin "overcome" the official Catholic religion, or
Hegel "overcomes" Fichte and Kant, Rousseau with his
republican Social Contract indirectly "overcomes" the
constitutional Montesquieu, this is a process which remains
within theology, philosophy or political science, represents

a stage in the history of these particular spheres of thought and never passes beyond the sphere of thought. Since the bourgeois illusion of the eternality and finality of capitalist production has been added as well, even the overcoming of the mercantilists by the physiocrats and Adam Smith is accounted a sheer victory of thought, not as the reflection in thought of changed economic facts, but of the finally achieved correct understanding of actual conditions substituting always and everywhere.'[2]

Engels's objection is twofold: first, he is protesting against the habit in the history of ideas of representing a new dogma as the *development* of an earlier one, a new school of poetry as a *reaction* to a preceding one, a new style as the *overcoming* of an older one; second, it is clear that he also implicitly objects to the custom of representing such new entities in isolation from their effect on people and their intellectual and economic processes of production. His argument destroys the claim of the humanities to be the history of constitutions or natural sciences, of religion or art. But the explosive power of these thoughts, which Engels carried with him for half a century,[3] goes deeper. It calls in question the hermetic self-sufficiency of the various disciplines and their subjects—in the case of art, the works which the concept of art purports to encompass. For a dialectical historian, these works incorporate both their prehistory and their after-history—an after-history in virtue of which their prehistory, too, can be seen to undergo constant change. They teach him how their function can outlast their creator, can leave his intentions behind; how its reception by the artist's contemporaries forms part of the effect that the work of art has on us ourselves today, and how this effect derives from

our encounter not just with the work, but with the history
that has brought the work down to us. This is what Goethe
intimated to Chancellor von Müller in a conversation about
Shakespeare: 'Nothing that has had a great impact can really
be judged any longer.' There could be no apter evocation
of the disquiet that marks the beginning of any critique
of history worthy to be called dialectical, which must
renounce a calm, contemplative attitude towards its subject
to become aware of the critical constellation in which precisely this fragment of the past is found with precisely this
present. 'Truth will not run away from us'—this dictum,
by Gottfried Keller, indicates the exact spot where historical
materialism breaks through the historicist view of the past.
For it is an irrecoverable picture of the past that threatens
to vanish with every present instant that does not see itself
prefigured in it.

The more one reflects on Engels's remarks, the clearer it
becomes that the price of any dialectical account of history is
abandonment of the contemplative approach characteristic
of historicism. The historical materialist must sacrifice the
epic dimension of history. The past for him becomes the
subject of a construction whose locus is not empty time, but
the particular epoch, the particular life, the particular work.
He breaks the epoch away from its reified *historical continuity*, and the life from the epoch, and the work from the life's
work. But the result of his construction is that *in* the work
the life's work, *in* the life's work the epoch, and *in* the epoch
the course of history are suspended and preserved.[4]

Historicism presents an eternal image of the past, historical materialism a specific and unique engagement with
it. The substitution of the act of construction for the epic

dimension proves to be the condition of this engagement. In it those powerful forces that lie bound in the 'once-upon-a-time' of historicism are set free. The task of historical materialism is to set to work an engagement with history original to every new present. It has recourse to a consciousness of the present that shatters the continuum of history.

Historical materialism conceives historical understanding as an after-life of that which is understood, whose pulse can still be felt in the present. This understanding has its place in Fuchs's scheme, but by no means an undisputed one. An old, dogmatic and naive notion of 'reception' coexists in him with the new and more critical one. The former consists essentially in the assertion that what should count for most in our reception of a work is the way it was received at the hands of the artist's contemporaries. It forms an exact analogy to Ranke's 'what it was actually like', which is 'after all the only thing that matters'.[5] Cheek by jowl with this, however, we find a dialectical insight into the significance of a history of reception—an insight that opens the widest horizons. Fuchs complains that the question is ignored in art history. 'This omission is a failure in our overall appreciation of art. And yet it seems to me that uncovering the real reasons for the greater or lesser success of an artist, for the duration of his success, and no less so for the opposite, is one of the most important problems of art.'[6] This was also the view taken by Mehring, the starting point of whose analyses in his *Lessing-Legende* was the reception accorded to the poet, whether by Heine or Gervinus, Stahr or Danzel or, finally, Erich Schmidt. It was not for nothing that Julian Hirsch's 'On the Genesis of Fame', a valuable study in terms of its contents if not its methods, appeared not long afterwards. Fuchs had the same question in mind. Its solution affords a criterion for the standards of historical materialism. This fact does not, however, justify the suppression of another: that such a solution is still wanting. It is better to concede without reservations that only in isolated cases has it been possible to apprehend the historical import of a work of art in such a way as to make it more transparent for us as a *work of art*. All attempts to court a work of art must remain futile unless its sober historical content is illumined by the shafts of dialectical insight. That is only the first of the truths by which the work of Eduard Fuchs the collector was guided. His collections are the practical man's answer to the paradoxes of theory.

2

Fuchs was born in 1870. He was not predisposed to a life of scholarship. And notwithstanding the great erudition to which he attained in later life, he never became the typical scholar. His work constantly overshot the bounds of the researcher's field of vision. So it was with his achievements as a collector; so, too, with his activity as a politician. Fuchs started to earn his living in the mid-1880s. It was the time of Bismarck's law against socialists. Fuchs' position as an apprentice brought him together with politically concerned proletarians, and he was soon involved in what today seems the idyllic struggle of the illegal militants of that time. This apprenticeship ended in 1887. A few years later, the Bavarian organ of the Social Democrats, the *Münchener Post*, solicited the services of the young book-keeper Fuchs from a Stuttgart printer's; it believed it had found in him the man who could clear up the paper's administrative difficulties. Fuchs went to Munich, to work there with Richard Calver.

The publishers of the *Münchener Post* also brought out a magazine of socialist lampoons, the *Süddeutsche Postilion*. It happened one day that Fuchs, to help out, had to assume responsibility for making up an issue of the *Postilion*, and filled some gaps with contributions of his own. This issue was unusually successful. Then, the same year, appeared the May issue of this paper, colourfully illustrated—coloured newspaper illustration was just then getting started—and put together by Fuchs. Sixty thousand copies were sold, compared with an annual average of 2,500. Thus Fuchs became editor of a magazine devoted to political satire. At the same time he turned to the history of his field; this, together with his day-to-day work, was the origin of the illustrated studies on the year 1848 in caricature and on the Lola Montez affair. By contrast with history books illustrated by living artists (e.g. Wilhelm Blos's popular books on the revolution, with pictures by von Jentsch), these were the first historical works with documentary illustration. At Harden's invitation, Fuchs himself announced the second of these works in *Die Zukunft*, remarking that it was only an excerpt from the comprehensive work he planned on caricature among the European peoples. A ten-month spell in prison, after a conviction for *lèsemajesté* in the press, stood him in good stead in his studies for this work. The idea was plainly an auspicious one. A certain Hans Kraemer, who had some experience in the production of illustrated almanacs, approached Fuchs with the news that he was already working on a history of caricature; he proposed to contribute his own studies to a joint work. His contributions, however, failed to materialize, and before long it was clear that Fuchs would have to shoulder the entire considerable work-load by himself. The name of the presumptive co-author, which still appeared on the title page of the first edition of the work on caricature, was dropped in the second. But Fuchs had given the first convincing proof of his stamina and of his mastery of his material. The long series of his major works was launched.[7]

Fuchs emerged at a time when, as *Die Neue Zeit* once put it, 'the trunk of the Social Democratic Party was expanding in ring after ring of organic growth'.[8] This meant new tasks in the party's educational work. The more the working masses flocked to the party, the less could it content itself with their mere political and scientific enlightenment, with popularizing the theories of surplus value and of evolution. It also had to start including historical material in its lecture courses and in the feature supplements of the party press. This raised the whole problem of the *popularization of knowledge*. It was not solved. And no solution could be approached so long as the object of this educational work was thought of as the *public* rather than as a class.[9] If the educational work of the party had been directed at the class, it would not have lost its feel for the scientific tasks of historical materialism. The historical material, ploughed over by Marxist dialectics, would have become the soil in which the seed sown by the present could have sprouted. That did not happen. The slogan 'Work and Education', under which the patriotic associations of Schultze-Delitzsch had conducted workers' education, was countered by Social Democracy with the slogan 'Knowledge is power'. But the party failed to perceive its double meaning. It thought the same knowledge that secured the rule of the bourgeoisie over the proletariat would enable the proletariat to free itself from that rule. In reality, knowledge with no outlet in praxis, knowledge that could teach the proletariat nothing about its situation as a class, was no danger to its oppressors. This was especially true of knowledge relating to the humanities. It lagged far behind economics, remaining untouched by the revolution in economic theory. It sought only to *stimulate*, to *offer variety*, to *arouse interest*. History was shaken up, to relieve the monotony; the result was *cultural history*. This is where Fuchs's work came into its own: in its reaction to this state of affairs lay its greatness, in its participation in it, its problematic dimension. From the beginning Fuchs had made a point of tailoring his work for the reading masses.[10]

Few recognized at the time how much in reality depended on the work of materialist education. It was the hopes, and even more the misgivings, of those few that found expression in a debate reflected in *Neue Zeit*. The most important contribution was an essay by Korn entitled 'The Proletariat and the Classics'. It dealt with the notion of heritage, a concept which has again become important today. Lassalle saw in German idealism, Korn argued, a heritage of which the working class took possession. But Marx and Engels held a different view. 'They did not derive the social priority of the working class from an inheritance, but rather from its decisive position in the production process itself. Besides, what need is there to talk of possessions, even cultural possessions, on the part of a parvenu class, like the modern proletariat, that daily and hourly demonstrates its *right* through ... its work that is constantly reproducing the entire apparatus of culture? ... For Marx and Engels the showpiece of Lassalle's educational ideal, speculative philosophy, is thus no tabernacle ... and both felt more and more strongly drawn to natural science.... Indeed for a class whose essence is its function, natural science may as well be called knowledge pure and simple, just as for the ruling and possessing class everything that is historical composes the given form of its ideology.... In actual fact history represents for consciousness the category of possession, exactly as capital represents for economics the control of past labour.'[11]

This critique of historicism has some weight. However, the reference to natural science—'knowledge pure and simple'—for the first time permits a clear view of the dangerous problematic of the educational question. The prestige of the natural sciences had dominated debate since Bebel. His major work, *Women and Socialism*, sold 200,000 copies in the thirty years between its appearance and that of Korn's work. Bebel's appreciation of natural science does not rest on the mathematical exactness of its results alone, but above all on its practical applicability.[12] Later it occupies a similar position in Engels's thought, when he tries to refute Kant's phenomenology by pointing to the triumph of technology, which shows that we do indeed recognize 'things in themselves'. Natural science, which in Korn appears as knowledge *tout court*, does so above all as the foundation of technology. But technology is obviously not a purely scientific phenomenon. It is also an historical one. As such, it forces us to investigate the positivist and undialectical separation between natural science and the humanities. The questions which mankind asks of nature are determined among other things by its level of production. This is the point where positivism breaks down. In the development of technology it saw only the progress of science, not the retrogression of society. It overlooked the fact that capitalism has decisively conditioned that development. It also escaped the positivists among the theoreticians of Social Democracy that the development of technology made it more and more difficult for the proletariat to take possession of it—an act that was seen to be more and more urgently necessary. They failed to perceive the destructive side of technology because they were alienated from the destructive side of the dialectic.

A prognosis was needed, and it was not forthcoming. This set the seal on a trend that was characteristic of the last century: the defective reception of technology. It consisted in a series of vigorous and repeated attempts to get round the fact that technology serves this society solely for the production of commodities. The disciples of Saint-Simon started the ball rolling with their industrial poetry; then came the realism of a Du Camp, who saw the locomotive as the saint of the future; and a Ludwig Pau brought up the rear: 'It is quite unnecessary to become an angel', he wrote, 'since the locomotive is worth more than the finest pair of wings.'[13] This romantic view of technology is straight out of *Die Gartenlaube*. It may fairly be wondered whether the *Gemütlichkeit* in which the century's bourgeoisie rejoiced may not stem from a vague satisfaction at never having to experience at first hand the development of the forces of production. That experience was really reserved for the following century. It is discovering that traffic speeds, like the capacity to duplicate both the spoken and the written word, have outstripped human needs. The energies that technology develops beyond their threshold are destructive. They serve primarily to foster the technology of warfare, and of the means used to prepare public opinion for war. It may be said of this development, which was thoroughly class-determined, that it occurred behind the back of the last century—which was not yet aware of the destructive energies of technology. This was particularly true of Social Democracy at the turn of the century. If it sought to puncture the illusions of positivism in certain specific areas, by and large it remained under their sway. It saw the past as having been brought once and for all into the granaries of the present; if the future held work in store, it also promised the certainty of a rich harvest.

3

This was the age in which Eduard Fuchs grew up, and some essential features of his work are derived from it. To put it simply, his work partakes of the problematic that is inseparable from cultural history. This problematic goes back to the Engels text quoted above. Indeed, the passage may be seen as the *locus classicus* that defines historical materialism as the history of culture. Must that not be its real meaning? Must not the study of individual disciplines, now stripped of their apparent autarky, be subsumed in the study of cultural history as that of the inventory mankind has to date preserved? In reality anyone asking questions of this sort would only be replacing the many and problematical unities embraced by intellectual history (as the history of literature and art, of law or religion) with a new and even more problematical one. The historical materialist understands

that the abstract mode in which cultural history presents
its material is an illusion, established by false consciousness.[14] He approaches this abstraction with reserve. He
would be justified in this reserve by the mere inspection of
the actual past: whatever he surveys in art and science has
a descent that cannot be contemplated without horror. It
owes its existence not just to the efforts of the great geniuses
who fashioned it, but also in greater or lesser degree to the
anonymous drudgery of their contemporaries. There is no
cultural document that is not at the same time a record of
barbarism. No history of culture has yet done justice to this
fundamental fact, or can well hope to do so.

Yet this is not the crux of the matter. If the concept of
culture is a problematical one for historical materialism, the
disintegration of culture into commodities to be possessed
by mankind is unthinkable for it. Historical materialism does
not regard the work of the past as over and done with. It
does not see that work, or any part of it, as falling with con-
venient quiddity into the lap of any epoch. The concept of
culture as the embodiment of entities that are considered
independently, if not of the production process in which
they arose, then of that in which they continue to survive,
is fetishistic. Culture appears reified. Its history is then
nothing but the residue of memorable things and events that
never broke the surface of human consciousness because
they were never truly, that is politically, experienced. One
must recognize that no historiography undertaken on the
basis of cultural history has ever managed to escape this
problematic. It is manifest in the ambitious *German History*
of Lamprecht, to which the critics of *Neue Zeit* more than
once addressed themselves, for obvious reasons. 'Of the

bourgeois historians', writes Mehring, 'Lamprecht is known as the one who has come closest to historical materialism'. Nevertheless, 'Lamprecht stopped half way ... Any concept of historical method vanishes ... when Lamprecht tries to apply a particular method to his account of economic and cultural developments, yet compiles the political developments of the same period from other historians.'[15] To represent cultural history on the basis of pragmatic storytelling certainly makes no sense. But the absurdity of a dialectical history of culture as such lies deeper, since the continuum of history, blown apart by dialectics, is nowhere scattered over a wider area than in that part people call culture.

In short, cultural history only seems to represent a deepening of insight; it does not present even the appearance of progress in dialectics. For it lacks the destructive element that guarantees the authenticity of dialectical thought and of the dialectician's experience. It may well increase the burden of the treasures that are piled up on humanity's back. But it does not give mankind the strength to shake them off, so as to get its hands on them. The same applies to the educational work of socialism around the turn of the century, which made cultural history its lodestar.

4

Fuchs' work takes on sharper historical definition against this background. Where it has lasting value, it was wrested from an intellectual constellation that has rarely been more unfavourable. And here it is Fuchs the collector who taught the theoretician many things to which his time barred access. It was the collector who found his way into grey areas—caricature, pornography—where the models of conventional art history sooner or later come to grief. In the first place it should be noted that Fuchs broke right across the board with the classicist conception of art, whose traces can still be recognized even in Marx. The ideas employed by the bourgeoisie in developing this conception of art no longer operate in Fuchs: not beauty of appearance, not harmony, not unity in diversity. And the same robust self-assertiveness of the collector which estranged the writer from the classicist theories sometimes sets its face, in the bluntest terms, against classical antiquity itself. In 1908, pointing to the work of Rodin and Slevogt, he prophesied a new beauty, 'which in its end result promises to be infinitely greater than the ancient world. For where the latter was only the highest animal form, the new beauty will be imbued with a grandiose intellectual and spiritual content'.[16]

In brief, the values that had dictated the aesthetic views of Winckelmann or Goethe lose all influence in the work of Fuchs. It would of course be a mistake to conclude that the dialectical critique of art was itself revolutionized. That cannot be the case before the *disiecta membra*, which idealism keeps handy in the form of *historical representation* and *appreciation*, have become one and as such have been superseded. That task is reserved for a science of history whose subject matter is not a tangle of purely factual details, but consists rather of the numbered group of threads that represent the weft of the past as it feeds into the warp of the present. (It would be a mistake to equate this weft with the mere nexus of causation. Rather, it is thoroughly dialectical, and threads may have been lost for centuries that the present course of history erratically, inconspicuously picks up again.) The subject matter of history, once released from pure facticity, needs no *appreciation*. For it offers not vague analogies to the present, but constitutes the precise dialectical problem that the present is called upon to resolve. That is indeed Fuchs' purpose. If in nothing else, his intention would be felt in the sententiousness that often makes his text sound more like a lecture. On the other hand, it also shows that much the author intended remained inchoate. What is basically new in the intention finds coherent expression principally where the subject meets it half way. This happens in the interpretation of iconography, in the consideration of mass art, and in the study of the technology of reproduction. These parts of Fuchs's work are pioneering. They are essential elements of any future materialist critique of works of art.

The three topics mentioned have one thing in common: they lead to insights that cannot prove other than destructive to the traditional view of art. Attention to the technology of reproduction reveals, as does scarcely any other line of inquiry, the decisive importance of reception; it thereby allows the correction, within limits, of the process of reification undergone by the work of art. Consideration of mass art leads to a revision of the concept of genius; it is a reminder not to overlook the invoice which alone allows the inspiration involved in the genesis of a work of art to become fruitful. Finally, explication of iconography not only proves indispensable for the study of reception and mass art; above all it guards against the excesses to which any formalism soon beckons.[17]

Fuchs had to concern himself with formalism. Wölfflin's teachings were in the ascendant at the time Fuchs was laying the foundations of his work. In his *Problem of the Individual* he refers to a principle from Wölfflin's *Classical Art*. This principle reads: 'The Quattrocento and Cinquecento as stylistic concepts can thus not be characterized by a mere account of their subject matter. The phenomenon ... points to a development of the artistic vision which is essentially independent of a particular mentality or a particular ideal of beauty.'[18] This formulation is certainly offensive to the historical materialist. But it does contain something useful; for it is precisely the historical materialist who is interested in tracing the change in artistic vision not so much to a changed ideal of beauty as to more elementary processes—processes brought about by economic and technical transformations in production. In this particular case, a fruitful line of inquiry would be to ask what economically determined changes in residential building were introduced by the Renaissance, and what role Renaissance painting played as a prospectus for the new architecture and as an illustration of the manners made possible by it.[19] Admittedly Wölfflin only touches on this question in passing. But when Fuchs retorts that 'It is precisely these formal points that can be accounted for only in terms of a change in the mood of the times',[20] he points straight to the dubiousness of the categories of cultural history discussed above.

It can be seen from more than one passage that Fuchs the writer was not interested in argument, or even discussion. The eristic dialectic, which according to Hegel's definition 'enters into the strength of the opponent so as to destroy him from within', is not to be found in Fuchs's arsenal, combative as he may appear. In those who pursued the inquiry initiated by Marx and Engels the destructive power of thought subsided, for it no longer dared to take on the century single-handed. It had already lost some of its tension in Mehring, from the sheer number of skirmishes fought. Even so, his *Lessing-Legende* is a considerable achievement. It showed what a host of political, but also scientific and theoretical, energies were mustered in the great classics. He thus made good his distaste for the bellettristic plodding of his contemporaries. He came to the noble insight that art could hope to be reborn only in the economic and political victory of the proletariat, and also to the incontestable conclusion: 'Art has no power to intervene deeply in the struggle for the emancipation of the proletariat.'[21] The subsequent development of art bore him out. Mehring's insights sent him with redoubled conviction to the study of science. In that study he earned the solidity and the rigour that made him invulnerable to revisionism. Traits were thus formed in his character that can be called in the best sense bourgeois, yet are far from guaranteeing the dialectician. They are to be met with no less in Fuchs. And they are perhaps the more conspicuous in his case for being embodied in a more expansive and sensual disposition. Be that as it may, one can easily imagine his portrait in a gallery of scholars. Next to him one might put Georg Brandes, whose rationalist fervour and passion to shed the light of the ideal (progress, science, reason) over broad vistas of history he shared. On his other side one might imagine Adolf Bastian, the ethnologist. Fuchs is reminiscent of him above all in his insatiable hunger for material. Bastian was legendary for his readiness to pack his grip and set off on expeditions that kept him away from home for months, whenever there was a question to be clarified. So too Fuchs always obeyed the impulse that drove him on to the quest for new evidence. The works of both will remain an inexhaustible mine of information for research.

5

For the psychologist it must be a significant question how an enthusiast, a nature turned towards the positive, can arrive at the passion for caricature. Answer it as he will, so far as Fuchs is concerned the facts allow of no doubt. From the start his interest in art differs from what might be called *joy in the beautiful*. From the start, truth enters the game. Fuchs never tires of emphasizing the source value, the authority, of caricature. 'Truth lies in extremes', he says somewhere. He goes further: caricature is for him 'to some extent the form from which all objective art arises. One look at the museums of ethnography will vindicate this proposition.'[22] When Fuchs brings prehistoric peoples and children's drawings into the area of caricature, the concept may become problematic; yet the vehement interest he brings to bear on the graphic content of the work of art, whether substantive[23] or formal, appears all the more original. This interest runs through the whole broad range of his work. Even in the late *T'ang Sculpture* we read: 'The grotesque is the ne plus ultra of the visual imagination ... In this sense grotesque forms are at the same time an expression of the exuberant health of an age ... There is of course no question that the driving force behind the grotesque may also be the exact opposite. Decadent times and sick brains, too, tend to produce grotesque forms. In such cases the grotesque is a shocking reflection of the fact that for the times and individuals concerned, the problems of the world and existence appear insoluble … Which of these two tendencies is the creative force behind a grotesque fantasy can be recognized at a glance.'[24]

The passage is instructive. It shows particularly clearly what it was that made Fuchs's work so popular. It was the gift of immediately combining his basic concepts with value judgments. This often occurs on a grand scale.[25] The judgments are always extreme. As such they polarize the concept with which they are amalgamated. So in the representation of the grotesque; so too in erotic caricature. In times of decline it is 'smut' and 'risque', when things are looking up 'the expression of overflowing pleasure and exuberant strength'.[26] Sometimes Fuchs brings in the value concepts of hey-day and decadence, sometimes those of health and sickness. He steers clear of borderline cases, that might reveal the problematic character of such terms. He prefers to stick to the 'truly great', whose prerogative is to give free rein to 'rapture in the simplest things'.[27] Transitional periods like the Baroque he has little time for. Even for him, the great age is still the Renaissance. Here his cult of the creative gets the better of his aversion to the classics.

The concept of the creative in Fuchs's work has a strongly biological slant. While genius is credited with attributes that at times border on the priapic, artists from whom the author keeps his distance seem reduced in their masculinity. Typical of such quasi-biological views is his judgment of Greco, Murillo and Ribera: 'All three are classic representatives of the Baroque in that each in his way was a pornographer *manqué*'.[28] One must not lose sight of the fact that Fuchs developed his basic concepts in an age that

regarded *pathography* as the ultimate standard of the psychology of art, and Lombroso and Möbius as authorities.
The concept of genius, furnished at the same time with a
wealth of illustrative material by Burkhardt's influential
Culture of the Renaissance, contributed from other sources
to the widespread conviction that creativity was above all
a manifestation of superabundant strength. It was related
trends that later led Fuchs to conceptions akin to psychoanalysis; he was the first to apply them fruitfully to aesthetics.

The eruptive immediacy, which in this view gives artistic
creation its special character, is no less important for Fuchs
as a criterion for approaching works of art. So for him it is
often no more than a single leap from perception to judgment. Indeed, Fuchs regards the *impression* the observer gets
from a work of art not only as an immediate and self-evident
experience, but as an actual category of contemplation. For
instance, when Fuchs reports his critical reservations about
the artistic formalism of the Ming period, he clinches his
argument by saying that the works 'in the final analysis ...
make no more, and very often not even as much impression
as, say, the T'ang period did with its bold lines'.[29] This is
how Fuchs the writer comes to the particular and apodictic,
not to say rustic, style expressed in masterly fashion in his
dictum, in the *History of Erotic Art*: 'From the correct intuition to the correct and comprehensive deciphering of the
energies operating in a work of art is always but a single
step.'[30] This style is not within reach of everyone; Fuchs had
to pay a price for it. To indicate the price in a word: Fuchs
the writer had not the gift of surprise. He was undoubtedly
aware of this lack. He tries to compensate for it in the most
various ways, and likes nothing better than to talk about

the mysteries he tracks down in the psychology of creation, or the riddles of history that find their solution in materialism. But the urge to the most immediate mastery of the facts, which is already decisive for his conception of creation and of reception too, finally prevails in his analysis as well. The course of art history is seen as *necessary*, styles in art as *organic*, even the most disconcerting art forms as *logical*. One gets the impression that these terms occur less frequently as his analysis proceeds. But he can still describe the fabulous creatures of the T'ang period with wings of flame and horns as *absolutely logical, organic*. 'Even the enormous elephant ears seem logical; logical, too, the posture. ... These are no mere constructs, but invariably an idea clothed in living, breathing form.'[31]

This was a series of ideas that had the closest possible connection with the Social-Democratic doctrines of the age. We know what a profound effect Darwinism had on the development of the socialist conception of history. In the time of the persecution by Bismarck, this effect helped to keep the party's self-confidence intact and its fighting spirit unbroken. Later, in the epoch of revisionism, the evolutionary view of history laid increasing emphasis on *development*, in direct proportion to the party's growing reluctance to risk what had been achieved in the struggle against capitalism. History began to look deterministic; the triumph of the party was 'inevitable'. Fuchs always held aloof from revisionism; his political instincts as well as his combative nature inclined him to the left. But as a theoretician he was powerless to escape these influences. They can be felt throughout his work. In those days a man like Ferri could derive not just the principles but even the tactics of Social Democracy from natural laws. Anarchist deviations he blamed on insufficient knowledge of geology and biology. It is true that leaders like Kautsky took issue with such deviations.[32] Yet many found satisfaction in theses that sorted historical processes into 'physiological' and 'pathological', or claimed that scientific materialism in the hands of the proletariat had 'automatically' been promoted to historical materialism.[33] Similarly, Fuchs saw the progress of human society as a process which 'can no more be held back than a glacier can be stopped in its inexorable advance'.[34] The determinist view is thus coupled with a robust optimism. Yet in the long run, without self-confidence, no class can engage in political action with any success. But it makes a difference whether the optimism is felt for the active strength of the class, or for the circumstances *in* which it operates. Social Democracy inclined towards the second, more questionable kind of optimism. The prospects of incipient barbarism, which had dawned on Engels in his *Condition of the Working Class in England*, and on Marx in his predictions of the course of capitalist development, and which are today familiar even to the most mediocre politician, were invisible to lesser lights around the turn of the century. When Condorcet spread the doctrine of progress, the bourgeoisie was on the brink of power; the proletariat a hundred years later was in a different position. In the proletariat it could breed illusions. These illusions in fact still form the background which Fuchs's account of the history of art now and then reveals: 'The art of our time', he maintains, 'has enriched us in a hundred ways that in the most various directions go far beyond the achievements of Renaissance art, and the art of the future will unquestionably take us to still greater heights.'[35]

6

The pathos that runs through Fuchs's conception of history is the democratic pathos of 1830. Its echo was the orator Victor Hugo. The echo of the echo are those books in which Hugo as orator speaks to posterity. Fuchs's conception of history is that celebrated by Hugo in *William Shakespeare*: 'Progress is God's very footstep.' Universal suffrage is the cosmic clock by which the pace of that step is measured. 'Qui vote règne,' wrote Victor Hugo, raising the standard of democratic optimism. This optimism long continued to beget strange fantasies. One of them was the illusion that 'all intellectual workers, including materially and socially prominent persons, should be considered proletarians'. For it was 'an undeniable fact that all who offer their services for money, from the puffed-up privy councillor in his gold-frogged uniform down to the exhausted wage earner ... are defenceless victims of capitalism.'[36] The banner raised by Victor Hugo still waves over the work of Fuchs. Besides, Fuchs stands squarely in the democratic tradition in his special attachment to France: the scene of three great revolutions, the home of exiles, the wellspring of utopian socialism, the fatherland of the tyrant-haters Quinet and Michelet, the earth in which the Communards lie buried. This was the image of France that lived in Marx and Engels, this was how Mehring came to see it, and this, too, as 'the vanguard of culture and freedom',[37] was the country as it appeared to Fuchs. He compares the winged irony of the French with heavy-footed German ridicule; he compares Heine with those who stayed at home; he contrasts German naturalism with French satirical novels. In this way he was led, like Mehring, to make sound predictions, especially in the case of Gerhardt Hauptmann.[38]

France is also a home for Fuchs the collector. The figure of the collector, which improves on closer acquaintance, has not often been given its due. One might think that nothing could have offered the romantic story-tellers a more tempting subject. But one looks in vain for the collector, moved by dangerous if domesticated passions, among the characters of Hoffmann, Quincey or Nerval. The traveller is a romantic figure, of the *flâneur*, the gambler, the virtuoso. The collector is not among their number. You will seek him in vain in the 'Physiologies', which from the newsvendor to the literary lion allowed no other figure of the Paris waxworks under Louis Philippe to escape them. All the more significant, then, is the place occupied by the collector in Balzac. Balzac raised a monument to him which is in no way romantic. He had always been a stranger to romance. There are few passages in his work where the anti-romantic position is given its due as amazingly as in the sketch of Cousin Pons. The most significant thing is this: no matter how much we learn about the objects in the collection for which Pons lives, we are told virtually nothing about how they were acquired. There is no passage in *Le Cousin Pons* to compare with the pages from the diary of the Goncourt Brothers where they describe the breath-taking excitement of a rare find. Balzac does not portray the hunter out in the bush tracking down his quarry, the way any collector can be seen. The feverish exaltation that fills his Pons, his Elie Magus, who are very poorly dressed.... They look as if they guard with tireless vigilance. Balzac puts the whole emphasis on the *possessor*, and he uses *millionaire* as a synonym for *collector*. He talks

about Paris. 'There', he says, 'you can often meet a Pons, an
Elie Magus, who are very poorly dressed ... They look as
if they cared for nothing and bothered about nothing; they
heed neither the women nor the shop windows. They walk
along as if in a dream, their pockets are empty, their gaze
is blank, and you wonder to what class of Parisians they
actually belong.—These people are millionaires. They are
collectors; the most passionate people that walk the earth.'[39]

Balzac's picture of the collector comes closer to Fuchs,
to the passionate intensity of his interests, than one could
have expected from a romantic. Indeed, pointing to the
very quick of the man, one may say that Fuchs as a collector was truly Balzacian; he was a Balzacian figure who
outgrew the author's conception. What could be more in
keeping with that conception than a collector whose pride,
whose expansiveness, were such that merely in order to
bring his collections before the public eye, he would put
them on sale in the form of reproductions, and—a no less
Balzacian twist—in this way became a rich man? It was not
just the conscientiousness of a man who knows himself to be
a custodian of treasures, it was also the exhibitionism of the
great collector that prompted Fuchs, in each of his works,
to publish exclusively unpublished pictures, drawn almost
exclusively from his own collections. For the first volume of
Caricature of the European Peoples alone he brought together
no fewer than 68,000 items, in order to pick out some 1,500
of them. He never had any item reproduced in more than
one single place. The volume of his documentation and the
breadth of his grasp belong together. Both show him to be a
true descendant of the race of bourgeois giants around 1830,
as characterized by Drumont. 'Almost all leaders of the

school of 1830', writes Drumont, 'had the same extraordinary constitution, the same fertility, and the same penchant
for the grandiose. Delacroix throws epics onto the canvas,
Balzac portrays an entire society, Dumas's novels range
over 4,000 years of human history. They all have backs for
which no burden is too heavy.'[40] When the revolution came
in 1848, Dumas published an appeal to the workers of Paris,
in which he presented himself as their like. In twenty years,
he said, he had produced 400 novels and 35 plays; he had
provided a living for 8,160 people: proofreaders and type-
setters, machine operators and cloakroom attendants; he
even spares a thought for the claque. The feeling with which
the world historian Fuchs laid the economic foundations of
his magnificent collections is perhaps not altogether unlike
this *amour propre* of Dumas. Later, these foundations were
to give him almost as free a hand in the Paris market as in his
own private preserves. The chairman of the Paris art dealers
used to say of him around the turn of the century: 'C'est le
Monsieur qui mange tout Paris.' Fuchs is an example of the
ramasseur type; he takes a Rabelaisian joy in quantity, which
is noticeable even in the luxuriant redundancy of his texts.

7

Fuchs' pedigree on the French side is that of the collector,
on the German side that of the historian. The moral auster-
ity which is typical of Fuchs the historiographer gives him
the Teutonic stamp—just as it did Gervinus, whose *History
of National Poetic Literature* could be called one of the first
attempts at a history of German thought. It is characteristic of Gervinus, and later of Fuchs too, that they represent

the great creative minds so to say in martial guise—the active, masculine, impetuous side of their natures getting the better of the more contemplative, feminine, receptive side. Admittedly this was easier for Gervinus. At the time he was writing his book, the bourgeoisie was in the ascendant; its art abounded in political energies. Fuchs wrote in the age of imperialism; he argued for the political energies of art in an epoch when they were dwindling daily. But his criteria were still the same as those of Gervinus. Indeed, they can be traced back further, as far as the eighteenth century, with the aid of Gervinus himself, whose commemorative address on F. C. Schlosser gave resounding expression to the unbending rectitude of the bourgeoisie in the age of revolution. Schlosser had been reproached with a 'dour puritanism'. 'What Schlosser could and would have retorted to such reproaches', Gervinus argued, 'would *be* this: that in general life, like history but unlike fiction, does not instruct even the most light-hearted and optimistic in a superficial *joie de vivre*; that the contemplation of life and history is conducive not, of course, to a disdainful misanthropy, but surely to a stern view of the world and serious principles about life; that the impression produced by existence on the greatest of all those who have judged the world and men, those whose own inner life was the measure of their outer experience, the impression produced at least on a Shakespeare, a Dante, a Machiavelli—has always been conducive to just such seriousness and sternness.'[41] That is the origin of Fuchs's moralism: a German Jacobinism, whose memorial is Schlosser's world history, which Fuchs came to know in his youth.[42]

As is hardly surprising, this bourgeois moralism contains elements that conflict with Fuchs's materialism. If Fuchs had realized this, he might perhaps have succeeded in muting the clash. But he was convinced that his moralistic view of history was in perfect accord with historical materialism. This was an illusion. It was based on the widespread view, much in need of revision, that the bourgeois revolutions—as celebrated by the bourgeoisie itself—were the direct ancestors of a proletarian revolution.[43] For a decisive counter to this, one must look to the spiritualism that runs through these revolutions. Its golden threads were spun by morality. The morality of the bourgeoisie—the reign of terror is already symptomatic—is inner-directed. Its touchstone is the individual conscience, whether of Robespierre's *citoyen*, or of Kant's citizen of the world. The behaviour of the bourgeoisie, which tended to advance its own interests but was dependent on complementary action by the proletariat that did *not* correspond to *its* interests, proclaimed conscience the arbiter of morality. Conscience is concerned with altruism. It advises the property-owner to act in accordance with concepts whose application is indirectly advantageous to his fellow property-owners, and it cheerfully advises non-property-owners to do likewise. If the latter go along with this advice, the usefulness of their behaviour to the property-owners is the more immediately visible the more questionable it is for those so behaving and for their class. Hence this behaviour bears the price tag of virtue. This is how class morality gets its way. But it does so unconsciously. The bourgeoisie was not so greatly in need of consciousness in order to erect this class morality as is the proletariat in order to overturn it. Fuchs misses this point, since he believes it his duty to direct his attacks against the conscience of the bourgeoisie. Its ideology seems to him a tissue of lies. 'The sanctimonious drivel', he says, 'that is talked about the subjective honesty of the judges even in the most shameless class judgments merely demonstrates the lack of character of those who say or write such things, or at best their obtuseness.'[44] It does not occur to Fuchs to indict the very notion of bona fides (good conscience). Yet that would be the natural reaction of a historical materialist. Not only because he perceives this concept to be a carrier of bourgeois class morality, but also because he will not fail to notice that it sustains the bond between moral disorder and economic anarchy. More recent Marxists have at least hinted at the truth of the matter. Thus it has been remarked of the politics of Lamartine, who made excessive use of bona fides: 'Bourgeois ... democracy ... needs this value. The democrat ... is professionally upright. Thereby he feels he can rise above the need to inquire into the real state of affairs.'[45] Treatments which focus on the conscious interests of individuals, rather than on the often unconscious reactions of their class to its position in the production process, lead to an overestimation of the role of conscious elements in the formation of ideology. This is obvious in Fuchs when he says: 'Art is in all essentials the idealized mask of a particular social order. For it is an eternal law ... that every ruling political or social order strives to idealize itself, in order morally to justify its existence.'[46] Here we approach the essential misunderstanding. It consists in the idea that the main reason why exploitation gives rise to a false consciousness, at least on the part of the exploiters, is that a true consciousness would be morally burdensome to them. This thesis may have some limited validity in the present day, when the class struggle has powerfully invested the entire bourgeois way of life. But the 'bad conscience' of the privileged is certainly not self-evident as regards the earlier forms of exploitation. For reification not only obscures relations among people; it also befogs the real subjects of such relations. Between the ruling powers of economic life and the exploited there arises an array of judicial and administrative bureaucracies, whose members no longer function as fully responsible moral subjects; their sense of duty is nothing but the unconscious expression of this deformity.

8

Psychoanalysis, too, failed to shake the moralism that left its mark on Fuchs's historical materialism. His verdict on sexuality: 'All forms of sensual behaviour that manifest the creative principle inherent in this law of life are justified.... Those forms are to be condemned on the other hand, which debase this highest of instincts to a mere instrument of sophisticated pleasure-seeking.'[47] This moralism bears an obviously bourgeois stamp. A proper mistrust for the bourgeois proscription of pure sexual pleasure and the more or less fantastic ways it is created remained outside Fuchs's experience. He does allow in principle that one can speak 'of morality and immorality only in relative terms'. But in the very next breath he decrees an exception for the 'absolute immorality' exemplified by 'offences against the social instincts of society, i.e. offences that are so to speak against nature'. Characteristic of this view is what Fuchs regarded as the historically inevitable victory of 'the masses, who are always capable of development, over degenerate individuality'.[48] In short, it can be said of Fuchs that he 'does not challenge the legitimacy of condemning allegedly corrupt instincts, but rather the usual view of their history and their extent'.[49]

Elucidation of the psycho-sexual problem is thereby hampered—a problem which has assumed particular importance since the bourgeoisie assumed power. This is where the taboo on more or less wide areas of sexual pleasure comes in. For the repressions it induces in the masses generate sado-masochistic complexes to which the ruling powers deliver up those objects best suited to their purposes. A coeval of Fuchs, Wedekind, looked into these connections. Fuchs neglected to undertake their social critique. All the more significant, then, is the passage where he makes good this omission, in an aside on natural history. It is a brilliant apologia for the orgy. According to Fuchs 'orgiastic pleasure is among the most valuable tendencies of culture ... it must be understood that the orgy is one of the signs that distinguish us from animals. By contrast with man, animals do not have orgies.... The animal turns away from the lushest fodder and the clearest stream when its hunger and thirst are assuaged, and its sexual drive is mostly restricted to brief and clearly defined periods of the year. Human beings are entirely different, especially creative human beings. For them there is simply no such thing as enough'.[50] The force of Fuchs's psycho-sexual observations lies in the ideas he uses to criticize conventional standards. It is these ideas that enable him to dispel certain petty-bourgeois illusions—the fallacy of nudism for instance, which he rightly sees as 'a revolution of narrow-mindedness'. 'Man is happily no longer a beast of the field and we ... want fantasy, including erotic fantasy, to play a role in dress. What we do not want is a social organization of humanity that ... depraves all this.'[51]

Fuchs's psychological and historical outlook proved very fruitful for the history of clothing. Indeed, there is scarcely any subject that lends itself better to the author's threefold interest—the historical, the social, and the erotic—than does fashion. This can be seen in his very definition of it, which is couched in terms reminiscent of Karl Kraus. Fashion, says Fuchs in his history of manners, announces 'how people mean to carry on the business of public morality'.[52] Incidentally, Fuchs did not fall into the error, common among interpreters of manners (think of Max von Boehn), of investigating fashion merely from the aesthetic and erotic standpoints. He did not fail to note its role as an instrument of domination. Just as fashion articulates the nuances of status, so is its main function to supervise the grosser class differences. In the third volume of his history of manners Fuchs devoted a long essay to fashion, whose argument the supplementary volume summarized in a list of its key elements. The first such element is 'the interests of class distinction'; the second is 'the private capitalist mode of production', which seeks to increase its sales potential through repeated changes of fashion; in third place we must not forget 'the erotically stimulating purposes of fashion'.[53]

The cult of creativity, which runs through the whole of Fuchs's work, drew fresh nourishment from his psycho-analytic studies. They enriched his originally biologically-determined conception, though admittedly without correcting it. Fuchs enthusiastically espoused the theory of the erotic origin of the creative impulse. But his conception of the erotic remained close to a rigorous, biologically determined view of sensuality. He steered clear as far as possible of the theory of repression and the complexes, which might perhaps have modified his moralistic view of social and sexual relations. Just as historical materialism, in Fuchs's understanding, traced the origin of things to the conscious economic interest of the individual rather than to the interests of the class unconsciously at work within him, so he saw the creative impulse as lying closer to conscious sensuous intention than to the unconscious imagination.[54] The symbolic significance of erotic imagery, as revealed by Freud in *The Interpretation of Dreams*, Fuchs acknowledges only where he feels a strong sense of personal identification. When that happens, his writing is filled with it, even when any reference to it is avoided. Thus, in his masterly description of the graphic art of the revolutionary period: 'Everything is taut, rigid, military. People do not lie, for the parade ground allows of no "Stand easy". Even when they sit, it is as if they were about to spring up. The whole body is tense, like an arrow on the bowstring. As with line, so with colour. The pictures produce a cold, brassy effect ... by contrast with those of the rococo ... The colour had to be harsh ..., metallic, it had to match the content of the pictures.'[55] More explicit is a revealing observation on fetishism, which traces its historical equivalents. It turns out that 'the increasing incidence of shoe and foot fetishism' appears to point to 'the substitution of the cult of the vulva for the cult of the phallus', whereas the growing incidence of breast fetishism points to a reverse trend. 'The cult of the clothed foot and leg mirrors the dominion of woman over man; the worship of the breast mirrors the role of woman as the object of man's pleasure.'[56] Fuchs's deepest insights into the realm of symbols were prompted by Daumier. His comment on the trees in Daumier's paintings is one of the happiest finds of his whole work. He sees them as 'a quite unique symbolic form …, which expresses Daumier's sense of social responsibility and his conviction that it is society's duty to protect the individual … Typically, Daumier depicts trees with outspread branches, especially when someone is standing or resting beneath. The branches of such trees extend like a giant's arms, they seem to reach out for the infinite. They thus form an impenetrable roof that keeps from harm all who have sought their protection.'[57] This lovely image leads Fuchs on to the dominance of the maternal in Daumier's work.

9

No one became more alive for Fuchs than Daumier. The figure of Daumier accompanied him through his working life; one could almost say that it was through him that Fuchs became a dialectician. He certainly grasped the breadth and living contradiction of the man's character. If he perceived the maternal in Daumier's art and vividly conveyed it to his readers, he was no less aware of the other pole, the masculine, pugnacious side of Daumier. He rightly pointed out that Daumier's work is lacking in the idyllic; not only the landscape, the animal painting, and the still life, but also the erotic motif and the self-portrait. What really impressed Fuchs about Daumier was the element of classical conflict in him, the agonistic element. Or would it be too daring to seek the source of Daumier's great caricatures in a question: how, Daumier seems to ask, would the bourgeois of my time look if one were to conceive their struggle for existence so to speak in terms of a palaestra? Daumier translated the public and private life of the Parisians into the language of the agon. His highest enthusiasm is aroused by the athletic tension of the whole body, its muscular excitements. This is in no way contradicted by the fact that perhaps nobody has depicted the utter enervation of the body more arrestingly than Daumier. His conception, as Fuchs observes, is closely akin to the sculptor's. And so he waylays the types offered him by his time and puts them on show in a convulsed travesty of Olympic champions. It is above all the studies of judges and lawyers that may be seen in this light. The elegiac humour with which Daumier likes to approach the Greek pantheon points more directly to this inspiradon. Perhaps it offers a solution to the riddle that had already teased Baudelaire: how was it that the master's caricatures, for all their force and penetration, could yet be so free of rancour?

Fuchs has only to speak of Daumier, and all his energies come alive. There is no other subject that struck such sparks of insight from his connoisseur's intelligence. Here the least impulse can set him off. A sketch, so fleeting that to call it unfinished would be a euphemism, suffices to give Fuchs a deep insight into Daumier's productive mania. It shows only the upper half of a head, in which the eyes and nose alone speak. That the sketch is restricted to this part, that it presents only a person looking, alerts Fuchs to the fact that here the painter's central interest is in play. For, he says, every painter sets about the execution of his pictures at the very spot where he instinctively feels most involved.[58] 'There are innumerable figures in Daumier's paintings', says Fuchs in his work on the artist, 'engaged in the most concentrated looking, whether they gaze into the distance, or contemplate particular things, or look no less intently into their own inner selves. Daumier's people look literally with the tip of their nose.'[59]

10

Daumier was the happiest subject for the scholar. He was no less the collector's luckiest strike. Fuchs remarks with justified pride that it was not the state but he himself, on his own initiative, that started the first collections of Daumier (and Gavarni) in Germany. He is not alone among the great collectors in his aversion to museums. The Goncourts preceded him in this; their distaste was even more vehement. If public collections may be socially less problematic and scientifically more useful than private ones, they have not the latter's biggest advantage. The collector's passion gives him a divining rod that guides him to new sources. This was true of Fuchs, and it was therefore inevitable that he should feel himself at odds with the spirit that prevailed in the museums under Wilhelm II. They had concentrated on so-called showpieces. 'Of course,' says Fuchs, 'today's museum is limited to this kind of collecting if only for reasons of space. But that does not alter the fact that because of it we get only a very imperfect conception of the culture of the past. We see it dressed up in its Sunday best, and only very rarely in its mostly shabby workaday clothes.'[60]

The great collectors are usually distinguished by the originality of their choice of object. There are exceptions: the Goncourts were not after objects so much as the ensemble that was to house them; they undertook the transfiguration of the interior just as it had expired. But as a rule collectors have been guided by the object itself. A great example on the threshold of the modern age is the humanists, whose Greek acquisitions and travels testify to the single-mindedness with which they collected. With Marolles, the model for Damocède, the collector was introduced by La Bruyère into literature (and at once unflatteringly). Marolles was the first to recognize the importance of prints: his 125,000 piece collection forms the ground floor of the Cabinet des Estampes. The seven-volume catalogue of his collections, published by Count Caylus in the following century, is the first great achievement of archaeology. The gem collection of von Stosch was catalogued by Winckelmann, on commission from the collector. Even where the scientific conception purportedly embodied in such collections was not destined to last, the collection itself sometimes was. This happened with the collection of Wallraf and Boisserée, whose founders, basing themselves on the romantic Nazarene theory that the art of Cologne was inherited from that of ancient Rome, laid the foundations of the Cologne Museum with their German paintings of the Middle Ages. Fuchs belongs in the ranks of these great, systematic, and unswervingly single-minded collectors. His idea was to restore the work of art to its existence in society, from which it had been so completely cut off that the place where he came upon it was the art market, where, as far removed from those who produced it as from those who were capable of understanding it, shrunk to mere merchandise, it yet survived. The fetish of the art market is the old master's name. Historically it will perhaps be seen to have been Fuchs' greatest service that he initiated the emancipation of art history from the fetish of the master's name. 'The complete anonymity of these tomb furnishings', says Fuchs about the sculpture of the T'ang period, 'the fact that in no single instance do we know the individual creator of such a work, is an important proof that what we confront here is never the experience of a particular artist, but rather the way the world and things were seen in those days by society at large.'[61] Fuchs was one of the first to elucidate the special character of mass art, and with it impulses he had received from historical materialism.

The study of *mass* art necessarily leads to the question of the technical reproduction of works of art. 'Every age has its own quite specific techniques of reproduction. They represent the technological potential of the period concerned and are … a response to the requirements of the time. It is therefore no cause for wonder that every major historical upheaval that brings other classes to power than those who have ruled hitherto, also regularly produces a change in the techniques of graphic reproduction. This fact needs to be made particularly clear.'[62] Fuchs was a pioneer with such insights. In them he pointed to subjects in whose study historical materialism can train itself. The technical standard of the arts is one of the most important criteria. Proper attention to it can make good some of the havoc wrought in the usual view of intellectual history (and sometimes even in Fuchs himself) by the vague concept of culture. That 'thousands of the simplest potters were capable of producing, literally off the cuff, work that was both technically and artistically daring' quite rightly strikes Fuchs as concrete proof of the value of ancient Chinese art.[63] Technical considerations now and then lead him to luminous aperçus that are ahead of his time: as witness his explanation of the fact that there was no caricature in the ancient world. The idealistic view of history would inevitably see this as corroboration of the classicist conception of Greece: its noble simplicity and tranquil greatness. And what is Fuchs' explanation? Caricature, he says, is a mass art. There is no caricature without the mass circulation of its products. Mass circulation means cheapness. But 'there was no cheap form of reproduction in the ancient world, apart from coins'.[64] The coin offers too small an area for caricature. So there was no caricature in antiquity.

The caricature was mass art, so was genre painting. This made forms already held in low esteem by conventional art history seem even more contemptible. Not in Fuchs's eyes; looking at the despised and apocryphal was his strength. And he beat his own path to them as a collector, a path which Marxism had done little more than broach. That took a passion bordering on mania. It left its mark on Fuchs's features, in what sense may best be seen by going through Daumier's long series of lithographs of art-lovers and dealers, of admirers of painting and connoisseurs of sculpture. They resemble Fuchs, even to the very build. They are tall, gaunt figures, and their eyes blaze fire. It has been not inaptly remarked that in these figures Daumier conceived the descendants of the gold-seekers, necromancers and misers to be found in the paintings of the old masters.[65] As a collector Fuchs is one of their kind. And just as the alchemist, with his *base* wish to make gold, experiments with chemicals in which the planets and elements combine to form images of spiritual man, so did this collector, while satisfying the *base* wish for possession, undertake the exploration of an art in whose creations the productive forces and the masses combine to form images of historical man. Even in the late books one can feel the passionate interest Fuchs took in these images. 'It is not the least glory of the Chinese ridge turrets', he writes, 'that they represent an anonymous folk art. There are no heroic epics to celebrate their creators.'[66] Whether such contemplation of unknown craftsmen and the work of their hands does not contribute more to the humanizing of mankind than the cult of the leader, which is apparently once more to be inflicted on it—that, like so much about which the past has vainly sought to instruct us, only the future can tell.

1937

Bibliographical Note

The first publication of the texts included in this volume was as follows:

'One-Way Street': *Einbahnstrasse*, Rowohlt, Berlin 1928.

'Fate and Character': *Die Argonauten*, I, 1921.

'Critique of Violence': *Archiv für Sozialwissenschaft and Sozialpolitik*, XLVII, 1920/1921.

'The Destructive Character': *Frankfurter Zeitung*, LXXVI, November 20, 1931.

'Naples': *Frankfurter Zeitung*, LXX, August 19, 1925.

'Moscow': *Die Kreatur*, II, 1927.

'Marseilles': *Neue Schweizer Rundschau*, XXII, 1929.

'Hashish in Marseilles': *Frankfurter Zeitung*, LXXVII, December 4, 1932.

'Surrealism': *Literarische Welt*, V, 1929, in four instalments.

'A Small History of Photography': *Literarische Welt*, VII, 1931, in three instalments.

'Karl Kraus': *Frankfurter Zeitung*, LXXVI, 1931, in four instalments.

'Eduard Fuchs, Collector and Historian': *Zeitschrift für Social-forschung*, October 1937.

Texts unpublished in Benjamin's life-time first appeared posthumously thus:

'On Language as Such and on the Language of Man': *Schriften*, Vol. I, Suhrkamp Verlag, Frankfurt 1955.

'Theologico-Political Fragment': *Schriften*, Vol. I, Frankfurt 1955.

'On the Mimetic Faculty': *Sehriften*, Vol. I, Frankfurt 1955.

'A Berlin Chronicle': *Berliner Chronik*, edited by Gershom Scholem, Suhrkamp Verlag, Frankfurt 1970.

Notes

Introduction

1 Gershom Scholem, 'Walter Benjamin', in *On Jews and Judaism in Crisis* (Schocken, 1976). Scholem, five years younger than Benjamin, relates that they did not actually meet until 1915, during Scholem's first term at the University of Munich, which Benjamin attended after leaving the University of Berlin. Unless otherwise indicated, the Scholem quotations come from this essay, written in 1964, or from 'Walter Benjamin and His Angel', written in 1972, in the same volume.

2 In 'Agesilaus Santander', a short text that Benjamin wrote in Ibiza in August 1933, found in his notebooks and first published by Scholem in 'Walter Benjamin and His Angel'.

3 The long Goethe essay was written in 1922 and appeared in two parts in 1924 and 1925 in the *Neue Deutsche Beiträge*, a magazine published in Vienna and edited by Hugo von Hofmannsthal. In 1937 Benjamin excerpted the section about Goethe's Saturnine character and published it in French translation in *Les Cahiers du Sud* as '*L'angoisse mythique chez Goethe*'.

4 Benjamin's brief essay 'Robert Walser' was first published in *Das Tagebuch* in 1929; it is still untranslated.

5 *Der Ursprung des deutschen Trauerspiels* (1928). Benjamin's study of the Baroque *Trauerspiel* is published in English as *The Origin of German Tragic Drama*, trans. John Osborne, London/NLB, 1977.

6 Asja Lacis and Benjamin met in Capri in the summer of 1924. She was

a Latvian communist revolutionary and theatre director, assistant to Brecht and to Piscator, with whom Benjamin wrote 'Naples' in 1925 (pp. 187–96) and for whom he wrote 'Programme for a Proletarian Children's Theatre' in 1928 (translated in *Performance*, No. 5, March/April 1973). It was Lacis who got Benjamin an invitation to Moscow in the winter of 1926–1927 and who introduced him to Brecht in 1929. Benjamin hoped to marry her when he and his wife were finally divorced in 1930. But she returned to Riga and later spent ten years in a Soviet camp.

7 For an excellent essay, written in 1961, on *Berlin Childhood as* a reading of the past for omens of the future, see Peter Szondi, 'Hope in the Past: Walter Benjamin', translated in *Critical Inquiry*, Vol. 4, No. 3, Spring 1978.

8 Scholem continues: 'And to deal with Benjamin one had to have the greatest patience oneself. Only very patient people could gain deeper contact with him.' Scholem cites the testimony of someone who was with Benjamin during his internment in a camp near Paris and in Nevers in the autumn of 1939, that he made an indelible impression on his fellow prisoners 'by his infinite and stoic patience, which he demonstrated without any ostentation whatever and under the most difficult conditions'.

9 See H. W. Belmore, 'Some Recollections of Walter Benjamin', in *German Life and Letters*, Volume XXVIII, No. 2, January 1975. This spiteful and unadmiring portrait of Benjamin is a document of the unquenchable bitterness about being dropped still felt, sixty years later, by one of these friends. Herbert Belmore was a Gymnasium class-mate of Benjamin; the earliest letters (Nos. 1–10) in the two-volume Suhrkamp edition of Benjamin's letters are written to him.

10 Letter to Christian Florens Rang (No. 126 in the Suhrkamp *Briefe*), December 9, 1923.

11 Scholem tells the story in 'Walter Benjamin'. But see Benjamin's letter to Scholem from Paris (No. 156 in the *Briefe*) of May 29, 1926, a long letter toward the end of which he writes: 'I couldn't build a Lilliputian state with this, as it were, Marxist letter. But let me tell you that in the Jewish section of the Musée Cluny I have discovered the Book of Esther written on a page a little more than half the size of this one. That should perhaps speed your visit to Paris.'

Scholem argues that Benjamin's love for the miniature underlies his taste for brief literary utterances, evident in *One-Way Street*. Perhaps; but books of this sort were common in the 1920s, and it was in a specifically Surrealist montage style that these short independent texts were presented. *One-Way Street* was published by Ernst Rowohlt in Berlin, in booklet form with typography intended to evoke advertising shock effects; the cover was a photographic montage of aggressive phrases in capital letters from newspaper announcements, ads, official and odd signs. The opening passage, in which Benjamin hails 'prompt language' and denounces 'the pretentious, universal gesture of the book', does not make much sense unless one knows what kind of book, physically, *One-Way Street* was designed to be.

12 Cf. Benjamin's letter (No. 326 in the *Briefe*) to Gretel Adorno, written in Paris on January 17, 1940.

13 In *Illuminations*, London, 1970, an earlier selection of Benjamin's writings, edited by Hannah Arendt, which includes the essays on Kafka and Proust.

14 Letter to Werner Kraft (No. 259 in the *Briefe*), written from Paris on May 25, 1935. At his death in 1940, Benjamin left thousands of pages of draft manuscript, only a small portion of which has been published. *Charles Baudelaire: A Lyric Poet in the Era of High Capitalism* (New Left Books, 1973) contains translations of the material from Benjamin's Paris project published in German so far.

15 In a letter from Adorno to Benjamin, written from New York on November 10, 1938, translated in *Aesthetics and Politics* (New Left Books, 1977). Benjamin and Adorno met in 1923 (Adorno was twenty), and in 1935 Benjamin started to receive a small stipend from Max Horkheimer's Institut für Sozialforschung, of which Adorno was a member.

16 Letter to Adorno (No. 260 in the *Briefe*), written from Paris on May 31, 1935.

17 Benjamin had his Krausian side in reviews. See his 'Left-Wing Melancholy', written the same year (1931) as the Kraus essay, a withering pan of a volume of poems by Erich Kästner, which pillories—through Kästner-shallow, philistine melancholy. Translated in *Screen*, Vol. 15, No. 2, Summer 1974.

18 In Adorno's essay 'A Portrait of Walter Benjamin', in *Prisms*, NLB, 1979.

Publisher's Note

1 See Michael Löwy, *Georg Lukács from Idealism to Bolshevism*, London NLB, 1979, Chapter II. Lukács's essay of 1912, *Von der Annul am Geist*, mingling appeals to Meister Eckhardt, Brahminism and Dostoevsky, is a particularly clear expression of this outlook.

2 *Der Geist der Utopie*, Frankfurt 1971 re-edition, pp. 298–299.

3 Scholem testifies that in discussions of *On the Mimetic Faculty* in 1938, Benjamin spoke unmetaphorically of the 'Word of God' as the foundation of any theory of language. See Gerhard Scholem, *Walter Benjamin—Die Geschichte einer Freundschaft*, Frankfurt 1975, p. 260.

4 '*Zweigleisigkeit*': see *Geschichte einer Freundschaft*, p. 156.

5 See Bernd Witte, *Walter Benjamin—Der Intellektuelle als Kritiker*, Stuttgart 5976, pp. 100–5. Witte's excellent study is indispensable for an understanding of Benjamin's early development.

6 Letter of 7.7.1924: *Briefe*, Frankfurt 1966, p. 355.

7 Scholem, *Geschichte einer Freundschaft*, p. 156.

8 *Geschichte einer Freundschaft*, p. 168.

9 The first draft is contained in the matchless scholarly apparatus provided by the contemporary editors of Benjamin's Collected Works: see *Gesammelte Schriften*, IV, Bd. 2, p. 931.

10 Letter of 9.8.1935: *Briefe*, pp. 684–685. See also his letter of 15.3.1929: *Briefe*, p. 491.

11 Letter of 8.2.1928: *Briefe*, p. 459.

12 Letter of 30.1.1928: *Briefe*, p. 455.

13 It may be significant that Benjamin later displayed frequent admiration for the work of Trotsky, well after the official denunciations of the latter, both in his articles and lectures (see, for example, 'Surrealism' below, p. 278, and 'The Author as Producer' in *Understanding Brecht*, NLB 1977), and in his private correspondence, expressing particular enthusiasm for *My Life* and the *History of the Russian Revolution:* see *Geschichte einer Freundschaft*, p. 229. Earlier, he had been very struck by *Where Is Britain Going?:* ibid., p. 161.

14 *Geschichte einer Freundschaft*, p. 161.

15 For a discussion of Benjamin's relationship to these papers, see Witte, pp. 141–144.

16 Theodor Adorno, 'Zu Benjamin Gedächtnis' (1940), in *Über Walter Benjamin*, Frankfurt 1970, p. 9.

17 Letter of 7.3.1931: *Briefe*, p. 523. The direction which a more materialist version of *The Origin of German Tragic Drama* might have taken can be surmised from Benjamin's declaration in his review of a history of Silesian literature: 'We need a book that represents baroque tragedy in close connection with the formation of bureaucracy, dramatic unity of time and action with the dark offices of Absolutism, wanton love poetry with the inquisitions into pregnancy of the emergent police state, operatic apotheoses with the juridical structure of sovereignty' (*Gesammelte Schrsften*, III, p. 193).

18 Letter of 7.3.1931: *Briefe*, p. 523.

19 Ibid., p. 524.

20 Letter of 30.3.1931: *Briefe*, p. 526.

21 Letter of 17.4.1931: *Briefe*, p. 532.

22 For this episode, see the judicious editorial account in *Gesammelte Schriften*, II, Bd. 3, pp. 1078–1130. Kraus' comments were published in *Die Fackel* in May 1931.

23 Letter of 27.9.1934: *Briefe*, p. 620. 'Demon', 'man' and 'monster' refer to the categories of his essay on Kraus.

24 Scholem's phrase: see his afterword to *Berliner Chronik*, Frankfurt 1970, p. 127.

25 For the editorial decision to restore this paragraph in the text printed in the Collected Works, see *Gesammelte Schriften*, II, Bd. 3, p. 1355.

Critique of Violence

1 One might, rather, doubt whether this famous demand does not contain too little, that is, whether it is permissible to use, or allow to be used, oneself or another in any respect as a means. Very good grounds for such doubt could be adduced.

2 Unger, *Politik and Metaphysik*, Berlin 1921, p. 8.

3 But see Unger, pp. 18 ff.

4 Sorel, *Réflexions sur la violence*, 5th ed., Paris 1919, p. 250.

5 Hermann Cohen, *Ethik des reinen Willens*, 2nd ed., Berlin 1907, p. 362.

6 Kurt Hiller in a yearbook of *Das Ziel*.

Moscow

1 Soviet Federated Socialist Republic [NLB].

A Small History of Photography

1 Helmuth Bossert and Heinrich Guttmann, *Aus der Frühzeit der Photographie 1840–1870. Ein Bildbuch nach 200 Originalen*. Frankfurt 1930. Heinrich Schwarz, *David Octavius Hill, der Meister der Photographic*. With 80 plates. Leipzig 1931.
2 Karl Blossfeldt, *Urformen der Kunst. Photographische Pflanzen bilder*. Published with an Introduction by Karl Nierendorf. £20 plates. Berlin 1931.
3 Eugène Atget, *Lichtbilder*, Paris and Leipzig 1931.
4 August Sander, *Des Antlitz der Zeit*. Berlin 1930.

Karl Kraus

1 The journal edited by Kraus from 1899 until his death in 1936 [NLB].
2 Karl Kraus translated and edited Offenbach's *La Vie Parisienne* [NLB].
3 *Granat* means 'pomegranate'; *Granate*, 'grenade' or 'shell' [Trans.].

A Berlin Chronicle

1 Benjamin is referring to Paris [NLB].
2 The beginning of this passage is missing in the manuscript; Benjamin is talking about his school experiences [Nix].
3 *Die Aktion*, a political journal of revolutionary tendency, founded in 1911 by Franz Pfemfert, dedicated to the revolution in literature and the visual arts.
4 Traute, Carla, and Rika Seligson [NLB].
5 Alfred Cohn [NLB].
6 Jula Cohn married Fritz Radt, whose sister, Grete Radt, became the wife of Alfred Cohn [NLB].
7 The sentence breaks off without punctuation at the end of a page, and the continuation is no doubt missing. The sonnet is likely to have been by Benjamin but has not been preserved [NLB].

8 See Hauff's fairy tale, 'The Cold Heart', [NLB].
9 Professor R. Renvers lived at 24 Nettelbeckstrasse. [NLB].

Eduard Fuchs, Collector and Historian

1 Karl Kautsky, 'Franz Mehring', in *Die Neue Zeit*, XXII, Stuttgart 1904, I, pp 103–104.
2 Marx-Engels, *Selected Correspondence*, Moscow 1964, pp 541–542. Cited in Gustav Mayer, *Friedrich Engels*, Vol II, *Friedrich Engels and der Aufstieg der Arbeiterbewegung in Europa*, Berlin, pp 450–451.
3 They appear in the earliest studies on Feuerbach, where Marx writes: 'There is no history of politics, of law, of science … of art, of religion'. *Marx-Engels Archive*, I, ed. David Ryazanov, Frankfurt am Main 1928, p 301.
4 It is the dialectical construction which distinguishes that which is our original concern with historical engagement from the patchwork findings of actuality. 'That which is original is never revealed in the naked and manifest existence of the factual; its rhythm is apparent only to a dual insight. It … is related to its history and subsequent development.' Walter Benjamin, *The Origin of German Tragic Drama*, London NLB, 1977, pp 45–46.
5 *Erotische Kunst*, I, p 70.
6 *Gavarni*, p 13.
7 These have been published by Albert Langen of Munich as *Hauptwerke*. They include: *Illustrierte Sittengeschichte vom Mittelalter bis zur Gegenwart*, Vol I: *Renaissance*, Vol II: *Die galante Zeit*, Vol III: *Des bürgerliche Zeitalter*, also Supplementary Vols I–III (here cited as *Sittengeschichte*); *Geschichte der erotischen Kunst*, Vol I: *Das zeitgeschichtliche Problem*, Vol II: *Das individuelle Problem*, Part One, Vol III: *Das individuelle Problem*, Part Two (here cited as *Erotische Kunst*); *Die Karikatur der europäischen Volker*, Vol I: *Vom Altertum bis zum, Jahre 1848*, Vol II: *Vom Jahre 1848 bis zum Vorabend des Weltkrieges* (here cited as *Karikatur*); *Honore Daumier: Holzschnitte and Lithographien*, Vol 1: *Holzschnitte*, Vols II–IV: *Lithographien* (here cited as *Daumier*); *Der Maler Daumier; Gavarni; Die grossen Meister der Erotik; Tang-Plastik. Chinesische Grab-Keramik des 7.-10. Jahrhunderts; Dachreiter and verwandte chinesische Kerarnik des 15.-18. Jahrhunderts*. Apart from these works, Fuchs devoted special studies to the caricature of women, of Jews, and of the World War.

8 A. Max, 'Zur Frage der Organisation des Proletariats der Intelligenz', *Die Neue Zeit*, XIII/I, Stuttgart 1895, p 645.

9 Nietzsche wrote as early as 1874: 'The final … result is the generally approved "popularization" … of science, that is the notorious cutting of the coat of science to the figure of the "mixed public", to use a tailor-like German [*sic*] for a tailor-like activity', Friedrich Nietzsche, 'Vom Nutzen und Nachteil der Historie für das Leben', *Unzeitgemässige Betrachtungen*, I, Leipzig 1893, p 168.

10 'A cultural historian who takes his task seriously must always write for the masses' (*Erotische Kunst*, II, foreword).

11 C. Korn, 'Proletariat und Klassik', *Die Neue Zeit*, XXVI/II, Stuttgart 5908, pp. 414–15.

12 See August Bebel, *Die Frau und der Sozialismus*, Stuttgart 1891, pp. 177–9 and pp. 333–6, on the changes in housework effected by technology, and pp. 200–1 on woman as inventor.

13 Cited in D. Bach, 'John Ruskin', *Die Nate Zeit*, XVIII/I, Stuttgart 1900, p. 728.

14 This illusion found characteristic expression in Alfred Weber's welcoming address to the German Sociological Convention of 1912: 'Culture only emerges when life has become a form which rises above its necessities and utilities.' This concept of culture contains seeds of barbarism which have since germinated. Culture appears as something 'which is superfluous for the continued existence of life but which we feel to be the very reason for which life is there.' In short, culture exists after the fashion of a work of art 'which perhaps disarrays entire modes of living and life principles, may be dissolving and destructive, but whose existence we feel to be higher than everything healthy and living which it destroys'. Alfred Weber, 'Der soziologische Kulturbegriff', *Verhandlungen des zweiten deutschen Soziologentages: Schriften der deutschen Gesellschaft für Soziologie*, I: I, Tubingen 1913, pp. 11–12. Twenty-five years after this was said, 'cultured States' have made it a point of pride to resemble, even to be, such works of art.

15 Franz Mehring, 'Akademisches', *Die Neue Zeit*, XVI, Stuttgart 1898, 1, pp. 195–6.

16 *Erotische Kunst*, I, p. 125. A constant reference to contemporary art is among the most important impulses of Fuchs the collector. It, too, comes to him partially through the great creations of the past. His incomparable knowledge of older caricature allows Fuchs an early recognition

of the works of a Toulouse-Lautrec, a Heartfield and a George Grosz. His passion for Daumier leads him to the work of Slevogt, whose conception of Don Quixote he deems alone able to hold its own beside Daumier. His studies in ceramics give him the authority to sponsor an Emil Pottner. All his life Fuchs enjoyed friendly relations with creative artists. Hence it is not surprising that his manner of addressing works of art is often more that of an artist than of a historian.

17 The master of iconographic interpretation is probably Emile Mâle. His research is confined to the sculpture of French cathedrals from the twelfth to the fifteenth centuries, and so does not overlap with Fuchs' studies.

18 Heinrich Wölfflin, *Die klassische Kunst*, Munich 1899, p. 275.

19 Older panel painting granted no more than the outline of a house to men for their quarters. The painters of the early Renaissance were the first to depict interior space in which the figures represented have room to move. That is what made Uccello's invention of perspective so overpowering to his contemporaries and to himself. From then on painterly creations, dedicated more than before to inhabitants rather to suppliants, presented them with patterns of dwelling and never tired of unfolding before them perspectives of the villa. The High Renaissance, although much more sparing in the representation of actual interiors, continued to build on this foundation. 'The Cinquecento has a particularly strong feeling for the relation between man and building, for the resonance of a beautiful room. It can scarcely imagine an existence which is not architecturally framed and founded'. Wölfflin, p. 227.

20 *Erotische Kunst*, II, p. 20.

21 Franz Mehring, *Geschichte der deutschen Sozialdemokratie*, Part Two: *Von Lassalles offenem Antwartschreiben bis turn Erfurter Programm* (*Geschichte des Sozialismus in Einzeldarstellungen*, III, 2). Stuttgart 1898 p. 546.

22 *Karikatur*, I, pp. 4–5.

23 See his fine comment on Daumier's figures of proletarian women: 'Whoever views such subjects merely as sentimental motifs proves that the *ultimate* impulses necessary to create powerful art are a sealed book to him. Precisely because these pictures represent something altogether different from "sentimental motifs" they will live forever … as powerful monuments to the enslavement of maternal woman in the nineteenth century.' *Der Maler Daumier*, p. 28.

24 *Tang-Plastik*, p. 44.

25 See his thesis on the erotic effects of works of art: 'The more intense the effect, the greater the artistic quality.' *Erotische Kunst*, I, p. 68.

26 *Karikatur*, I, p. 23.

27 *Dachreiter*, p. 39.

28 *Die grossen Meister der Erotik*, p. 115.

29 *Dachreiter*, p. 48.

30 *Erotische Kunst*, II, p. 186.

31 *Tang-Plastik*, pp. 30–1. This immediate, intuitive approach becomes problematic when it attempts to fulfil the demands of a materialist analysis. It is well known that Marx nowhere really divulged how the relationship between superstructure and infrastructure should be conceived in individual cases. All that can be said with confidence is that he envisaged a series of mediations, as it were transmissions, interpolated between the material relationships of production and the remoter realms of the superstructure, including art. So also Plekhanov: 'When art, which is created by the higher classes, stands in no direct relation to the process of production, then this must ultimately be explained on economic grounds. The materialist interpretation of history … is applicable here as well. Obviously, however, the undoubted causal connection between being and consciousness, between the social relations founded on "labour" and art, are in this case not so easy to establish.… There are some intermediate stations between them.' G. Plekhanov, 'Das französische Malerei im neunzehnten Jahrhundert vom Standpunkt der materialistischen Geschichtsauffassung', *Die Neue Zeit*, XXIV, Stuttgart 1911, pp. 543–4. So much is clear, however; Marx's classic historical dialectic takes the existence of causal dependencies as given. Later practice *became* more lax and was often content with analogies. Possibly this was linked to the ambition to replace bourgeois histories of literature and art by materialist works planned on an equally grand scale—a hallmark of the epoch that was part of the Wilhelmine ethos. This ambition took its toll on Fuchs as well. A favourite idea of the author, expressed in various ways, prescribed epochs of realism for trading states—for Holland of the seventeenth century as much as for China of the eighth and ninth centuries. Starting from an analysis of Chinese horticulture, as the explanation of many characteristics of the Empire, Fuchs then turns to the new sculpture which emerged under T'ang rule. The monumental rigidity of the Han style was relaxed: the anonymous masters who created the new pottery

responded to the movements of men and animals. 'Time', Fuchs goes on, 'awoke from its long sleep in China in those centuries ... for commerce always quickens life and movement. So life and movement come to the forefront in the art of the T'ang period. This is the first characteristic it displays. While the whole bearing of the animals of the Han period is heavy and cumbersome, for example, those of the T'ang period vivaciously stir in every limb'. *Tang-Plastik*, pp. 41–2. This kind of treatment rests on mere analogy—movement in trade as in sculpture: one might almost call it nominalistic. Fuchs' attempts to elucidate the reception of Antiquity in the Renaissance remains equally trapped in analogy. 'In both epochs the economic basis was the same, only in the Renaissance this basis was at a higher stage of development. Both were founded on commerce in commodities.' *Erotische Kunst*, I, p. 42. Finally trade itself appears *as* the subject of the exercise of art. Fuchs writes: 'Trade must calculate with given quantities and it can only take into account concrete and verifiable quantities. That is how trade has to approach the world and things if it wants to master them economically. Consequently its aesthetic outlook is in every respect realistic.' *Tang-Plastik*, p. 42. One may disregard the fact that a 'realistic' representation 'in every respect' cannot be found in art. But one would have to say that any connection which claims equal validity for the art of Ancient China and of early modern Holland appears questionable in principle. In effect, no such connection exists, as a glance at the Republic of Venice suffices to show. Venice flourished because of its trade. Yet the art of Palma Vecchio, of Titian or of Veronese could scarcely be called 'realistic in every respect'. The aspect of life we encounter in it is rather festive and symbolic. On the other hand, commercial life in all stages of its development demands a considerable sense of reality. The materialist cannot deduce any manifestations of style from this.

32 Karl Kautsky, 'Darwinismus und Marxismus', *Die Neue Zeit*, XIII/I, Stuttgart 1895, pp. 709–10.

33 H. Laufenberg, 'Dogma und Klassenkampf', *Die Neue Zeit*, XXVII/I, Stuttgart 1909, p. 574. The notion of self-activity has sunk to a sad state here. The zenith of the idea is to be found in the eighteenth century as markets started to be equalized. It celebrated its triumph in Kant in the form of 'spontaneity', and in technology in the form of automatic machines.

34 *Karikatur*, I, p. 312.

35 *Erotische Kunst*, I, p. 3.

36 A. Max, 'Zur Frage der Organisation des Proletariats der Intelligenz', p 652.

37 *Karikatur*, II, p. 238.

38 Mehring commented on the trial occasioned by 'The Weavers' in *Die Neue Zeit*. Parts of the speech by the lawyer for the defence have become as topical today as they were in 1893: he said that 'he had to point out that the allegedly revolutionary passages in question are offset by others which are soothing and appeasing in character. The poet in no way stands on the side of the revolt, he rather permits the victory of order through the intervention of a handful of soldiers'. Franz Mehring, 'Entweder-Oder', *Die Neue Zeit*, XI/I, Stuttgart 1893, p. 780.

39 Honoré de Balzac, *Le Cousin Pons*, Paris 1925, p. 162.

40 Edouard Drumont, *Les Héros et les Pitres*, Paris, pp. 107–8.

41 G. G. Gervinus, *Friedrich Christoph Schlosser: Ein Nekrolog*, Leipzig 1861, pp. 30–1.

42 This element in Fuchs's work proved useful when the imperial prosecutors started to accuse him of 'distributing obscene writings'. His moralism was naturally depicted with particular emphasis in an expert testimonial submitted in the course of one of his trials, all of which without exception ended in his acquittal. Written by Fedor von Zobeltitz, its most important passage reads as follows: 'Fuchs seriously considers himself a preacher of morals and an educator. This deeply serious outlook on life, this inner conviction that his work in the service of the history of humanity must be informed by the highest morality, is alone enough to protect him against the suspicion of any profiteering speculation. Anyone who knows the man and his enlightened idealism must smile at the very idea'.

43 This revision has been inaugurated by Max Horkheimer in his essay 'Egoismus and Freiheitsbewegung', *Zeitschrift für Sozialforschung*, V, 1936, p. 161 ff. The documents assembled by Horkheimer find confirmation in a series of interesting materials on which the Ultra Abel Bonnard bases his charges against those bourgeois historians of the French Revolution whom Chateaubriand calls 'L'école admirative de la terreur'. See Abel Bonnard, *Les Modérés*, Paris, pp. 179 ff.

44 *Der Maler Daumier*, p. 30.

45 Norbert Guterman and Henri Lefebvre, *La Conscience mystifiée*, Paris 1936, p. 151.

46 *Erotische Kunst*, II/I, p. 11.

47 Ibid., I, p. 43. His moral-historical image of the Directory has traits reminiscent of a popular ballad. 'The frightful book of the Marquis de Sade, its plates as bad as they were infamous, lay open in all shop windows.' Barras expressed 'the desolate fantasy of the shameless libertine'. (*Karikatur*, I, pp. 201–2).

48 *Karikatur*, I, p. 188.

49 Max Horkheimer, 'Egoismus und Freiheitsbewegung', p. 166.

50 *Erotische Kunst*, II, p. 283. Here Fuchs is on the track of an important phenomenon. Would it be too rash to link the threshold between human and animal, which Fuchs sees in the orgy, directly to that other threshold, of erect posture? With its appearance, the partners can for the first time in natural history look into each other's eyes during orgasm. Therewith the orgy becomes possible. Not through an increase in visual attractions, but rather because the expression of satiety and even impotence can now become an erotic stimulant itself.

51 *Sittengeschichte*, III, p. 234. A few pages later this confident judgment disappears—proof of the force with which it had to be wrested away from convention. He now writes: 'The fact that thousands of people become sexually excited at the sight of a female or male *nude* photograph … proves *that the eye* is no longer capable of perceiving the harmonious whole but only the piquant detail.' Ibid., III, p. 269. If there is anything sexually arousing here, it is more the idea of the naked body displayed before the camera, than the sight of nakedness in the photograph itself. This is probably the effect intended by most of these photographs.

52 Ibid., *III*, p. 189.

53 Ibid., *Ergänzungsband*, pp. 53–4.

54 For Fuchs art is immediate sensuousness, as ideology is immediate expression of interests. 'The essence of art is: sensuousness. Art is sensuousness. Indeed it is sensuousness in its most potent form. Art is sensuousness become form, become visible, at the same time the highest and noblest sensuousness.' *Erotische Kunst*, I, p. 61.

55 *Karikatur*, I, p. 223.

56 *Erotische Kunst*, II, p. 390.

57 *Der Mater Daumier*, p. 30.

58 Compare the following reflection: 'My observations have led me to conclude that the dominant elements in each artist's palette can be seen with particular clarity in his erotically pointed paintings. Here ... they acquire their highest luminosity.' *Die grossen Meister der Erotik*, p. 14.

59 *Der Maler Daumier*, p. 18. The famous 'Art Expert', a water colour in several versions, must be numbered among the figures in question. One day Fuchs was shown a hitherto unknown version of the painting, to authenticate it. He picked up the main representation of the motif in a good reproduction and then proceeded to a very instructive comparison. No variation, however small, remained unnoticed, as he sought to determine whether each was the product of the master's hand or that of impotence. Again and again Fuchs reverted to the original. Yet the way he did so suggested that he could well have dispensed with it, so familiar was it to him—as can only occur with a painting one has had in mind for years. Doubtless this was the case for Fuchs. Only so could he discern the most covert uncertainties of contour, the least evident discolorations of shadow, the slightest deflections of line, which enabled him to place the painting—not as a forgery but as a good old copy which might have been the work of an admirer.

60 *Dachreiter*, pp. 5–6.

61 *Tang-Plastik*, p. 44.

62 *Honoré Daumier*, I, p. 13. These thoughts may be compared with Victor Hugo's allegorical interpretation of the Wedding at Cana. 'The miracle of the loaves represents the multiplication of readers. The day that Christ hit upon this symbol he had a premonition of the art of the book printer.' Victor Hugo, 'William Shakespeare', cited by Georges Batault, *Le pontife de la démagogic: Victor Hugo*, Paris 1934, p. 142.

63 *Dachreiter*, p. 46.

64 *Karikatur*, I, p. 19. The exception proves the rule. A mechanical technique of reproduction served to produce terracotta figures. Among these many caricatures may be found.

65 See Erich Klossowski, *Honoré Daumier*, Munich 1908, p. 113.

66 *Dachreiter*, p. 45.

Index